Fodor's

6th Edition

New Zealand

D0431058

Fodor's Travel Publications • New York, Toronto, London, Sydney, Auckland
www.fodors.com

CONTENTS

MAPS

Circled letters in text correspond to letters on the photographs. For more information on the sights pictured, turn to
the indicated page number ⒶＤ on each photograph.

DESTINATION
NEW ZEALAND

The promise of fabulous scenery is what brings most travelers to New Zealand, and it's hard to imagine anyone coming away disappointed. Alone, the spectacle of Mt. Cook reflected in Lake Matheson at sunrise is worth the trip, and similarly dramatic views of steaming geysers, the island-strewn coast, crystal-clear fjords, and dense, ferny rain forests reveal themselves at almost every turn. You can fish, kayak, rock climb, and otherwise exert yourself on countless outdoor adventures—or just take it easy, sipping wine in the Marlborough vineyards, soaking up the atmosphere at a Maori *hangi* (feast), or simply exploring cosmopolitan Auckland or prettily British Christchurch. The open-hearted Kiwi hospitality you find at every corner of this amazing nation is an unexpected pleasure that adds a shine to every experience, however you spend your time.

Ⓐ 42

AUCKLAND
AND THE NORTH

Ⓑ 50

When Aucklanders introduce their city, they tend to concentrate first on what's *outside* it. For starters, the talk usually turns to the coastal views and multitude of beaches that lie within an easy drive of the city, many in the undulating countryside of Ⓕ**Northland.** Then come boasts about the lush, rolling hills that run down to the sand and sea of the Bay of Islands. Next you'll be steered to the historic Treaty House, set in the lovely Ⓑ**Waitangi National Reserve,** where the native Maoris signed the Treaty of Waitangi and ceded governorship of New Zealand to the British in 1840. When the conversation finally turns to

Ⓒ 25

D⟩ 25

E⟩ 19

Auckland, the advice is inevitably to begin a tour with a boat ride on ⒠**Waitemata Harbour,** where it's easy to understand why residents of the so-called "City of Sails" prefer boats to cars.

Back on land, a stroll through leafy suburbs (as neighborhoods are called) provides glimpses of cosmopolitan pleasures—picture-gazing at the ⒞**Auckland Art Gallery,** admiring the products of New Zealanders' horticultural genius at the ⒟**Wintergardens,** or watching the action of the Kiwis' favorite rugby team, the ⒜**All Blacks.**

F⟩ 46

Ⓐ 88

ROTORUA TO WELLINGTON

Ⓑ 126

After Northland's peaceful green hills and sea views the landscape of Ⓐ**Waiotapu,** near Rotorua, is a stark contrast. Here geysers hiss and spout, hot spots bubble and spit, and ponds send wisps and clouds of steam into the air that is often suffused with the rotten-egg smell of hydrogen sulfide. Meanwhile, all around the central North Island, nature serves up adventure and

Ⓒ 101

beauty for rafters, anglers, and wildlife watchers. Rotorua rivers like the Ⓔ**Rangitaiki** sprint through magnificent stands of forest. The limestone caves at Waitomo glimmer with glowworms, and active volcanic peaks in Tongariro National Park provide the backdrop for pine forests, crater lakes, and barren lava fields. Farther south, at ©**Cape Kidnappers,** a spectacular gannet colony shelters more than 15,000 of the graceful birds. Out west, near the peak of Mt. Taranaki, gorgeous gardens bloom from the rich, volcanic soil. But it's not always nature that steals the show in these parts. Local Maori still practice age-old crafts and customs that include preparing a feast for visitors in villages such as Ⓓ**Te Tawa Ngahere Pa.** When mod-

Ⓓ 88

ern society does intrude, it's with graceful panache, as in the art deco seaside town of Napier, or with cosmopolitan pleasures such as those found in Wellington, the capital. Not the least of these is Ⓑ**Te-Papa–Museum of New Zealand,** where exhibits on the natural and cultural wonders may inspire you to hit the road again and experience it all firsthand.

Ⓔ 91

9

UPPER SOUTH ISLAND

As you ferry across Ⓓ**Cook Strait** and near the rock-faced entrance to South Island at labyrinthine Marlborough Sounds, you're entering a realm of jagged mountain peaks and desolate seascapes, a land far less mellow than North Island. Even so, you might take South Island to be almost gentle if you were to begin by wine-tasting your way through inland Marlborough and Ⓔ**Blenheim,** where vines producing striking sauvignon blancs and Rieslings rise toward the mountain ranges that are omnipresent on the island's horizon. In the Nelson region,

⑩⟩ 144

in the northwest, you find balmy weather, sunny skies, and ©**Abel Tasman National Park,** whose cove-notched shore and rugged Coastal Track attract travelers all year long. A taste for adventure comes in handy on the wild, primeval West Coast, whose fantastic, mazelike Ⓐ**Pancake Rocks** typify the area's surreal terrain. The rocks are the geological result of the fog and constant, wind-driven rain that have also, inevitably, made their mark on the hardy character of the locals. Inland is Ⓑ**Fox Glacier,** one of several dozen that squeak, creak, groan, and gurgle as they edge down the mountainsides in Westland National Park at a rate of up to 3 feet a day. The crush of thousands of tons of ice makes hiking a risky business and a guide a necessity. At Ⓕ**Lake Matheson** nature relaxes somewhat and offers what's often called the view of views: It lives up to every bit of its promise.

Ⓔ⟩ 152

Ⓕ⟩ 177

CHRISTCHURCH AND LOWER SOUTH ISLAND

Natural wonders never cease on Lower South Island. In fact it just gets more amazing as you move south from the high-country grassland near 12,283-foot Ⓕ**Aoraki** (Mt. Cook) to Ⓐ**Fiordland National Park,** the nation's largest, where 5,560-foot Mitre Peak shoots straight up from rockbound Milford Sound. A cruise into this long, deep canyon leaves every traveler awestruck, and the four-day trek along the preserve's famous, lush Milford Track—past waterfalls and glowworm caves—may well be, as Kiwis attest, the finest walk in the world, though the region's Kepler, Hollyford, and Routeburn tracks are glorious as well. Not

that your heart won't have taken a few extra beats by the time you get this far south. This is especially true if you dare to attach a bungy cord to your ankles and plunge head first from the ©**Kawarau Suspension Bridge** near the former gold-mining center of Arrowtown, or sample some of the other extreme sports that have made Queenstown New Zealand's adventure capital. Once you're accustomed to the South Island

Ⓓ▷186

Ⓔ▷186 wilds, Ⓓ**Christchurch** may take you by surprise, with its trim brick houses, church spires, and gentle, willow-shaded Ⓔ**Avon River,** a stream ideal for genteel punting. This lovely place is said to be the most English city outside England. The surefire antidote to its civility? Head farther south to Ⓑ**Stewart Island,** the most southerly of New Zealand's trio of main islands. Remote, raw, and untouched even by New Zealand standards, it's a good place to see the natural nighttime light show known as the aurora australis. It's also the surest place to encounter a kiwi bird in the wild.

Ⓕ▷202

GREAT ITINERARIES

Highlights of New Zealand
13 or 14 days

From the subtropical Bay of Islands in the north to the icy fjords and glaciers of the southwest, this itinerary knits together the best that New Zealand has to offer. After a day of strolling in Auckland and neighboring Devonport, drive north to Pahia and the Bay of Islands.

BAY OF ISLANDS
2 days. Sail or cruise the islands, scuba dive, or go marlin fishing in New Zealand's balmy, lush summer playground. Spend half a day touring the historic sites around the former whaling port of Russell, and don't miss the Treaty House at Waitangi.
☞ *Northland and the Bay of Islands in Chapter 1.*

ROTORUA
2 days. Drive south to ⒶRotorua and its bubbling, spitting thermal wonders. Visit Waiotapu, then relax on a short lunch-time cruise aboard the MV *Reremoana* on Lake Tarawera. Returning to

Ⓐ 86

Rotorua, stop in at the excavations at Te Wairoa, the buried village, and at Whakarewarewa, another spectacular thermal area. In the evening, take in a Maori *hangi* (feast).
☞ *Rotorua, Lake Taupo, and Tongariro National Park in Chapter 2.*

LAKE TAUPO
1 day. Drive to peaceful Lake Taupo, stopping along the way to marvel at the multicolored terraces and hissing streams of Orakei Korako. Arrive at Taupo in time for a cruise and some of the world's best trout fishing.
☞ *Rotorua, Lake Taupo, and Tongariro National Park in Chapter 2.*

WELLINGTON
1 day. Drive south to New Zealand's charming, cosmopolitan capital. Take the Kelburn Cable Car to the heights of the city and then spiral down on foot through the Botanic Garden and past the old wooden houses of Tinakori Road. End your day learning everything you want to know about New Zealand at Te Papa, the interactive National Museum.
☞ *Wellington in Chapter 2.*

CHRISTCHURCH
1 or 2 days. Fly to Christchurch, where you'll find the splendid Botanic Gardens and the diverse Arts Centre complex. If you feel like some relaxation, drive out to Akaroa and explore this historic settlement and its varied surroundings of steep volcanic hills and quiet bays.
☞ *Christchurch and Side Trips from Christchurch in Chapter 4.*

THE WEST COAST
2 days. Catch the Tranz-Alpine Express train ride across the Canterbury Plains and through the rugged peaks of the Southern Alps. At Greymouth, rent a car and drive south to the ethereal Fox and Franz Josef glaciers, where you can take a guided glacier hike or a private flight for dazzling views of the Alps.
☞ *The West Coast in Chapter 3.*

SOUTHLAND
3 days. Drive south to Queenstown and get a view of the adventure capital of New Zealand from the

Skyline Gondola trip to the heights of Bob's Peak. Thrill to a ride on the Shotover Jet or even a bungy jump, and take the half-day Dart River Jet Boat Safari through spectacular country. Don't miss a full-day side trip to Fiordland National Park, including a cruise on awe-inspiring Milford Sound.
☞ *Southland in Chapter 4.*

Ⓑ 158

New Zealand Adventures
14 days

Aimed at those who want to experience New Zealand's diverse natural wonders in hiking boots, in crampons, or with a paddle in their hands, this itinerary is confined to the South Island so as to maximize time in the wilderness. The trip could be

Franz Josef Glacier
Fox Glacier
Routeburn Track
Hollyford Track
Milford Sound
Queenstown
Milford Track
Kepler Track
Invercargill

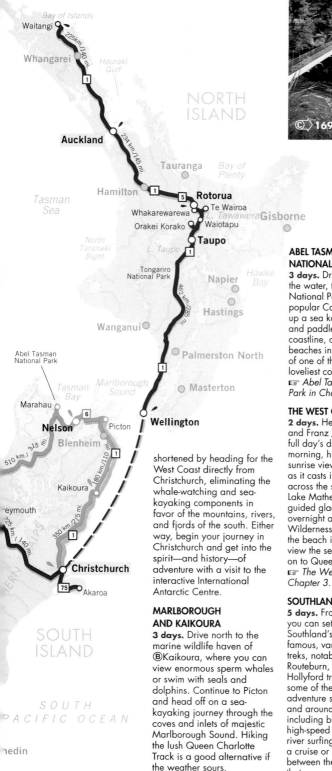

©169

ABEL TASMAN NATIONAL PARK

3 days. Drive west, along the water, to ©Abel Tasman National Park. Hike the popular Coastal Track or pick up a sea kayak in Marahau and paddle along the rugged coastline, camping on the quiet coves of one of the country's loveliest coastal parks. ☞ *Abel Tasman National Park in Chapter 3.*

THE WEST COAST

2 days. Head south to Fox and Franz Josef glaciers—a full day's drive. Early next morning, hike to the famous sunrise view of Mount Cook as it casts its mirror image across the smooth waters of Lake Matheson. Take a guided glacier hike and overnight at Lake Moeraki Wilderness Lodge. Hike to the beach in the morning to view the seals, then continue on to Queenstown. ☞ *The West Coast in Chapter 3.*

SOUTHLAND

5 days. From Queenstown, you can set out on one of Southland's many world-famous, varied, and glorious treks, notably the Milford, Routeburn, Kepler, and Hollyford tracks. Sample some of the wildest extreme adventure sports on earth in and around Queenstown—including bungy jumping, high-speed jet boating, or river surfing. Be sure to take a cruise or sea-kayaking trip between the sheer rock walls that surround breathtaking Milford Sound. ☞ *Southland in Chapter 4.*

shortened by heading for the West Coast directly from Christchurch, eliminating the whale-watching and sea-kayaking components in favor of the mountains, rivers, and fjords of the south. Either way, begin your journey in Christchurch and get into the spirit—and history—of adventure with a visit to the interactive International Antarctic Centre.

MARLBOROUGH AND KAIKOURA

3 days. Drive north to the marine wildlife haven of ⑧Kaikoura, where you can view enormous sperm whales or swim with seals and dolphins. Continue to Picton and head off on a sea-kayaking journey through the coves and inlets of majestic Marlborough Sound. Hiking the lush Queen Charlotte Track is a good alternative if the weather sours. ☞ *Marlborough and Kaikoura in Chapter 3.*

1 AUCKLAND AND THE NORTH

The mighty 1,200-year-old kauri trees, ferny semitropical forests, and miles of island-strewn coastline of Northland and the Coromandel Peninsula are the perfect counterpoint to Auckland, New Zealand's largest city, and its neighborhood bustle and sprawl.

By Michael
Gebicki and
Stu Freeman

As YOU FLY INTO AUCKLAND, New Zealand's gateway city, you might wonder where the city is. Most people arriving for the first time, and even New Zealanders coming home, are impressed by the seascape and green forest that dominate the view on the approach to the airport.

The drive from the airport does little to dispel the clean, green image so many people have of the country. The scenery is commanded by some of the city's 46 volcanic hills, their grass kept closely cropped by those four-legged lawn mowers known as sheep. And reading the highway signs will begin to give you a taste of the unusual and sometimes baffling Maori place-names around the country.

Yet a couple of days in this city of about 1 million will reveal a level of development and sophistication that belies first impressions. In the past 10 years Auckland has grown up in more ways than one. Many shops are open seven days, central bars and nightclubs welcome patrons well into the night, and a cosmopolitan mix of Polynesians, Asians, and Europeans all contribute to the cultural milieu. Literally topping things off is the 1,082-ft Sky Tower, dwarfing everything around it and acting as a beacon for the casino, hotel, and restaurant complex that opened early in 1996. This is the newest, if least pervasive, face of modern New Zealand.

In the midst of the city's activity, you'll see knots of cyclists and runners. Like all other New Zealanders, Aucklanders are addicted to the outdoors—especially the water. There are some 70,000 powerboats and sailing craft in the Greater Auckland area—about one for every four households. And a total of 102 beaches lie within an hour's drive of the city center. The city is currently working to enhance its greatest asset, Waitemata Harbour—a Maori name meaning "Sea of Sparkling Waters." The city staged its first defense of the America's Cup in the year 2000, and the regatta was a catalyst for major redevelopment of the waterfront. The area is now known as Viaduct Village and has some of the city's most popular bars, cafés, and restaurants.

Auckland is not easy to explore. Made up of a sprawling array of neighborhoods (Kiwis call them suburbs), the city spreads out on both shores of Stanley Bay and Waitemata Harbour. It's best to have a car for getting around between neighborhoods, and even between some city-center sights. If you are nervous about driving on the left, especially when you first arrive, purchase a one-day Link Pass or, for a circuit of the main sights, an Explorer Bus Pass, and get acquainted with the city layout. One good introduction to the city, particularly if you arrive at the end of a long flight and time is limited, is the commuter ferry that crosses the harbor to the village of Devonport, where you can soak up the charming suburb's atmosphere on a leisurely stroll.

As you put Auckland behind you, you'll find yourself in the midst of some of the great open space that defines New Zealand. North of the city, the Bay of Islands is both beautiful—for its lush forests, splendid beaches, and shimmering harbors—and historic—as the place where westernized New Zealand came into being with the signing of the Treaty of Waitangi in 1840. Southeast of the Auckland is the rugged and exhilarating Coromandel Peninsula, with mountains stretching the length of its middle and a Pacific coastline afloat with picturesque islands.

Note: For more information on bicycling, diving, deep-sea fishing, hiking, and sailing in Auckland and the north, *see* Chapter 5.

Pleasures and Pastimes

Beaches

When the sun comes out, Aucklanders head to the beach. With seas both to the west and the east, few people in the city live more than a 15-minute drive from the coast. Generally speaking the best surfing is at the black-sand beaches on the west coast, and the safest swimming is on the east coast. Beaches that do have a reputation for large waves and rips are patrolled in the summer, so play it safe and swim between the flags. The only other danger is from the sun itself. The ozone layer is weak above New Zealand, so slap on the sunscreen and resist the temptation to bake.

Boating

Auckland is dubbed "City of Sails," and for good reason. The population is crazy about boating and any other recreation associated with the sea. A variety of ferries and high-speed catamarans operate on Waitemata Harbour. Even better, go for a sail on the *Pride of Auckland*. Northland and the ravishing Bay of Islands also have a choice of boat and sailing trips, and taking a small boat out to Cathedral Cove on the Coromandel Peninsula is a great way to see its stunning coastline.

Dining

Auckland is one of the great dining cities of the Pacific Rim, with a cosmopolitan mix of cafés, restaurants, brasseries, and bars spreading from the city center to the closest suburbs. Appropriately enough, given the maritime climate, the local style leans to the Mediterranean, with a strong sideways glance toward Asia. Seafood abounds. Don't miss such delicacies as Bluff oysters, from the tiny town of the same name (in season March–August), Greenshell mussels (also known as green-lipped or New Zealand green mussels), scallops, crayfish, and two clamlike shellfish, *pipi* and *tuatua*. In spring, many restaurants will feature whitebait, known to Maori as *inanga,* which are the juvenile of several fish species. They are eaten whole, usually in an omelet-like fritter. You'll also encounter plenty of opportunities to try *kumara,* a local sweet potato and staple of the Maori diet.

The downtown waterfront area was extensively rebuilt for the America's Cup yachting series that straddled the millennium changeover. Princes Wharf and adjoining Viaduct Quay, an easy stroll from the city's major thoroughfare, Queen Street, now burst at the seams with dozens of eateries in every style from cheap-and-cheerful to superposh. Names and chefs are constantly changing, so ask the locals for recommendations—or simply follow the crowds.

Away from the city center, the top restaurant strips are Ponsonby and Parnell roads, both a 10-minute bus or cab ride from the city center. Dominion and Mount Eden roads in the city, as well as Hurstmere Road in the suburb of Takapuna, over the Harbour Bridge, are also worth exploring. The mix is eclectic—Indian, Chinese, Japanese, and Thai eateries sit comfortably alongside casual taverns, pizzerias, and high-end restaurants. At hole-in-the-wall spots in and around the city center a few dollars will buy you anything from fish-and-chips to nachos, noodles, or naan bread. Ponsonby Road leads the field in outdoor dining, but Hurstmere Road is catching up fast.

As you put Auckland behind you, the choice of fare reduces sharply, though there are increasing numbers of enlightened cooks in countryside nooks. That said, tradition does have its place when cutting-edge cuisine palls. At least once, give old-style roast lamb and veggies a try—if you don't like New Zealand lamb, chances are you won't like it anywhere.

For price category information, see the chart *under* Dining *in* Smart Travel Tips A to Z.

Lodging

Around Auckland and the north, a great variety of accommodation is available, from flashy downtown hotels to comfortable B&Bs to mom-and-pop motels. Because Kiwis are so naturally hospitable, it's hard not to recommend lodgings where you have a chance to talk with your hosts—unless you prefer anonymity.

For price category information, see the chart *under* Lodging *in* Smart Travel Tips A to Z.

Volcanoes and Vistas

Auckland is built on and around 48 volcanoes, and the tops of many of them provide sweeping views of the city. Mt. Eden is probably the most popular, and several bus tours include this central site. Rangitoto Island has an even better vista. This volcano emerged from the sea just 600 years ago, no doubt much to the wonder of the Maori people living next door on Motutapu Island. Take a ferry to the island, then either a short ride or an hour's walk to the top will give you a 360-degree view of the city and the Hauraki Gulf islands. The best views from the city itself are not surprisingly from the Sky Tower. The main observation deck turns under its own power so you'll get a 360-degree view without moving.

Walking and Hiking

There is superb bushwalking (hiking) around Auckland, Northland, and the Coromandel Peninsula. New Zealand's largest city is fringed by bush (wilderness) to the west, and the Waitakere Ranges are an ideal way to experience the country's flora if you have limited time. The Northland and Coromandel bush is full of impressive ancient kauri trees (a local species of pine) and interesting birds, such as *tuis* (*too*-ees), fantails, and wood pigeons.

Exploring Auckland and the North

Northland and the Coromandel Peninsula have beautiful countryside, coasts, and mountains—some of the finest in North Island. Auckland is a thoroughly modern, car-oriented metropolis, with good restaurants and a handful of suburbs to poke around. Interestingly enough, Aucklanders seem to talk as much about what surrounds the city as what's in it: the beaches, the Waitakere Ranges, and the vineyards of Waiheke Island. To get to most of these and to happening suburbs like Ponsonby, you will need a car, which you can then use to go farther afield: up to Northland and southeast to the Coromandel Peninsula.

Great Itineraries

Numbers in the text correspond to numbers in the margin and on the maps.

IF YOU HAVE 2 DAYS

Spend your nights in 🏨 **Auckland** ①–⑭, and divide your days between the city's attractions and nearby destinations. Take a full day to see the best of Auckland. Next day, head west to the Waitakere Ranges and explore the bush or west coast beaches with their volcanic black sand. Or take the day and visit the beaches and vineyards of Waiheke Island. Be sure to work in a short foray (at the least) to charming 🏨 **Devonport**—taking in the harbor views on the ferry.

IF YOU HAVE 5 OR MORE DAYS

Spend the first day or two looking around metropolitan Auckland and its beautiful environs. Then head either to the popular Bay of Islands or the less-trodden Coromandel Peninsula. With more than a week, you could see both, but the drive connecting the two is more than six hours, making it more sensible to choose one of the two places. Heading north to the Bay of Islands, stop in **Warkworth** ⑯ for a look at some great old kauri trees. Wine enthusiasts should head for nearby Matakana, one of the country's most exciting new grape-growing areas. ⌘ **Whangarei** ⑰ is also on the way—a good place for a picnic by the harbor or at the waterfall. This area is steeped in history and has superb coastal scenery. Continue north and spend a couple of days exploring the beaches, water sports, and history of ⌘ **Paihia and Waitangi** ⑱, the nearby Waitangi Treaty House, and the historic port of ⌘ **Russell** ⑲. When you return south, take the western route to **Waipoua State Forest** ㉒, and stop farther down at the **Matakohe Kauri Museum** ㉓ to learn about the area's incredible native trees. If you want to stay off the main road dropping back into Auckland, go past the scenic Kaipara Harbour, then through Helensville.

The Coromandel Peninsula is an easy two-hour drive south and east of Auckland. Historic ⌘ **Thames** ㉔ is a logical first stop, then wind your way up the Firth of Thames coast to the town of ⌘ **Coromandel** ㉕, a good base for exploring the upper peninsula. Then turn to the east coast, where you'll find some of the best Coromandel beaches. **Hot Water Beach** ㉘ is a combination of thermal activity and surf—dig a hole in the sand, and you've got a hot bath—and you can overnight in nearby ⌘ **Tairua** ㉙. A range of mountains runs in a line up the Coromandel, and from just about any point you can head into the hills for great hiking through lush ferny forests. To the south are the popular surf beaches of **Whangamata** ㉚ and Wahi. If you have extra time, you could linger here or even head toward the coastal Bay of Plenty. The town with the most country-style charm in the area is ⌘ **Katikati** ㉛, and ⌘ **Tauranga** ㉜ is a handy base for exploring the surrounding bush and beach. The best swimming beaches are found at **Mt. Maunganui** and **Whakatane** ㉝.

When to Tour Auckland and the North

Snow doesn't fall on this part of New Zealand, and the weather doesn't exactly get frigid. Still, to see these areas at their finest, mid-November through mid-April are the beautiful months, with December through March being the highest season for tourism. If you plan to come around the Christmas holidays, reserve well in advance, especially in seaside places. The Bay of Islands is a summertime hot spot for vacationing Kiwis, and the Coromandel town of Whangamata, for example, gets overrun by surfies (surfers) around New Year's.

AUCKLAND

According to Maori tradition, the Auckland isthmus was originally peopled by a race of giants and fairy folk. When Europeans arrived in the early 19th century, however, the Ngati-Whatua tribe was firmly in control of the region. The British began negotiations with the Ngati-Whatua in 1840 to purchase the isthmus and establish the colony's first capital. In September of that year the British flag was hoisted to mark the township's foundation and Auckland remained the capital until 1865 when the seat of government was moved to Wellington. Since then development has been haphazard and the urban sprawl has made this city of approximately 1 million people one of the largest geographically in the world.

These days, New Zealand's largest city is considered too bold and brash for its own good by many Kiwis who live in other parts of the country. The glass towers, crawling rush-hour traffic, and cell-phone culture set it apart from points north and south. Visitors will see beyond all that. Indeed, much of Auckland's charm lies in the fact that you can enjoy a cappuccino in a downtown café watching the city bustle pass you by—knowing that within 30 minutes' driving time you could be cruising the spectacular harbor, playing a round at a public golf course, or even walking in subtropical forest while listening to the song of a native tui.

Exploring Auckland

Auckland isn't the easiest place to figure out in a couple of days, the way you can get a sense of the character of other New Zealand cities. It has built out, rather than up, and the sprawl makes the greater city close to impossible to explore on foot. What might look like reasonable walking distances on maps can turn out to be 20- to 30-minute treks, and stringing a few of those together can get frustrating. If you want to see the city center close to the harbor, Devonport, and Parnell, you can get around by walking, busing, and ferrying between places. To explore suburbs farther afield, it's best to rent a car.

City Center and Parnell

Auckland's city center includes the port area, much of it reclaimed from the sea in the latter half of the 19th century. Most visitors start exploring by walking along Queen Street toward the waterfront, making detours from this main drag. Turn right to head to the Albert Park and university side of town, left to reach Sky Tower. Just keep going straight ahead to reach the Ferry Building, the Maritime Museum, and downtown shopping malls. The Auckland Domain and Parnell areas are where you'll find the city's largest museum as well as historical homes and shops. Parnell was Auckland's first suburb, established in 1841, and is a good place to look for arts and crafts or sample some of Auckland's most popular cafés, bars, and restaurants.

A GOOD TOUR

It's relatively easy to travel around the main inner city sights with a combination of short bus and ferry trips and some shoe leather. Auckland is a harbor city and the following tour gives plenty of opportunity for views both out to and back from the sea.

Start at the **Civic Theatre** ①, a recently restored mid-city landmark close to most major hotels and the Visitor Information Centre. Right next door is the **Force Entertainment Centre** ②. Step in to check out its futuristic architecture and eclectic shops. Walk out of the complex onto Queen Street, face down toward the harbor, and then turn immediately right into Wellesley Street East. A short walk will get you to the two buildings that comprise the **Auckland Art Gallery** ③. For historic works, look around the Heritage Art Gallery, but for more modern art spend time at the New Art Gallery. At the main entrance to the gallery you are right on the edge of **Albert Park** ④, which divides the city from the university. It's a good place to take a break and watch the students studying and chatting under the trees.

Walk back down the stairs and right onto Kitchener Street. Make your first left onto Victoria Street East. Head downhill toward Queen Street and past a bevy of student-oriented shops and cafés. Continue across Queen Street and up the other side of Victoria Street to the **Sky Tower** ⑤ at Sky City. Before ascending, take a moment to glance up from the base. It's an awesome experience but nothing compared with the view from the top.

Leave Sky City and double back to Queen Street and turn left, toward the waterfront. Malls, travel agents, and myriad retail outlets line both sides of the road. Walk all the way to the end, cross QEII square, and you'll be at the **Ferry Building** ⑥. Follow the signs to the Devonport Ferry but instead of buying a ticket for that trip alone, spend the same amount of money ($7) on a full-day pass, good on Link buses as well. The ferry crosses between Auckland city and Devonport regularly and the round-trip only takes 20 minutes. It's the best way to get onto the harbor if you're pressed for time and gives great views of the city, the Harbour Bridge, the North Shore, and Rangitoto Island.

Back in Auckland, walk out of the Ferry Building, turn right, and walk a few minutes along Quay Street to the **National Maritime Museum** ⑦, which is dedicated to New Zealand's seafaring past and present.

To continue this tour of Auckland, catch an Explorer Bus ($20 for a full day) in front of the museum or at the better-marked stop back at the Ferry Building. Once on the Explorer Bus go to the left side of the top level for the best views. After the bus passes some industrial ports, you'll get excellent views of Devonport, Rangitoto Island, and the Hauraki Gulf. A little farther along is Okahu Bay—the closest swimming beach to the city. The Explorer Bus travels to Mission Bay, a popular swimming and picnic spot, and then stops at **Kelly Tarlton's Underwater World and Antarctic Encounter** ⑧, where you view sharks, giant stingrays, and other species. Continue by Explorer Bus to the **Parnell Rose Gardens** ⑨. You'll have to tell the driver if you want to disembark here, as it is a "request stop." In flowering season (November to March) you should make the effort, but if it's wintertime you can continue straight on to the **Auckland Museum** ⑩ to view the most comprehensive collection of Maori artifacts in the country. The museum is set in the attractive parklands known as **Auckland Domain** ⑪.

Head away from the museum by foot, back down Maunsell Road, then cross the road and turn left on Parnell Road. Take a right onto Ayr Street where you'll find the historic **Ewelme Cottage** ⑫. Walk back up Ayr Street, turn right into Parnell Road, and you will quickly reach the Church of the Holy Trinity and **Cathedral Church of St. Mary** ⑬, a Gothic-style church built in 1886. Walk down the hill just a bit and you'll reach charming **Parnell Village** ⑭. The last Explorer Bus passes through Parnell at 4:35 PM, but if you prefer to stay in Parnell for dinner, you can head back downtown later by taxi or on a Link bus. Catch a bus at any Link bus stop on the left-hand side of the road as you face the sea. They run every 10 minutes. A convenient stop is at the corner of Parnell Road and Birdwood Crescent.

TIMING

This tour can be done in a full day, but you'd be restricting your gallery, museum, and Kelly Tarlton's visits to about an hour each. If you have two days, it would make sense to walk the first part of this tour on day one, and get off the ferry at Devonport, spending some time in this quaint, seaside suburb. On the second day, you could head to Kelly Tarlton's first and then explore the Auckland Museum and Parnell area in a more leisurely manner. You might want to pack a picnic lunch to eat in the Domain.

Another way to have more museum time is to save Kelly Tarlton's for an evening visit, since the last admission is 8 PM. At that time of night you would have to drive or take a taxi both to and from Kelly Tarlton's.

Sights to See

 Albert Park. These 15 acres of formal gardens, fountains, and statue-studded lawns are a favorite for Aucklanders who pour out of nearby

Auckland

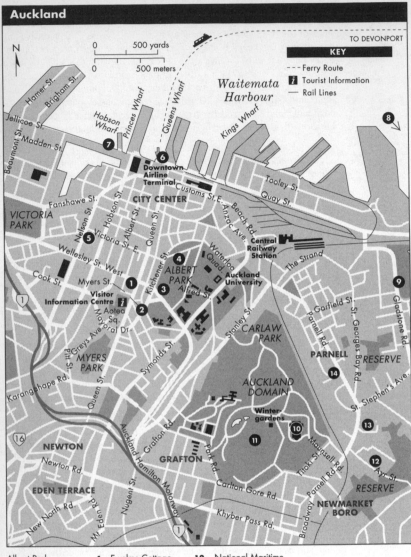

KEY

- - - - Ferry Route
i Tourist Information
———— Rail Lines

TO DEVONPORT

Waitemata Harbour

N

0 ————— 500 yards
0 ————— 500 meters

office blocks and the university and polytechnic to eat lunch on sunny days. The park is built on the site of a garrison from the 1840s and 1850s that was used to protect settlers from neighboring Maori tribes. There are still remnants of its stone walls (with rifle slits) behind university buildings on the east side of the park. ⊠ *Wellesley St. W, Kitchener St., Waterloo Quad.*

❸ Auckland Art Gallery. The country's finest collection of contemporary art hangs here as well as paintings of New Zealand dating from the time of Captain Cook. Look for works by Frances Hodgkins, New Zealand's best-known artist. The older **Heritage Art Gallery** houses many of the historic paintings and in 1995 the gallery expanded with the opening of the more modern **New Art Gallery** across the street. On some winter Sunday afternoons the museum presents jazz and classical music concerts. ⊠ *5 Kitchener St., at Wellesley St. E,* ☎ *09/307–7700.* ☒ *Heritage Gallery free, except for special exhibits; New Gallery $3.* ☉ *Daily 10–5.*

⓫ Auckland Domain. Sunday picnickers and morning runners are two types of Aucklanders who you'll see enjoying the rolling, 340-acre Domain. Watch the local paper for free summer weekend evening concerts, which usually include opera and fireworks displays. Take a bottle of wine and a basketful of something tasty and join in with the locals— up to 300,000 of them per show. Within the Domain, the domed **Wintergardens** house a collection of tropical plants and palms and seasonally displayed hothouse plants—a good stop for the horticulturally inclined. ⊠ *Entrances at Stanley St., Park Rd., Carlton Gore Rd., and Maunsell Rd.* ☒ *Free.* ☉ *Wintergardens daily 10–4.*

❿ Auckland Museum. Dominating the Domain atop a hill, the Greek Revival museum is known especially for its Maori artifacts, the largest collection of its kind. Portraits of Maori chiefs by C. F. Goldie are splendid character studies of a fiercely martial people. Other exhibits in the museum are dedicated to natural history, geology, and local history, including a reconstructed streetscape of early Auckland. Check out **Weird and Wonderful,** an interactive display for kids of all ages. ⊠ *Auckland Domain, Park Rd., Grafton,* ☎ *09/309–0443,* ☒ *09/379–9956.* ☒ *Free ($5 suggested donation).* ☉ *Daily 10–5.*

⓭ Cathedral Church of St. Mary. Gothic Revival wooden churches don't get much finer than this one. Built in 1886, it's one of a number of churches commissioned by the early Anglican missionary Bishop Selwyn. The craftsmanship inside the church is remarkable, as is the story of its relocation. St. Mary's originally stood on the other side of Parnell Road, and in 1982 the entire structure was moved across the street to be next to the new church. Photographs inside show the progress of the work. The church now forms part of the Cathedral of the Holy Trinity. ⊠ *Parnell Rd. and St. Stephen's Ave.* ☉ *Daily 8–6.*

❶ Civic Theatre. This extravagant Art Nouveau movie theater was the talk of the town when it opened in 1929, but just nine months later the owner, Thomas O'Brien, went bust and fled, taking with him the week's revenues and an usherette. During World War II a cabaret show in the basement was popular with Allied servicemen in transit to the battlefields of the Pacific. One of the entertainers, Freda Stark, is said to have appeared regularly wearing nothing more than a coat of gold paint. The building reopened in late 1999 after being closed for extensive refurbishment. To see the best of the Civic, don't restrict your visit to standing outside. Sit down to a show or movie, look up to the ceiling, and you'll see a simulated night sky. ⊠ *Queen and Wellesley Sts.,* ☎ *09/307–5075.*

⑫ **Ewelme Cottage.** Built by the Reverend Vicesimus Lush and inhabited by his descendants for more than a century, this historic cottage stands behind a picket fence. The house was constructed of kauri, a resilient timber highly prized by the Maori for their war canoes and later by Europeans for ship masts. Ewelme Cottage contains much of the original furniture and personal effects of the Lush family. ⊠ *14 Ayr St.,* ☎ *09/379–0202.* ☞ *$3.* ☉ *Wed.–Sun. 10:30–noon and 1–4:30.*

⑥ **Ferry Building.** This magnificent Edwardian building was built in 1912 and it continues to stand out on Auckland's waterfront. The building is still used for its original purpose and it's here that you can catch the ferry to Devonport as well as to Waiheke and other Huaraki Gulf islands. The building also houses bars and restaurants—more recent additions. Nearby, and easily seen from the Ferry Building, is Marsden Wharf, where French frogmen bombed and sank the Greenpeace vessel *Rainbow Warrior* in 1985. On Friday and Saturday after 7 PM, the regular Devonport boat is replaced by the MV *Kestrel*, a turn-of-the-last-century ferry with restored wood and brass and fitted with a bar and a jazz band. ⊠ *Quay St.*

② **Force Entertainment Centre.** With design concepts that could be from a science-fiction movie (actually, some of them are), the Force is worth a walk even if you don't intend to partake in the entertainment and eclectic shopping available here. Spiral staircases, bridges designed to look like film, and elevators in the shape of rockets regularly attract design and architecture students and enthusiasts. The Force incorporates New Zealand's only **IMAX Theatre**, an Internet café, a 12-screen cineplex, an international food court, and several bars, including the **Playhouse Pub**, an English-style tavern with a Shakespearean theme. A video arcade, bookstore, photo developer, and New Zealand's first **Planet Hollywood** add to the diverse mix. ⊠ *291–297 Queen St.,* ☎ *09/303–3346.* ☉ *8 AM–midnight.*

🖐 ⑧ **Kelly Tarlton's Underwater World and Antarctic Encounter.** The creation of New Zealand's most celebrated undersea explorer and treasure hunter, this harborside marine park offers a fish's-eye view of the sea. A submerged transparent tunnel, 120 yards long, makes a circuit past moray eels, lobsters, sharks, and stingrays. In Antarctic Encounter, you enter a replica of explorer Robert Falcon Scott's 1911 Antarctic hut at McMurdo Sound, then circle around a deep-freeze environment aboard a heated Sno-Cat (snowmobile) that winds through a penguin colony and an aquarium exhibiting marine life of the polar sea. You emerge at Scott Base 2000 for a glimpse of the next century's Antarctic research and exploration. Kelly Tarlton's is 5 km (3 mi) from downtown Auckland, west on Tamaki Drive. ⊠ *Orakei Wharf, 23 Tamaki Dr.,* ☎ *09/528–0603.* ☞ *$20.* ☉ *Daily 9–9 (last admission 8 PM).*

🖐 ⑦ **National Maritime Museum.** New Zealand's rich seafaring history is on display in a marina complex on Auckland Harbour. Experience what it was like to travel steerage class in the 1800s or check out a replica of a shipping office from the turn of the last century. There are detailed exhibits on early whaling and a collection of outboard motors, yachts, ship models, and Polynesian outriggers. A scow conducts short trips on the harbor. The museum also hosts workshops, where traditional boatbuilding, sail making, and rigging skills are kept alive. The pride of the museum is the *KZ1*, the 133-ft racing sloop built for the America's Cup challenge in 1988. ⊠ *Eastern Viaduct, Quay St.,* ☎ *09/358–3010.* ☞ *$12, heritage cruise $10 extra.* ☉ *Oct.–Easter, daily 9–6; Easter–Sept., daily 9–5.*

9 Parnell Rose Gardens. When you tire of boutiques and cafés, take a 10-minute stroll to gaze upon and sniff this collection of some 5,000 rosebushes. The main beds contain mostly modern hybrids, with new introductions being planted regularly. The adjacent **Nancy Steen Garden** is the place to admire the antique varieties. And don't miss the garden's incredible trees. There is a 200-year-old *pohutukawa* (puh-hoo-too-*ka*-wa) whose weighty branches touch the ground and rise up again and a *kanuka* that is one of Auckland's oldest trees. The Rose Garden Restaurant serves lunch (closed Saturday). ⌧ *Gladstone and Judges Bay Rds.,* ☎ *09/302–1252.* ⌧ *Free.* ☉ *Daily dawn–dusk.*

10 Parnell Village. The pretty Victorian timber villas along the slope of Parnell Road have been transformed into antiques shops, designer boutiques, street cafés, and restaurants. Parnell Village is the creation of Les Harvey, who saw the potential of the quaint but run-down shops and houses and almost single-handedly snatched them from the jaws of the developers' bulldozers by buying them, renovating them, and leasing them out. Harvey's vision has paid handsome dividends, and today this village of trim pink-and-white timber facades is one of the most delightful parts of the city. At night its restaurants, pubs, and discos attract Auckland's chic set. Parnell's shops are open Sunday. ⌧ *Parnell Rd. between St. Stephen's Ave. and Augustus Rd.*

5 Sky Tower. The joke among Auckland residents is that your property value rises if you *can't* see this 1,082-ft beacon. Yet it's also the first place Aucklanders take friends and relatives visiting from overseas in order to give them a view of the city. Up at the main observation level, the most outrageous thing is the glass floor panels—looking down at your feet, you see the street hundreds of yards below. Adults usually step gingerly onto the glass, and kids delight in jumping up and down on it. More educational are the audio guides to Auckland and touch-screen computers that you'll find on the deck. There is also an outdoor observation level, where you'll feel the wind on your face as you see the sights. ⌧ *Victoria and Federal Sts.,* ☎ *09/912–6000.* ⌧ *$15.* ☉ *Sun.–Fri. 8:30 AM–11 PM (last elevator 10:30 PM), Sat. 8:30 AM–midnight (last elevator 11:30 PM).*

Devonport

The 20-minute ferry to Devonport across Waitemata Harbour provides one of the finest views of Auckland. The first harbor ferry service began with whaleboats in 1854. Later in the century the Devonport Steam Ferry Co. began operations, and ferries scuttled back and forth across the harbor until the Harbour Bridge opened in 1959. The bridge now carries the bulk of the commuter traffic, but the ferry still has a small, devoted clientele.

Originally known as Flagstaff, after the signal station on the summit of Mt. Victoria, Devonport was the first settlement on the north side of the harbor. Later the area drew some of the city's wealthiest traders, who built their homes where they could watch their sailing ships arriving with cargoes from Europe. These days, Aucklanders have fixed up and repopulated its great old houses, laying claim to the suburb's relaxed, seaside atmosphere.

The Esplanade Hotel is one of the first things you'll see as you leave the ferry terminal. It stands at the harbor end of **Victoria Road,** a pleasant street for taking a stroll, stopping at a shop, a bookstore, or a café, or for picking up some fish-and-chips to eat next to the giant Moreton Bay fig tree on the green across the street.

Long before the era of European settlement, the ancient volcano now called **Mt. Victoria** was the site of a Maori *pa* (fortified village) of the local Kawerau tribe. On the northern and eastern flanks of the hill you can still see traces of the terraces once protected by palisades of sharpened stakes. Don't be put off by its name—this is more molehill than mountain, and the climb isn't much. Mt. Victoria is signposted on Victoria Road, a few minutes' walk from the Esplanade Hotel. ⊠ *Kerr St. off Victoria Rd.*

New Zealand's navy is hardly a menacing global force, but the small **Naval Museum** has interesting exhibits on the early exploration of the country and information on its involvement in various conflicts. The museum is five blocks west of Victoria Wharf along Queens Parade. ⊠ *Queens Parade.* 🎫 *Small donation.* ⊙ *Daily 10–4.*

North Head is an ancient Maori defense site, and its position jutting out from Devonport into Auckland's harbor was enough to convince the European settlers that they, too, should use the head for strategic purposes. Rumor has it that veteran aircraft are still stored in the dark, twisting tunnels under North Head, but plenty of curious explorers have not found any. You can still get into most tunnels, climb all over the abandoned antiaircraft guns, and get great views of Auckland and the islands to the east. North Head is a 20-minute walk east of the ferry terminal on King Edward Parade, left onto Cheltenham Street, and then out Takarunga Road. ⊠ *Takarunga Rd.*

Around Auckland

🐾 **Auckland Zoo.** Like many of the world's zoos, this one has had its fair share of controversy over the merits of keeping caged animals. The past decade has seen a real shift of priorities, and emphasis is now on displaying animals in as natural a habitat as possible as well as on breeding and conservation. The best examples of this new approach are the new primates area and Pridelands section. To catch a glimpse of New Zealand flora and fauna, spend time in the New Zealand Aviary (where you walk among the birds) and the Kiwi and Tuatara Nocturnal House, which are at opposite ends of the zoo. By car, take Karangahape Road (which turns into Great North Road) west out of the city, past Western Springs. Take a right onto Motions Road. ⊠ *Motions Rd., Western Springs,* ☎ *09/360–3819,* 𝖥𝖠𝖷 *09/360–3818.* 🎫 *$12.* ⊙ *Daily 9:30–5:50 (last entry 4:30).*

★ **Beaches.** Auckland's beaches are commonly categorized by area—east, west, or north. The ones closest to the city are the east-coast beaches along Tamaki Drive on the south side of the harbor, which do not have heavy surf. **Judge's Bay** and **Mission Bay** are particularly recommended for their settings. The best swimming is at high tide.

West-coast black-sand beaches are popular in summer, but the sea is often rough, and sudden rips and holes can trap the unwary. The most visited of these is **Piha,** some 40 km (25 mi) west of Auckland, which has pounding surf as well as a sheltered lagoon dominated by the reclining mass of Lion Rock. **Whatipu,** south of Piha, is a broad sweep of sand offering safe bathing behind the sandbar that guards Manukau Harbour. **Bethells,** to the north, often has heavy surf. In the vicinity, **Karekare** is the beach where the dramatic opening scenes of Jane Campion's *The Piano* were shot. Across Waitemata Harbour from the city, a chain of magnificent beaches stretches north as far as the WhangaTheraoa Peninsula, 40 km (25 mi) from Auckland.

🐾 **Museum of Transport and Technology.** This fascinating collection of aircraft, telephones, cameras, locomotives, steam engines, and farm equipment is a tribute to Kiwi ingenuity. One of the most intriguing exhibits is the remains of an aircraft built by Robert Pearse, who made a successful powered flight barely three months after the Wright broth-

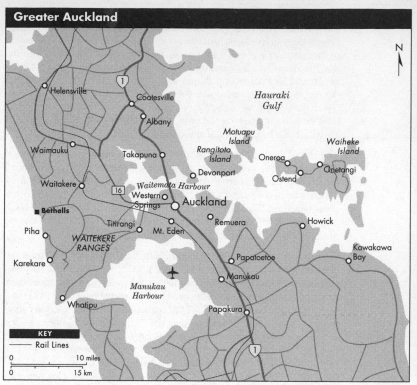

Helensville · Coatesville · Albany · *Hauraki Gulf* · *Motuapu Island* · *Rangitoto Island* · Waimauku · Takapuna · Devonport · Oneroa · *Waiheke Island* · Onetangi · Ostend · Waitakere · *Waitemata Harbour* · Western Springs · **Auckland** · **Bethells** · Titirangi · Mt. Eden · Remuera · Howick · Piha · *WAITEKERE RANGES* · Kawakawa Bay · Karekare · Papatoetoe · Manukau · *Manukau Harbour* · Whatipu · Papakura

N

KEY
— Rail Lines

0   10 miles
0   15 km

ers first took to the skies. The flight ended inauspiciously when his plane crashed into a hedge, but Pearse, considered a wild eccentric by his farming neighbors, is recognized today as a mechanical genius. The museum is west of the city, near the Auckland Zoo. ⊠ *825 Great North Rd., off Northwestern Motorway, Rte. 16, Western Springs,* ☎ *09/846–0199.* ☜ *$10.* ☉ *Daily 10–5.*

Rangitoto Island. When Rangitoto Island emerged from the sea in a series of fiery eruptions 600 years ago, it had an audience. Footprints in the ash on its close neighbor **Motutapu Island** prove that Maori people watched Rangitoto's birth. It is now the largest and youngest of about 50 volcanic cones and craters in the Auckland volcanic field, though scientists are confident that it will not blow again. During the 1920s and 1930s hundreds of prisoners built roads and trails on the island, some of which are still used as walkways. Small beach houses were also erected on the island in the early 20th century but it now has no permanent residents.

The most popular activity on the island is the one-hour summit walk, beginning at Rangitoto Wharf and climbing through lava fields and forest to the peak. At the top, walkers are rewarded with panoramic views of Auckland and the Hauraki Gulf. Short detours will lead to lava caves and even to the remnants of a botanical park planned in 1915, and you can walk around the rim of the crater. **Fullers Cruise Centre** (☎ 09/367–9111) operates ferries to Rangitoto at 9:30 AM and 11:45 AM weekdays, plus 2 PM weekends. Return trips are at 12:30 PM and 3 PM weekdays, plus 5 PM weekends. The fare is $18 round-trip. The **Volcanic Explorer,** operated by Fullers, will take you on a guided ride to the summit in a covered carriage towed by a tractor. The cost (including ferry fare) is $35.

Waiheke Island. Once a sleepy suburb of Auckland, Waiheke was mainly used as a weekend and summer vacation retreat, with beach houses dotting its edges. Since the late 1980s more people have moved to the island as a lifestyle choice, commuting each day by ferry to the city. The island is also earning an international reputation for its vineyards, and local cafés sometimes stock wines that aren't available on the mainland—vintners make them purely for island enjoyment. Ferries make the trip from the Ferry Building at least a dozen times a day, even on Sunday. However, it pays to phone first (☎ 09/367–9111), as crossings can be canceled if the seas are rough.

The ferry lands at **Matiatia Wharf.** Buses meet ferries at the terminal and make a loop around the island. Or you can walk five minutes to the small town of **Oneroa.** Another minute's walk gets you to **Oneroa Beach,** one of the island's finest and most accessible beaches. Another great beach on Waiheke is **Onetangi,** on the north side of the island, 20 minutes from Matiatia by bus. **Whakanewha Regional Park** is on the south of the island and has hiking and picnic options.

There are around 30 vineyards on Waiheke Island, but because most are rather new, less than a dozen are producing wine. First to plant grapes were Kim and Jeanette Goldwater, whose eponymous wines have earned a reputation for excellence. The **Goldwater Estate** (✉ 18 Causeway Rd., Putiki Bay, ☎ 09/372–7493) cabernet sauvignon–merlot–cabernet franc blend is outstanding, and the Esslin Merlot has been hailed as the best Kiwi interpretation of this popular variety. The winery is open for tastings in summer months only, daily between 11 AM and 4 PM. Stephen White's **Stonyridge Vineyard** (✉ 80 Onetangi Rd., Ostend, ☎ 09/372–8822, FAX 09/372–8766) has the island's highest profile, and his Stonyridge Larose, also made from the classic Bordeaux varieties, is world class—and priced accordingly. Stephen gets faxed orders months before release and is usually sold out hours later. Call before you visit—he may have nothing left to taste or sell. A good place to try wines that never make it to the mainland is **Mudbrick Vineyard and Restaurant** (✉ Church Bay Rd., Oneroa, ☎ 09/372–9050), which produces a small portfolio of whites and reds of its own, and serves them and those of other tiny producers alongside food generally regarded as the island's best.

If you're planning on going farther afield on the island, you can purchase an all-day bus pass from **Fullers Cruise Centre** (☎ 09/367–9111). The $30 pass includes the ferry trip and bus travel on regular services to Oneroa, Palm Beach, Onetangi, and Rocky Bay. To use the pass, you need to take the 8:15, 10, or noon ferry. Return time is optional. **Fuller's Island Explorer Tour and Ferry** costs $34 and stops at Onetangi Beach. Their **Waiheke Vineyard Explorer Tour** takes 5½ hours and costs $55, ferry included. After either explorer tour, on the same day, passengers may use their ticket to travel free on regular island buses to visit additional attractions. Reservations for Waiheke tours are essential during the summer. You can also take a shuttle to beaches or vineyards; **Waiheke Island Shuttles** (☎ 09/372–7756) has reliable service. The best way to get to Whakanewha Regional Park is by shuttle.

Waitakere Ranges. This scenic mountain range west of Auckland is a favorite walking and picnic spot for locals. The 20-minute **Arataki Nature Trail** is a great introduction to kauri and other native trees. The highlight of another great trail, **Auckland City Walk,** is Cascade Falls. The **Arataki Visitors Centre** displays modern Maori carvings and has information on the Waitakeres and other Auckland parks. To get to the Waitakeres, head along the Northwestern Motorway, Route 16, from central Auckland, take the Waterview turnoff, and keep heading west to the gateway village of Titirangi. A sculpture depicting fungal growths tells you you're heading in the right direction. From here the best route to follow is Scenic Drive, with spectacular views of Auckland and its two harbors. The visitor center is 5 km (3 mi) along the drive.

Dining

City Center

$$$–$$$$ ✕ **Five City Road.** Dietmar Sawyere is the owner and executive chef of this very upmarket establishment—quite a feat, given that he holds the same positions at Level 41 in Sydney! The food is contemporary, but Dietmar's classical training shows through. Various Asian flavors are interestingly combined in dishes such as Chinese-style roast duck served with tiny scallops and drizzled with a Vietnamese-inspired dressing, but there are plenty of options to please the traditionalists. The decor is elegant and the atmosphere rather hushed; this is the place for serious dining. ⊠ *5 City Rd.,* ☎ *09/309–9273. AE, DC, MC, V. Closed Sun. No lunch.*

$–$$ ✕ **Sun World.** In the last six years, Auckland has absorbed a huge num-
★ ber of immigrants from Hong Kong and Taiwan, and the standard of Chinese restaurants has improved dramatically as a result. Sun World is the place to go for *yum char* (dim sum), that admirable institution that allows you to choose from a variety of dishes (not all of them recognizable) as they're carried past your table. It's on every day from 11 AM, and it is enthusiastically supported by Asian family groups. You'll think you're in Kowloon or Taipei, you'll have a great time, and you'll eat really cheaply. Choose a well-priced bottle of wine from the modest list or save cash by sticking to almost-free fragrant tea. ⊠ *56 Wakefield St.,* ☎ *09/373–5335. AE, DC, MC, V.*

Devonport

$$–$$$ ✕ **Porterhouse Blue.** Devonport's main street is chock-full of casual cafés and delicatessens, but it's worth leaving the shopping strip and heading up the hill to this popular spot. Chef Craig McKenzie has an innovative style that often combines Asian, French, and Italian influences on one plate. Three different preparations of salmon are served as a trio, and the Porterhouse tuatua (shellfish) fritters are regarded as the best in town. Phone first, and you can arrange a pickup from the ferry. ⊠ *58 Calliope Rd., Devonport,* ☎ *09/445–0309. AE, DC, MC, V. Closed Sun. No lunch.*

Harborside

$$$–$$$$ ✕ **Kermadec.** This complex's two restaurants are owned by a major fishing company, so naturally, the emphasis is on seafood. Take in the harborside views and dramatic Pacific-theme decor, then decide which area takes your fancy. In the more casual brasserie, start with shellfish, then seek the kitchen's advice on the best way to enjoy the catch of the day. The adjacent Ocean Fresh restaurant prepares great sushi and sashimi, or you could start with spiced *simi* (Japanese shellfish) scampi and water chestnuts with tandoori-spiced melon and mint yogurt, followed by herb-crusted orange roughy (a mild fish) on citrus and kumara *rösti* (sweet potato fritters). Can't decide? Share a platter—it will probably include smoked salmon, scallops, prawns, mussels, smoked eel, scampi, John Dory, and snapper. Desserts are equally imaginative. ⊠ *1st floor, Viaduct Quay Building, Quay and Lower Hobson Sts.,* ☎ *09/ 309–0413 brasserie, 09/309–0412 restaurant. AE, DC, MC, V.*

$$$ ✕ **Cin Cin on Quay.** Auckland's original seaside brasserie is still one of
★ the best. Look for innovative pizza—tandoori chicken with avocado-mango chutney and red onion has been here since day one—and clever starter and main course selections like rare, peppered yellowfin tuna with

Auckland Dining and Lodging

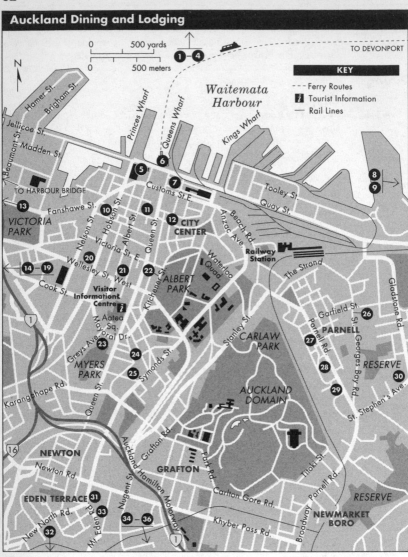

Dining

Antik's **32**
Antoine's **29**
Atomic Café **14**
Burger Wisconsin . . . **15**
Catalonia **13**
Cibo **26**
Cin Cin on Quay **6**
Dizengoff **16**
Five City Road **25**
The French Café **31**

Galbraith's
Ale House **33**
GPK **17**
Harbourside Seafood
Bar and Grill **7**
Iguaçú **28**
Kermadec **5**
Non Solo Pizza **27**
Porterhouse Blue **4**
Provence **18**
Saint's Waterfront
Brasserie **8**

Sun World **24**
Vinnie's **19**

Lodging

Albion Hotel **20**
Ascot Parnell **30**
Brooklands Country
Estate **34**
Carlton **23**
Centra **21**
Devonport Villa Inn . . .**1**
Florida Motel **9**

Grand Sommerset
Metropolis Hotel **22**
Heritage Aukland . . . **10**
Hotel DeBrett **12**
Hotel du Vin **35**
Hyland House **3**
Peace and
Plenty Inn **2**
Sedgwick-Kent
Lodge **36**
Stamford Plaza **11**

a green-tea noodle salad and sesame dressing, or pink-roasted lamb rack with a pumpkin and goat cheese strudel and sweet peppers. The wine list includes several vintages of local icons like Kumeu River Chardonnay and Stonyridge Larose, a power-packed cabernet-based blend from Waiheke Island. If you're in town on the weekend, reserve an outside table overlooking the harbor for the good-value breakfast. ⊠ *Auckland Ferry Building, 99 Quay St.,* ☎ *09/307–6966. AE, DC, MC, V.*

$$$ ✕ **Harbourside Seafood Bar and Grill.** Overlooking the water from the upper level of the restored ferry building (above Cin Cin), this sprawling, modish seafood restaurant is a fine choice for warm-weather dining. Some of the finest New Zealand fish and shellfish, including tuna, salmon, snapper, pipi, and tuatua, appear on a menu with a fashionably Mediterranean accent—or choose the seafood platter and try the lot. Lobster fresh from the tank is a house specialty. Non-fish–eaters have their choice of *cervena* (farmed venison), lamb, and poultry. On warm nights, reserve ahead and request a table outside on the deck. ⊠ *Auckland Ferry Building, 99 Quay St.,* ☎ *09/307–0486. AE, DC, MC, V.*

Parnell

$$$$ ✕ **Antoine's.** Owners Tony and Beth Astle have run this stately Par-
★ nell institution for a quarter century, and it still enjoys a reputation as *the* special occasion spot in town. The decor is old-style stately, the service immaculate, and the food classy—and expensive. Tony is still at the stove, and his current menu reads as if it were designed by a chef half his age. The classics are there—oxtail casserole, braised lamb shanks, and creamy tripe are big sellers—but they are joined by the likes of a seaweed and garlic flan topped with oysters, whitebait, and flying fish caviar, or a trio of tuna preparations that presents the rich red flesh sliced thinly as carpaccio, chopped as tartare, and sliced, seared, and tucked inside a spring roll. All three versions are drizzled with a dressing based on sesame and chilli oils. Prefer your tuna cooked? Try it coated in toasted sesame seeds, cooked rare (unless requested otherwise), and served on a green tomato relish with salmon caviar. The wine list is extensive and international. ⊠ *333 Parnell Rd.,* ☎ *09/379–8756. AE, DC, MC, V. Closed Sun. No lunch Sat.*

$$$ ✕ **Cibo.** A little bit away from the main Parnell restaurant strip, but well worth searching out, Cibo won three categories in a recent restaurant competition—a feat no other establishment has managed, before or since. A few mod-Kiwi classics are available here, but food leans towards Asia, with an emphasis on Nonya, Singapore's distinctive Chinese-Malaysian cuisine. The winning competition menu included a salad of lemongrass-poached prawns on *soba* (Japanese buckwheat) noodles that one judge deemed perfect, followed by oven-roasted venison with red lentils and eggplant. The wine list is well thought out and expertly presented, and the surroundings are interestingly eclectic, combining plush, red velvet drapes with lots of steel and glass. ⊠ *81 St. Georges Bay Rd.,* ☎ *09/309 2255. AE, DC, MC, V.*

$$–$$$ ✕ **Iguaçú.** With flares blazing near the entrance, dappled red ocher walls, a terra-cotta tiled floor, enormous mirrors in Mexican metalwork frames, a glass ceiling, and a pair of chandeliers made from copper tubing, the decor borrows from several cultures, and the menu follows suit. The kitchen goes nationalistic with fritters based on tuatua (shellfish) and kumara, served with mayo flavored with *kina* (sea urchin) roe. Or picture yellowfin tuna, crusted with sesame seeds, seared, and arranged over Malaysian noodles and a papaw salsa. Befitting its fashionable status, the restaurant is generally full of patrons who come to see and be seen as much as to enjoy the food. ⊠ *269 Parnell Rd.,* ☎ *09/309–4124. AE, DC, MC, V.*

$$–$$$ ✕ **Non Solo Pizza.** The name means "not only pizza," and that tells it
  ★   like it is. This uncompromisingly Italian eatery offers pasta as a single
       serving or in table-sharing bowls that feed four or more. Try the egg-
       plant, panfried and layered with mozzarella, tomato, basil, and Parme-
       san, or look for spaghetti with fresh cockles. And there's always pizza
       with traditional toppings followed by a masterfully prepared green salad.
       The same team runs Toto, on the other side of town, so if you can't
       get a seat here, ask if the sister restaurant is also full. ✉ *259 Parnell
       Rd.,* ☎ *09/379–5358. AE, DC, MC, V.*

Ponsonby

$$$ ✕ **Provence.** You'll think you've swapped continents when you step
       into this small but perfectly formed restaurant. Wide, ornately framed
       mirrors and lots of timber and exposed brick all add to the French provin-
       cial atmosphere, and chef Laurance Brunacci's food is thoroughly Gal-
       lic. Snails, brains, rabbit, pig's trotters, duck—you'll find them all in
       various guises, and they will all be delicious. The wine list, too, has
       French leanings, but nationalism is sensibly suspended to give New
       Zealand bottles pride of place. ✉ *44 Ponsonby Rd.,* ☎ *09/376–8147.
       AE, DC, MC, V.*

$$–$$$ ✕ **GPK.** The initials stand for Gourmet Pizza Kitchen or Gourmet
       Pizza Konnection—take your pick. This corner eatery was the city's
       pioneer posh-pizza place, and soon afterwards spawned a sister es-
       tablishment at 234 Dominion Road, Mount Eden. Some of the top-
       pings would make a traditionalist squirm (tandoori chicken with
       banana and yogurt), but there are plenty of offerings more typically
       Italian. The wine and beer list is impressively comprehensive. ✉ *262
       Ponsonby Rd.,* ☎ *09/360–1113. Reservations not accepted. AE, DC,
       MC, V.*

$–$$ ✕ **Dizengoff.** The food is Jewish, but not strictly kosher, and with owner-
       chef Brendan Turner's background as a cooking school instructor, it's
       right up to the minute. The most popular breakfast dish is a combi-
       nation of eggs, lox, and butter sauce on a brioche. The lunch menu
       has chopped liver as well as Israeli classics, but they share the menu
       with the likes of a salad of finely diced chicken, tossed with chopped
       parsley, lemon juice, and fruity olive oil. Or try the beet salad—Bren-
       dan mixes baby beets with fava beans in a balsamic dressing, then lay-
       ers on extra flavor with pesto and shaved Parmesan. ✉ *256 Ponsonby
       Rd.,* ☎ *09/360–0108. AE, DC, MC, V. No dinner.*

$ ✕ **Atomic Café.** Chris Priestley was a Ponsonby pioneer, and he still
       runs one of the best coffee bars on the strip. There's food for vegetar-
       ians, vegans, macrobiotics, meat-eaters—and even children. Young
       ones are also catered to in the outside courtyard, where scattered toys
       and other distractions keep them amused while Mom and Dad nibble
       on the likes of noodle or rice bowls, or eclectic salads, followed by cof-
       fee made from beans roasted on the premises. The decor is bohemian,
       and the service is supercasual and friendly. ✉ *121 Ponsonby Rd.,* ☎
       09/376–4954. No credit cards. BYOB. No dinner Sat.–Wed.

$ ✕ **Burger Wisconsin.** Traveling Americans consistently rate Wiscon-
       sin's five Auckland outlets as the best burger joints in town. The
       bunned delights include chicken breast with cream cheese and apricot
       sauce, Malaysian *satay* (marinated, grilled meat skewers), bacon and
       beef with coconut mayonnaise, and a vegetarian soy and sesame-seed
       burger. At this branch—if the weather's warm—you can order your
       burger to go, then wander over to nearby Western Park. ✉ *168 Pon-
       sonby Rd.,* ☎ *09/360–1894. AE, DC, MC, V.*

Other Suburbs

$$$ ✕ **Catalonia.** The name sounds Spanish, but it refers to the French side
★ of the Catalan district. That's where chef Franck Bocamy hails from,
and the menu has been largely transplanted from his homeland. Mar-
seille-style seafood soups, classic steak tartare, and an authentic cas-
soulet are all favorites with the regulars. Franck's partner, Catherine
Finlayson, learned her waiting and greeting skills working for the Ori-
ent Express group, but she's grafted on a bit of Kiwi casualness. Take
her word for it when it comes to desserts—the *crème Catalan*, Franck's
hometown adaptation of a classic crème brûlée, is fabulous. ⊠ *129
Hurstmere Rd., Takapuna,* ☎ *09/489–3104. AE, DC, MC, V.*

$$$ ✕ **The French Café.** It's not really a café, and it's not particularly
★ French, but don't let the inaccurate nomenclature put you off—the food's
great. Simon Wright has a light touch that translates to clean, focused
flavors, and his partner, Creghen Molloy, greets guests with style and
a smile. Order classic New Zealand ingredients like *paua* (black
abalone), Greenshell mussels, crayfish, or spring lamb and be guaranteed
they will be marvelous. In season, Simon's whitebait fritter, sometimes
served with braised bell peppers, aioli, and an herb salad, is the best
in the land. The wine list includes a few finds, and the staff knowledge
is impeccable. ⊠ *210B Symonds St., at Khyber Pass,* ☎ *09/377–1911.
AE, DC, MC, V.*

$$$ ✕ **Saint's Waterfront Brasserie.** This stylish brasserie, a 15-minute
drive east of the city, is the perfect place to enjoy the City of Sails along
with good, modern New Zealand fare. The gray carpet and white table-
cloths under glass create a smart, clean atmosphere, and full-width,
folding glass doors frame an impressive sea view. Start with tuatua (shell-
fish) fritters with fresh tomato and basil sauce, then get serious with
beef tenderloin on grilled summer vegetables marinated in balsamic vine-
gar, served with soft kumara. The weekend brunch menu includes
obligatory muesli and other healthy options, but what the heck—
you're on vacation! Head for berry pancakes with soft whipped cream
and ice cream, or French toast with bacon, tomato, and maple syrup.
⊠ *425 Tamaki Dr., St. Heliers,* ☎ *09/575–5210. AE, DC, MC, V.*

$$$ ✕ **Vinnie's.** Serious foodies rate David Griffith's food as the best
★ around. Vinnie's recently beat 80 other contestants to take the top award
in the Corbans Wine & Food Challenge, in which restaurants compete to serve three courses perfectly matched with three wines. The decor
in this shop-front suburban restaurant is fresh and clean, with just a
hint of Paris bistro, but the food leans more toward the gutsy styles of
Provence and southern Italy—with the obligatory glance towards Asia.
Let David's partner, Pru Barton, tempt you with the likes of prosci-
utto-wrapped quail with mortadella stuffing, Chinese five-spice duck
confit with pineapple-sherry vinegar dressing and wild greens, or
thyme-roasted lamb rack with summer ratatouille and goat cheese
tortellini. Desserts are equally imaginative. ⊠ *166 Jervois Rd., Herne
Bay,* ☎ *09/376–5597. AE, DC, MC, V. No lunch Jan.–Nov.*

$$–$$$ ✕ **Antik's.** The eccentric wall hangings at this pioneer café in the city's
newest foodie strip include antique skis, a pair of crutches, and a gro-
cer's bicycle. Owner Tim Holman serves his customers with panache
and humor: anyone finding the menu hard to read is handed a flashlight and glasses (sponsored by a local optician)—or a magnifying
glass if the glasses aren't strong enough. The menu is eclectic, with dishes
like tandoori chicken with cubed pumpkin, banana salad, and a curry-
cream reduction sauce, or *hangi*-style stuffed chicken breast with crispy
bacon and sautéed mushrooms (a hangi is a Maori earth oven, but this
facsimile is cooked above ground). ⊠ *248A Dominion Rd.,* ☎ *09/638–
6254. AE, DC, MC, V. Licensed and BYOB.*

$ ✕ **Galbraith's Ale House.** Brew lovers and Brits craving a taste of home head straight for Keith Galbraith's traditionally decorated ale-house. The English-style ales are made on the premises and served at proper cellar temperature—i.e., not too cold. Keith learned the art of brewing in the United Kingdom, and he sticks religiously to the style. Order a half or dig into pub classics like pea-pie-pud—a hearty British import that tops a steak pie with mashed potatoes, minted green peas, and gravy—or bangers and mash (seriously good sausages atop creamy mashed potatoes). Well-prepared salads, steaks, and poultry satisfy less medieval palates. ✉ *2 Mt. Eden Rd., Grafton,* ☎ *09/379–3557. AE, MC, V.*

Lodging

City Center

$$$$ ⊞ **Carlton.** Its proximity to the Aotea Centre and downtown makes the Carlton a favorite with business travelers. Guest rooms are spacious and elegantly furnished, and bathrooms are particularly well equipped. The best views are from the rooms that overlook the park-lands and the harbor to the east. Polished granite and warm, earthy tones have been used liberally throughout the building. The hotel's restaurants have occasional food festivals and cooking classes. ✉ *Mayoral Dr. and Vincent St.,* ☎ *09/366–3000,* 𝖥𝖠𝖷 *09/366–0121. 286 rooms. 2 restaurants, 2 bars, coffee shop, tennis court. AE, DC, MC, V.* 🐾

$$$$ ⊞ **Grand Somerset Metropolis Hotel.** Auckland's old magistrate's court
★   house has been converted to provide an elegant lobby, restaurant, and bar for this all-suite hotel. The guest rooms are all situated in a new tower built just behind the court. Though most rooms have decent views, the best sea views are available higher up on the east side of the hotel. On a clear day you'll be able to see right across the harbor to the Coromandel Peninsula. Units are either one- or two-bedroom; most have balconies, and all come with a kitchenette and washing machine and dryer. ✉ *1 Courthouse La.,* ☎ *09/300–8800,* 𝖥𝖠𝖷 *09/300–8899. 315 suites. Bar, restaurant, kitchenettes, indoor pool, 2 hot tubs, sauna, health club. AE, DC, MC, V.* 🐾

$$$$ ⊞ **Heritage Auckland.** Transformed from one of Auckland's land-mark buildings, the Farmers Department Store, this hotel opened in 1998 and quickly earned a reputation as one of the finest in the city. Since then it has added a tower wing, making it New Zealand's largest hotel as well. The size has not detracted from character—the main building has retained its original 1920s art deco design including high ceilings, large jarrah wood columns, and native timber floors. The tower wing is more contemporary and includes New Zealand art especially commissioned for the rooms and public areas. Ask for a room with a harbor view. ✉ *35 Hobson St.,* ☎ *09/379–8553,* 𝖥𝖠𝖷 *09/379–8554. 467 rooms. 2 restaurants, 2 bars, indoor lap pool, outdoor pool, sauna, spa, tennis court, health club. AE, DC, MC, V.* 🐾

$$$$ ⊞ **Stamford Plaza.** This mid-city hotel brought a dash of style to Auckland when it opened as a Regent in the mid-1980s, and, despite some energetic competition, its service, sophistication, and attention to detail keep it on top. Standard rooms are large and furnished extensively with natural fabrics and native woods in an updated art deco style. The marble bathrooms are luxuriously appointed. The best rooms are on the harbor side—the higher the better. Make sure you check out the rooftop area, with its expansive views over Auckland's harbor, or, on a rainy day, take high tea in the lobby. ✉ *Albert St.,* ☎ *09/309–8888,* 𝖥𝖠𝖷 *09/379–6445. 332 rooms. 3 restaurants, bar, pool. AE, DC, MC, V.* 🐾

$$$ ⊞ **Centra.** Rooms at this city landmark are equal to those in just about any of Auckland's leading hotels, but cutting down on facilities and glossy public areas has reduced prices substantially. Accommodations begin on the 16th floor, and every room has a view. The suites on the 28th floor have great views and bigger bathrooms for just a slightly higher price. The hotel opened in 1991 and is aimed primarily at business travelers. Service is keen and professional. ⊠ *128 Albert St.,* ☎ *09/302–1111,* ℻ *09/302–3111. 252 rooms. Restaurant, bar, exercise room. AE, DC, MC, V.* ✎

$$ ⊞ **Ascot Parnell.** Accommodations and facilities in this sprawling guest house are comfortable and functional, but space and character have been sacrificed to provide rooms with private bathrooms at a reasonable price. The room with the attached sunroom at the back of the house is small but pleasant. The house stands on a relatively busy street, within easy walking distance of the shops and nightlife of Parnell Village. Smoking is not permitted inside. ⊠ *36 St. Stephens Ave., Parnell,* ☎ *09/309–9012,* ℻ *09/309–3729. 9 rooms. AE, MC, V. BP.*

$ ⊞ **Albion Hotel.** If you'd like comfortable accommodations in the heart of the city and outstanding value, look no farther. Rooms are modest in size and have no views, but all are neat and well kept. The best room in the house, the Hobson Suite, is equipped with a water bed and bath with jets and costs only slightly more than a standard room. Despite the busy corner location, the area is quiet after 6 PM. However, rooms on the lower floors can be affected by noise from the ground-floor pub, which is especially busy on Friday night. Sky City, the Aotea Centre, and the shops of Queen Street are only a few blocks away. ⊠ *Hobson and Wellesley Sts.,* ☎ *09/379–4900,* ℻ *09/379–4901. 20 rooms. Brasserie, pub. AE, DC, MC, V.*

$ ⊞ **Hotel DeBrett.** This is a good downtown option, especially if you want to save your money for the nearby cafés, bars, and nightclubs. Built in an art deco style, this hotel has had its ups and downs, but reopened recently with a new lease on life. It now offers fairly spacious, comfortable rooms. The hotel's own Saloon Bar, or the quieter Corner Bar, also on-site, are good places to meet locals who come in after work for drinks. ⊠ *2 High St.,* ☎ *09/377–2389,* ℻ *09/377–2391. 21 rooms. 2 bars. MC, V.* ✎

Devonport

$$$$ ⊞ **Hyland House.** Carol and Bruce Hyland are well known in New
★ Zealand's lodging scene as providers of service with flair. They work their magic in this restored 1907 house with added little touches like fresh cookies and locally roasted coffee in the guest rooms and a different table setting each morning for breakfast. The largest guest room is the Aatea Suite, which features works by local artist Cynthia Taylor on the walls. Many a guest has taken the short walk to Flagstaff Art Gallery and purchased one of Taylor's works as a reminder of their stay in Devonport. The suite's bathroom has an antique clawfoot tub. Upstairs, the Provence Room has a French sleigh bed and collection of books about France. Don't leave without admiring the ornately plastered original ceiling and cornice in the guest lounge. ⊠ *4 Flagstaff Terr.,* ☎ *09/445–9917,* ℻ *09/445–9927. 2 rooms. AE, MC, V. BP.* ✎

$$$$ ⊞ **Peace and Plenty Inn.** Devonport's neighborhoody atmosphere
★ makes for a pleasant alternative to staying in central Auckland, and Carol and Graham Ward's beautiful Victorian B&B is one of the treats of the town. In guest rooms, milk-painted walls, country antiques, thoughtfully combined decorative objects, cushy duvets, and abundant flowers create a feeling of earthy sophistication. Two rooms have small private verandas, and one garden-level room has its own entrance. On the main floor, there is a spacious lounge where you can make coffee,

tea, or pour yourself a glass of sherry or port. Breakfasts are an all-out display of culinary finesse and Kiwi hospitality. ⊠ *6 Flagstaff Terr., Devonport,* ☎ *09/445–2925,* FAX *09/445–2901. 4 rooms. AE, MC, V. BP.*☜

$$ ⊞ **Devonport Villa Inn.** This gracious timber villa combines tranquil,
★   historic surroundings and fresh sea air, a 20-minute ferry ride from the city. Rooms are individually decorated and have handmade quilts, queen-size beds with Edwardian-style headboards, lace curtains, and colonial furniture. Cheltenham Beach, which offers safe swimming, is a two-minute walk away, and the picture-book village of Devonport is a short walk. Arriving guests can be collected from the Devonport ferry terminal. ⊠ *46 Tainui Rd., Devonport,* ☎ *09/445–8397,* FAX *09/445–9766. 4 rooms. Lounge. AE, V. BP.* ☜

Other Suburbs and Auckland Environs

$$$$ ⊞ **Brooklands Country Estate.** A fine alternative in the country only a 90-minute drive south of Auckland, Brooklands is ideal if you are short of time and want a taste of rural hospitality. The turn-of-the-last-century homestead is set among gardens and surrounded by a 2,000-acre sheep, cattle, and deer station. Drink in the homey atmosphere in the library and lounge, where you will find plenty of timber, leather furnishings, and books from the owner's family. An open fire is the centerpiece of the dining room in cooler months, and in summer, dinner is often served outside by the pool. The watercolors around the lodge were painted by the owner's father, Robert Gower. Antique oak furniture and Persian rugs on the old kauri floors give rooms a pleasant country atmosphere. ⊠ *R.D. 1, Ngaruawahia,* ☎ *07/825–4756,* FAX *07/825–4873. 10 rooms. Pool, tennis court, croquet, billiards, helipad. AE, DC, MC, V.*☜

$$$$ ⊞ **Hotel du Vin.** There can be no finer introduction to New Zealand
★   than to head south from the Auckland International Airport to this smart, luxurious hotel, surrounded by native forests and the grapevines of the de Redcliffe estate. Standard rooms are palatial, and the newer rooms at the far end of the resort are the best. The decor is crisp and modern, and the central restaurant and reception areas glow with honey-color wood and rough stone fireplaces. The restaurant has an excellent reputation, though prices are high. The hotel is 64 km (40 mi) from Auckland, a 45-minute drive from both Auckland airport and the city via the motorway. Casual visitors are welcome to taste the wines or stop for an evening meal—a pleasant way to break the journey between Auckland and the Coromandel region. ⊠ *Lyons Rd., Mangatawhiri Valley,* ☎ *09/233–6314,* FAX *09/233–6215. 46 rooms. Restaurant, bar, indoor pool, spa, tennis courts, exercise room, bicycles. AE, DC, MC, V.*☜

$$–$$$$ ⊞ **Sedgwick-Kent Lodge.** On a quiet street in the suburb of Remuera,
★   between the airport and downtown, this single-story Edwardian villa is a wonderful retreat from the city. Entering through a garden courtyard, you immediately sense the lodge's graceful style. Inside, native timber trims doorways that open onto rooms fitted with writing desks and luxurious antique bedsteads. Hosts Wort and Helma van der Lans take good care of guests and offer delightful breakfasts: you can give in and ask for a sumptuous hot dish or restrain yourself and stick with freshly squeezed orange juice, muffins, fruit, and homemade muesli and yogurt. For anyone wanting a touch of romance, a candlelit dinner is available by arrangement. ⊠ *65 Lucerne Rd., Remuera,* ☎ *09/524–5219,* FAX *09/520–4825. 5 rooms, 1 apartment. AE, DC, MC, V. BP.* ☜

$$ ⊞ **Florida Motel.** In a harborside suburb a 15-minute drive east of the city center (and close to a major bus route into the city), this motel offers exceptional value. Rooms come in three versions: studios or one- or two-bedroom units. The units have a lounge room separate from

the bedroom, and the two-bedroom units are particularly good for families. All rooms have separate, fully equipped kitchens and a few nice touches, such as wall-mounted hair dryers, French-press coffeemakers, and irons with ironing boards. As the motel is immaculately maintained and extremely popular, rooms must be booked several months in advance. ⊠ *11 Speight Rd., Kohimarama,* ☎ *09/521–4660,* ℻ *09/ 521–4662. 8 rooms. AE, DC, MC, V.*

Nightlife and the Arts

The Arts

For tickets, **Ticketek** (☎ 09/307–5000) is the central agency for all theater, music, and dance performances, as well as for major sporting events.

ART GALLERIES AND STUDIOS

A group of 30 artists living and working in Waitakere, west of Auckland, have set up the **Art Out West Trail,** by which visitors can view and purchase art in artists' private studios. Many of the studios require advance warning and you'll need a car if you want to really explore the trail. Brochures are available at the Auckland Travel and Information Centre (☞ Visitor Information *in* Auckland A to Z, *below*).

For a one-stop sample of West Auckland art, visit **Lopdell House Gallery** (⊠ Titirangi and S. Titirangi Rds., Titirangi, ☎ 09/817–8087). The gallery shows local works, but also has regular exhibitions by national and international artists.

MUSIC AND OPERA

The **Aotea Centre** (⊠ Aotea Sq., Queen and Myers Sts., ☎ 09/309–2678 or 09/307–5060) is Auckland's main venue for music and the performing arts. The **Auckland Philharmonia Orchestra** performs regularly at the center, and the **New Zealand Symphony Orchestra** performs both at the Town Hall and at the Aotea Centre. For general inquiries check by the information desk in the Owens Foyer, Level Two of the complex.

Dame Kiri Te Kanawa often performs at the Aotea Centre on return visits to her homeland. Tickets are usually sold out months in advance.

Nightlife

After sunset the liveliest area of the city is Parnell, which has several restaurants, bars, and nightclubs. For a late-night café scene, head to Ponsonby Road, southwest of the city center off Karangahape Road, where you will find street-side dining, small dessert-only restaurants, and intimate bars. If you prefer to stay in the city center, the place to be for bars and late-night dancing is High Street and nearby O'Connell Street and Vulcan Lane. At the Queen Street end of Karangahape Road (just north of Highway 1) you'll find shops, lively bars, cafés, and nightspots, but as you head toward Ponsonby Road these give way to strip clubs and sex shops. Auckland usually has three or four lively nightclubs running at any one time, but they are transient animals with names and addresses changing as young Aucklanders follow the trend of the day. From Sunday to Wednesday most bars close at 10 PM and nightclubs at about midnight or 1 AM. From Thursday to Saturday, many city bars close at 11 PM or midnight but some do have 24-hour licenses. Nightclubs keep rocking until at least 2 AM and some for a couple of hours after that. For the latest information on nightclubs check with the information center (☞ Visitor Information *in* Auckland A to Z, *below*).

BARS AND LOUNGES

At the heart of the city center, the **Civic Tavern** (⊠ 1 Wellesley St., ☎ 09/373–3684) houses three bars. The **London Bar** has a vast selection of beer and an impressive variety of Scotch whiskey. **The London Underground Bar** is a sports bar with 8-ball pool tables and casino-style poker machines. For a glass of Irish stout, stay on the ground floor and visit **Murphy's Irish Bar.**

Classic Comedy & Bar (✉ 321 Queen St, ☎ 09/373–4321) is housed in what used to be an X-rated movie theater, so if you get a funny look when you ask for directions, you'll know why. These days it is Auckland's only regular venue for live comedy. The caliber of the acts varies, and you'll find a mix of well-known Kiwi comedians, new faces, and the occasional international act.

Part of the new Viaduct Village development, the **Loaded Hog** (✉ 104 Quay St., ☎ 09/366–6491) has a vaguely nautical feel. This popular brewery and bistro has indoor and outdoor dining and drinking and can get crowded late in the week, so try to arrive early. Jazz musicians perform most evenings.

An atmospheric city-center brewpub, the **Shakespeare Tavern** (✉ Albert and Wyndham Sts., ☎ 09/373–5396) has beer with colorful names like Willpower Stout and Falstaff's Real Ale. There are several bars inside.

NIGHTCLUBS

Pappa Jacks Voodoo Lounge (✉ 9 Vulcan La., ☎ 09/358–4847) has disco dance music late into the night. You'll find things slightly quieter in the adjacent **Dragon Bar** if you want a break from the dancing.

Rakinos (✉ 35 High St., ☎ 09/358–3535) has live jazz in an easy-to-miss upstairs location. It's open Thursday to Saturday and music ranges from the soft and gentle to stomping blues.

Outdoor Activities and Sports

Biking
Auckland is good for cycling, especially around the waterfront. **Penny Farthing Cycle Shop** (✉ Symonds St. and Khyber Pass Rd., ☎ 09/379–2524) rents mountain bikes for $25 per day or $100 per week.

Golf
Chamberlain Park Golf Course (✉ Linwood Ave., Western Springs, ☎ 09/846–6758) is an 18-hole public course in a parkland setting a five-minute drive (off Northwestern Motorway, Route 16) from the city. The club shop rents clubs and carts. Greens fees are $16 weekdays, $20 weekends.

Titirangi Golf Course (✉ Links Rd., New Lynn, ☎ 09/827–5749), a 15-minute drive south of the city, is one of the country's finest 18-hole courses. Nonmembers are welcome to play provided they contact the course's professional in advance and show evidence of membership at an overseas club. Clubs and golf carts can be rented; the greens fee is $75.

Running
Auckland's favorite running track is **Tamaki Drive,** a 10-km (6-mi) route that heads east from the city along the south shore of Waitemata Harbour and ends at St. Heliers Bay. The **Auckland Domain** (☞ City Center and Parnell, *above*) is popular with executive lunchtime runners.

Swimming
The **Tepid Baths** (✉ 102 Customs St. W, ☎ 09/379–4794) near the heart of Auckland has a large indoor swimming pool, a whirlpool, saunas, and a steam room.

Tennis
ASB Tennis Centre (✉ 72 Stanley St., ☎ 09/373–3623) has 12 hard courts indoors and outdoors, 1 km (½ mi) east of the city center.

Spectator Sports
Eden Park is the city's major stadium for sporting events. This is the best place in winter to see New Zealand's sporting icon, the rugby team All Blacks, consistently among the world's top three teams. Cricket is played in summer. For information on sporting events, *Auckland Alive* is a quarterly guide available from the Auckland Travel and Information Centre (☞ Visitor Information *in* Auckland A to Z, *below*). Tickets can be booked through **Ticketek** (☎ 09/307–5000).

Shopping

Department Store
Smith and Caughey Ltd. (✉ 253–261 Queen St., ☎ 09/377–4770) extends over four floors and is a comprehensive department store. You'll even find a hairdresser.

Districts
Ponsonby, about 1½ km (1 mi) west of the city center, is known for its antiques shops and fashion boutiques. Auckland's main shopping precinct for clothes, outdoor gear, duty-free goods, greenstone jewelry, and souvenirs is **Queen Street.**

Mall
Dress-Smart (✉ 151 Arthur St., Onehunga, ☎ 09/622–2400) is a whole mall of factory outlets and is the place to go for quality, low-priced goods. As the name suggests it started as a clothing mall, but has recently doubled in size and diversified. You'll now find books, records, children's toys, bags, jewelry, and housewares. Expect to pay 30% to 50% less than you would retail. Take the inexpensive shuttle service (☎ 0800/188–988) or, if you're driving, take the Penrose turnoff from the Southern Motorway, then follow the signs to Onehunga. This is the heart of Auckland suburbia, so a detailed road map will help. Dress-Smart is close to Onehunga Mall.

Street Markets
The beautiful countryside of the Waitakere Ranges have attracted artists seeking an alternative lifestyle, close to a major population (and customer) base but away from the hustle and bustle. Many of their wares are on sale at the **Titirangi Village Market** (✉ Titirangi Memorial Hall, S. Titirangi Rd., ☎ 09/817–3584). It is held on the last Sunday of each month.

Auckland's main bazaar, **Victoria Park Market** (✉ Victoria and Wellesley Sts., ☎ 09/309–6911), consists of 2½ acres of clothing, footwear, sportswear, furniture, souvenirs, and crafts at knockdown prices. It's housed in the city's former garbage incinerator.

Specialty Stores
BOOKS AND MAPS
Legendary Hard to Find (but worth the effort) Quality Second-hand Books, Ltd. (✉ 171–175 The Mall, Onehunga, ☎ 09/634–4340) has a name that pretty much says it all. It's a local favorite and very large. Its smaller sister in Devonport, **Hard to Find North Shore** (✉ 81A Victoria St., ☎ 09/446–0300), is a great spot to stop into for a browse.

Unity Books (✉ 19 High St., ☎ 09/307–0731) is a general bookstore that specializes in travel, fiction, science, biography, and New Zealand–related books.

RUGBY: A NATIONAL OBSESSION

WHEN THE NEW ZEALAND national rugby team, the All Blacks, lost its world cup semifinal to France in October 1999, it seemed the whole nation plunged into mourning. The unexpected loss dominated television, newspapers, and talk radio for days. But how did a sport invented half a world away in Europe—which has become popular in few other countries—develop into such an integral part of the nation's culture? Rugby evolved out of soccer in 19th-century Britain. It was born at the elitist English school of Rugby, where in 1823 a schoolboy by the name of William Webb Ellis became bored with kicking a football and picked up the ball and ran with it. Rugby developed among the upper classes of Britain, while soccer remained a predominantly working-class game. Since it was primarily fashionable among British gentlemen, its following remained small. However in colonial New Zealand, a country largely free from the rigid class structure of Britain, the game developed as the nation's number-one sport. From early on, New Zealanders felt such passion about rugby that in many ways their national identity was formed around it. One reason for this was undoubtedly the success of New Zealand teams in the late 19th and early 20th centuries. This remote outpost of the British empire, with a population of only 750,000 in 1900, was an impressive force at rugby, and this became a source of great national pride. Today, in a country of nearly 4 million, the national sport is played by 250,000 New Zealanders at club level and embraced by huge numbers with an almost religious fervor.

The sport is very similar to American football, except that players are not allowed to pass the ball forward and they wear no protective gear. Like American football, rugby is not a worldwide sport. Although many countries, including the United States, take part in international rugby matches, the only nations to play it at a high level are Australia, New Zealand, South Africa, England, Ireland, Scotland, Wales, and France. Countries such as Argentina, Italy, and the Pacific islands of Fiji, Tonga, and Samoa are also showing signs of catching up with the leading nations. Despite its limited worldwide following, rugby administrators have organized a world cup for the sport every four years since 1987, which New Zealand has won once. The New Zealand team was a hot favorite to win the most recent world cup played in Britain in 1999. So when the All Blacks not only failed to win the trophy, but failed to reach the final, the national team's failure sparked off a huge bout of introspection about what went wrong with not just the national sport but with the country as a whole.

SOUVENIRS

Follow elephant footprints down an alley in Parnell Village to **Elephant House** (✉ 237 Parnell Rd., ☎ 09/309–8740) for an extensive collection of souvenirs, many unavailable elsewhere.

At **Wild Places** (✉ 28 Lorne St., ☎ 09/358–0795), proceeds from posters, T-shirts, books, and cards on the themes of whales, rain forests, and native birds all go to conservation projects in New Zealand and the Pacific.

SPORTS AND HIKING

If you haven't brought your own, **Kathmandu** (✉ 350 Queen St., ☎ 09/309–4615) sells quality New Zealand–made clothing and equipment for the outdoor enthusiast.

One of a nationwide chain of stores, **Outdoor Heritage** (✉ 75 Queen St., ☎ 09/309–6571) sells high-quality outdoor clothing.

The extensive range of outdoor gear at **Tisdall's Sports** (✉ 176 Queen St., ☎ 09/379–0254) is made especially for New Zealand conditions.

Auckland A to Z

Arriving and Departing

BY BUS

The terminal for **InterCity Coaches** (☎ 0800/802–802) is the Auckland Central Railway Station (☞ *below*). **Newmans Coaches** (☎ 09/309–9738) arrive and depart from the Downtown Airline Terminal (✉ Quay and Albert Sts.).

BY PLANE

Auckland International Airport lies 21 km (13 mi) southwest of the city center, around a 30-minute drive.

A free **Interterminal Bus** links the international and domestic terminals, with frequent departures in each direction 6 AM–10 PM. Otherwise, the walk between the two terminals takes about 10 minutes along a signposted walkway. Luggage for flights aboard the two major domestic airlines, Air New Zealand and Ansett New Zealand, can be checked at the international terminal.

Major international carriers serving Auckland include **Air New Zealand** (☎ 0800/737–000), **Canadian Airlines International** (☎ 09/309–0735), **Cathay Pacific** (☎ 09/379–0861), **Qantas** (☎ 09/357–8900), **Singapore Airlines** (☎ 09/379–3209), and **United Airlines** (☎ 09/379–3800).

Domestic carriers with services to Auckland are **Air New Zealand** (☎ 0800/737–000), **Air Nelson** (☎ 09/379–3510), **Ansett New Zealand** (☎ 09/302–2146), and **Mount Cook Airlines** (☎ 0800/800–737).

The **Airbus** (☎ 09/275–9396) costs $12 one way and $20 return and leaves the international terminal every 20 minutes between 6:20 AM and 8:20 PM. The fixed route between the airport and the Downtown Airline Terminal, on the corner of Quay Street and Albert Road, includes a stop at the railway station and, on request, at any bus stop, hotel, or motel along the way. Returning from the city, the bus leaves the Downtown Airline Terminal at 20-minute intervals between 6:20 AM and 9 PM. Travel time is 35–45 minutes.

Hallmark Limousines and Tours (☎ 09/629–0940) operates Ford LTD limousines between the airport and the city for approximately $65.

Super Shuttle (☎ 09/275–1234) has service between the airport and any address in the city center. The cost is $18 for a single traveler and $6 extra for each person accompanying them.

Taxi fare to the city is approximately $35.

BY TRAIN

The terminal for all InterCity train services is **Auckland Central Railway Station** (☎ 0800/802–802) on Beach Road, about 1½ km (1 mi) east of the city center. A booking office is inside the **Auckland Travel and Information Centre** (✉ 287 Queen St., ☎ 09/979–2333).

Getting Around

BY BUS

The easily recognizable white **Link Buses** are city buses that circle the inner city, including many of the most popular stops for visitors, every 10 minutes between 6 AM and 6 PM weekdays, and then every 20 minutes until 10 PM. The weekend service is every 20 minutes from 7 AM to 11 PM. The route includes the **Downtown Bus Terminal** at the Britomart Centre between Customs Street and Quay Street. The buses stop at Queens Street, Parnell, Newmarket (where passengers can disembark for the Auckland Museum), Ponsonby, and Krangahape Road among other places. The fare anywhere on the route is a dollar, payable as you get onto the bus. To get travel farther afield you'll need to get onto a **Stagecoach Bus**, which is run by the same company and has services as far north as Orewa on the Hibiscus Coast and south to Pukekohe. A one-day **Link Pass** at $7 for unlimited travel is easily the best value for anyone planning extensive use of the buses (both Link and Stagecoach), particularly because it is also valid for travel on Link ferries between the city and the North Shore. For timetables, bus routes, fares, and lost property, stop by the **Information Kiosk** (✉ Britomart), which is open weekdays 8–7, weekends 9–5, or call **RideLine** (☎ 09/366–6400), open Monday–Saturday 7–7.

BY CAR

By the standards of most cities, Auckland traffic is moderate, parking space is inexpensive and readily available, and highways pass close to the heart of the city. Getting used to driving on the left, if you'll be traveling by car, can be especially difficult when trying to figure out where to get onto motorways. Taking a close look at a city map before you set out is a good idea.

BY FERRY

Various companies serve Waitemata Harbour; one of the best and least expensive is the **Devonport commuter ferry** (☎ 09/367–9118). The ferry terminal is on the harbor side of the Ferry Building on Quay Street, near the corner of Albert Street. Boats leave here for Devonport Monday–Thursday 6:15 AM–11 PM, Friday and Saturday 6:15 AM–1 AM, and Sunday 7 AM–11 PM. On weekdays they depart on the hour between 10 and 3, and at half-hour intervals during the morning and evening commuter periods; on Saturday and Sunday they leave every hour. The cost is $7 round-trip. Ferries also make the 35-minute run to Waiheke Island approximately every two hours, beginning at 6:30 AM, at a cost of $23 round-trip. Return ferries leave about every two hours on odd-numbered hours.

BY TAXI

Taxis can be hailed in the street but are more readily available from taxi stands throughout the city. Auckland taxi rates vary with the company, but are listed on the driver's door. Most taxis will accept major credit cards. **Alert Taxis** (☎ 09/309–2000), **Auckland Cooperative Taxi**

Service (☎ 09/300–3000), and **Eastern Taxis** (☎ 09/527–7077) are reliable operators with radio-controlled fleets.

Contacts and Resources

CAR RENTAL

Avis, Budget, and **Hertz** have offices inside the Auckland International Airport (☞ Car Rental *in* Smart Travel Tips A to Z).

CONSULATES

Australian Consulate. ✉ *Union House, 32–38 Quay St.,* ☎ 09/303–2429. ۞ *Weekdays 8:30–4:45.*

British Consulate. ✉ *Fay Richwhite Building, 151 Queen St.,* ☎ 09/303–2971. ۞ *Weekdays 9:30–12:20.*

Canadian Consulate. ✉ *Jetset Centre, 48 Emily Pl.,* ☎ 09/309–3690. ۞ *Weekdays 8:30–4:30.*

U.S. Consulate. ✉ *General Assurance Building, Shortland and O'Connell Sts.,* ☎ 09/303–2724. ۞ *Weekdays 9:30–12:30.*

CURRENCY EXCHANGE

Two **Bank of New Zealand** branches inside the international terminal of Auckland International Airport are open for all arriving and departing flights. In the city, there are several currency-exchange agencies on Queen Street between Victoria and Customs streets offering the same rate as banks (open weekdays 9–5 and Saturday 9–1). Foreign currency may also be exchanged daily 8–4 at the cashier's office above Celebrity Walk at the Drake Street entrance of **Victoria Park Market** (☎ 09/309–6911). A 24-hour exchange machine outside the **Downtown Airline Terminal** on Quay Street will change notes of any major currency into New Zealand dollars, but the rate is significantly less than that offered by banks.

EMERGENCIES

Dial 111 for **fire, police, or ambulance** services.

Auckland Hospital. ✉ *Park Rd., Grafton,* ☎ 09/379–7440.

St. John's Ambulance. St. John's can refer you to the nearest dentist on duty. ☎ *09/579–9099.*

Southern Cross Central. ✉ *122 Remuera Rd., Remuera,* ☎ 09/524–5943 or 09/524–7906.

GUIDED TOURS

Explorer Bus (☎ 09/360–0033, ☎ 0800/439–756) is a convenient introduction to Auckland. The blue-and-gray double-decker bus travels in a circuit, stopping at eight of the city's major attractions; you can leave at any stop and reboard any following Explorer bus. The loop begins at the Downtown Airline Terminal every hour between 9 and 4 daily; tickets are available from the driver. A one-day pass is $20.

Fullers Cruise Centre (☎ 09/367–9111) has a variety of cruises around the harbor and to the islands of Hauraki Gulf. The two-hour coffee cruise ($20) departs daily at 9:30, 11:30, and 2:30, with an extra afternoon cruise from late December to April. The Jetraider cruise ($50) to Great Barrier Island, the most distant of the Hauraki Gulf Islands, is a popular day trip for Aucklanders; however, the voyage can be canceled due to rough seas. You may want to take a guided bus tour of the island ($17). The cruise departs Tuesday, Thursday, Friday, and weekends at 9, returning to Auckland at about 6. Reservations are essential.

The **Gray Line** (☎ 09/377–0904) runs a Morning Highlights tour, which includes admission to Kelly Tarlton's Underwater World. This tour departs daily from the Downtown Airline Terminal on Quay Street at 9 and costs $51.

The **Pride of Auckland Company** (☎ 09/373–4557) sails for lunch and dinner on the inner harbor. The 1½-hour lunch cruise ($30) departs at 11 and 1, and the three-hour dinner cruise ($75) departs at 6. An Experience Sailing trip ($30) departs at 3. Boats leave from the wharf opposite the Downtown Airline Terminal on the corner of Quay and Albert streets.

Red Feather Expeditions Ltd. (✉ Box 60243, ☎ 09/817–9396) is run by expat American Beth Coleman, who has built up a love for the wilderness and culture of New Zealand. Tours are tailor-made and can be restricted to the greater Auckland area (Beth has a special knowledge of the Waitakere Ranges) or extended farther afield. The company is happy to include activities such as kayaking, horseback riding, or canyoning into an itinerary.

Scenic Tours (☎ 09/634–0189) operates a three-hour City Highlights guided bus tour, which takes in the main attractions in the city and Parnell and the view from the lookout on Mt. Eden. Tours leave at 9:30 and 2, and tickets are $35.

LATE-NIGHT PHARMACY
Late-Night Pharmacy. ✉ *60 Broadway*, ☎ *09/520–6634.* ⊙ *Weekdays 5:30 PM–7 AM, weekends 9 AM–7 AM.*

TRAVEL AGENCIES
American Express Travel Service. ✉ *101 Queen St.*, ☎ *09/379–8243.*

Thomas Cook. ✉ *107 Queen St.*, ☎ *09/379–3924.*

VISITOR INFORMATION
The Thursday *Auckland Tourist Times* is a free newspaper with the latest information on tours, exhibitions, and shopping. The paper is available from hotels and from the Travel and Information Centre.

Auckland International Airport Visitor Centre. ✉ *Ground floor, International Airport Terminal*, ☎ *09/275–6467*, 🗏 *09/256–8942.* ⊙ *Daily 5 AM–last flight.*

Auckland Travel and Information Centre. ✉ *287 Queen St.*, ☎ *09/979–2333*, 🗏 *09/979–2334.* ⊙ *Weekdays 8:30–5:30, weekends 9–5.*

NORTHLAND AND THE BAY OF ISLANDS

Beyond Auckland, North Island stretches a long arm into the South Pacific. This is Northland, an undulating region of farms, forests, and marvelous beaches. The Bay of Islands is the main attraction, an island-littered seascape with a mild, subtropical climate and some of the finest game-fishing waters in the country—witness its record catches of marlin and mako shark. Big-game fishing is expensive, but small fishing boats can take you out for an evening of trawling for around $50.

It was on the Bay of Islands that the first European settlement was established and where modern New Zealand became a nation with the signing of the Treaty of Waitangi in 1840. The main town is Paihia, a strip of motels and restaurants along the waterfront. If you plan to spend more than a day in the area, the town of Russell, just a ride or short ferry trip away, makes for a more atmospheric and attractive base.

You can explore Northland in an easy loop from Auckland, driving up Highway 1 and returning on Highway 12 with little revisiting of sights on the way back. Bay of Islands is a favorite vacation spot for

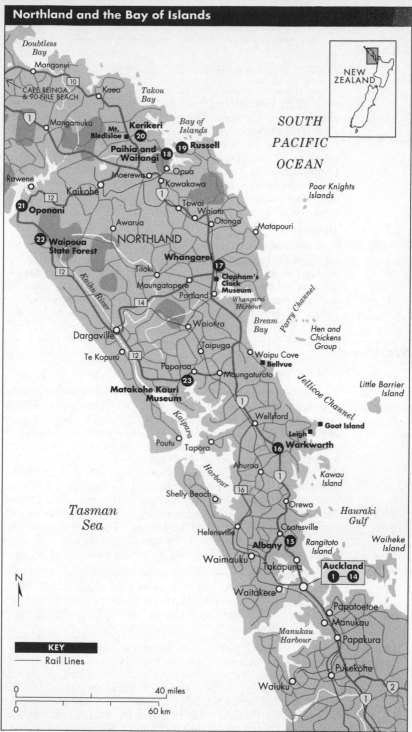

Northland and the Bay of Islands

Doubtless Bay

Mangonui

10

CAPE REINGA & 90-MILE BEACH

Kaeo

Takou Bay

1

Mangamuka

Mt. Bledisloe ■

Kerikeri
20

Bay of Islands

Paihia and Waitangi **18**

19 Russell

Rawene

12

Kaikohe

Moerewa

Opua

Kawakawa

1

21 Opononi

Awarua

Towai

Waiotu

Otonga

Matapouri

22 Waipoua State Forest

Kauihu River

NORTHLAND

Titoki

Whangarei

17

Clapham's Clock Museum ■

Poor Knights Islands

SOUTH

PACIFIC

OCEAN

Maungatapere

Portland

Whangarei Harbour

Parry Channel

12

Dargaville

Waiotira

Bream Bay

Hen and Chickens Group

14

Te Kopuru

12

Taipuga

Waipu Cove

Bellvue ■

Jellicoe Channel

Little Barrier Island

Paparoa

Maungaturoto

Matakohe Kauri Museum

23

Kaipara

1

Wellsford

Leigh ■ **■ Goat Island**

16 Warkworth

Poutu

Tapora

Harbour

Ahuroa

1

Kawau Island

16

Shelly Beach

Orewa

Hauraki Gulf

Helensville

Coatesville

Albany 15

Rangitoto Island

Waiheke Island

Tasman Sea

Waimauku

Takapuna

Auckland
1 14

N

Waitakere

Papatoetoe

Manukau

Papakura

Manukau Harbour

KEY
— Rail Lines

Pukekohe

0 ——— 40 miles
0 ——— 60 km

Waiuku

2

1

NEW ZEALAND

Kiwis, particularly from mid-December to the end of January, when accommodations are often filled months in advance.

Albany

⑮ *12 km (7 mi) north of Auckland.*

Albany is a small village north of Auckland, the first town north after the northern motorway narrows. In December the pohutukawa trees along the roadside blossom for the Kiwi Christmas by erupting in a blaze of scarlet, hence their *Pakeha* (European) name—the New Zealand Christmas tree. To the Maori, the flowers had another meaning: the beginning of shellfish season. The spiky-leaved plants that grow in clumps by the roadside are New Zealand flax. The fibers of this plant, the raw material for linen, were woven into clothing by the Maori. The huge tree ferns—common throughout the forests of North Island, where they can grow as high as 30 ft—are known locally as *pungas*.

Dining

$$–$$$ ✕ **Quattro.** Break your journey north at this country pub, run by a couple of big-city weekend refugees who also operate a café in trendy Ponsonby. The food is generous, with an emphasis on casseroles and slow-cooked meats in winter, grilled food and salads in summer. The wine and beer lists are wide-ranging and generally well-priced. Dine indoors or out—although the only view is of a parking lot. ⊠ *276 Main St.,* ☎ *09/415–9515. AE, DC, MC, V.*

Warkworth

⑯ *47 km (29 mi) north of Albany.*

One of the great natural features of the north half of North Island is one native pine species, the kauri tree. Two giants stand in Warkworth, near the **Warkworth Museum** (☞ *below*). The larger one, the **McKinney Kauri,** measures almost 25 ft around its base, yet this 800-year-old colossus is a mere adolescent by kauri standards. Kauri trees, once prolific in this part of the North Island, were highly prized by Maori canoe builders, because a canoe capable of carrying a hundred warriors could be made from a single trunk. Unfortunately these same characteristics—strength, size, and durability—made kauri timber ideal for ships, furniture, and housing, and the kauri forests were rapidly depleted by early European settlers. Today the trees are protected by law, and infant kauri are appearing in the forests of North Island, although their growth rate is painfully slow.

The **Warkworth Museum** contains a collection of Maori artifacts and farming and domestic implements from the pioneering days of the Warkworth district. The museum also has a souvenir shop with kauri bowls and other wooden items. ⊠ *Tudor Collins Dr.,* ☎ *09/425–7093.* ⌷ *$3.* ☉ *Daily 9–4.*

En Route   Even if you aren't a hortomaniac, come to Daniel and Vivian Papich's **Bellvue** for its spectacular views of the Pacific Ocean. The Hen and Chickens Islands lie right off the coast, and on clear days you can even see the Poor Knights Islands, a good 70 km (45 mi) away. This hillside garden has been designed on several levels to take advantage of its topography. The bold foliage of agaves, bromeliads, succulents, and *puka* trees is abundant, and sets off the more delicate exotics. Vivian's container plantings—300 at last count—are everywhere, even hanging from the trees. Conceived as a way to keep more demanding plants from struggling in the hard clay soil here, the containers have evolved into an art form. They are often composed of unconventional materials and used in inventive seasonal displays. Birders, keep your eyes and ears open for the fantails, whiteyes, and tuis that frequent the garden. The distance from Warkworth to Waipu and the garden is 55 km (34 mi). ⊠ *Coastal Hwy., Langs Beach, southeast of Waipu,* ☎ 09/432–0465. ⬛ *Small entry fee.* ⊘ *By appointment.*

For a glimpse of what the New Zealand coast must have been like 200 years ago, take a trip to the **Goat Island** marine reserve. Fishing is prohibited here, and marine life has returned in abundance, with prominent species including blue *maomao,* snapper, and cod. You can put on a snorkel and easily glide around the island, just a little way offshore. You can rent mask, snorkel, and flippers ($8) at the beach from Maria Anthoni of **Seafriends** (☎ 09/422–6212). **Habitat Explorer** (☎ 09/422–6334) has a glass-bottom boat that runs around the island ($15). But you needn't get even this serious to see plenty of fish. Just walk into the water up to your waist and look around you. To drum up more action, throw some bread or noodles into the sea and watch the fish congregate just inches from you. The beach area is good for a picnic as well.

To get to Goat Island head toward Leigh, 21 km (13 mi) northeast of Warkworth. From Leigh, take a left turn and follow the signs for a couple of miles. The area can get crowded, but if you arrive by 10 AM or earlier, you should avoid the masses. Department of Conservation leaflets detailing Goat Island can be obtained from the Warkworth Visitor Information Centre (☞ Contacts and Resources *in* Northland and the Bay of Islands A to Z, *below*). If it's mealtime when you're in Leigh, ask for directions to **Leigh Sawmill** (⊠ Pakiri Rd, ☎ 09/422–6019), the best country restaurant in the region.

Whangarei

⑰ *127 km (79 mi) north of Warkworth, 196 km (123 mi) north of Auckland.*

Many people on the way to the Bay of Islands bypass Whangarei (*fahng*-ar-ay), but it is well worth taking the turnoff from the main highway, especially since the area known as the **Whangarei Town Basin** has been improved. Here you will find a **Museum of Fishes**, which in New Zealand means looking at exhibits of species that you wouldn't see back home. Also at the basin is **Ahipupu Maori and Pacific Arts and Crafts**, where you will find both traditional and contemporary works.

Claphams Clock Museum is another Town Basin site. Just about every conceivable method of telling time is represented in this collection of more than 1,400 clocks, from primitive water clocks to ships' chronometers to ornate masterworks from Paris and Vienna. Some of the most intriguing examples were made by the late Mr. Clapham himself, like his World War II air-force clock. Ironically, the one thing you won't find here is the correct time. If all the bells, chimes, gongs, and cuckoos went off together, the noise would be deafening, so the clocks are set to different times. ⊠ *Quayside Whangarei,* ☎ 09/438–3993. ⬛ *$3.50.* ⊘ *Daily 10–4.*

The oldest kauri villa in Whangarei, **Historical Reyburn House** contains the Northland Society of Arts exhibition gallery, which hosts a free exhibition each month. It is separated from the Town Basin by a playground. ⊠ *Lower Quay St.,* ☎ 09/438–3074. ⊘ *Tues.–Sun. 10–4.*

You'll find a lovely picnic spot at **Whangarei Falls** on Ngunguru Road, 5 km (3 mi) northeast of town. There are viewing platforms atop the falls and a short trail through the local bush.

Early settlers anxious to farm the rich volcanic land around Whangarei found their efforts constantly thwarted by an abundance of rock in the soil. To make use of the stuff they dug up, they built walls—miles of walls. The current settlers at **Greagh,** Kathleen and Clark Abbot, have carried on this tradition, giving their gardens the Celtic name for "land among the stone." The walls form a handsome framework for perennials and roses and the plantings, in turn, emphasize the beauty and strength of the stone on terraces and in five separate walled gardens. ⊠ *Three Mile Bush Rd., Whangarei,* ☎ *09/435–1980.* ⊒ *Small entry fee.* ⊙ *Oct.–mid-Dec., daily 10–4; mid-Dec.–Apr. by appointment.*

Dining and Lodging

$$$ ✕ **Tonic.** Neil Smith has cooked at a couple of top establishments in Britain, and is enjoying himself in New Zealand's far north. Tonic seats only around 30 diners, which suits him fine. He puts an emphasis on seafood, creating imaginative dishes like salmon fillet with a sauce based on red bell peppers and cockles (tiny shellfish). ⊠ *239 Kamo Rd.,* ☎ *09/437–5558. AE, DC, MC, V. Closed Sun.–Mon.*

$$ ▥ **Parua House.** On the edge of Parua Bay, 17 km (11 mi) from central Whangarei, this is a great base from which to explore the towering Whangarei Heads that enclose the bay. Owners Pat and Peter Heaslip are solid practitioners of Kiwi hospitality who lived in England for more than 20 years before purchasing the house a few years ago. Parua House dates from 1882, and retains much of its colonial charm, enhanced by the French oak table brought from England and two sideboards in the dining room, one of which is some 300 years old. Furnishings and decorations in guest rooms also have touches of old England. You can take a walk through the nearby bush or even help milk their cow. ⊠ *Whangarei Heads Rd., R.D. 4, Parua Bay,* ☎ *09/436–5855,* ℻ *09/436–5855. 2 rooms. Dining room, hot tub. No credit cards. BP.*

Paihia and Waitangi

⑱ *69 km (43 mi) north of Whangarei.*

As the main vacation base for the Bay of Islands, Paihia is an unremarkable stretch of motels at odds with the quiet beauty of the island-studded seascape and the rounded green hills surround it. Nearby Waitangi, however, is one of the country's most important historic sites. It was near here that the Treaty of Waitangi, the founding document for modern New Zealand, was signed.

Waitangi National Reserve is at the northern end of Paihia. Inside the visitor center a 23-minute video, shown every hour on the hour, sketches the events that led to the Treaty of Waitangi. The center also displays Maori artifacts and weapons, including a musket that belonged to Hone Heke Pokai, the first Maori chief to sign the treaty. After his initial display of enthusiasm for British rule, Hone Heke was quickly disillusioned, and less than five years later he attacked the British in their stronghold at Russell. From the visitor center, follow a short track (trail) through the forest to **Nga Toki Matawhaorua** (ng-ga to-ki ma-ta-*fa*-oh-*roo*-ah), a Maori war canoe. This huge kauri canoe, capable of carrying 150 warriors, is named after the vessel in which Kupe, the Polynesian navigator, is said to have discovered New Zealand.

Treaty House in Waitangi National Reserve is a simple white timber cottage that has a remarkable air of dignity despite its size. The interior is fascinating, especially the back, where exposed walls demonstrate the difficulties that early administrators faced—such as an acute shortage of bricks (since an insufficient number had been shipped

MAORI HISTORY AND THE WAITANGI TREATY

THE HISTORY OF COLONIALISM is rife with broken promises, and New Zealand's legacy is no different. The first recorded contact between a European and the indigenous people of New Zealand was in 1642 by Dutch explorer Abel Tasman. In October 1769, Captain James Cook landed at Poverty Bay and claimed the country for Britain. When the first Europeans arrived, the indigenous New Zealanders—who had arrived between AD 850 and 1300—had settled most of what they called *Aotearoa* (land of the long white cloud). A rich culture had developed: the family and *hapu* (tribe) were the central units of society. Tribal ancestors were venerated along with gods representing elemental forces. Complex systems for health, education, justice, spirituality, ecological preservation, art, and governance were in place.

The initial settlement by European whale and seal traders and missionaries was welcomed by Maori chiefs. They enjoyed the trade and quickly adapted the religion and literacy bought by missionaries. But settlers also arrived with diseases and demonstrated a growing need for more land. In the face of these conditions, North Island Maori chiefs banded together to set up a regulated system for land sales and laws to contain unruly settlers. They also desired opportunities to trade across the Tasman and farther afield.

On February 6, 1840, a confederation of North Island chiefs signed the Treaty of Waitangi with England. But there were significant differences between the Maori and English translations of this first treaty. In the first article, the English version said Maori would cede sovereignty to Queen Victoria. But the Maori version used the word *kawanatanga* (governorship), which did not mean that the Maori were ceding the right to *mana* (self-determination).

The second article in English and Maori versions guaranteed the chiefs, the "full, exclusive and undisturbed possession of their lands, estates, forests, fisheries and other properties" and allowed the Crown the right to buy and sell land from Maori. The third article granted Maori protection as British citizens, though the English version said they were British subjects.

On top of the problems of translation, basic breaches of the treaty began almost as soon as it was signed. What wasn't confiscated after the 1861 New Zealand Land Wars was taken by legislation. In 1877 Chief Justice Prendergast ruled that the treaty was "a simple nullity" that lacked legal validity because one could not make a treaty with "primitive barbarians." At first European contact, 66.5 million acres of land was under Maori control, but by 1979 only 3 million remained—of mostly marginal lands.

But the battle to have the treaty honored has continued despite the government assimilation policies through which Maori language and cultural practices were actively discouraged or banned. And the Maori population, which had been decimated by 1900, began to resurge over the course of the 20th century.

By the 1970s some urban Maori pushed for policies to allow Maori language to be taught in schools, and for Maori to have greater say in social services and government. Under the Labour Government, the Waitangi Tribunal was established in 1975 to allow Maori to rule on alleged breaches of the treaty, and in 1985 the tribunal's powers were made retrospective to 1840. Today, Maori have more than 20 representatives in Parliament and Maori hold key government portfolios.

Many would agree that the key issue facing the country is what to do about the claims for alleged grievances under the Treaty of Waitangi. The Maori are a growing political force. By 2040 some predict that 50% of the country's population will be of Maori or Polynesian descent. Despite many economic and social troubles, Maori are making inroads into participating in New Zealand society at every level. And the government is, finally, grappling with how to implement the partnership.

from New South Wales, as Australia was known at the time) with which to finish the walls.

The Treaty House was prefabricated in New South Wales for the British Resident James Busby, who arrived in New Zealand in 1832. Busby had been appointed to protect British commerce and put an end to the brutalities of the whaling captains against the Maori, but Busby lacked either the judicial authority or the force of arms necessary to impose peace. On one occasion, unable to resolve a dispute between Maori tribes, Busby was forced to shelter the wounded of one side in his house. While tattooed warriors screamed war chants outside the windows, one of the Maori sheltered Busby's infant daughter, Sarah, in his cape.

The real significance of the Treaty House lies in the events that took place here on February 6, 1840, the day that the **Treaty of Waitangi** was signed by Maori chiefs and Captain William Hobson, representing the British crown. Under the treaty, the chiefs agreed to accept the authority of the crown; in return, the British recognized the Maori as the legitimate landowners and granted them all the rights and privileges of British subjects. The treaty also confirmed the status of New Zealand as a British colony, forestalling French overtures in the area, and legitimized—at least according to European law—the transfer of land from Maori to European hands. In recent years the Maori have used the treaty successfully to reclaim land that they maintain was misappropriated by white settlers.

The Treaty House has not always received the care its significance merits. When Lord Bledisloe bought the house and presented it to the nation in 1932, it was being used as a shelter for sheep.

Whare Runanga (fah-ray roo-nang-ah) is a Maori meetinghouse with an elaborately carved interior. Inside, an audio show briefly outlines traditional Maori society. The house is on the northern boundary of Waitangi National Reserve. ⊠ *Waitangi Rd., Waitangi,* ☎ *09/402–7437.* ⌸ *$5.* ☉ *Daily 9–5.*

🍃 The Tui, high and dry on the banks of the Waitangi River, is an historic kauri sailing vessel that was built to carry sugar to a refinery in Auckland. Below decks is an exhibition of artifacts recovered from shipwrecks by the famous New Zealand salvage diver Kelly Tarlton. In addition to the brass telescopes, sextants, and diving helmets that you can try on for size, there is an exquisite collection of jewelry that belonged to Isidore Jonah Rothschild (of the famous banking family), which was lost when the SS *Tasmania* sank in 1897. Rothschild was on a sales trip to New Zealand at the time. ⊠ *Waitangi Bridge, Paihia,* ☎ *09/402-7018.* ⌸ *$5.* ☉ *Daily 10–5.*

Mt. Bledisloe offers a splendid view across Paihia and the Bay of Islands. The handsome ceramic marker at the top showing the distances to major world cities was made by Doulton in London and presented by Lord Bledisloe in 1934 during his term as governor-general of New Zealand. The mount is 3 km (2 mi) from the Treaty House, on the other side of the Waitangi Golf Course. From a small parking area on the right of Waitangi Road, a short track rises above a pine forest to the summit.

Dining and Lodging

$$ ✕ **Saltwater Café.** Fresh ingredients, mostly local, are prepared here with innovation and style. Orongo Bay oysters come from nearby waters, and are matched with a mango and chilli salsa. Spinach and mesclun are tossed with honey-spiked vinaigrette, and partnered with

the kitchen's interpretation of Peking duck. There's good vegetarian fare here and one and all will have a chuckle at the restaurant's whimsical fish sculptures. ⊠ *Kings Rd., Paihia,* ☎ *09/402–7783. AE, DC, MC, V. Licensed and BYOB.*

$–$$ ✕ **Waikokupu Café.** With a view straight out to sea, this pleasant spot has a lot going for it. Chunky sandwiches, delicious cakes, and other goodies are available through the day, but things get more serious in the evening. Try the loin of tuna infused with lemongrass, pink ginger, and sesame, served on a bed of shiitake mushrooms with baby bok choy, or the flour tortilla filled with Mexican-rubbed lamb loin, with roasted corn, grilled bell peppers, and bean salsa. For most of the winter, from May to September, the café is closed for dinner. It's best to phone first to check. ⊠ *Tau Henare Dr., Waitangi,* ☎ *09/402–6275. MC, V. Licensed and BYOB. No dinner May–Sept.*

$$$–$$$$ 🖭 **Abri.** These new studio apartments take advantage of the bush setting just behind the Pahia beachfront, offering lovely sea views. The two units feature *rimu* flooring and *macrocarpa* timber walls and jet baths, and have large living room areas that open onto outside decks. The apartments have their own kitchen facilities, even a small barbecue on the deck, but most guests take the short walk to the restaurants in town for meals. The owners know the little touches that make visitors feel welcome, and you'll find fresh fruit and flowers in your room daily. Listen for the "resident" kiwi bird, and if you do hear some shuffling outside at night, grab a flashlight and attempt some bird spotting. ⊠ *10 Bayview Rd., Paihia,* ☎ *09/402–8003. 2 studios. In-room VCRs. MC, V.* ✍

$$$ 🖭 **Copthorne Resort Waitangi.** The biggest hotel north of Auckland and a favorite with tour groups, this complex sprawls along a peninsula within walking distance of the Treaty House. Units face the sea, and garden-facing rooms are decorated in a French provincial style, with yellows and blues and wrought-iron light fixtures. ⊠ *Waitangi Rd., Waitangi,* ☎ *09/402–7411,* 𝔽𝔸𝕏 *09/402–8200. 138 rooms. 3 restaurants, 2 bars, pool, coin laundry. AE, DC, MC, V.*

$$ 🖭 **Austria Motel.** The large, double-bed rooms here are typical of motel accommodations in the area—clean and moderately comfortable but almost totally devoid of charm. The motel also has a family unit on the ground level of the two-story wing. The shops and waterfront at Paihia are a two-minute walk away. ⊠ *36 Selwyn Rd.,* ☎ 𝔽𝔸𝕏 *09/402–7480. 7 rooms. Kitchenettes. AE, DC, MC, V.*

Outdoor Activities and Sports

BOATING

Moorings Yacht Charters (☎ 09/402–7821, Wharf, Opua) has charter boats for sailors of various abilities. A catamaran operated by **Straycat Day Sailing Charters** (⊠ Doves Bay Rd., Kerikeri, ☎ 09/407–7342 or 025/96–9944) makes one-day sailing trips in the Bay of Islands from Russell and Paihia at $60 per person.

DIVING

The Bay of Islands has some of the finest scuba diving in the country, particularly around Cape Brett, where the marine life includes moray eels, stingrays, and grouper. The wreck of the Greenpeace vessel *Rainbow Warrior,* sunk by French agents, is another Bay of Islands underwater highlight. Water temperature at the surface varies from 62°F in July to 71°F in January. From September through November, underwater visibility can be affected by a plankton bloom. **Paihia Dive Hire and Charter** (⊠ Box 210, Paihia, ☎ 09/402–7551) offers complete equipment rental and regular boat trips for accredited divers for about $145 per day.

FISHING

The Bay of Islands is one of the world's premier game-fishing grounds for marlin and several species of shark. **NZ Billfish Charters** (✉ Box 416, Paihia, ☎ 09/402–8380) goes for the big ones. A far less expensive alternative is to fish for snapper, kingfish, and John Dory in the inshore waters of the bay. **Skipper Jim** (☎ 09/402–7355) and **MV Arline** (☎ 09/402–8511) offer a half day of fishing, including bait and rods, for about $50 per person.

Russell

🔞 *4 km (2½ mi) east of Paihia by ferry, 13 km (8 mi) by road.*

Russell is regarded as the "second" town in the Bay of Islands, but it is far more interesting, and pleasant, than Paihia. Hard as it is to believe these days, sleepy little Russell was once dubbed the "Hellhole of the Pacific." In the early 20th century (when it was still known by its Maori name, Kororareka) it was a swashbuckling frontier town, a haven for sealers and for whalers who found the east coast of New Zealand to be one of the richest whaling grounds on earth. Tales of debauchery were probably exaggerated, but British administrators in New South Wales were sufficiently concerned to dispatch a British Resident in 1832 to impose law and order. After the Treaty of Waitangi, Russell was the national capital, until in 1844 the Maori chief Hone Heke attacked the British garrison and most of the town burned to the ground. Hone Heke was finally defeated in 1846, but Russell never recovered its former prominence, and the seat of government was shifted first to Auckland, then to Wellington. Today Russell is a delightful town of timber houses and big trees that hang low over the seafront, framing the yachts and game-fishing boats in the harbor. The atmosphere can best be absorbed in a stroll along the Strand, the path along the waterfront.

Pompallier House, at the southern end of the Strand, was named after the first Catholic bishop of the South Pacific. Marist missionaries built the original structure out of rammed earth (mud mixed with dung or straw—a technique known as *pise* in their native France), since they lacked the funds to buy timber. For several years the priests and brothers operated a press here, printing bibles in the Maori language. The original building forms the core of the elegant timber house that now stands on the site. ✉ *The Strand, Russell,* ☎ *09/403–7861.* 🎟 *$5.* ☉ *Daily 9–5.*

The **Russell Museum** houses a collection of Maori tools and weapons and some fine portraits. The pride of its display is a ⅕-scale replica of Captain Cook's ship, HMS *Endeavour,* which entered the bay in 1769. The museum was previously known as the Captain Cook Memorial Museum, and some locals still refer to it by that name. The museum is set back slightly from the waterfront, some 50 yards north of Pompallier House. ✉ *York St.,* ☎ *09/403–7701.* 🎟 *$2.50.* ☉ *Daily 10–5.*

Christ Church is the oldest church in the country. One of the donors to its erection in 1835 was Charles Darwin, at that time a wealthy but unknown young man making his way around the globe on board the HMS *Beagle.* Behind the white picket fence that borders the churchyard, gravestones tell a fascinating and brutal story of life in the early days of the colony. Several graves belong to sailors from the HMS *Hazard* who were killed in this churchyard by Hone Heke's warriors in 1845. Another headstone marks the grave of a Nantucket sailor from the whaler *Mohawk.* As you walk around the church, look for the musket holes made when Hone Heke besieged the church. The interior is simple and charming—embroidered cushions on the pews are examples of a folk-art tradition that is still very much alive. ⊠ *Church and Robertson Sts., Russell.* ◷ *Daily 8–5.*

You can drive between Russell and Paihia, but the quickest and most convenient route is by ferry. Three passenger boats make the crossing between Paihia and Russell, with departures at least once every 30 minutes in each direction from 7:30 AM to 11 PM. The one-way fare is $1.50. The car ferry is at Opua, about 5 km (3 mi) south of Paihia. This ferry operates from 6:40 AM to 8:50 PM (Friday until 9:50 PM), with departures at approximately 20-minute intervals from either shore. The last boat leaves from Russell at 8:50 (Friday 9:50), from Opua at 9 (Friday 10). The one-way fare is $7 for car and driver plus $1 for each adult passenger.

Dining and Lodging

$$$ ✕ **The Quarterdeck.** The specialty of this waterfront restaurant is fish alfresco—*hapuku* (grouper), scallops, mussels, and oysters are all served with chips and salad. The prices are pretty steep for less-than-glamorous dining, but the indoor-outdoor tables on the enclosed deck overlooking the lively harbor are a pleasant place to relax on a warm evening and it's a welcoming spot for families. ⊠ *The Strand, Russell,* ☎ *09/403–7761. AE, DC, MC, V. BYOB.*

$$$ ✕ **Sally's.** Overlooking Kororareka Bay in the pretty cream-and-green timber Bay of Islands Swordfish Club building, this seaside restaurant has a varied menu, with plenty to please seafood lovers. The dishes are mostly old-fashioned, but the kitchen does them well. Oysters are served raw, or topped with bacon and cheese and grilled. Mussels are steamed open in herb-laced white wine, then topped with a creamy sauce. The fish medley is a bit more adventurous—it spikes bacon-wrapped scallops, shrimp, and fish onto bamboo skewers, sits them on a bed of lemon couscous, and drizzles them with hollandaise sauce. Ask for a window table, or dine outdoors when it's sunny. ⊠ *The Strand, Russell,* ☎ *09/403–7652. MC, V. Licensed and BYOB.*

$$$$ ▥ **The Homestead at Orongo Bay.** Tucked away in gardens off the road between the car-ferry landing and Russell, this lodge, built in 1865, has a welcoming atmosphere of peace and quiet. The current owners, Chris Wharehinga Swannell and Michael Hooper, bought the homestead in the mid-1990s and immediately saw its potential as a fine boutique lodge. The rooms upstairs in the main house each have their own character. The Oyster Bay is a smaller room with a tasteful green-and-blue color scheme and a shared bath. The Consol is larger and the Retreat, which is detached from the main homestead, offers a more private setting, with private decks, views over the lake, and a country decor. Set even farther back, the two Barn Rooms each occupy two levels and are more contemporary, with angled roofs and skylights. Four-course dinners or light suppers are available by prior arrangement, and it's advisable to eat at the homestead at least once. Management can recommend Russell restaurants as well. ⊠ *Aucks Rd., R.D. 1, Russell,* ☎ *09/403–7527. 6 rooms, 5 with bath. AE, MC, V.* ◈

$$$$ ▥ **Kimberley Lodge.** This splendid white timber mansion occupies a
★ commanding position overlooking Russell and Kororareka Bay. The house has been designed with big windows and sunny verandas to take maximum advantage of its location. Below, terraced gardens fall away down a steep hillside to the sea. The house is opulently furnished in contemporary style, and the bathrooms are very well equipped. Only one bedroom at the rear of the house—Pompallier—lacks impressive views. The best room in the house is the Kimberley Suite, which costs more than the standard suites. A new management team has brought fresh ideas, including events like wine tastings and a winter ball to add

appeal outside of the summer months. Smoking is not allowed indoors. ⊠ *Pitt St.,* ☎ *09/403–7090. 4 rooms. No-smoking rooms, pool, massage. AE, DC, MC, V. BP.*

$$$$ ⊞ **Okiato Lodge.** Okiato is high up on Okiato Point—hence its name—and has views of Opua, Paihia, and other Bay of Islands locales. If you happen to be sipping predinner drinks on the lawn on a Wednesday evening, you'll even see vessels from the local yacht club sailing by in the harbor below. Spacious rooms with step-down lounge areas, high vaulted ceilings, plenty of timber furnishings, and large windows with great views add up to a high standard of comfort. Rates include drinks and a four-course dinner, which emphasizes New Zealand produce such as scallops, venison, and lamb. The lodge's hosts have in-depth knowledge of the surrounding area and are happy to help with arranging activities and sightseeing. Most guests do some fishing or golf, but the most exhilarating activity might be a day visiting 90 Mile Beach and Cape Reinga at the northern tip of North Island. ⊠ *Okiato Point, R.D. 1, Russell,* ☎ *09/403–7948. 8 rooms. Bar, dining room, lounge. AE, DC, MC, V.*

$$ ⊞ **Duke of Marlborough Hotel.** This historic hotel is a favorite with the yachting fraternity, for whom ready access to the harbor and the bar downstairs are the most important considerations. Owner Dell Gifford has been busy spiffing up the rooms in recent years, and has added character by putting antique furnishings and new art around the hotel. The stairwell leading to the rooms has a traditional feel and features a 1780s clock and the family coat of arms on a stained-glass window. The rooms are much brighter, with plenty of yellows and floral designs. The front rooms with harbor views are the priciest, fairly small, and can be noisy, especially on weekends. Best in the house, especially if you like a bit of room, are the suites (rooms 7 and 8). ⊠ *The Strand,* ☎ *09/403–7829,* FAX *09/403–7760. 27 rooms. Restaurant, bar. DC, MC, V.*

$ ⊞ **Russell Lodge.** Surrounded by quiet gardens two streets back from the waterfront, this lodge—owned and operated by the Salvation Army—offers neat, clean rooms in several configurations. Family units have a separate bedroom with two single beds and either a double or a single bed in the main room. The largest room is Unit 15, a two-bedroom apartment with a kitchen, which will sleep six. Backpacker-style accommodations are also available in rooms for four; towels and sheets are not provided in these rooms but may be rented. Five rooms have kitchen facilities. ⊠ *Chapel and Beresford Sts., Russell,* ☎ *09/ 403–7640. 24 rooms. Pool, coin laundry. AE, MC, V.*

Outdoor Activities and Sports

FISHING

Bay of Islands Sportsfishing (⊠ Box 78, Russell, ☎ 09/403–7008) represents several operators who can meet most sportfishing requirements. **Dudley Smith** (⊠ Box 203, Russell, ☎ 09/403–7200) and **Nighthawk** (⊠ Russell, ☎ 09/407–8999) are two fishing outfitters.

Kerikeri

㉠   *20 km (12 mi) north of Paihia.*

Kerikeri is often referred to as the cradle of the nation because so much of New Zealand's earliest history, especially in terms of interaction between Maori and European, took place here. The main town itself is a small but pleasant enough shopping center.

The **Historic Kerikeri Basin,** just north of the modern town, is where most of the interest lies. Missionaries arrived in this area in 1819, having been invited to Kerikeri by its most famous historical figure, the great Maori chief Hongi Hika. The chief visited England in 1820, where he was showered with gifts. On his way back to New Zealand, during a stop in Sydney, he traded many of these presents for muskets. Having the advantage of these prized weapons, he set in motion plans to conquer other Maori tribes, enemies of his own Ngapuhi people. The return of his raiding parties over five years, with many slaves and gruesome trophies of conquest, put considerable strain between Hongi Hika and the missionaries. Eventually his warring ways were Hongi's undoing. He was shot in 1927 and died as a result of complications from the wound a year later.

Adjacent to the Stone Store (☞ *below*), the 1821 **Kemp House** is otherwise known as Mission House. It has gone through many changes since 1821, but ironically a major flood in 1981 inspired its "authentic" restoration. The flood washed away the garden and damaged the lower floor, and during repair much information about the original structure of the house was revealed. As a result, its ground floor and garden have been restored to the style of missionary days, and the upper floor, which remained unharmed by the flood, is still presented with its Victorian decoration. ✉ *Kerikeri Historic Basin, Kerikeri Rd.,* ☎ *09/407–9236.* 🖼 *$5.* ☉ *Nov.–Apr., daily 10–5; May–Oct., Sat.–Wed. 10–5.*

Across the road from the Stone Store is a path leading to the historic site of **Kororipo Pa,** the fortified headquarters of chief Hongi Hika. Untrained eyes will have a bit of difficulty working out exactly where the *pa* (hilltop fortification) was, as there are no structures left. Information boards and drawings aid the imagination. The pa was built on a steep-sided promontory between the Kerikeri River and the Wairoa Stream. You'll still get a fine view over both.

Rewi's Village museum re-creates a *kainga* (unfortified fishing village) where local Maori would have lived in peaceful times. (In times of siege they would have taken refuge in nearby Kororipo Pa; ☞ *above*.) The village-museum was built in 1969, when the local community wanted to save the area from threatened urban development. A video plays near the entrance, with a history of chief Hongi Hika. In the village itself are replicas of the chief's house, the weapons store, and the family enclosure, as well as two original canoes dug up from local swamps and original hangi stones (used to cook traditional Maori feasts) found onsite. ✉ *Kerikeri Historic Basin, Kerikeri Rd.,* ☎ *09/407–6454.* 🖼 *$2.50.* ☉ *Nov.–Apr., daily 9–5; May–Oct., daily 10–4.*

The **Stone Store** is Kerikeri's most picturesque attraction and is the most striking building in the historic basin. Built between 1832 and 1836, it is New Zealand's oldest existing stone building. It was part of the Kerikeri Mission Station and was built to hold stores for the whole New Zealand mission of the time. In November 1998, after a three-year-long renovation, it opened in what is close to its original state. ✉ *Kerikeri Historic Basin, Kerikeri Rd.,* ☎ *09/407–9236.* 🖼 *$2.* ☉ *Nov.–Apr., daily 10–5; May–Oct., Sat.–Wed. 10–5.*

Lodging

$$$ 🏠 **The Summer House.** Hosts Christine and Rod Brown both come from artistic families and the evidence is displayed throughout this B&B. The prints are Christine's mother's, Rod's sister has provided the impressive sculpture at the main doorway, and his father supplied the watercolors. The downstairs room, slightly detached from the house, is done in browns and creams with a South Pacific theme that uses tapa cloth. It has the most space, a kitchenette, and a higher room rate. The two upstairs rooms in the main house share a guest lounge. One room has an 1860 French bed with furniture to match, and the other has a Victorian brass bedstead that traveled south from Scotland in the early 20th century. Christine's breakfasts are wonderful, featuring fresh or poached fruits, Greek yogurt, homemade muesli, eggs on request, croissants, and freshly baked orange muffins. ⊠ *Kerikeri Rd. (south end),* ☎ *09/407–4294,* FAX *09/407–4297. 3 rooms. Lounge. MC, V. BP.* ✑

\$\$ ⬚ **Kauri Park.** This small cluster of chalets is a notch above the usual, with modern decor and a beautiful setting among fruit trees adjacent to farmland. Owners Alexander Gramse and Helene Henriksen have combined a touch of European hospitality—a free drink on arrival, a guest lounge—with the usual Kiwi warmth. Each unit has a veranda and colorful furnishings. Kauri Park is a little bit out of town, which gives it a rural feeling, but it's still only a few minutes' drive from the historic sights. ⊠ *Kerikeri Rd. (south end),* ☎ *09/407–7629. 7 rooms. Lounge. AE, DC, MC, V.*

Opononi

㉑ *85 km (53 mi) west of Paihia.*

Opononi is a small town near the mouth of the Hokianga Harbour. It is the place where Opi, a tame dolphin, came to play with swimmers in the mid-1950s, putting the town on the national map for the first and only time in its history. There is a statue in front of the pub commemorating the much-loved creature. If you're driving and approaching the town from the south, be sure check out some of the signposted lookouts en route.

㉒ **Waipoua State Forest** contains the largest remnant of the kauri forests that once covered this part of the country, along with some delicious forest air. A short path leads from the parking area through the forest to **Tane Mahuta,** "Lord of the Forest," standing nearly 173 ft high and measuring 43 ft around its base. The largest tree in New Zealand, it's said to be 1,200 years old. The second-largest tree, but older by some 800 years, is **Te Matua Ngahere.** It takes about 20 minutes to walk to it from the road. There are other trees of note in the forest, among them the **Four Sisters,** four trees that have grown together in a circular formation. If you have three hours to spare, hike the Yakas Track, which links the Four Sisters to the **Department of Conservation Visitor Centre** (☎ 09/439–0605). It's possible to camp in the forest, as long as you check at the visitor center before you pitch a tent. Facilities include toilets, hot showers, and a communal cookhouse. When it's wet, you may spot some large kauri snails in the forest. Also, the recent successful eradication of predators such as weasels and stoats has led to a rise in the number of kiwis in the forest. Visitors are beginning to report sightings, but it's still very much a case of being in the right place at the right time. You'll need a flashlight to spot one, because the birds only come out at night.

Dining and Lodging

\$\$\$ ✕⬚ **Waipoua Lodge.** Owners Raewyn and Tony Lancaster have taken what were once working farm areas and turned them—very tastefully—into guest lodgings. The names of the rooms record their past lives: the Calf Pen, the Wool Shed, and the Stables. All the rooms have plenty of space and natural light, with an emphasis on country comfort. The original farmhouse is now used as the reception area and restaurant and is packed with antique objects such as an old pedal organ, photographs, and saws. Raewyn's cooking is legendary: country fare with a twist. Past delights have included rack of lamb with braised summer fruits and wild berry sauce and set in a kumara basket. Tony was once the local policeman and still serves as the fish-and-game ranger in the area. He can advise you on fly-fishing, bushwalks, and other outdoor activities in the area. The lodge is just a kilometer (½ mi) south of Waipoua Forest. ✉ *State Hwy. 12, Waipoua,* ☎ *09/439–0422,* FAX *09/439–0422. 3 rooms. Restaurant, bar. MC, V.*

Matakohe

95 km (59 mi) south of Opononi.

㉓ Matakohe Kauri Museum is one of the most intriguing museums in the country. Its vast collection of artifacts, tools, photographs, documents, and memorabilia tells the story of the pioneers who settled this part of the country in the second half of the 19th century—a story interwoven with the kauri forests. Here you'll find superb examples of craftsmanship: furniture and a complete kauri house, as well as an early example of an American-built Caterpillar bulldozer, which was used to drag logs from the forest. One of the most fascinating displays is of kauri gum, the transparent lumps of resin that form when the sticky sap of the kauri tree hardens. This gum, which was used to make varnish, can be polished to a warm, lustrous finish that looks remarkably like amber—right down to the insects that are sometimes trapped and preserved inside. At one time collecting this gum was an important rural industry. **Volunteers Hall** contains a huge kauri slab running from one end of the hall to the other, and there is also a Women in the Bush display, a replica of a cabinetmaker's shop, and an exhibition dedicated to fishing in Kaipara Harbour. The latest display, the Steam Saw Mill, illustrates how the huge kauri logs were cut into timber. The life-size mannequins in the exhibit, like others in the museum, are modeled on living descendants of the actual pioneers of the region. If you like the whirring of engines, the best day to visit is Wednesday, when much of the museum's machinery is started up. ✉ *Church Rd., Matakohe,* ☎ *09/431–7417.* ⊡ *$7.* ☉ *Daily 9–5.*

Northland and the Bay of Islands A to Z

Arriving and Departing

BY BUS
Northliner Express (☎ 09/913–6100), **InterCity** (☎ 09/358–4085), and **Newmans** (☎ 09/913–6200) run several times daily between Auckland and Paihia.

BY CAR
The main route from Auckland is Highway 1. Leave the city by the Harbour Bridge and follow signs to Whangarei. Driving time for the 250-km (150-mi) journey to Paihia is about four hours.

Contacts and Resources

EMERGENCIES
Dial 111 for **fire, police, or ambulance** services.

GUIDED TOURS
The **4x4 Dune-Rider** is a novel way to get to Cape Reinga—via the vast strip of 90 Mile Beach. The company uses four-wheel-drive vehicles for small groups and makes slightly unusual stops, such as a visit to the "world-famous" Mangonui fish-and-chips shop. The drive gives you a chance to dig for the shellfish known as tuatua and goes to the dramatically set Cape Reinga Lighthouse. ✉ *Box 164, Paihia,* ☎ *09/402–8681.* ⊡ *$75.* ☉ *Departs Paihia daily at 7:30* AM, *Kerikeri 8:15.*

Fullers Northland, based out of Auckland, has one-, two-, and three-day tours from Auckland to the Bay of Islands. Its three-day Bay Explorer includes a tour of the historic Waitangi Treaty House, a trip to Cape Reinga, a swim with dolphins, a voyage around the bay aboard a schooner, and accommodations in Russell. ✉ *Bay of Islands Travel*

Centre, Shop 2, Downtown Shopping Centre, Customs St., Auckland,
☎ *09/358–0259.* ⌾ *$459.*

Fullers Northland, based in Paihia, runs cruises in the Bay of Islands,
departing from both Paihia and Russell. The most popular is the half-
day catamaran cruise to Cape Brett, at the eastern extremity of the bay.
This includes a journey through a large hole in Motukako Island,
known naturally enough as "the hole in the rock." The Cream Trip is
an enjoyable six-hour cruise that stops in at many of the bay islands.
⊠ *Maritime Building, Paihia,* ☎ *09/402–7421.* ⌾ *Cape Brett $52,*
Cream Trip $65. ⊙ *Cape Brett cruise departs Paihia daily at 9 and*
1:30. Cream Trip departs Paihia Oct.–May, daily at 10; June–Sept.,
Mon., Wed., Thurs., and Sat. at 10.

Russell Mini Tours' one-hour tours of the historic sights of Russell depart from the Fullers office, opposite the wharf. ⊠ *Box 70, Russell,*
☎ *09/403–7891.* ⌾ *$12.* ⊙ *Tours daily at 11, 1, 2, and 3:30.*

VISITOR INFORMATION
Bay of Islands Visitor Information Centre Paihia. ⊠ *Maritime Reserve,*
Paihia, ☎ *09/402–7426.* ⊙ *Nov.–Mar., daily 7:30–7:30; Apr.–Oct.,*
daily 8–5.
Bay of Islands Visitor Information Centre Russell. ⊠ *The Strand, Rus-*
sell, ☎ *09/403–7866.* ⊙ *Daily 8–4:30.*
Warkworth Visitor Information Centre. ⊠ *1 Baxter St., Warkworth,*
☎ *09/425–9081,* ℻ *09/425–7584.* ⊙ *Daily 9–5.*

THE COROMANDEL PENINSULA

New Zealand has countless pockets of beauty that are not included in
standard itineraries. One of the most accessible is the Coromandel Peninsula, which juts out like a hitchhiker's thumb east of Auckland. As with
so many lands "discovered" by Europeans, the peninsula was looted
for its valuable resources: kauri trees, then Kauri gum, and finally gold
in the 1870s. Relative quiet since the 1930s has allowed the region to
recover a little, and without question natural beauty abounds.

The center of the peninsula is dominated by a craggy spine of volcanic
peaks that rises sharply to a height of almost 3,000 ft. The west coast
cradles the Firth of Thames, and along the east coast the Pacific has
carved out a succession of beaches and inlets separated by rearing headlands. Due to its rich volcanic soil, the peninsula has many spectacular gardens, several of which are open to the public. From the town of
Thames, the gateway to the region, Highway 25 and the 309 Road circle the lower two-thirds of the peninsula—an exhilarating drive with
the sea on one side and great forested peaks on the other. Hiking in
the peninsula's lush forest is a great pleasure, and the east-coast beaches
are breathtaking. Especially considering the Coromandel's proximity
to Auckland, it would be difficult to find a finer introduction to the
wonders of New Zealand.

Thames

㉔ *120 km (75 mi) southeast of Auckland.*

Thames is an historic town in the southwest corner of the peninsula
about an hour and a half from Auckland. Since the 1920s the city has
changed from a gold-mining center to a center for local agriculture.
Locals have a saying that when the gold ran out, "Thames went to sleep
awaiting the kiss of a golden prince—and instead it awoke to the
warm breath of a cow." At the **Historical Museum** (⊠ Pollen and
Cochrane Sts., ☎ 07/868–8509; ⌾ $2.50, ⊙ daily 1–4) you can look

The Coromandel Peninsula

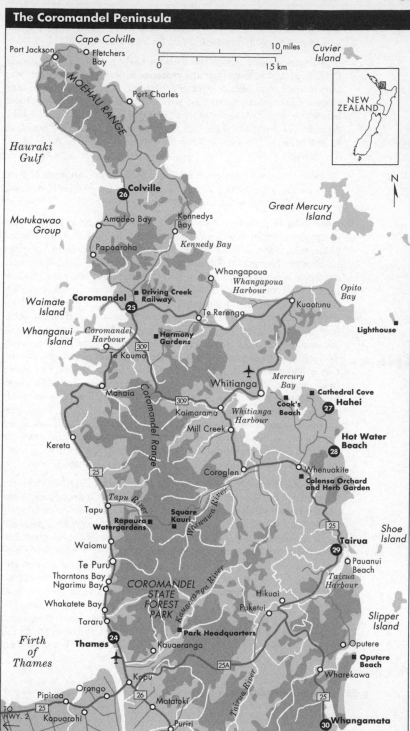

Cape Colville

Port Jackson

Fletchers Bay

Cuvier Island

0 — 10 miles
0 — 15 km

MOEHAU RANGE

Port Charles

Hauraki Gulf

NEW ZEALAND

Colville 26

Motukawao Group

Amodeo Bay

Kennedys Bay

Great Mercury Island

Papaaroha

Kennedy Bay

Whangapoua

Whangapoua Harbour

Opito Bay

Waimate Island

Coromandel 25

Driving Creek Railway

Te Rerenga

Kuaotunu

Lighthouse

Whanganui Island

Coromandel Harbour

Harmony Gardens

309

Te Kouma

Whitianga

Mercury Bay

Cathedral Cove
Hahei 27

Manaia

309

Kaimarama

Whitianga Harbour

Cook's Beach

Mill Creek

Kereta

Coroglen

Whenuakite

Hot Water Beach 28

Colenso Orchard and Herb Garden

Tapu River

Tapu

Rapaura Watergardens

Square Kauri

Shoe Island

Waiomu

Waiwawa River

Tairua 29

Te Puru

Pauanui Beach

Thorntons Bay
Ngarimu Bay

COROMANDEL STATE FOREST PARK

Tairua Harbour

Whakatete Bay

Hikuai

Slipper Island

Tararu

Kauaeranga River

Puketui

Park Headquarters

Oputere

Firth of Thames

Thames 24

Kauaeranga

Oputere Beach

Kopu

25A

Wharekawa

Pipiroa

Orango

26

Matatoki

Tairua River

25

TO HWY. 2

Kapuarahi

Puriri

Whangamata 30

Coromandel Range

into earlier ways of life in the town. Rock lovers will enjoy the geologic take on local history at the **Mineralogical Museum** (✉ Brown and Cochrane Sts., ☎ 07/868–6227; 🎫 $2.50, ⊙ Tues.–Sun. 11–4).

If you want to learn even more about early gold-mining efforts in the Coromandel, stop in at the **stamper battery,** north on the way out of town, and take a brief underground tour of the old Golden Crown Claim, which was first worked in 1868. Five hundred feet below this site, the Caledonia strike was one of the richest in the world. A guide will describe the geological and historical interest of the mine. ✉ *State Hwy. 25, north of Waiotahi Creek Rd.,* ☎ *07/868–7448.* 🎫 *$5.* ⊙ *Daily 9–5.*

While in Thames, take a quick look into **St. George's Anglican Church.** The interior is unpainted, and the kauri wood used to build it is gorgeous. ✉ *Willoughby and MacKay Sts.*

Meonstoke is probably New Zealand's most unusual garden, and nothing printed here will quite prepare you for it. For more than 35 years, Pam Gwynne has been working every square inch of her quarter-acre lot. Numerous paths wind through a junglelike space, where the world appears before you as it did in childhood. There are no lookouts or vistas to distract you from taking in the magic around you. Pam is a collector, not only of top horticultural specimens, but of found objects as well, which she ingeniously incorporates into surreal and often humorous tableaux with plants. On one path, a row of a ceramic pitchers is suspended from a rod (to collect rainwater?), and an overflowing bird feeder serves two hungry porcelain doves. Elsewhere, tiny winking porcelain Asian figures festoon bonsai plants, and an old black tricycle looks as if a young boy has just left it there. Although the garden is small, allow yourself plenty of time. There are hundreds of delights, many of which you'll miss the first time around. Pam's passion continues indoors, and if you are interested in dolls, ask to see her collection. Remember that this is a private home, and visitors are welcome only by appointment. The small entry fee goes to local charities. ☎ *07/868–6560 or 07/868–6850.* ⊙ *By appointment only.*

The **Tropical Butterfly Garden** is just a few minutes' drive north on the way out of Thames, but it's easy to miss unless you're specifically looking for the signs. Owners Roger and Sabine Gass have brought some color to the Coromandel, with a garden where the star attraction is a flock of fluttering butterflies from Australia. Up to 12 species and 250 butterflies may be on view at any time, including large birdwing butterflies. Look for the chrysalis box at the entrance to the garden and the glassed-in display of the massive gum emperor moth kept near the garden's waterfall. Adding to the attraction are exotic birds such as finches, doves, and quails, plus about 100 different plant species. The orchids are particularly stunning. Make sure you leave time to sit and relax in the garden. ✉ *Dickson Holiday Park, Victoria St.,* ☎ *07/868–8080,* 📠 *07/868–5648.* 🎫 *$8.* ⊙ *Summer, daily 9–5; winter, daily 11–4.*

Lodging

$-$$ 🏨 **Brian Boru Hotel.** This much-photographed period piece has a stunning black-and-white exterior. Built in 1868, the hotel and its reception area, bar, and dining room all have a charm that newer places in town can't match, with mining paraphernalia and historical photographs adorning the walls. Inside the hotel rooms, however, be prepared for very basic comforts—a bed, a desk, a chair, and rather tired carpets and wallpaper. If you're after a higher standard of amenities, look at the motel units just at the back of the main building, which were built more recently. Despite this unevenness, the combination of a central town location, good room rates, and a sense of history makes the Brian Boru a good bet. Because of the hotel's legendary resident (fortunately friendly) ghosts, manager Barbara Doyle offers highly regarded mystery and murder weekends. During these weekends, someone in the hotel pretends to be "murdered" and other guests have to follow clues to find out who among them is guilty of the crime. ✉ *200 Richmond St., Thames,* ☎ *07/868–6523,* ℻ *07/868–9760. 25 rooms, 13 with bath; 15 motel units. Dining room, bar. MC, V.*

$–$$ 🏠 **Te Kouma Harbour Farmstay.** A little off the beaten track, this set of single-story wooden chalets set on a deer farm is excellent for families, with outdoor options like kayaking, nearby bushwalking, and a soccer field, *petanque* (the French game *boules*), and pool on-site—enough to keep you busy for a couple of days. Large, bright multiroom cabins have contemporary furniture and kitchen areas with cooking facilities. Breakfast is available by arrangement, but most guests cook for themselves. There are also barbecue areas on the grounds. The cabins are down a long drive that is well signposted from Highway 25 north out of Thames. ✉ *Te Kouma Harbour,* ☎ *07/866–8747. 6 rooms. Picnic area, pool, boating, recreation room. No credit cards.*

Outdoor Activities and Sports

Coromandel State Forest Park has more than 30 walking trails, which offer anything from a 30-minute stroll to a three-day trek, overnighting in huts equipped with bunks. The most accessible starting point is the delightful Kauaeranga Valley Road, where the **Coromandel Forest Park Headquarters** provides maps and information (☎ 07/868–6381). The office is open weekdays 8–4. Keep in mind that the park can be very busy from late December to mid-January. If you're traveling then, plan to visit the park midweek. To reach the Kauaeranga Valley, head south from Thames and on the outskirts of the town turn left on Banks Street, then right on Parawai Road, which becomes Kauaeranga Valley Road.

En Route The Coromandel Ranges drop right down to the seafront Highway 25 as it winds up the west coast of the peninsula. Turn upon turn makes each view seem more spectacular than the last, and when you top the hills north of Kereta on the way to Coromandel, mountains, pastures, and islands in the Firth of Thames open out before you—spectacular.

Tapu

25 km (16 mi) north of Thames.

The unpaved **Tapu-Coroglen Road** turns off Highway 25 in the hamlet of Tapu to wind into the mountains. It's a breathtaking route where massive tree ferns grow out of the roadside hills. About 6½ km (4 mi) from Tapu you will come to the magical **Rapaura Watergardens** (☞ *below*). Travel another 3½ km (2 mi) along the road and pull over to climb the 178 steps up to the huge, 1,200-year-old **Square Kauri,** so named for the shape that a cross section of its trunk would have. At 133 ft tall and 30 ft around, this is only the 15th-largest kauri in New Zealand. From a tree-side platform there is a splendid view across the valley to Mau Mau Paki, one of the Coromandel Ranges peaks. Continuing east across the peninsula, the road passes through forests and sheep paddocks—a shimmeringly beautiful ride in sun or mist.

Rapaura Watergardens, full of native and exotic flowering species, has been sculpted from the wilderness in a 65-acre sheltered valley in the Coromandel Ranges. Rapaura (running water) is a wonderful place to witness the role water plays in New Zealand gardens and the tranquillity that can result. In the garden's various streams, waterfalls, fountains, and 14 ponds, fish and ducks swim among colorful water lilies and other bog plants while songbirds lilt overhead. Paths wind among the waters through collections of grasses, flaxes, gunneras, rhododendrons, and camellias, all organically gardened. Giant tree ferns and rimu, *rata*, and kauri trees form a lush canopy overhead. The combination of delicacy and rugged grandeur may have been what inspired the philosophic messages that you'll find painted on signs around the garden, such as KEEP YOUR VALUES IN BALANCE AND YOU WILL ALWAYS FIND HAPPINESS. Be sure to take the easy 10-minute walk to the cascading falls known as Seven Steps to Heaven, especially if you aren't planning on spending much time in the native bush. Rapaura has a tearoom and a crafts shop with work by Coromandel artisans. ⊠ *Tapu–Coroglen Rd., 6 km (4 mi) east of Tapu,* ☎ FAX *07/868–4821.* ⊑ *$6.* ☉ *Daily 10–5.*

Coromandel

㉕ *60 km (38 mi) north of Thames, 29 km (18 mi) northwest of Whitianga.*

Coromandel became the site of New Zealand's first gold strike in 1852 when sawmiller Charles Ring found gold-bearing quartz at Driving Creek, just north of town. The find was important for New Zealand, since the country's workforce had been severely depleted by the gold rushes in California and Australia. Ring hurried to Auckland to claim the reward that had been offered to anyone finding "payable" gold. The town's population soared, but the reef gold could be mined only by heavy and expensive machinery. Within a few months Coromandel resumed its former sleepy existence as a timber town—and Charles Ring was refused the reward.

☉ **Driving Creek Railway** is one man's magnificent folly. Barry Brickell is a local potter who discovered that clay on his land was perfect for his work. The problem was that the deposit lay in a remote area at the top of a steep slope; so he hacked a path through the forest and built his own miniature railroad to haul the stuff. Visitors to his studio began asking if they could go along for a ride, and Brickell now takes passengers on daily tours aboard his toy train. The route that the diesel-powered, narrow-gauge locomotive follows incorporates a double-decker bridge, two tunnels, a spiral, and a switchback. The round-trip takes about 50 minutes. The "station" is 3 km (2 mi) north of Coromandel township. ⊠ *410 Kennedy's Bay Rd., Coromandel,* ☎ *07/866–8703.* ⊑ *$12.* ☉ *Late Oct.–Apr., daily at 2, 4, and 10:30.*

Dining and Lodging

$–$$ ✕ **Pepper Tree Restaurant and Bar.** Coromandel seafood takes precedence on the menu of this pleasant eatery. Locally farmed oysters are served simply on the half shell, and Greenshell mussels are steamed open and piled into bowls, or turned into fritters and offered with a dipping sauce. Organic produce, including meat, is used whenever possible. Nachos, potato wedges, and other easygoing nibbles dominate the all-day menu, but things get more serious after sundown with dishes like local lamb shanks with a sauce based on dark beer, and panfried snapper with a preserved lemon and bell pepper salsa. ⊠ *Kapanga Rd., Coromandel,* ☎ *07/866–8211. AE, DC, MC, V.*

$$$$ ✕▦ **Buffalo Lodge.** Perched on a hillside and surrounded by bush just
★ out of Coromandel town, the lodge looks across the Hauraki Gulf toward Auckland. Original owners Raouf and Evelyne Siegrist-Huang made sure that all rooms, the dining room, and lounge area have great scenic backdrops. They've added personal touches as well—their own artwork adorns walls at the lodge's entrance and in guest rooms. Evelyne now runs the lodge alone, following Raouf's death in 1999. However the

lodge still reflects Raouf's love of wood, which is used in the ceilings, floors, and furnishings. In the evening the restaurant is popular with guests and others staying in town. A three-course meal costs $85, and specialties include New Zealand king salmon, venison, lamb fillet, and fish fresh from waters around the Coromandel. With a limit of six people staying at any one time, you'll never feel crowded. ⊠ *Buffalo Rd.,* ☎ *07/866–8960,* ⅢX *07/866–8960. 4 rooms. AE, DC, MC, V. Closed May–Sept. BP.* ◈

$$ 🏠 **Coromandel Colonial Cottages.** These eight immaculate timber cot-
★ tages offer spacious and comfortable self-contained accommodations for about the same price as a standard motel room. Six of the units have two bedrooms, a living room with convertible beds, a large, well-equipped kitchen, and a dining area. The two newer units have only one bedroom but still feel spacious. Arranged with military precision in two ranks, the cottages face each other across a tailored lawn surrounded by green hills on the northern outskirts of Coromandel. For vacation periods book several months in advance. ⊠ *Rings Rd., Coromandel,* ☎ *07/ 866–8857. 8 cottages. Pool, playground. AE, DC, MC, V.*

Colville and Beyond

㉖ *30 km (19 mi) north of Coromandel.*

If you find yourself possessed with the urge to reach land's end on the wilds of the peninsula—with more rugged coastline, beautiful coves, beaches, and pasturelands—follow the paved road up to Colville. Beyond that, a gravel road will take you to the **Mt. Moehau** trail that climbs to the peninsula's highest point (2,923 ft); to the sands at **Port Jackson**; or all the way to the tip, at **Fletcher's Bay** (60 km, or 38 mi, from Coromandel). Colville's classic counterculture **General Store** (☎ 07/866–6805) sells foodstuffs, wine, and gasoline and has a café with vegetarian meals. It is the northernmost supplier on the peninsula, so don't forget to fill up before you move on.

En Route On your way south from Coromandel, **Harmony Gardens** is delightful, tranquil, noted for its rhododendrons, and filled with the sounds of birds and running water. From Coromandel, drive down Highway 25 for about 4 km (2½ mi) and turn inland where a sign points to WHITIANGA—309 ROAD. After about 2 km (1 mi), this road passes the gardens. ☎ 07/866–8487. ⊡ $4. ◷ *Spring–fall, daily 10–4.*

Hahei

㉗ *14 km (9 mi) northeast of Whenuakite on Hahei Beach Rd., 57 km (35 mi) southeast of Coromandel, 64 km (40 mi) northeast of Thames.*

The beaches and seaside land formations in and around Hahei make for a great day of exploring—or lounging. Past Hahei on Pa Road, **Te Pare Historic Reserve** is the site of a Maori pa (fortified village), though no trace remains of the defensive terraces and wooden spikes that ringed the hill. (A much larger pa was on the hilltop overlooking this site.) At high tide, the blowhole at the foot of the cliffs will add its booming bass note to the sound of waves and the sighing of the wind in the grass. To reach the actual pa site, follow the red arrow down the hill from the parking area. After some 50 yards take the right fork through a grove of giant pohutukawa trees, then through a gate and across an open, grassy hillside. The trail is steep in places and becomes increasingly overgrown as you climb, but persist until you reach the summit, then head toward more pohutukawas off to your right at the south end of the headland.

Cathedral Cove is a beautiful white-sand crescent with a great rock arch. It is only accessible at low tide, about a 45-minute walk each way. To get there, travel along Hahei Beach Road, turn right toward town and the sea, and then, just past the shops, turn left into Grange Road and follow the signs. From the parking lot you will get excellent views over Mahurangi Island, a marine reserve.

Cook's Beach lies along Mercury Bay, so named for Captain James Cook's observation of the transit of the planet Mercury in November 1769. The beach is notable because of the captain's landfall here—it was the first by a European, and it is commemorated by a beachside plaque. The beach itself is one of the less attractive ones in the area.

★ ㉘ The popular **Hot Water Beach** is a delightful thermal oddity. A warm spring seeps beneath the beach, and by scooping a shallow hole in the sand, you can create a pool of warm water; the deeper you dig, the hotter the water becomes, but the phenomenon occurs only at low to mid tide, so time your trip accordingly. Hot Water Beach is well signposted off of Hahei Beach Road from Whenuakite (fen-oo-ah-*kye*-tee). For a swim without the spa treatment, nearby, at the end of Hahei Beach Road, you'll find one of the finest well-protected coves on the coast, with sands tinted pink from crushed shells.

NEED A   **Colenso Orchard and Herb Garden** (✉ Main Rd., Whenuakite, ☎ 07/
BREAK?   866–3725), on Highway 25 just south of the Hahei turnoff, is a relaxed cottage café that you might find yourself wishing would franchise across rural New Zealand. Set in a garden full of lavender and kitchen herbs, Colenso serves fresh juices (from its own orchards), daily soups, focaccia sandwiches, those addictive chocolate fudge biscuits (also called slices) that are a real Kiwi treat, and Devonshire teas—simple, wholesome fare that goes with the droning of bees and the sound of wind chimes. Before getting back on the road, buy a bag of the freshly harvested fruit at the roadside stand. Colenso is open from 10 to 5 daily, September through July.

Tairua

㉙ *28 km (18 mi) south of Hahei, 37 km (23 mi) north of Whangamata.*

A town that you'll actually notice when you pass through it, Tairua is a harborside center where you can find food stores and a seafood joint or two. The twin volcanic peaks of Paku rise up beside the harbor.

Dining and Lodging

$$$$ ✕🏨 **Puka Park Resort.** This stylish hillside hideaway, which attracts a largely European clientele, lies surrounded by native bushland on Pauanui Beach, at the seaward end of Tairua Harbour on the east coast of the peninsula. Timber chalets are smartly furnished with black cane tables and wooden Venetian blinds. Sliding glass doors lead to a balcony perched among the treetops. Bathrooms are well equipped but small. The lodge offers a full range of activities for those who want to take advantage of the splendor of the surrounding beaches and forests. Rates are comparatively low for accommodations of this standard. Food and service in the international restaurant are outstanding. The turnoff from Highway 25 is about 6 km (4 mi) south of Tairua. ✉ *Private Bag, Pauanui Beach,* ☎ *07/864–8088,* 🆅 *07/864–8112. 48 rooms. Restaurant, bar, pool, spa, tennis court, bicycles. AE, DC, MC, V.* 🍽

$$$ ✕🏨 **Pacific Harbour Motor Lodge.** Clustered between the road and an ocean inlet, these stand-alone cottages are attractively designed in a Fijian style, with shell paths between them. Peak-ceilinged interiors are trimmed with New Zealand rimu wood, and furnishings are pleasant

and tasteful. All units have fully equipped kitchenettes. The motor lodge has its own bar and restaurant, with local seafood on the menu, and there is a helpful local activities list available at the front desk. ⊠ *Hwy. 25, Box 5, Tairua,* ☎ ℻ *07/864–8581. 25 suites. Restaurant, bar, hot tub. AE, DC, MC, V.*

$$$ ▦ **Pauanui Pines.** This modern motor lodge provides a less expensive but still comfortable alternative to Puka Park. Owners Ian and Sue Wilkinson have gone for light, bright decor to suit a beach vacation, and even the designs on the crockery closely match the colors of the furniture. The units here are self-contained, with French-press coffeemakers a nice extra. Continental breakfast is available by arrangement, but for other meals guests cook their own or wander to the nearby Pauanui township, where there are a restaurant and café. Portable gas barbecues are available as well. ⊠ *168 Vista Paku, Pauanui Beach,* ☎ *07/864–8086,* ℻ *07/864–7122. 15 one-bedroom units, 3 two-bedroom units. Pool, putting green, tennis court. AE, DC, MC, V.*

En Route On the road between Tairua and Whangamata you'll pass the mountainous wilderness around the second branch of the Tairua River, which is the remarkable domain of Doug Johansen. Over the past 20 years he has cut his own trails in the valley's lush rain forest—not that you could find them even if you were walking on one. Their minimal invasiveness is uncanny. Heading into the woods with a knowledgeable, and in this case entertaining, guide to point out native plants and their uses can make later hikes on your own even more rewarding. *See* Kiwi Dundee Adventures *in* Coromandel A to Z, *below.*

While on the road between Tairua and Whangamata, you can also stop at Oputere Beach and the Wharekawa (fah-ray-*ka*-wa) Wildlife Refuge for a 15-minute stroll through the forest to another great stretch of white sand. The long beach is bounded at either end by headlands, and there are stunning views of Slipper Island. An estuary near the parking lot is a breeding ground for shorebirds. In the late afternoon waterfowl are often present as the sun slants across the Coromandel Ranges to the west. A handsome bridge arches over the river to the forest walk.

Whangamata

 37 km (23 mi) south of Tairua, 60 km (38 mi) east of Thames.

Whangamata (fahng-a-ma-*ta*) is another harborside village backed by the Coromandel Ranges. The modest houses and main strip of this town of 4,000 won't exactly bowl you over. Its harbor, surf beaches, mangroves, and coastal islands, however, are glorious. It is a great spot for deep-sea fishing, and its bar break brings in some of the best waves in New Zealand. Around the Christmas holidays and into January, it's a favorite for throngs of surfers.

Dining and Lodging

$ ✗ **Ginger's Health Shop & Cafe.** If you need breakfast or a sandwich
★ to take to the beach, you're sure to find something here. About half the dishes are vegetarian, and the sandwiches and savory and sweet scones (ooh, those date scones) are uniformly delicious. Homemade apricot-muesli bars and other treats make Ginger's a popular spot for fueling up. A full range of alternative health products, including homeopathic remedies, is also available. ⊠ *601 Port Rd., Whangamata,* ☎ *07/865–7265. AE, DC, MC, V. No dinner.*

$$$ ▦ **Brenton Lodge.** Looking out over Whangamata and the islands in
★ its harbor from your hillside suite, you'll have no trouble settling into a luxurious mood. Fresh flowers and a tray of fruit and muffins greet you on arrival, as do cheerful furnishings: a couch, breakfast table and

chairs (for a private breakfast), a wonderfully comfortable bed, and terry robes. The lodge's only rooms are two suites on the second floors of attractive outbuildings. Stroll around the garden, peep at the birds in the aviary, and in springtime breathe in the scent of orange and jasmine blossoms. ⊠ *Box 216, Whangamata,* ☎ *07/865–8400. 2 suites. AE, MC, V. BP.*

The Coromandel A to Z

Arriving and Departing

BY BUS

The **Coromandel Bus Plan** is the cheapest and most flexible way to travel around the region by bus. It is valid for three months, and you can get on and off where you wish. A rate of $49 covers the Thames–Coromandel–Whitianga–Tairua–Thames loop, and you can take round-trips to Hahei, Hot Water Beach, and Whangamata. ⊠ *Thames Visitor Information Centre, 206 Pollen St.,* ☎ *07/868–7284.*

InterCity (☎ 07/868–7251) links Whitianga, Thames, and Auckland daily.

BY CAR

From Auckland take the Southern Motorway, following signs to Hamilton. Just past the narrowing of the motorway, turn left onto Highway 2, then take the turnoff to Highway 25, signposted between the small towns of Maramarua and Mangatarata. Follow the signs to Thames. Allow 1 to 2½ hours for the 118-km (73-mi) journey.

Contacts and Resources

EMERGENCIES

Dial 111 for **fire, police, or ambulance** services.

GUIDED TOURS

Kiwi Dundee Adventures. A trip to New Zealand really wouldn't be complete without a day or more with Doug Johansen and Jan Poole or one of their expert associate guides. Their total enthusiasm for the region inevitably rubs off on anyone who takes a Kiwi Dundee tour. There are one- to five-day or longer experiences of the majesty of the Coromandel, or all of New Zealand if you'd like. The spectacular natural phenomena that they know intimately and respect deeply and the odd bits of history and bush lore are all rolled into their hikes and walks. They have a great time as conservationists and guides, and you're sure to have one with them in their beautiful neck of the woods. ⊠ *Box 198, Whangamata,* ☎ ℻ *07/865–8809.* ✿

Mercury Bay Safaris has a swim-with-the-dolphins program, plus a glass-bottom boat trip and a journey around islands in the area. Departures from Whitianga Wharf are subject to weather conditions. ⊠ *Whitianga Visitor Information Centre, Whitianga,* ☎ *07/866–5555,* ℻ *07/866–2205.* ⚑ *Dolphin Quest $90, glass-bottom boat $40, Seven Island Safari $75.*

VISITOR INFORMATION

Thames Visitor Information Centre. ⊠ *206 Pollen St., Thames,* ☎ *07/ 868–7284.* ☉ *Weekdays 8:30–5, weekends 9–4.* ✿

Whitianga Visitor Information Centre. ⊠ *66 Albert St.,* ☎ *07/866–5555.* ☉ *Spring–fall, weekdays 9–5, weekends 10–1; summer, daily 9–5.*

THE BAY OF PLENTY

Explorer Captain James Cook gave the Bay of Plenty its name for the abundant sources of food he found here; these days it is best known

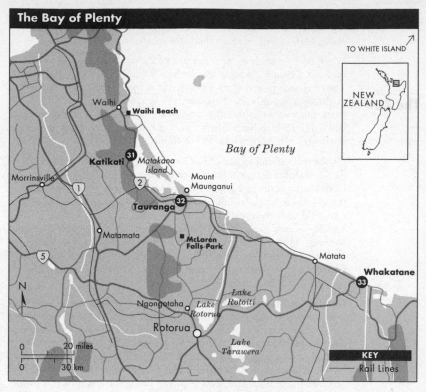

The Bay of Plenty

TO WHITE ISLAND

NEW ZEALAND

Waihi
Waihi Beach
Bay of Plenty
Katikati
Matakana Island
Morrinsville
Mount Maunganui
Tauranga
Matamata
McLaren Falls Park
Matata
Whakatane
N
Ngongotaha
Lake Rotoiti
Lake Rotorua
Rotorua
Lake Tarawera

0   20 miles
0   30 km

KEY
Rail Lines

for its plentiful supply of beaches. Places like Mt. Maunganui and Whakatane overflow with sunseekers during peak summer vacation periods (especially over Christmas and New Year's), but even at the busiest times you only need to travel a few miles to find a secluded stretch of beach.

The gateway to the region is the small country town of Katikati, but the central base for the area is Tauranga, which has managed to retain its relaxed vacation-town atmosphere despite its recent spurts of development. From Tauranga you can take day trips to beaches, the nearby bush, and offshore attractions such as Mayor Island marine reserve and the volcanic White Island.

Katikati

③ *62 km (39 mi) southeast of Thames, 35 km (22 mi) northwest of Tauranga.*

In its early days, the Katikati area was heavily populated by Maori, and many pa (fortified village) sites have been found—an indication of frequent tribal warfare. These days, fruit growing keeps the economy afloat. Katikati's most noticeable features are the 26 murals that locals have painted on buildings around town. Look for the Returned Servicemen's Association's *Those Who Served* murals, and those that depict the arrival of the Maori by *waka* (canoe).

Waihi Beach, 19 km (12 mi) north of Katikati, is ideal for swimming and surfing and has access to numerous walkways. At low tide, people bent over digging in the sand are looking for tuatua and pipi—delicious shellfish that you boil until they open. Don't miss the drive to the top of the Bowentown heads at the southern end of Waihi Beach.

This is an old Maori pa (fortified village) with stunning views. A short but steep walk from here leads to Cave Bay directly below the view point. Don't swim here, as there are dangerous currents.

You'll find great views over the Bay of Plenty at the **Lindemann Road Lookout** a couple of minutes north of Katikati on State Highway 2. The only sign pointing to the lookout is right at the turnoff, so you might come upon it fairly suddenly. The road is good but narrow in parts. Once at the lookout (where the road ends) you'll find a map embedded in rock to help orient you. Look for Mayor Island just to the north and Mt. Maunganui to the south.

On the main road just out of Katikati township to the south you'll spot the Cape Dutch design of the **Morton Estate** winery building. Wine maker Evan Ward produces a large range and has won a stack of awards over the years. He has also talked the company's accountants into letting him hold some bottles back until he thinks they're drinking at their best, so you are likely to find earlier vintages here than you will in most wineries. Most of the grapes come from Hawke's Bay, but Evan also occasionally uses Marlborough fruit. The top-of-the-line Black Label Chardonnay is particularly recommended. ⊠ *Main Rd. Katikati,* ☎ *09/300–5053.* ⊘ *Daily 10:30–5.*

Dominating Moffat Road in the town of Bethlehem, the impressive **Mills Reef Winery** stands out from the local farmland. Owner–wine maker Paddy Preston used to make kiwi-fruit wine, but he hasn't looked back since he turned to the real thing. Paddy seems particularly good with riesling and sauvignon blanc varieties, but his whole range is worth trying. The complex includes a classy tasting room and a reliable restaurant, open for lunch all year, and dinner for most of it. ⊠ *Moffat Rd., Bethlehem,* ☎ *09/576–8800.* ⊘ *Tastings daily 10–5.*

Dining and Lodging

$$$ ✕ **Somerset Cottage.** This is regarded by many locals as the best in the whole region, including Tauranga. The name says it all—Somerset is a genuine country cottage with indoor-outdoor dining. The menu is modern and eclectic, featuring dishes like panfried squid with lemon zest, chilli, and roasted peanuts, or lamb short loin on roasted eggplant with a feta anchovy and bread-crumb crust. The wine list is moderately comprehensive, but you're welcome to take your own bottle— perhaps one you've just purchased at nearby Mills Reef Winery or Morton Estate. ⊠ *30 Bethlehem Rd.,* ☎ *07/576–6889. AE, DC, MC, V. Licensed and BYOB. No lunch Sat.–Tues.*

$$$$ 🏨 **Fantail Lodge.** Expat Harrie Geraerts has brought some European charm to the region with his lodge's Bavarian-style exterior. His enthusiasm for his new country is infectious, though, and even locals are likely to advise you to "ask Harrie" if you have questions about the Katikati area. His friendships and alliances with local landowners mean he can get you places (like a nearby glowworm grotto) that you wouldn't find alone, and your adventures will likely cost you no more than a bottle of wine for the farmer who owns the property. If you're planning a few days' stay, consider one of the two-bedroom villas. Each has two bathrooms, a kitchenette, and a private terrace. Rooms in the main lodge are all done in natural colors with timber ceilings. The plantings around the grounds have been especially selected to attract birds, and the fresh flowers in your room on arrival usually come from the lodge's garden. ⊠ *117 Rea Rd.,* ☎ *07/549–1581,* 𝖥𝖠𝖷 *07/ 549–1417. 11 rooms, 2 two-bedroom villas. Restaurant, bar, kitchenettes (some), pool, tennis court. AE, DC, MC, V.* ❧

Tauranga

32 *216 km (134 mi) southeast of Auckland, 88 km (55 mi) north of Rotorua.*

The population center of the Bay of Plenty, **Tauranga** is a pleasant town—one of New Zealand's fastest growing, thanks to retirees and young families escaping the bustle (and housing prices) of Auckland. To explore the town center, start at the **Strand**, an attractive tree-lined street that separates the shops from the sea. You'll find bars, restaurants, and cafés along this road and its side streets.

The **Tauranga Community Village** is a watered-down version of what was once a more impressive historic museum. It's worth a visit though, if just to check out the **House of Bottles Wood Museum** where Keith Godwin takes old fence posts originally used in New Zealand's pioneering farms, and turns them into handcrafted bottles. They make unusual and attractive souvenirs. ⊠ *17th Ave. W,* ☎ *07/571–3700,* 🕿 *07/571–3701.* 🖅 *Free.* ⊙ *Daily 9–5.*

Tauranga is also one of the places in New Zealand to swim with dolphins. **Dolphin Seafaris** (⊠ Coronation Pier, Tauranga, ☎ 🕿 07/577–1061 or 0800/326–8747) will take you out to frolic with these delightful creatures. Wet suits, dive gear, and towels are included in the $80 price tag. Trips depart daily at 8; check-in is at 7:30.

The formerly volcanic **Mt. Maunganui** is the geological icon of the region, with its conical, rocky outline rising 761 ft above sea level. Regarded as one of the best beach and surfing areas in New Zealand, "the Mount" gets quite crowded around Christmas and New Year's Eve. To see it at its best, come in November, early December, or between mid-January and late March. A system of trails around Mauao—Maunganui's local Maori name—includes an easy walk around its base and the more strenuous Summit Road from the campground by the Pilot Bay boat ramp.

The **Mt. Manganui Hot Pools** include a cool pool with marked lanes for anyone who wants some serious exercise, but most visitors prefer to soak in the hotter saltwater pools. It's a relaxing way to spend a few hours if the weather turns cold and wet. ⊠ *Adams Way,* ☎ *07/575–0868.* 🖅 *$3.* ⊙ *Mon.–Sat. 6 AM–10 PM, Sun. 8 AM–10 PM.*

McLaren Falls Park is just a 15-minute drive south of Tauranga off State Highway 29. You can take the 10-minute easy bushwalk to the falls, or tackle the more strenuous walks to Pine Tree Knoll or the Ridge where your efforts will be rewarded with great vistas across the park. ⊠ *State Hwy. 29,* ☎ *07/578–8103.*

Dining and Lodging

$$$ ✕ **Harbourside Brasserie and Bar.** The Oregon timber floor of this rustic Tauranga institution is supported by piles sunk into the seabed, giving it the most nautical atmosphere in town. The building began as a yacht club back in the 1930s, but it's been better known as a restaurant for much of its life. In the past, the food was hearty but dated, but since chef Stephen Barry took over the stoves the standard has lifted considerably. If the seafood chowder is on, order it—it's his signature dish. ⊠ *Strand Extension, Tauranga,* ☎ *07/571–0520. AE, DC, MC, V.*

$$$ ✕ **Spinnaker's.** This pleasant indoor-outdoor restaurant has great views of Mt. Maunganui across a sea of pleasure craft in one direction, and Tauranga township in the other. There's a big emphasis on seafood, with at least three fish-of-the-day options. Seared yellowfin tuna is one popular choice, but despite the nautical leaning, roast lamb

loin with sweetbreads often outsells it. ⊠ *Tauranga Bridge Marina,* ☎ *07/574–4147. AE, DC, MC, V.*

$$ ✕ **Bella Mia.** The owner comes from Rome, and he has succeeded in re-creating a little piece of home in this cozy suburban eatery. The table-cloths are red-and-white checked, the floor is tiled with terra-cotta, and grapes hang from the ceiling. The food is as authentic as the decor. Much of the pasta is made in the kitchen, and turned into cannelloni, tortellini, or lasagna. Pizzas are thin-crusted and flavorsome, and main dishes cover the field. Be sure to leave room for dessert—Bella Mia makes its own gelato, sorbets, and tiramisu. ⊠ *73A Devonport Rd., Tauranga,* ☎ *07/578–4996. MC, V. BYOB. No lunch Sun.*

$$ ✕ **Sandrock Café.** Floors of native rimu and comfortable chairs crafted from timber and chrome give this place a light, contemporary feel. Dine indoors or out—the deck is elevated so that parked cars don't inter-fere with the panoramic ocean view. The food is well priced, and cov-ers the gamut of seafood and meat options. The most popular item is an unlikely combination of steak with scallops and oysters, but less-confused choices include strips of venison stir-fried with sliced red onions and served with a sauce based on reduced port, pink-cooked rack of lamb with kumara mash, and scallops in an old-fashioned but well-executed cream sauce. ⊠ *4 Marine Parade, Mt. Maunganui,* ☎ *07/574–7554. AE, MC, V. Licensed and BYOB.*

$ ✕ **Sirens.** This 90-seat café has been in business less than two years, but it has already gained a great reputation. Take a seat in the quiet back section, or choose a table up front or outside where it's bright and bustling. Food is served from the counter, and includes a big range of bagels, croissants, and lengths of French bread, all with tasty and imaginative fillings such as shredded chicken with Camembert, smoked salmon with avocado, and sweet Thai-flavored chilli. ⊠ *801 Cameron Rd., Tauranga,* ☎ *07/578–5857. AE, DC, MC, V. No dinner.*

$$$–$$$$ 🏠 **Taiparoro House.** This restored Victorian villa has the best views in town, overlooking Tauranga harbor, and it's also close to the shop-ping and dining district. It was built by a well-known local family in 1882, and was the home of the town's mayor during World War I. Cur-rent owners Kevin and Lois Kelly immediately saw the house's potential as a B&B and went about collecting "pre-loved" furniture to match the colonial atmosphere they were after. All the bedrooms are furnished differently and are on the top floor, with atticlike slanting ceilings. A favorite for honeymooners is the pricier Harbourview Suite, which has the best views, a superb clawfoot bath, a (decorative) mosquito net over the bed, and an old kauri dresser. Be sure to relax by the open fire in the conservatory lounge. The house can be hard to find if you're coming from the harbor, so call for directions. ⊠ *11 5th Ave.,* ☎ *07/577–9607,* 𝖥𝖠𝖷 *07/577–9264. 4 rooms. Lounge. MC, V. BP.* ❧

$$$ 🏠 **Copthorne Suites Puriri Park Tauranga.** If you're seeking modern accommodations close to town this is easily the best of Tauranga's mass of lodging choices. This all-suites establishment is priced just above mo-tels in the vicinity, but is still less expensive than its location and fa-cilities would suggest. The rooms are spacious, with kitchen facilities, private balconies, and furniture imported from the United States—in-cluding solid oak work tables. For lunch and dinner, guests can walk to a selection of nearby restaurants that have a "charge back" ar-rangement with the hotel. ⊠ *32 Cameron Rd.,* ☎ *07/577–1480,* 𝖥𝖠𝖷 *07/577–1490. 21 suites. Bar, pool. AE, DC, MC, V.* ❧

Whakatane

㉝   *100 km (62 mi) southeast of Tauranga.*

For yet another chance to laze on the beach, **Whakatane** (fah-kah-*tah*-nee) claims to be North Island's sunniest town. This was landfall on New Zealand for the first migratory Maori canoes, and the fertile hinterland was the first part of the country to be farmed. The most popular and safest swimming beach in the area is Ohope beach, east of Whakatane.

Whakatane is also a base from which to explore **White Island,** where you can deep-sea fish or swim with dolphins. The island is an active volcano, and whether you see it by plane, boat, or on foot, its billowing steam makes for a typically awesome Pacific Rim geothermal experience.

The least expensive way to get to White Island is by boat. Options include tours on the *Te Kahurangi* (☎ 07/323–7829), a 37-ft SuperCat vessel that only carries small groups. The cost is $85 and includes lunch and a two-hour tour of White Island. **Vulcan Helicopters** (☎ 0800/804–354) has a nine-seat helicopter; pilot-owner Robert Fleming is an authority on the island. Two-hour flights cost $315 and include a landing. **East Bay Flight Centre** (☎ 07/308–8446) has aircraft that fly over the island's crater; 50-minute trips cost $150.

For closer aqueous encounters of the mammalian kind, **Dolphins Down Under** (✉ 19 Quay St., Whakatane, ☎ 07/308–4636 or 0800/354–7737) has four-hour cruises during which you can swim with or simply view dolphins. Wet suits and snorkels are provided. Cruises leave at 7:30 AM and cost $85 per person.

The Bay of Plenty A to Z

Arriving and Departing

BY BUS

Intercity links Auckland, Thames, Waihi, Katikati, Mt. Maunganui, and Tauranga daily. The Tauranga depot is on 97 Willow Street (☎ 07/571–3211). Intercity links Auckland to Whakatane through Rotorua. The Whakatane depot is on Pyne Street (☎ 07/308–6169).

The **Pacific Coast Highway Traveller** (☎ 09/913–6100, ✉ $149) is a pass for a bus that follows the Pacific Coast Highway tourist route from Auckland through to Napier in Hawke's Bay. The pass allows for stops in Tauranga and Whakatane and nicely links these towns to the Coromandel Peninsula, Rotorua, and Gisborne.

BY CAR

From Auckland take the Southern Motorway, following signs to Hamilton. Just past the narrowing of the motorway, turn left onto Highway 2, and travel through Paeroa. Stay on Highway 2 all the way to Tauranga, driving through Waihi and Katikati on the way. The driving time between Auckland and Katikati is around 2 hours and 40 minutes. Between Auckland and Tauranga, it is 3 hours and 15 minutes.

BY TRAIN

Tranz Scenic operates the 3½-hour *Kamai Express* between Auckland and Tauranga daily. The train departs Auckland at 6:05 PM and departs Tauranga at 8:05 PM. ✉ *Tauranga Railway Station, the Strand,* ☎ *0800/802–802.* ✉ *$30.*

Contacts and Resources

EMERGENCIES

Dial 111 for **fire, police, and ambulance** services.

GUIDED TOURS

Sea Spray Charters (☎ 07/572–4241) combines knowledge of the region with Kiwi-style hospitality. The company offers customized tours that can include fishing, spearfishing, and scuba diving, or simply cruising around and enjoying the coastal sights.

VISITOR INFORMATION

Katikati Visitor Information ⊠ *Centre Main Rd.,* ☎ *07/549–1658.* ☉ *Daily 9–4:30.*

Mt. Maunganui Visitor Information Centre ⊠ Salisbury Ave., ☎ 07/575–5099. ☉ Weekdays 9–5.

Tauranga Visitor Information Centre ⊠ *97 Willow St.,* ☎ *07/571–3211.* ☉ *Weekdays 7–5:30, weekends 8–4.*

Whakatane Visitor Information Centre ⊠ *Boon St.,* ☎ *07/308–6058.* ☉ *Weekdays 9–5, Sat. 9–1, Sun. 10–2.*

2 ROTORUA TO WELLINGTON

Sulfuric Rotorua bubbles and oozes with surreal volcanic activity. It's one of the population centers of New Zealand's pre-European inhabitants, the Maori—try dining at a traditional *hangi* feast. Great hiking abounds in a variety of national parks, glorious gardens grow in the rich soil of the Taranaki Province, and the nation's capital in Wellington and charming, art deco Napier are friendly urban counterpoints to the countryside.

N ORTH AND SOUTH ISLANDS have different sorts of natural beauty. South Island's better-known heroic landscapes are generally flat or precipitous. North Island's rolling pasturelands have a more human scale—some think of Scotland. Parts of North Island do break the rhythm of these verdant contours: the majestic, Fuji-like Mt. Taranaki, the rugged wilderness areas of Te Urewera and Tongariro national parks, the gorges and valleys of the Wanganui river region, the rocky forms in the Wairarapa district northeast of Wellington, and the bizarre geological plumbing around Rotorua.

Rotorua is the mid-island's population center, and it has been a tourist center since Europeans first heard of the healing qualities of local hot springs. All around, nature has crafted a gallery of surreal wonders that include limestone caverns, volcanic wastelands, steaming geysers, and hissing ponds. From the shores of Lake Taupo—the country's largest lake and the geographic bull's-eye of North Island—Mt. Ruapehu, the island's tallest peak, is plainly visible. Site of New Zealand's largest ski area, the mountain is the dominant feature of Tongariro National Park, a haunting landscape of craters, volcanoes, and lava flows that ran with molten rock as recently as 1988 and were throwing up some threatening clouds in 1996.

Southeast of Lake Taupo, on the shores of Hawke Bay, the town of Napier has an interesting aggregation of art deco architecture. Around Napier, the Hawke's Bay region is one of the country's major wine routes. A diversion to the north will take you to relatively isolated Gisborne and Eastland, which are often overlooked but extremely rewarding: the largely agricultural East Cape juts out above Gisborne, coursing with trout-rich streams and ringed with stunning beaches and coves.

The lush Taranaki region literally sprang from the ocean floor in a series of volcanic blasts, forming that odd hump down the west coast of North Island. The now-dormant cone of Mt. Taranaki is the breathtaking symbol of the province and the site of great hiking tracks (trails). Agriculture thrives in the area's volcanic soil, and Taranaki's gardens are some of the country's most spectacular, from a massive rhododendron trust to smaller private gardens. It almost goes without saying that the Maori were the province's first settlers, and their local mythology and historical sites deepen any experience of the area.

More and more people are finding their way to Wellington—New Zealand's capital—by choice rather than necessity. Arguably the country's most cosmopolitan city, it is gaining a reputation for fostering the arts and preserving its culture in a way that the more brash Auckland to the north does not. Charming and small enough to explore easily on foot, Wellington has an excellent arts complex, the popular Te Papa–Museum of New Zealand, scores of fashionable cafés, contemporary clothing designers, and music of all kinds. Because it is perched at the southern tip of North Island, Wellington is the jumping-off point for the ferry south—but don't jump south too quickly. It's worth considering taking a side trip east to the Wairarapa, a rugged coastal area with some of the country's finest wineries, or north to the isolated settlements of the Wanganui river region.

Note: For more information on bicycling, fishing, hiking, kayaking, rafting, rock climbing, and skiing in central North Island, *see* Chapter 5.

Pleasures and Pastimes

Dining

Between Rotorua and Wellington, you'll come across a number of small towns with little more than a country-style pub or a dairy (convenience store) to satisfy the appetite. They may lack big-city sophistication, but they're certain to be friendly. If you're lucky, the pub might have an attached restaurant offering honest home cooking, but mostly you'll have to settle for a sandwich and a sweet bun from the dairy. Two sandwich fillings that never fail to fascinate visitors are spaghetti and baked beans, both from a can. You'll find this weird combination only in New Zealand and Australia.

Rotorua is the best place to try the Maori feast known as a hangi. Traditionally, meat and vegetables placed in flax baskets were gently steamed in an earth oven lined with heated stones and wet leaves—lamb, pork, chicken and seafood along with potatoes, pumpkin, and *kumara* (sweet potato), a staple of the Maori diet that holds spiritual significance to some tribes. Nowadays, the food may well be prepared above ground, but when it's done well, it doesn't lose much in the translation. Almost without exception, a Rotorua hangi will be followed by a Maori concert, usually a commercialized but entertaining performance of traditional songs and dances, with often hilarious audience participation.

In the central North Island, particularly around Taupo, you might be lucky enough to taste freshly caught trout. Laws prohibit trout from being sold commercially, so you'll probably have to hook one for yourself, or get to know someone who has, then ask your host or a local chef to cook it. (Not long ago, an enterprising restaurateur tried to bypass the law by offering the trout free and charging $28 for the sauce. Nice try, but he didn't get away with it.) Also look for game food such as wild boar, venison (the farmed version is usually called *cervena*), and hare—with a Hawke's Bay merlot or a Martinborough or Central Otago pinot noir. On the Whanganui River, the local catch is eel—try it smoked at the Flying Fox.

For price category information, *see* the chart *under* Dining *in* Smart Travel Tips A to Z.

Fishing

Central North Island is trout country. You can get out on any of the designated lakes and waterways if you have your own gear and a fishing license. It is worthwhile, however, to engage a local guide to take you to the right spots. On the lakes around Rotorua, and perhaps even more on Lake Taupo, few people leave disappointed. For extensive information on central North Island fishing, *see* Chapter 5.

Lodging

New Zealand's lodges are often small and exclusive, set in places of great beauty. Some of the best are in central North Island, the most famous being Huka Lodge, just outside Taupo and Solitaire, near Rotorua. They tend to attract people keen on fishing, hunting, or other outdoor activities, and the area's best guides are always nearby. Decor and ambience vary greatly from lodge to lodge, but the best places combine a relaxed country-house atmosphere—perhaps mixing antique furniture and contemporary design—with high-quality, unobtrusive service and exhaustive facilities. The wine and food available at lodges is another point of appeal. If your budget allows, even one night at one of these lodges will be an experience you won't soon forget.

The up and down fortunes of New Zealand's rural communities over the last decade or so have persuaded farming families to supplement their incomes by offering farm-stay accommodations. Farm stays usually aren't luxurious, but the best provide hands-on involvement with the working life of the farm. And the New Zealanders whom you meet often have the pioneering spirit of those who work the land for a living. Standards can vary, as the hosts have often not had extensive hospitality training, but you will be safe sticking to farm stays recommended in this book. Or ask for guidance at the nearest information center.

In Rotorua and Taupo there are many more hotel beds than visitors for much of the year, and a number of hotels and motels offer significant discounts on their standard rates. The exception is school holidays, for which you should book well in advance. Also note that peak season in Tongariro National Park and other ski areas is winter (June–September), which means summer visitors can always find empty beds and good deals.

For price category information, *see* the chart *under* Lodging *in* Smart Travel Tips A to Z.

Soaking

In Rotorua and Taupo, thermal springs are literally on tap. You can soak in your own thermal bath in even the cheapest hotels in Rotorua, or take advantage of public facilities such as Polynesian Spa. Many Taupo motels and hotels also have their own thermal baths or pools. Lie on your back and close your eyes. You'll be amazed how relaxed you feel afterward.

Tramping and Walking

Central North Island doesn't have the world-famous walking tracks of South Island, but it does have equally serious bushwalking and plenty of pleasant trails. Excellent longer trails circle Mt. Taranaki or climb through the alpine areas in Tongariro National Park. Some of the most rugged bush in the country is in Te Urewera National Park southeast of Rotorua, and hiking opportunities abound around Rotorua, Taupo, and the Wairarapa.

Exploring Central North Island and Wellington

You could easily spend a month traveling between Auckland and Wellington and still touch on only the major sights. Realistically, you're most likely to travel either straight through the middle or down the east or west coasts. The difficulty comes in deciding which coast and which smaller areas to explore. If you're interested in the bizarre thermal activity of Rotorua, start there. If you're a garden lover, starting in Taranaki to the west and stopping at other spots on the way to Wellington is the way to go. If wine routes are more appealing, you can take in three on the east coast: Gisborne, Hawke's Bay, and Wairarapa. If you want to get into some astonishing backcountry, Tongariro and Te Urewera national parks are unbeatable, as are parts of the Wairarapa. And Wellington is a charming city for refreshing yourself for a couple of days before hopping over to South Island.

Great Itineraries

Numbers in the text correspond to numbers in the margin and on the Central North Island, Napier, Wellington, and Greater Wellington and Wairarapa maps.

IF YOU HAVE 3 DAYS

Three days will only allow you to see one of the major areas covered in the chapter or to scratch the surface of two—especially taking travel

Central North Island

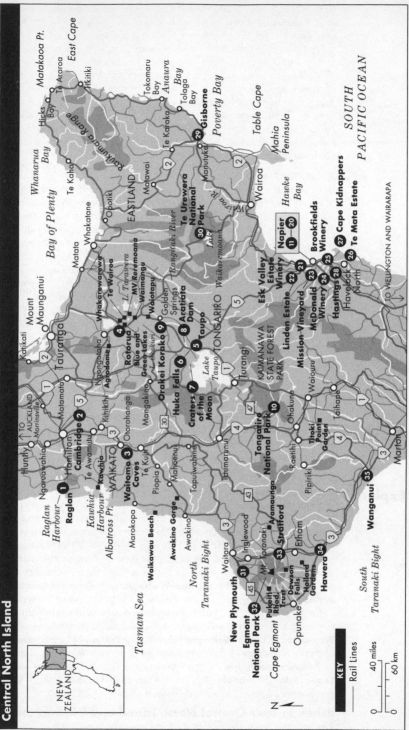

NEW ZEALAND

SOUTH PACIFIC OCEAN

Tasman Sea

Bay of Plenty

EASTLAND

Poverty Bay

Hawke Bay

KEY
— Rail Lines

0   40 miles
0   60 km

N

time into account. If you do have only three days, spend all of them in ⊡ **Rotorua** ④ taking in its sights and smells, popping over to **Waitomo Caves** ③ for the glowworm spectacle and spending all or part of a day fishing; or take three in ⊡ **Napier** ⑪–⑳, with a day in the city and two days in the surrounding wine country and natural beauty; or ⊡ **Wellington** ㊱–㊿, taking a day or two in the city and the rest in the ⊡ **Wairarapa,** visiting wineries, hiking, or seeing rare native animals. You would have to fly in and out of New Plymouth for spending three days in ⊡ **Mt. Taranaki**'s gardens and hiking in Egmont National Park. If surface treatment will do, you could take a day in Rotorua before dropping down the next morning to Napier for the rest of the time. Fly from there to your next stop.

IF YOU HAVE 6 DAYS

With almost a week, you can put together a more diverse experience of a couple of regions. Pick a path for moving from north to south and leave a half day or more for travel between Rotorua and Napier or Taranaki, then another half day plus for the trip down to Wellington if you have a car. Start in ⊡ **Rotorua** ④, spending two to three days around the bubble and ooze, fishing, and going to a hangi at night; then continue either east to the art deco city of ⊡ **Napier** ⑪–⑳ and ⊡ **Hawke's Bay** ㉑–㉘ and the surrounding wine country, or west to ⊡ **Taranaki** for gardens, mountain walks, and beaches for the rest of the time. Or from Rotorua you could head south to ⊡ **Taupo** ⑤ and **Tongariro National Park** ⑩ for serious outdoor activities: fishing, canoeing, rafting, and hiking. The ⊡ **Wanganui River region** is another outdoors option, though you'll need to set aside at least two full days to see its remote river settlements. Going to Napier or Taupo would set you up for a stop in the ⊡ **Wairarapa** for more spectacular countryside, including rugged coastal scenery, one of the country's finest wildlife parks, and a wine tour in ⊡ **Martinborough** ㊿. In six days you could also combine Taranaki, the Wairarapa, and Wellington, with one day each in the last two. Or chuck it all and head straight for ⊡ **Gisborne** ㉙ and Eastland for six days of some of New Zealand's finest off-the-beaten-path travel.

IF YOU HAVE 9 DAYS

You might think that you can see it all in nine days, but try not to get too ambitious—always allow more time in each place to absorb the local atmosphere. In this case, the more you take on, the more travel time you'll have between places. One more word of caution: the small mountain roads on a Napier to Taranaki crossing will run you ragged, so don't try them. Allow one day of the nine for time on the road. So then, the two-day-in-each surface treatment options for nine-day stays are **Rotorua–Napier–Wairarapa–Wellington,** or **Rotorua–Taranaki–Wairarapa–Wellington.** To give yourself a better sense of place, each of the six following combinations will provide in-depth experiences of the delights of central and southern North Island: **Taranaki** (4 days)–**Wairarapa** (2 days)–**Wellington** (2 days); *or* **Eastland** (5 days)–**Napier** (3 days); *or* **Napier** (3 days)–**Wairarapa** (3 days)–**Wellington** (2 days); *or* **Rotorua and Taupo** (5 days)–**Wairarapa** (3 days); *or* **Rotorua and Taupo** (4 days)–**Taranaki** (4 days); *or* **Rotorua and Taupo** (4 days)–**Wanganui river region** (2 days)–**Wellington** (2 days). Pick one!

When to Tour Central North Island and Wellington

The months from December through mid-April are the best for central and southern North Island. Everything is open (though not in the few days between Christmas and New Year and over Easter) and the weather can be glorious. That said, Wellington and the exposed coastal regions do get more than their fair share of rain and southerly winds, so even in summer expect the odd very chilly day and slightly more frequent overcast days. Some say that Taranaki's Rhododendron Festival nearly always gets rained on, the answer to which is to skip the festival and go in late November for more than just rhodo blossoms. Of course if you want to do some skiing, August is the month to hit the slopes of Tongariro National Park and Egmont National Park, though the first major snows fall as early as June.

THE WAIKATO AND WAITOMO

Many think of the Waikato region as the heartland of the North Island—a fertile, temperate, agricultural district south of Auckland that boasts New Zealand's largest inland city (Hamilton) and some of its most important pre-European sites.

Polynesian sailors first landed on the region's west coast as early as the mid-14th century; by way of contrast, Europeans didn't settle here until the 1830s. By the 1860s, the Waikato's different Maori tribes had overcome their differences and united to elect a king in an attempt to resist white encroachment upon their lands. This Maori "King Movement," as it is known, is still a significant cultural and political force, centered in the small Waikato town of Ngaruawahia.

History intrudes only briefly as you speed down Highway 1 from Auckland: Ngaruawahia is the official residence of the reigning Maori monarch, but the ceremonial buildings are not open to the public; and Hamilton—though pleasantly sited on the banks of the Waikato River—is a city you can afford to miss if time is tight. Instead, visitors are funneled through Hamilton to three nearby attractions: the surfing hot spot of Raglan on the West Coast; attractive Cambridge, an agricultural town renowned as a horse-breeding center; and the extraordinary cave formations at Waitomo.

Raglan

❶ *176 km (110 mi) south of Auckland, 44 km (27 mi) west of Hamilton.*

It's hard to think of a more laid-back town in the country than Raglan. Set on sheltered Raglan Harbour, and in the lee of Mt. Karioi, the tiny town owes its easygoing ways to the legions of young surfers drawn to the legendary breaks at nearby Manu Bay and Whale Bay, both 8 km (5 mi) southwest of town. When the surf's up, drive out to the parking areas above the sweeping bays to see scores of surfers tackling what's reputed to be world's longest left-hand break.

The surfers have made Raglan cool and along the tree-lined main street, Bow Street, barefoot dudes in designer shades pad in and out of the few hip café-bars or hang in the smattering of craft and surfwear shops. Families vacation here, too, splashing and kayaking in the picturesque estuary waters and frequenting the sandy beaches on either side of the harbor entrance.

On hot days, the spectacular **Bridal Veil Falls** make an appealing target. A 10-minute, shaded hike from the parking lot leads to a viewing platform above the 150-ft drop; from here, another 10-minute walk down a steep, stepped trail puts you on a wooden platform at the base of the falls. Bring your swimsuit and, if you dare, plunge into the very cold water. The falls are 20 km (12 mi) south of Raglan; take the Kawhia road from town.

OFF THE
BEATEN PATH

KAWHIA – With time on your hands, explore the minor road from Raglan to this isolated, coastal harbor settlement 55 km (34 mi) to the south. It's a fine route, skirting the eastern flank of Mt. Karioi and passing the turnoff for the Bridal Veil Falls (☞ Raglan, *above*), though take care since much of the road is gravel. Kawhia was landfall in AD 1350 for some of the Waikato's earliest Polynesian settlers, the Tainui people, and permission is sometimes granted (inquire at the harborside museum) to visit the local *marae* (meetinghouse). What most come for, however, are the Te Puia hot springs at Ocean Beach, east of town, which are far less crowded than the Hot Water Beach at Hahei on the Coromandel Peninsula. There's road access to the beach (or it's a two-hour walk from Kawhia). Since you can only find the springs by digging into the sand a couple of hours either side of low tide, you should check the tide tables in Raglan before you set off.

Lodging

$ 🏨 **Raglan Backpackers & Waterfront Lodge.** Many rate this supremely agreeable, budget-price, harborside lodge the best of its type in the country. Designed by genial hosts Jeremy and Lynda Walton, the modern lodge provides real New Zealand "outdoor living." The small, very simple rooms open on to a pretty, wood-decked interior courtyard (complete with hammock) and the comfortable lounge provides access to a grassy lawn and barbecue area. Basic but spotless bathroom facilities are shared with other guests. There's a well-equipped self-catering kitchen, or you are just a two-minute walk from Raglan's eateries. And if you're feeling adventurous take a surfing lesson with Jeremy, who knows the coast like the back of his hand. ⊠ *6 Nero St.,* ☎ *07/825–0515. 8 rooms, 1 8-bed backpackers' dorm. Coin laundry. No credit cards.*

Cambridge

❷ *150 km (94 mi) southeast of Auckland, 23 km (14 mi) southeast of Hamilton, 85 km (53 mi) northwest of Rotorua.*

Cambridge is a place most people drive through in a hurry—en route to Rotorua from Auckland—and then wish they hadn't. Even a quick glance reveals that this is a charming town, with its historic buildings and rural English atmosphere.

The best way to check out its lovely trees and its craft and antique stores is simply to leave your car and take a walk along Victoria, Empire, and Commerce streets. Cambridge is also regarded as New Zealand's Kentucky, and, in fact, the Thoroughbred industry has become the most prominent local feature.

☺ **New Zealand Horse Magic** at Cambridge Thoroughbred Lodge is a must for anyone interested in horse racing or the Thoroughbred industry. Experienced presenters tailor shows for each audience, easily moving from expert-level information to antics for any kids that might be in the group. A two-year-old Thoroughbred is shown off in full racing gear. If you do come with children, they can go for a short ride while you have a cup of coffee and muffins. Auctions, which are interesting to drop in on if you're in the area, are held in March, May, August, and November. ⊠ *State Hwy. 1, 6 km (4 mi) south of town,* ☎ *07/827–8118.* 🎫 *$12.* ☉ *Tues.–Sun. tour and show at 10:30.*

Dining

$$–$$$ ✕ **Souter House.** In summer sit on the covered veranda of this stately, restored Edwardian villa, listed by the New Zealand Historical Places Trust. The innovative entrées might include panfried scallops on a bed of spinach or a delicate mousseline of smoked salmon. Cervena (farmed

venison) is rolled in roasted cumin and served rare on a sauce based on beets and red onions. Or try the rack of lamb, coated with toasted coriander, alongside a parsnip mousse. The wine list is far-, and high-, reaching, and the service formal but friendly. ⊠ *19 Victoria St.,* ☎ *07/827–3610. AE, DC, MC, V.*

$ ✕ **Fran's Café and Continental Cake Kitchen.** Dine in the main room, or wander past the kitchen to the courtyard out back. Once you're settled, choose from a big selection of homemade goodies including imaginative sandwiches or pasta. The grilled vegetable salad is tossed in balsamic vinegar, and the flans and quiches are equally up-to-date. Vegetarians note: Fran makes her own hummus and falafel. Don't forget to order a cuppa (Kiwi coffee or tea—Fran's doesn't have a license to sell wine) and a piece of cake. The food is well flavored, the servings generous, and the staff friendly. What more could you want? ⊠ *62 Victoria St.,* ☎ *07/827–3946. AE.*

Waitomo Caves

❸ *80 km (50 mi) southwest of Hamilton, 65 km (41 mi) southwest of Cambridge, 150 km (95 mi) west of Rotorua.*

The **Waitomo Caves** are parts of an ancient seabed that was lifted and then spectacularly eroded into a surreal underground landscape of limestone formations, gushing rivers, and contorted caverns. Many of the caves are still unexplored, although an increasing number are accessible on adventurous underground activity trips involving rafting, caving, and rappeling. But you don't need to be Indiana Jones to appreciate the magnificent underground structures. Two of the caves are open to the public for guided tours: the Aranui and the Waitomo, or Glowworm, Cave. **Waitomo Cave** takes its name from the Maori words *wai* and *tomo,* water and cave, since the Waitomo River vanishes into the hillside here. You ride through in a boat. In the grotto the larvae of *Arachnocampa luminosa,* measuring between 1 and 2 inches, live on cave ceilings. They snare prey by dangling filaments of tiny, sticky beads, which trap insects attracted to the light the worm emits by a chemical oxidation process. A single glowworm produces far less light than any firefly, but when massed in great numbers in the dark, their effect is a bit like looking at the night sky in miniature.

Aranui Cave, 2 km (1 mi) beyond Waitomo Cave, is a very different experience. Eons of dripping water have sculpted a delicate garden in pink-and-white limestone. The cave is named after a local Maori, Te Rutuku Aranui, who discovered the cave in 1910 when his dog disappeared inside in pursuit of a wild pig. Each cave tour lasts 45 minutes. Glowworm Cave is high on the list of every bus tour, so try to avoid visiting between 11 and 2, when groups arrive from Auckland. ⊠ *Te Anga Rd.,* ☎ *07/878–8227.* 🎟 *Waitomo Cave $20, both caves $30.* ⊙ *Waitomo Cave tour Nov.–Easter, daily every ½ hr 9–5:30; Easter–Oct., daily every hr 9–5; Aranui Cave tour daily at 10, 11, 1, 2, and 3.*

At the visitor center of Waitomo Caves Village the **Museum of Caves** provides an entertaining and informative look at the formation of the caves and the life cycle of the glowworm, with a number of interactive displays designed especially for children. ⊠ *Waitomo Caves Village,* ☎ *07/878–7640.* 🎟 *$4, combined ticket for Waitomo Cave plus museum $22.* ⊙ *Daily 8:30–5.*

The **Waitomo Walkway** is a 5-km (3-mi), 2½-hour walk that begins across the road from the Museum of Caves and follows the Waitomo River. The track passes through forests and impressive limestone outcrops and, though it is relatively easy, you have to walk back to Waitomo Caves Village on the same path. For an alternative to the complete walk, take Te Anga Road from the village, turn left into Tumutumu Road, park at **Ruakuri Reserve**, and walk the short (30-minute) final section of the track. There's a natural rock tunnel on the way, and many people come out here after dusk for a free view of the local glowworms—bring a flashlight.

<table>
<tr><td>OFF THE
BEATEN PATH</td><td>**TE ANGA-MAROKOPA ROAD –** This classic backcountry road works its way west out of Waitomo toward the coast. It makes for a spectacular detour—or the scenic long way to Taranaki—winding past stunning vistas. Some 26 km (16 mi) out of Waitomo, stop at the Mangapohue (mang-ah-po-*hoo*-ay) Natural Bridge. From the parking area, there are two approaches to the bridge. One to the right climbs over a hill, dropping into a valley strewn with boulders embedded with oyster fossils—the remains of a seismic shift that thrust up the seabed millions of years ago. The natural bridge rises off to the left of the boulders. The other path follows a stream through a gorge it has carved out. The gorge walls climb ever higher until they meet and form the bridge that closes over the path. The circular walk—going out on one path, returning on the other—only takes 15 to 20 minutes to complete.</td></tr>
</table>

About 5 km (3 mi) farther along the road to Marokopa, **Piripiri Caves** beckon with their interesting fossil legacy—the marks of giant oysters that resided here during the area's onetime subaqueous existence. The approach and entrance to the caves are steep and slippery, so wear appropriate shoes or boots, and bring a jacket for the cool air and a powerful flashlight to cut through the gloom if you really want to see the extensive underground network.

A couple of miles farther still, you can view the 120-ft **Marokopa Falls** from a small roadside platform or walk down a trail (15 minutes round-trip) to get closer. And a few miles beyond the falls, the Maori-run pub at **Te Anga** is a good place to stop for refreshment.

The road splits at Te Anga, heading north to Kawhia (☞ Raglan, *above*) or southwest for 14 km (9 mi) to the small hamlet of **Marokopa**, where there's a stupendous lookout point over the coast's black-sand beaches. At Marokopa you are 50 km (31 mi) from Waitomo; time either to turn back or keep on south on a more difficult (mostly gravel) stretch for an incredibly scenic route to the Taranaki region. If you're in for the duration, fill up your gas tank before turning off State Highway 1 for Waitomo.

Outdoor Activities and Sports

Most of Waitomo's adventure tours contain some element of black-water rafting, that is, floating through the underground caverns on inflated inner tubes, dressed in wet suits and equipped with cavers' helmets. Be prepared for the pitch-black darkness and the freezing cold water: your reward is an exhilarating trip gliding through vast glow-worm-lit caverns, clambering across rocks, and jumping over underground waterfalls. Waitomo Caves Visitor Information Centre (☞ Visitor Information, *below*) can advise on which of the various tours is most suitable—some involve steep rappeling or tight underground squeezes. Adventurous types will be able to cope with the basic trip offered by one of the longest-standing companies, **Black Water Rafting** (⊠ Black Water Rafting, Waitomo Caves, ☎ 07/878–6219 or 0800/228–464). The three-hour trip allows around an hour and a half underground, finishing with welcome hot showers and a mug of soup back at base. The cost is $65 per person and includes free admission to the Museum of Caves. Departure times vary, depending on demand.

The Waikato and Waitomo A to Z

Arriving and Departing

BY BUS

Newmans and **InterCity** buses (☎ 09/913–6100) run several times daily between Auckland and Hamilton, with onward services to Raglan or Cambridge. For Waitomo, take the bus from Auckland to Otorohanga, 50 minutes south of Hamilton, where there is also a train station. From here, the **Waitomo Shuttle** (☎ 0800/808–279) makes the half-hour trip from Otorohanga to Waitomo six times daily, connecting with all major bus and train arrivals. Outside of these times, you must pay taxi rates (around $30) for the shuttle service. There are also circular bus services between Waitomo, Rotorua, and Taupo—contact local visitor information centers for details.

BY CAR

Access to the Waikato region is straight down Highway 1 from Auckland—count on 90 minutes to Hamilton. Cambridge is another 20 minutes southeast on Highway 1. For Raglan, take Highway 23 west, a 40-minute drive. For Waitomo (1 hr from Hamilton), take Highway 3 south and turn off on to Highway 37 past Otorohanga.

Contacts and Resources

EMERGENCIES

Dial 111 for **fire, police, and ambulance** services.

GUIDED TOURS

Newmans (☎ 09/913–6100) offers a one-way bus tour from Auckland to the Waitomo Caves and on to Rotorua, or from Rotorua to the Waitomo Caves, ending in Auckland, including a brief stop at an historic battle site, a barbecue lunch, and admission to the Waitomo Caves. You'll be picked up at your Auckland accommodation and dropped at your Rotorua accommodation, or vice versa. Cost is $136 per person.

Raglan Harbour Cruises (☎ 07/825–0300) has daily boat trips throughout summer around the inlets and bays of Raglan's lovely harbor. Tickets are $15 and reservations are advised.

VISITOR INFORMATION

Cambridge Visitor Information Centre. ⊠ *Corner of Queen and Victoria Sts.,* ☎ *07/823–3456.* ◷ *Weekdays 9–5, weekends 10–4.*
Raglan Visitor Information Centre. ⊠ *7 Bow St.,* ☎ *07/825–0556.* ◷ *Weekdays 10–5, weekends 10–4.*
Waitomo Caves Visitor Information Centre. ⊠ *Museum of Caves,* ☎ *07/878–7640.* ◷ *Daily 9–5:30.*

ROTORUA, LAKE TAUPO, AND TONGARIRO NATIONAL PARK

New Zealand's most famous tourist attraction, Rotorua (ro-to-*roo*-ah) sits smack on top of the most violent segment of the Taupo Volcanic Zone, which runs in a broad belt from White Island in the Bay of Plenty to Tongariro National Park, south of Lake Taupo. The region's spurting geysers, sulfur springs, and bubbling mud pools have spawned an unashamedly touristy town that is largely undistinguished save for its dramatic surroundings. True, Rotorua has tidied up its act considerably in the past few years, particularly by landscaping the streets and lakefront, but the air in "Sulfur City" doesn't always encourage lingering outdoors. Drive outside the city limits, however, and you'll find yourself in magnificent, untamed country, where spring-fed streams sprint through native forests into lakes that are an abundant source of some of the largest rainbow trout on earth.

Fishing is big business, both in Rotorua and at Lake Taupo to the south. The region's lakes are some of the few places where tales of the "big one" can actually be believed. Meanwhile, the town of Taupo on the northeastern shore of Lake Taupo has blossomed into one of the country's major outdoor activity centers—with everything from rafting to skydiving—and is worth a visit in its own right to see even more examples of the region's geothermal wonders. South of the lake rise the three volcanic peaks that make up Tongariro National Park. This is a year-round magnet for skiers and trampers. Even if you don't have much time, skirting the peaks provides a rewarding route on your way south to Wanganui or Wellington.

Rotorua

 85 km (53 mi) south of Cambridge, 200 km (125 mi) southeast of Auckland.

It's one of the most extraordinary areas in the country. Everywhere you turn, the earth bubbles, boils, spits, and oozes. Drainpipes steam, flower beds hiss, rings tarnish, and cars corrode. The rotten-egg smell of hydrogen sulfide hangs in the air, and even the local golf course has its own mud-pool hot spots, where a lost ball stays lost forever. There's no question that Rotorua and its environs are, well, different.

It's also an historic region. There is a well-established Maori community here tracing its ancestry back through the Te Arawa tribe to the great Polynesian migration of the 14th century. For hundreds of years, the local Maori settled by Lake Rotorua and harnessed the unique geological phenomena, cooking and bathing in the hot pools and erecting buildings on the warm ground. Maori culture is still stamped indelibly on the area and most visitors make the effort to attend a hangi (a traditional feast) followed by a Maori concert.

The town you see today at Rotorua is almost entirely a product of the late-19th-century fad for spa towns, from which era date the elaborate bathhouse and formal gardens. In fact, the "Great South Seas Spa," as Rotorua was known, was among the very earliest tourist ventures in the country, with tours of the geothermal oddities being offered as far back as the 1860s. In keeping with those times, the **Lakeland Queen** paddle steamer (☎ 07/348–6634) sets off daily from the lakefront piers for hour-long cruises of Lake Rotorua.

The **Government Gardens** occupy a small lakeside peninsula that fronts the modern street grid, and they are the most attractive part of Rotorua. The Maori call this area Whangapiro (fang-ah-*pee*-ro, evil-smelling place)—an appropriate name for these bizarre gardens, where sulfur pits bubble and fume behind manicured rose beds and bowling lawns. The focus of interest here is the extraordinary neo-Tudor **Bath House.** Built as a spa at the turn of the last century, it is now Rotorua's **Art and History Museum.** One room on the ground floor is devoted to the eruption of Mt. Tarawera. A number of artifacts that were unearthed from the debris and a remarkable collection of photographs show the terraces of Rotomahana before the eruption. ✉ *Arawa St.,* ☎ *07/349–4350.* 🖾 *$7.50.* ⏱ *Daily 9:30–5.*

A trip to Rotorua would hardly be complete without a dip in the soothing, naturally heated **Polynesian Spa.** A wide choice of mineral baths is available, from large communal pools to family pools to small, private baths for two. Massage and saunas are also offered, and the

Lake Spa has exclusive bathing in four shallow rock pools overlooking Lake Rotorua. The pools are close to the Government Gardens. ✉ *Hinemoa St.,* ☎ *07/348–1328.* ✉ *Family or adult pool $10, private pool $10 per ½ hr, lake spa $25.* ⊙ *Daily 6:30 AM–11 PM.*

At the northern end of town on the shores of the lake stands **St. Faith's,** the Anglican church for the Maori village of Ohinemutu (which was one of the area's original settlements). The interior of the church, which is richly decorated with carvings inset with mother-of-pearl, deserves attention at any time, but it's at its best during Sunday services, when the sonorous, melodic voices of the Maori choir rise in hymns. The service at 8 AM is in the Maori language; the 10 AM service is in both Maori and English. ✉ *Memorial Dr.*

Whakarewarewa (*fa*-ka-*ree*-wa-*ree*-wa) is one mouthful of a name—locals just call it Whaka. This is the most accessible and popular of the Rotorua region's thermal spots—partly because it's closest to town—but it is also the most varied, as it provides an insight into Maori culture. You'll get the most from the experience if you take a free one-hour guided tour (every hour, on the hour) from the Arts and Crafts Institute near the ticket office. The trails winding through the **thermal valley** pass steaming pools, spitting mud ponds (known, due to the plopping sounds, as the Leaping Frog Pools), and smooth silica terraces that appear to be coated in melted candle wax. At the Cooking Pool, eggs and corncobs are placed in flax baskets, lowered into the steaming waters, and then served alfresco. **Pohutu** (the big splash) is a rather erratic geyser that can shoot to a height of more than 80 ft. Near the main entrance, there's a reconstructed **Maori village** with fortified gates, sleeping houses, a *pataka* (food storehouse), war canoe, and a marae (meetinghouse). A 45-minute Maori cultural performance takes place daily at 12:15 in the meetinghouse, where you'll be shown a traditional welcome followed by examples of war and love songs and chants, stick throwing, and *poi* (ball) twirling. Don't leave Whaka without a peep in the nocturnal **Kiwi House,** for a glimpse of these shy birds. And don't miss the displays and gifts in the Maori Arts and Crafts Institute (☞ Shopping, *below*). Whakarewarewa is 3 km (2 mi) along Fenton Street from the Rotorua Visitor Centre, heading toward Taupo. ✉ *Hemo Rd.,* ☎ *07/348–9047.* ✉ *$18, includes 12:15 concert; evening concerts separate charge.* ⊙ *Oct.–Mar., daily 8–6; Apr.–Sept., daily 8–5.*

The **Blue and Green lakes** are on the road to ☞ Te Wairoa (the buried village) and Lake Tarawera. The Green Lake is off-limits except for its viewing area, but the Blue Lake is a popular picnic and swimming area. To get to them, take Highway 30 east (Te Ngae Road) and turn right into Tarawera Road at the signpost for the lakes and buried village. It's a scenic ride as the road loops through forests and skirts the edge of the lakes.

At the end of the 19th century, **Te Wairoa** (tay why-*ro*-ah, the buried village) was the starting point for expeditions to the pink-and-white terraces of Rotomahana, on the slopes of Mt. Tarawera. As mineral-rich geyser water cascaded down the mountainside, it formed a series of baths, which became progressively cooler as they neared the lake. In the latter half of the 19th century these fabulous terraces were the country's major attraction, but they were completely destroyed when Mt. Tarawera erupted in 1886. The explosion, heard as far away as Auckland, killed 153 people and buried the village of Te Wairoa under a sea of mud and hot ash. The village has been excavated, and of special interest is the *whare* (*fah*-ray, hut) of the *tohunga* (priest) Tuhoto Ariki, who predicted the destruction of the village. Eleven days before the eruption, two separate tourist parties saw a Maori war canoe emerge from the mists of Lake Tarawera and disappear again—a vision the tohunga interpreted as a sign of impending disaster. Four days after the eruption, the 100-year-old tohunga was dug out of his buried whare still alive, only to die in the hospital a few days later. A path circles the excavated village, then continues on as a delightful trail, the lower section of which is steep and can be slippery in places. Te Wairoa is 14 km (9 mi) southeast of Rotorua, a 20-minute drive. ⊠ *Tarawera Rd.,* ☎ *07/362–8287.* 🖭 *$10.50.* ☉ *Daily 9–5:30.*

From the shores of Lake Tarawera, the **MV Reremoana,** a restored lake cruiser, makes regular scenic runs. The two-hour cruise is especially recommended; it departs daily at 11 and stops for 30 minutes at the foot of Mt. Tarawera, where you can picnic, swim, or walk across the isthmus to Lake Rotomahana. Forty-five–minute cruises depart from the landing at one-hour intervals from 1:30 to 4:30. Four kilometers (2½ mi) beyond the Buried Village, on Spencer Road, a sign points to LAUNCH CRUISES and the *Reremoana*'s parking lot. ⊠ *Tarawera Launch Cruises,* ☎ *07/362–8595.* 🖭 *2-hr cruise $27, 45-min cruise $15.*

When Mt. Tarawera erupted in 1886, destroying Rotomahana's terraces, not all was lost. A volcanic valley emerged from the ashes—**Waimangu**—extending southwest from Lake Rotomahana. It's consequently one of the world's newest thermal-activity areas, encompassing the boiling water of the massive Inferno Crater, plus steaming cliffs, bubbling springs, and bush-fringed terraces. A path (one–two hours) runs through the valley down to the lake, where a shuttle bus takes you back to the entrance. Or plan to spend around three hours at Waimangu, which allows time to take a scenic cruise on the lake as well. Waimangu is 26 km (16 mi) southeast of Rotorua; take Highway 5 south (Taupo direction) and look for the turn after 19 km (12 mi). ⊠ *Waimangu Rd.,* ☎ *07/366–6137.* 🖭 *$16, including cruise $36.* ☉ *Daily 8:30–5.*

★ If you've only got time for one visit to a thermal area around Rotorua, make it to **Waiotapu** (why-oh-*ta*-pu)—a freakish, fantastic landscape of deep, sulfur-crusted pits, jade-color ponds, silica terraces, and a steaming lake edged with red algae and bubbling with tiny beads of carbon dioxide. Be smart and get here early: the **Lady Knox Geyser** erupts precisely at 10:15 daily—but not through some miracle of Mother Nature. Soap powder is poured into the vent of the geyser, which reduces the surface tension, so that the boiling water below erupts, on schedule, to gasps of delight. Having seen the geyser, which is set apart from the main thermal area, you then drive back to the main entrance for the spectacular one- to two-hour circular walk. Waiotapu is 30 km (19 mi) southeast of Rotorua—follow Highway 5 south (Taupo direction) and look for the signs. ⊠ *State Hwy. 5,* ☎ *07/366–6333.* 🖭 *$12.* ☉ *Daily 8:30–5.* 🐾

☝ The **Agrodome** is a sprawling complex, part of a 320-acre farm, 10 minutes northwest of Rotorua off State Highway 5. Most of it is dedicated to the four-footed woolly New Zealander. Shows daily at 9:30, 11, and 2:30 demonstrate the different breeds of sheep, shearing techniques, and sheepdogs at work. There are farm buggy tours after the shows, and children can participate by feeding lambs and milking a cow. ⊠ *Riverdale Park, Western Rd., Ngongotaha,* ☎ *07/357–4350.* 🖭 *$13, farm tour $13, combined ticket $20.* ☉ *Daily 9–4:30.*

Dining and Lodging

In addition to some solid restaurants, Rotorua provides the best opportunities to experience a Maori hangi (feast). The **Tamaki Tours** (☎ 07/346–2823) hangi takes place at a Maori village, **Te Tawa Ngahere**

Pa. A coach picks you up at your hotel, and on the way to the village you get briefed on Maori protocol. Once there, you are formally welcomed before the important part—eating the food. The cost, including pickup, is $58. Hangis at the **Sheraton** (☎ 07/349 5200, $49) have a long-standing reputation for serving authentic-tasting food and having good concerts. The **Lake Plaza** hangi (☎ 07/348–1174, $47) has an equally strong reputation. Here you can watch the food being lifted out of the hangi—usually an hour before the food is served, but call ahead to confirm.

Most of Rotorua's budget backpacker lodges are pretty similar, but a few have distinctive characteristics and can be counted on for clean—if sometimes threadbare—rooms, self-catering kitchens, laundry facilities, and helpful staff. **Hot Rock Backpackers** (✉ 1286 Arawa St., ☎ 07/347–9469) has the highest profile in town, plus three hot pools, the popular Lava Bar, and a youthful buzz. **Central Backpackers** (✉ 1076 Pukuatua St., ☎ 07/349–3285) is quieter, with the largest rooms and best-equipped kitchen. **Kiwi Paka YHA** (✉ 60 Tarewa Rd., ☎ 07/347–0931) is a little way out of town, overlooking Kuirau Park, but has lodge rooms and chalets, a bar and brasserie, and a large pool.

$$$ ✕ **Poppy's Villa Restaurant.** This colorfully decorated restaurant is Rotorua's big-occasion spot, yet prices are relatively moderate. First courses might include mussels poached in an Italian-style tomato and basil sauce, or sweetbreads in wine and tarragon sauce served with walnut brioche. The restaurant was recently awarded a Hallmark of Excellence for its beef and lamb dishes, thanks to selections like pink-cooked lamb racks served with a simple rosemary glaze, grain-fed beef with chunky potatoes, or cervena (farmed venison) with poached pear in a beet-based sauce. It's not all meat—vegetarians are also well looked after. ✉ *4 Marguerita St.,* ☎ *07/347–1700. AE, DC, MC, V. No lunch.*

$$$ ✕ **You and Me.** Kaname Yamamato is one of the most creative chefs not just in Rotorua, but in the whole of New Zealand. Japanese-born and French-trained, he combines both culinary disciplines (and others) with dishes like a rosette of orange-scented smoked salmon with a *shiso* (a Japanese herb) and papaya salad, sautéed prawns with Thai green basil curry and wild rice, and a fillet of lamb coated with roasted cashew nuts and served with spiced plum chutney and a chilli-spiced sauce. This is the only restaurant in Rotorua to have achieved a notable culinary style of its own. ✉ *31 Pukuatua St.,* ☎ *07/347–6178. AE, DC, MC, V. BYOB. Closed Sun.–Mon. No lunch.*

$$–$$$ ✕ **Copper Crioli.** Cajun food in a town where the ground steams? Seems logical. This kinky eatery is worth visiting just for the decor. A turn-of-the-last-century bank teller's cage takes pride of place, and the espresso machine is in the center of the room, dramatically plumbed from above with antique copper piping. The dishes include Southern U.S. classics like jambalaya and gumbo—and there's even spicy chicken marinated in Coca Cola with peppers. But it's not all Cajun—the kitchen has an oven with a sandstone tray that seeks to duplicate the effect of a Maori earth oven. Look for the "earth-flavored food" heading on the menu. ✉ *1151 Arawa St.,* ☎ *07/348–1333. AE, DC, MC, V.*

$ ✕ **The Fat Dog Café and Bar.** The eclectic but homely decor attracts young, old, and everyone in between. Fish tanks, lots of oak, and even a few lounges give it atmosphere, and the food's cheap and cheerful. Lasagna and Thai curry are local favorites, but there's also a biggish list of nibbles like potato wedges and nachos, as well as soups and salads. ✉ *69 Arawa St.,* ☎ *07/347–7586. AE, DC, MC, V. Licensed and BYOB.*

$$$$ ▥ **Solitaire Lodge.** Set high on a peninsula that juts out into Lake
★ Tarawera, this paradisal, plush retreat is surrounded by lakes, forests, and volcanoes. At this sophisticated hideaway, a few guests at a time

can enjoy the scenery in a relaxed, informal atmosphere. All suites are luxuriously equipped and individually decorated, with contemporary furnishings and artwork; the best room is the Tarawera Suite, which has spectacular 180-degree views. Check out the volcanoes from the telescopes in the library-bar, or settle down in a shaded garden nook and sip a drink. The surroundings are perfect for hiking, boating, and fishing, and the lodge has boats and fishing gear. Smoking is not permitted indoors. Rates include all meals. ⊠ *Ronald Rd., Lake Tarawera,* ☎ *07/362–8208,* ℻ *07/362–8445. 8 suites, 1 two-bed villa. Restaurant, bar, spa, boating, fishing. AE, DC, MC, V.* 🐾

$$$ 🏨 **Princes Gate Hotel.** Across the road from the Government Gardens, this ornate timber hotel was built in 1897 on the Coromandel Peninsula. It was brought here in 1917, and efforts have been made to re-create a turn-of-the-last-century feeling. The decor may be a bit too floral for some tastes, but rooms are reasonably large, very comfortable, and have been upgraded to incorporate all modern conveniences, from TVs to hair dryers. Best of all though is the sheer look of the place— pull up a cane chair on the wooden deck, look across to the Government Gardens, and imagine yourself transported back in time. ⊠ *1 Arawa St.,* ☎ *07/348–1179,* ℻ *07/348–6215. 50 rooms. 2 restaurants, bar, pool, hot tub, mineral baths, tennis court. AE, DC, MC, V.*

$$$ 🏨 **Royal Lakeside Novotel.** The Royal Lakeside has the handiest position of any of the large downtown hotels—it overlooks the lake and is just a two-minute walk from the restaurants and shops. Furnishings are sleek and contemporary, and the guest rooms are decently sized, though you'll want to specify a lake view when booking. ⊠ *Tutanekai St.,* ☎ *07/346–3888,* ℻ *07/347–1888. 199 rooms. Restaurant, bar, brasserie, no-smoking rooms, pool, sauna, spa, concert hall. AE, DC, MC, V.* 🐾

$$ 🏨 **Cedar Lodge Motel.** These spacious, modern two-story units, about a half mile from the city center, are a good value, especially for families. All have a kitchen and lounge room on the lower floor, a bedroom on the mezzanine floor above, and at least one queen-size and one single bed, and some have a queen-size bed and three singles. Every unit has its own hot tub in the private courtyard at the back. Gray-flecked carpet, smoked-glass tables, and recessed lighting are clean and contemporary. Request a room at the back, away from Fenton Street. ⊠ *296 Fenton St.,* ☎ *07/349–0300,* ℻ *07/349–1115. 15 rooms. Coin laundry. AE, DC, MC, V.*

$ 🏨 **Eaton Hall.** There's a friendly welcome in this central B&B, where simplicity is the watchword. The rooms are hardly on the cutting edge of fashion (everything is pink, lilac, and cream—a bit like grandma's) but the price and location is right, and a big English-style breakfast sets you up for the day. All rooms have a washbasin, though if you need more space (and your own shower and toilet) ask for rooms 9 or 10 which open out on to a row of flower boxes at the front of the house. ⊠ *39 Hinemaru St.,* ☎ ℻ *07/347–0366. 10 rooms. Hot tub. AE, DC, MC, V. BP.*

$ 🏨 **Motel Monterey.** There's much to be said for driving right into Rotorua to the Monterey, a very central two-story motel with a touch of yesteryear about it. Accommodations are simple, the walls are bare, and the kitchens in each unit are a little old-fashioned, but there's a lovely, sunny rear garden with heated pool, private mineral pool, and barbecue area. ⊠ *Whakaue St.,* ☎ *07/348–1044,* ℻ *07/346–2264. 15 units. Pool, outdoor hot tub. AE, DC, MC, V.*

Outdoor Activities and Sports

EXTREME ADVENTURE

The folks in Rotorua keep coming up with ever more fearsome ways to part adventurers from their money (and their wits). Try white-water sledging with **Kaitiaki Adventures** (☎ 0800/338–736): $80–100 (depending on the destination) gets you up to two hours shooting rapids on a buoyant, plastic water raft the size of a Boogie board. You get a wet suit, helmet, fins, and gloves—you provide the "go for it attitude."

There's bungy-jumping (the New Zealand spelling for *bungee-jumping*) of course, but you would be better off waiting for the spectacular natural sites at Taupo and Queenstown rather than jumping from the 140-ft-high crane in Rotorua. So go Zorbing instead: the "zorbonaut" (that's you) is strapped into a huge plastic ball and rolled head-over-heels 200 yards down a hill. You'll find **Zorb Rotorua** (☎ 07/332–2768) outside of town on Western Road, near the Agrodome. Zorbing costs $40 a ride, $50 for two rides, or $60 for a tandem ride. **Rotorua Swoop** (☎ 07/357–4747) sounds innocuous enough—that is until you're strapped into the hang-gliding harness, raised 120 ft off the ground, and the rip cord is pulled. Is that the earth whizzing by at 130 km/hour? It most certainly is. The Swoop takes place out at the Agrodome complex and costs $40 a ride.

FISHING

If you want to keep the trout of a lifetime from becoming just another fish story, it pays to have a boat with some expert advice on board. Expect to pay about $70–80 per hour for a fishing guide and a 20-ft cruiser that will take up to six passengers. The minimum charter period is two hours, and fishing gear and bait are included in the price. A one-day fishing license costs $13 per person and is available on board the boat. In Rotorua fishing operators include **Clark Gregor** (☎ 07/347–1123), **Bryan Colman** (☎ 07/348–7766), and **Gordon Randle** (☎ 07/349–2555). *See* Chapter 5 for in-depth fishing information.

RAFTING AND KAYAKING

The Rotorua region has a number of rivers with Grade-3 to Grade-5 rapids that make excellent white-water rafting. For scenic beauty—and best for first-timers—the Rangitaiki River (Grade 3–4) is recommended. For experienced rafters who want a challenge, the Wairoa River has exhilarating Grade-5 rapids. The climax of a rafting trip on the Kaituna River is the drop over the 21-ft Okere Falls, among the highest to be rafted by a commercial operator anywhere. The various operators all offer similar trips on a daily schedule, though note that different rivers are open at different times of year, depending on water levels. All equipment and instruction is provided, plus transportation to and from the departure points (which can be up to 80 km/50 mi, from Rotorua). Prices start at around $65 for the short (one-hr) Kaituna run; a half day on the Rangitaiki costs from $90. All sorts of discounted combination trips are also available. Contact **Kaituna Cascades** (☎ 07/357–5032 or 0800/524–8862), **Wet'n Wild Adventure** (☎ 07/348–3191 or 0800/462–7238), **Raftabout** (☎ 07/345–4652 or 0800/723–822), or **River Rats** (☎ 07/347–6049 or 0800/333–900). *See* Chapter 5 for in-depth rafting information.

Gentler natures should opt for a serene paddle on one of Rotorua's lakes. **Adventure Kayaking** (☎ 07/348–9451) has a variety of tours, from half a day spent paddling on Lake Rotorua ($45) to a full day on Lake Tarawera ($60) including a swim in a natural hot pool. Especially magical is the twilight paddle ($50) on Lake Rotoiti that incorporates a dip in the Manupirua hot pools (which you can't otherwise reach).

Shopping

The Whakarewarewa thermal reserve funds the work of the **New Zealand Maori Arts and Crafts Institute** (☎ 07/348–9047), established in 1963 to preserve Maori heritage and crafts. At the Institute (inside the thermal reserve) you can watch wood-carvers and flax-weavers at work, and see New Zealand greenstone (jade) being sculpted into jewelry. The adjacent gift shop sells fine examples of this work, plus many other items, from small wood-carved kiwis to decorative flax skirts of the kind worn in the Maori cultural shows.

Taupo

❺ *82 km (51 mi) south of Rotorua, 150 km (94 mi) northwest of Napier, 335 km (210 mi) west of Gisborne.*

The neat and tidy town of Taupo is the base for Lake Taupo, the largest lake in New Zealand. It's a beautiful spot, its placid shores backed by volcanic mountains, and in the vicinity is more of the geothermal activity which characterizes this zone (and, unlike Rotorua, most of the natural sites are free to visit). Water sports are popular here—notably sailing, cruising, and waterskiing—but most of all Taupo is known for its fishing. The town is the rainbow trout capital of the universe: the average Taupo trout weighs in around 4 pounds, and the lake is open year-round. Meanwhile, the backpacker crowd converges upon Taupo for its plethora of adventure activities: the town is celebrated for its skydiving and bungy-jumping opportunities, and there's also whitewater rafting and jet boating available on the local rivers.

❻ At **Huka Falls,** the Waikato River thunders through a narrow chasm and over a 35-ft rock ledge. The fast-flowing river produces almost 50% of the North Island's required power and its force at this point is extraordinary, with the falls dropping into a seething, milky-white pool 200 ft across. The view from the footbridge is superb, though for an even more impressive look, both the Huka Jet and the Otuni paddleboat (☞ Outdoor Activities and Sports *and* Rotorua, Lake Taupo, and Tongariro National Park A to Z, *below*) get close to the maelstrom. The falls are 3 km (2 mi) north of town; turn right off Highway 1 onto Huka Falls Road.

❼ The construction of the local geothermal project had an impressive—and unforeseen—effect: the underground dynamics were so drastically altered that boiling mud pools, steaming vents, and large craters appeared in an area now known as **Craters of the Moon.** A marked walkway snakes for 2 km (1 mi) through the belching, sulfurous landscape, past boiling pits and hissing crevices; the walk takes approximately 45 minutes. Entrance (during daylight hours) is by donation. The craters are up Karapiti Road, across from the Huka Falls turnoffs on Highway 1, 3 km (2 mi) north of Taupo.

❽ The Waikato River is dammed along its length, the first construction being the **Aratiata Dam,** 10 km (6 mi) northeast of Taupo (turn right off Highway 5). The river below the dam is virtually dry for most of the time, but three times a day (at 10, noon, and 2), and four times a day in summer (Oct.–Mar., also at 4), the dam gates are opened and the gorge is dramatically transformed into a raging torrent. Watch the spectacle from the road bridge over the river or from one of two lookout points a 15-minute walk downriver through the bush. The whole thing lasts 30 minutes, after which the dam gates close, the river subsides, and the gorge returns to serenity.

❾ Even if you think you have seen enough bubbling pools and fuming craters to last a lifetime, the captivating thermal valley of **Orakei Korako** is likely to change your mind. Geyser-fed streams hiss and steam as they flow into the waters of the lake, and there is an impressive multicolor silica terrace, believed to be the largest in the world since the volcanic destruction of the terraces of Rotomahana. At the bottom of Aladdin's Cave, the vent of an ancient volcano, a jade-green pool was once used exclusively by Maori women as a beauty parlor, which is where the name *Orakei Korako* (a place of adorning) originated. The valley is 37 km (23 mi) north of Taupo (take Highway 1 out of town) and takes around 25 minutes to reach by car; you could always see it en route to or from Rotorua, which lies another 68 km (43 mi) northeast of the valley. ☎ *07/378–3131.* ⌕ *$17.* ☉ *Spring–fall, daily 8:30–4:30; winter, daily 8:30–4.*

Dining and Lodging

$–$$$ ✕ **Villino's.** Kiwi gal Carolyn Obel and her German-born husband, Alex, spent serious time eating their way around Italy before settling down in picturesque Taupo, which explains the Italian influence on the menu. Alex's heritage shows in dishes like duck livers with caramelized apples, or pork partnered with a smoky bacon and gherkin sauce. But mostly, the food is good, modern Mediterranean—innovative salads, antipasto, pasta, and risotto. Eat indoors or out, casually during the day, more seriously at night. ⌂ *45 Horomatangi Rd.,* ☎ *07/377–4478. AE, DC, MC, V.*

$ ✕ **The Replete Food Company.** The food is served at the counter from display cabinets, and there's no wine license, but Replete's trump card is its management team—it's largely owned by cookbook author Greg Heffernan, formerly executive chef at plush Huka Lodge down the road. Thailand rules the menu with a prawn broth and a chicken curry that's so good at least one customer gets it delivered to Wellington. *Panini* (Italian flatbread) is filled with various goodies, including eggplant with an Indian-spiced salsa. The enchilada stack is legendary, as is the "Complete Replete" breakfast—honey-cured bacon, poached eggs, and grilled mushrooms. In town for a while? Ask about the cooking classes. ⌂ *45 Heu Heu St.,* ☎ *07/377–3011. AE, DC, MC, V.*

$$$$ ✕⌂ **Huka Lodge.** Buried in parklike grounds at the edge of the frisky
★ Waikato River, this superb lodge is the standard by which New Zealand's other sporting lodges are judged. The large, lavish guest rooms, decorated in muted grays and whites, are arranged in blocks of two or three. All have sliding glass doors that open to a view across lawns to the river. In the interest of tranquillity, guest rooms are not equipped with telephones, televisions, or radios. The five-course formal dinners are gourmet affairs, while the wine list is a showcase of the very best New Zealand has to offer—its stores are housed in a wine cellar with more than 50,000 bottles. Meals are served either at a communal dining table or, on request, at one of a dozen private dining areas (including the wine cellar or on the outdoor terrace). Rates include a superb breakfast and dinner. ⌂ *Huka Falls Rd., Box 95, Taupo,* ☎ *07/378–5791,* ℻ *07/378–0427. 20 rooms, 1 cottage with 3 rooms. Restaurant, bar, spa, tennis court, fishing. AE, DC, MC, V.* ✆

$$$ ⌂ **Cascades Motor Lodge.** Set on the shores of Lake Taupo, these attractive brick-and-timber rooms are large, comfortable, and furnished and decorated in a smart contemporary style. The two-story "luxury" apartments, which sleep up to seven, have a lounge room, bedroom, kitchen, and dining room on the ground floor in an open-plan design, glass doors leading to a large patio, and a second bedroom and bathroom on the upper floor. Studio rooms have one bedroom. All rooms are equipped with a jet bath. Room 1 is closest to the lake and a small beach. ⌂ *Lake Terr., 3 km (2 mi) south of Taupo, just beyond the Hwy. 5 (Napier) turnoff,* ☎ *07/378–3774,* ℻ *07/378–0372. 22 rooms. Pool, coin laundry. AE, DC, MC, V.*

Outdoor Activities and Sports

BUNGY JUMPING

If you're not heading to the South Island and Queenstown—spiritual home of bungy jumping—then Taupo is your best bet. **Taupo Bungy** provides jumps from an awesome cantilevered platform projecting out from a cliff 150 ft above the Waikato River. Even if you have no intention of "walking the plank," go and watch the jumpers from the nearby lookout point. ⊠ *202 Spa Rd., off Tongariro St., 1 km north of town,* ☎ *0800/888–408.* ⊑ *$89 per jump.* ◷ *Daily 9–5.*

FISHING

Many operators offer great fishing in the Taupo area and prices are fairly standard, from around $70 per hour for the boat (minimum trip usually two–three hrs) with all equipment supplied. Contact **Richard Staines** (☎ 07/378–2736), **Punch Wilson** (☎ 07/378–5596), or the Maori-owned **Te Moana Charters** (☎ 07/378–4839). At the other end of the scale, a luxury cruiser on Lake Taupo costs about $150 per hour; for more information, contact **Chris Jolly Outdoors** (☎ 07/378–0623). *See* Chapter 5 for in-depth fishing information.

JET BOATING

For high-speed thrills on the Waikato River take a trip on the **Huka Jet** (☎ 07/374–8572 or 0800/485–2538), which spins and skips its way between the Aratiata Dam and Huka Falls. Departures are every 30 minutes throughout the day; cost is $55 per person.

RAFTING

The Grade-5 Wairoa and Mohaka rivers are accessible from Taupo, as are the Rangitaiki and more family-friendly Tongariro. Different rivers are open at different times of year, depending on water levels, and operators all run similarly priced trips, starting at around $75 per person. Call **Rapid Sensations** (☎ 07/378–7902 or 0800/227–238), who provide transportation, wet suits, equipment, and much-needed hot showers at the end. *See* Chapter 5 for in-depth rafting information.

SKYDIVING

Two companies operate tandem skydiving trips—**Great Lake Skydive Centre** (☎ 0800/373–335) and **Taupo Tandem Skydiving** (☎ 0800/275–934). Call at least one day in advance to arrange your jump—which goes ahead weather permitting—and expect to pay $150 per person per jump. Discounted combo tickets are also available with other adventure sports, so ask around if you plan to do more than one activity.

SOAKING

The laziest activity in Taupo is a few hours spent at the **Taupo Hot Springs,** a favored bathing spot for a century or more. Naturally occurring hot springs have been corralled into three interlinked pools and twin hot tubs, which sit in a natural chasm below De Bretts Thermal Resort. The waters are great for soothing aching limbs and there's a water slide and barbecue and picnic area if you'd like to make a day of it. ⊠ *Hwy. 5, 3 km (2 mi) southeast of Taupo (Napier Rd.),* ☎ *07/377–6502.* ⊑ *$7, water slide $4; bathing gear and towel rental available.* ◷ *Daily 7:30 AM–9:30 PM.*

Tongariro National Park

⑩ *110 km (69 mi) southwest of Taupo.*

Tongariro is the country's first national park, established on sacred land donated by a Maori chief. Southwest of Lake Taupo, the park is dominated by three active volcanic peaks: Tongariro, Ngauruhoe, and Ruapehu, which at 9,175 ft is the highest North Island mountain. Ruapehu last erupted in 1996, spewing forth ash and showers of rocks.

Tongariro's spectacular combination of dense *rimu* pine forests, crater lakes, barren lava fields, and bird life makes it the most impressive and popular of the island's national parks. It has numerous walking trails, the most famous the so-called Tongariro Crossing, a 16-km (10-mi)—six- to seven-hour—hike that traverses the mountain from one side to the other and is generally considered one of the finest walks in the country. You'll need to be reasonably fit to tackle it as some of the steep inclines and the harsh volcanic terrain can be punishing on a hot day. The longest hikes in the park are the three-day Northern Circuit and the four-day Round-the-Mountain Track, though you can just as well tackle short ½-hr to two-hour walks if all you want is a flavor of the region. Wherever you hike, be prepared for rapidly changing weather conditions with warm and waterproof clothing. If you want to stay in the wilderness overnight, there are trailside huts throughout the park.

Highway 1 skirts the east side of the park, but the most direct access is from Highway 47, on the north side; Highway 48, which leads to Whakapapa Village, branches off from here, about 10 km (6 mi) before the confusingly named village of National Park, which sits at the junction of Highways 4 and 47, just outside the park proper. At National Park village you'll find motels, cafés, a gas station, and other services.

The only settlement—with the only services—within the national park is **Whakapapa Village,** which lies just below the Whakapapa ski area, on the north side of Mt. Ruapehu. Accommodations in the village are wide ranging. Campsites and simple cabins are available at the **Whakapapa Holiday Park** (☎ 07/892–3897). **Skotel Alpine Resort** (☎ 07/892–3719) offers chalets and rooms. And you can find grander rooms at the Grand Chateau hotel (☞ Dining and Lodging, *below*). There is a second ski area on the south side of the mountain, Turoa, which generally has a longer ski season than Whakapapa's, from June through October. The nearest town to the Turoa ski slopes is the ski resort of **Ohakune,** just beyond the southern boundary of the park—take Highway 49, which runs between Highways 1 and 4.

For displays about Tongariro National Park, and helpful tramping and skiing advice, stop off at the **Whakapapa Visitor Centre.** This is also the best place to buy maps and guides, including the very useful Department of Conservation park map—essential for trampers—and individual local walk leaflets. ✉ *Whakapapa Visitor Centre, Hwy. 48, Mt. Ruapehu,* ☎ *07/892-3729.* ◔ *Daily 8–5.*

Dining and Lodging

$$$ ✕🏨 **The Grand Chateau.** Built in 1929 in a French chateau style, this property really catches the eye as you drive into Whakapapa Village. The recently refurbished rooms provide a comfortable base for hiking or skiing. In the premium rooms there's plenty of space and some fine mountain views. Meals are taken in the Ruapehu Restaurant—serving traditional New Zealand cuisine with a modern slant—or there's a less formal café. The hotel can arrange guided tramps on all the best-known routes in the park. Note that room rates increase by almost 50% in the busy winter ski season (July–September). ✉ *Hwy. 48,* ☎ *07/892-3809 or 0800/733-944,* 🖷 *07/892-3704. 64 rooms. Restaurant, bar, café, hot tub, 9-hole golf course, tennis court. AE, DC, MC, V.* ✎

Rotorua, Lake Taupo, and Tongariro National Park A to Z

Arriving and Departing

BY BUS

Newmans and **InterCity** buses (☎ 09/913–6100) run five times daily between Auckland and Rotorua, and there are three daily services from Auckland to Taupo. Rotorua is something of a transportation hub: it's easy to reach Taupo, Hamilton, Tauranga, Wellington, Gisborne, and Napier by buses at the Tourism Rotorua Visitor Information Centre.

It's more difficult to reach Tongariro National Park by public transportation, though there is a daily summer bus service (mid-October–April) between Taupo, Whakapapa Village, and the village of National Park. To tackle the Tongariro Crossing one-day walk—a one-way track between Mangatepopo and Ketetahi—call **Tongariro Track Transport** (☎ 07/892–3897) for bookings. Their bus to the trailhead leaves Whakapapa Visitor Centre daily at 8 AM. In addition, many of the motels and lodges in National Park village can arrange transport to the track.

BY CAR

Rotorua is about three hours from Auckland. Take Highway 1 south past Hamilton and Cambridge to Tirau, where Highway 5 breaks off to Rotorua. Taupo is four hours from Auckland (take Highway 1 the whole way) and 70 minutes from Rotorua. For Tongariro National Park, the main approach is along Highway 4 on the park's western side: turn off at National Park for Whakapapa and the northern ski slopes, or at Raetihi for Ohakune and the south.

BY PLANE

Air New Zealand (☎ 0800/737–000) and **Ansett New Zealand** (☎ 07/347–0146) have daily flights that link Rotorua with Auckland and Wellington, with further connections throughout New Zealand. Rotorua Airport is about 10 km (6 mi) from the city center. Taxi fare to the city is $18.

BY TRAIN

There's one daily train service from Auckland to Rotorua, which takes just over four hours: call **Tranz Rail** (☎ 0800/802–802). For Tongariro National Park, either the daily *Overlander* or *Northerner* services—with Tranz Rail—stop at National Park village and Ohakune.

Contacts and Resources

CRUISES

Cruises on Lake Taupo all feature a similar itinerary, usually involving a couple of hours out on the lake visiting local bays and a modern Maori rock carvings.

The **Barbary** (☎ 07/378–3444) is a 1920s wooden yacht believed once to be the property of Errol Flynn. Departures are at 10 and 2 ($25) and summer evenings at 5 PM ($20).

Otuni (☎ 07/378–5828), an old "sidewheel" paddle steamer, visits the Huka Falls for $20; an evening glowworm cruise ($25) takes you through starlit gorges.

EMERGENCIES

Dial 111 for **fire, police, and ambulance** services.

GUIDED TOURS

Carey's Tours has the largest selection of bus and boat tours in Rotorua and Taupo, with various combinations taking you out to every conceivable sight and attraction in the area. Prices start at $50 for a half-day Waimangu valley trip to $125 for a full day touring all the major thermal areas. ⊠ *1108 Haupapa St., Rotorua,* ☎ *07/347–1197.*

Mount Tarawera 4WD Tours (☎ 07/348–2814) has a sensational half-day, four-wheel-drive trip to the edge of the Mt. Tarawera crater. Departures are available at 8:30 and 1:30.

New Zealand Helicopters Rotorua (☎ 07/348–1223) offers a choice of scenic flights, from a short (10-minute) flight over the city and Whakarewarewa Thermal Reserve ($55 per person) to an hour's flight over crater lakes and the Waimangu Valley, with a landing on top of Mt. Tarawera ($345 per person).

The **Waimangu Round Trip** is probably the most complete tour of Rotorua. It includes an easy 5-km (3-mi) hike through the Waimangu Thermal Valley to Lake Rotomahana, where a cruiser takes you past steaming cliffs to the narrow isthmus that divides the lake from Lake Tarawera. After crossing the lake on a second cruiser, the tour visits the Buried Village and ends with a dip in the Polynesian Pools in Rotorua. Lunch is included. ⊠ *Reserve at Tourism Rotorua Visitor Information Centre,* ☎ *07/347–1197.* ⊠ *$140.*

Taupo Visitor Information Centre. ⊠ *13 Tongariro St., Taupo,* ☎ *07/ 378–9000.* ⊘ *Daily 8:30–5.*

Tourism Rotorua Visitor Information Centre. In addition to an information office, this modern complex houses a café, a film-processing service, a tour-reservation desk, a map shop operated by the Department of Conservation, and a lost-luggage facility. It is also Rotorua's main tour bus stop. ⊠ *67 Fenton St., Rotorua,* ☎ *07/348–5179.* ⊘ *Daily 8–5:30.*

Whakapapa Visitor Centre. ⊠ *Hwy. 48, Mt. Ruapehu,* ☎ *07/892–3729.* ⊘ *Daily 8–5.*

NAPIER AND HAWKE'S BAY

New Zealand prides itself on natural wonders. By that way of thinking, Napier is an exception. This city of 50,000, situated about two-thirds of the way down the east coast of North Island, is best known for its architecture. After an earthquake devastated Napier in 1931, citizens rebuilt it in the fashionable art deco style of the day. Its well-kept uniformity of style makes it a pleasant and comfortable sort of period piece. There's a similar aspect to Napier's less-visited twin city, Hastings, just to the south, which was also remodeled after the earthquake. After stretching your legs in either place, you can relax on a brief wine-tasting tour for the rest of the day—the region produces some of New Zealand's best. In addition, the mild climate and beaches of Hawke Bay make this a popular vacation area for New Zealanders. (*Hawke* Bay is the body of water; *Hawke's* Bay is the region.) You also should make a point of trying to visit the gannet colony at Cape Kidnappers—which you can see only between October and March.

Napier

150 km (94 mi) southeast of Taupo, 345 km (215 mi) northeast of Wellington.

The focus of any visit to Napier is its art deco buildings—many of which lie between Emerson, Herschell, Dalton, and Browning streets—and the city is a pleasure to tour on foot. Art deco was born at the 1925 International Exposition of Modern Decorative and Industrial Arts in

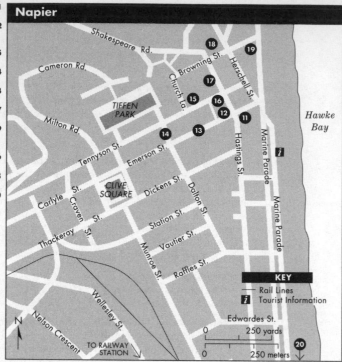

Napier

Paris. Its influences around the Western world are broad: from skyscrapers and diners to toasters and jewelry. The style is bold and geometrical, often using stainless steel to represent the sleekness of the machine age as it was seen in the 1920s, 1930s, and beyond. In Napier, the elements that remain are often found above the ground floor, so any walk will involve looking up frequently. The buildings aside, Napier's charming seafront also makes for a rewarding stroll. Marine Parade is lined with Norfolk pines, formal gardens, and children's attractions, and is backed by pastel-color houses; there is a town beach, though you should note that the waves and currents here make swimming dangerous.

⓫ One of Napier's notable buildings is the **ASB Bank,** at the corner of Hastings and Emerson streets. The Maori theme on the lintels above the main entrance is echoed in the ceiling inside the building.

⓬ The **Criterion Hotel** (⊠ Hastings St.) is typical of the Spanish Mission style, which Napier took on due to its success in Santa Barbara, California, where an earthquake had similarly wreaked havoc just a few years ⓭ before the New Zealand catastrophe. Along **Emerson Street** and its pedestrian mall, **Hannahs,** the **Bowman's Building, McGruers,** and the **Hawke's Bay Chambers** are among the city's finest art deco examples.

⓮ **Dalton Street** has its treasures as well. South of the intersection with Emerson Street, the pink **Countrywide Bank Building,** with its balcony, is one of Napier's masterpieces. **Hildebrand's,** at Tennyson Street, has an excellent frieze, which is best viewed from across Dalton. Hildebrand was a German who migrated to New Zealand—hence the German flag at one end, the New Zealand at the other, and the wavy lines in the middle to symbolize the sea passage between the two countries.

⑮ The **Daily Telegraph Building** (⊠ Tennyson St. and Church La.) is another Napier classic. If you can turn back the clock in your mind and imagine the city littered with heaps of rubble, you would see the **Market Reserve Building** (⊠ Tennyson and Hastings Sts.) as the first to rise following the earthquake. You would have seen Hartson's Music Shop survive the quake had you lived through it, and you may have lived to

⑰ see it turn into **Hartson's Bar** (⊠ Hastings St. between Browning and Tennyson Sts.), the facade of which has changed little since its change in ownership replaced songs with suds.

⑱ The **Ministry of Works** (⊠ Browning St.), with its decorative lighthouse pillar at the front, takes on the almost Gothic menace that art deco architecture sometimes has (like New York's Chrysler Building).

⑲ Using newspaper reports, photographs, and audiovisuals, the **Hawke's Bay Museum** re-creates the suffering caused by the earthquake. It also houses a unique display of artifacts of the Ngati Kahungunu Maori people of the east coast—including vessels, decorative work, and statues. ⊠ *65 Marine Parade,* ☎ *06/835-7781.* ⊡ *$4.* ☉ *Daily 10–4:30.*

👆 ⑳ Napier's waterfront aquarium has undergone long-term refurbishment during its restyling as New Zealand's **National Aquarium.** The facility provides hands-on environmental and ecological displays alongside a collection of sharks, rays, tropical fish, saltwater crocodiles, turtles, and piranha. Completion is expected during 2001; phone for details, or inquire about progress at Napier Visitor Information Centre. ⊠ *Marine Parade,* ☎ *06/834-1404.*

Dining and Lodging

$$$ ✕ **Bayswater Bistro.** This bay-side restaurant has had several differ-
★ ent owners, but it has managed to hold onto its status as one of Napier's finest eateries. The current chef is Stephen Tindall, who did serious kitchen time at London's Bibendum before moving to well-regarded Cibo in Auckland. Recent menu selections have included crab dumplings with Vietnamese dipping sauce, and salmon crusted with coriander and cooked medium-rare. The voguish white interior has a faintly art deco feeling, and the large doors open to a sparkling sea view. In warm weather request a table on the deck outside, or at least a table at the window. The restaurant can be hard to spot at night—take Marine Parade out of the city center, and it's about 1 km (½ mi) north of the port just after the playground. ⊠ *Harding Rd.,* ☎ *06/835-8517. AE, DC, MC, V. No lunch.*

$$ ✕ **Restaurant Indonesia.** Local wine maker Alan Limmer, who makes
★ the world-beating Stonecroft Gewürztraminer (once voted best in the show in London against competitors from Germany and Alsace), holds an annual gewürztraminer dinner at this tiny Hawke's Bay institution. The interior is like an Indonesian museum, thanks to the owners' regular trips back home. Try a large selection of the Dutch-Indonesian food by sharing a *rijsttafel,* which consists of 13 sampling dishes. Other favorites: marinated prawn *satay* (grilled skewers), and *babi panggang*—grilled pork loin with a sweet-and-sour sauce based on onions, pineapple, and lemon juice. ⊠ *409 Marine Parade,* ☎ *06/835-8303. AE, DC, MC, V.*

$$$ 🏠 **Anleigh Heights.** Built in 1900 as a town house for a wealthy sheep rancher, this sprawling hilltop guest house is one of Napier's landmark buildings and a fine example of the city's Edwardian timber architecture. The guest lounge—once a ballroom—is paneled in English oak, and the pick of the rooms is the north-facing Colenso Suite, with its large bathroom and sunny aspect. The owners are charming and attentive hosts. Two of the rooms have only showers and no baths. ⊠ *115 Chaucer Rd., North Napier,* ☎ *06/835-1188,* FAX *06/835-1032. 4 rooms. AE, DC, MC, V. BP.*

$$$ ⌹ **The County Hotel.** Built in 1909 as the headquarters of the Hawke's Bay County Council, this is one of the few Napier buildings that survived the 1931 earthquake. You can't help but feel with its refurbishment that you're stepping back in time—high ceilings, brass fittings, wood paneling, and art deco–style lights in the rooms are betrayed only by TVs and fax and modem plugs. Each room has a spacious white-tile bathroom with shower, and some have a clawfoot tub as well. The original hotel's doors are of native kauri wood, and there are a magnificent rimu stairway and a clubby library off the atrium. ⌂ *12 Browning St., Napier,* ☎ *06/835–7800,* ℻ *06/835–7797. 12 rooms. Restaurant, bar. AE, DC, MC, V.*

$$ ⌹ **Edgewater Motor Lodge.** Motels and inns line Marine Parade and the Edgewater is a prime choice here. The small studio units on the ground floor would suffice for a night or two, but for more space and comfort opt either for a spic-and-span spa unit (with jet bath and courtyard seating) or an upper-floor studio unit, with ocean views from a small private balcony. ⌂ *359 Marine Parade,* ☎ *06/835–1148,* ℻ *06/ 835–6600. 20 rooms. Pool, hot tub, coin laundry. AE, DC, MC, V.*

Hawke's Bay

The natural world provides as vital an experience of Hawke's Bay as the human factor does. The gannet colony on the coast southeast of the city is a beautiful and fascinating spot. Then there is the wine—Napier's surrounding countryside grows some of New Zealand's most highly esteemed grapes, reds being of particular note.

㉑ **Esk Valley Estate Winery** is terraced on a north-facing hillside, ensuring it full sun and a cherished location for grape growing. Wine maker Gordon Russell produces chardonnay, sauvignon blanc, chenin blanc, merlot, and flavorsome blends featuring cabernet sauvignon, merlot, cabernet franc, and malbec in various combinations, including a rare and expensive red simply called the Terraces. Look for the reserve version of any varietal to find out what he has done with the best grapes from given years. The winery is 12 km (8 mi) north of Napier, just north of the town of Bay View before Highways 2 and 5 split. ⌂ *Main Rd., Bay View, Napier,* ☎ *06/836–6411.* ☉ *Nov.–Mar., daily 9–5:30; Apr.– Oct., daily 9:45–5; tours by appointment.*

㉒ **Linden Estate** is next to an historic church, which manages to look thoroughly at home surrounded by vines. Wine maker Nick Chan makes reliably good sauvignon blanc, chardonnay, and cabernet-merlot blends, many of which have achieved medal success. His Linden Reserve Chardonnay is served to first-class Air New Zealand passengers. ⌂ *SH5, Napier-Taupo Hwy., Napier,* ☎ *06/836–6806.* ☉ *Daily 9–5.*

㉓ The **Mission Vineyard** at Taradale is the oldest in New Zealand, established by Catholic Marist brothers in the late 1850s after an earlier vineyard farther north at Poverty Bay was abandoned. Legend has it that in 1852 one of the brothers made a barrel of sacramental wine and shipped it to Napier; the seamen broached the cargo, drank the wine, and filled the empty cask with seawater. The Jewelstone label is reserved for the top wines, and the Mission Estate label is used for a wide range of well-made varietals including sauvignon blanc, gewürztraminer, riesling, pinot gris, and cabernet blends. Sample and buy to take with you, or try them in the pleasant attached restaurant. To reach the vineyard, leave Napier by Kennedy Road, heading southwest from the city center toward Taradale. Just past Anderson Park, turn right into Avenue Road and continue to its end at Church Road. ⌂ *Church Rd., Taradale,* ☎ *06/844–2259.* ☉ *Mon.–Sat. 8:30–5:30, Sun. 11–4.*

㉔ The **McDonald Winery** is owned by Montana, the country's largest wine company, but it operates pretty much as a separate entity. The wines are labeled Church Road: their chardonnay is a nationwide restaurant staple, and the various variations on the cabernet sauvignon and merlot themes are all worth sampling. The complex has a unique wine museum and beautifully restored cellars, as well as an indoor-outdoor casual café. ✉ *150 Church Rd., Taradale, Havelock North,* ☎ *06/877–2053.* ☞ *$3.* ⊘ *Daily 9–5; tours 10, 11, 2, 3.*

㉕ **Brookfields Winery** is one of the most attractive wineries in the area, befitting its status as a premier producer. The Reserve Chardonnay and Pinot Gris are usually outstanding, but the showpiece is the Reserve Vintage Cabernet Merlot, with its intense fruit and assertive oak. The winery restaurant (☞ Dining and Lodging, *below*) is casual and very good. From Napier take Marine Parade toward Hastings and turn right on Awatoto Road. Follow it to Brookfields Road and turn left. Signs will point to the winery. ✉ *Brookfields Rd., Meanee, Taradale,* ☎ *06/ 834–4615.* ⊘ *Mon.–Sat. 8:30–5:30, Sun. 11–4.*

㉖ **Te Mata Estate** is one of New Zealand's top wineries, and Coleraine, a rich but elegant cabernet-merlot blend named after the much-photographed home of the owner, John Buck, is considered the archetypal Hawke's Bay red. Elston Chardonnay and Cape Crest Sauvignon Blanc show similar restraint and balance. If there's any viognier open (it's made only in tiny quantities), try it—it's excellent. From Napier head south on Marine Parade through Clive and turn left at the Mingatere Tree School. Signs from there will lead you to Te Mata Road and the estate. ✉ *Te Mata Rd., Box 8335, Havelock North,* ☎ *06/ 877–4399.* ⊘ *Weekdays 9–5, Sat. 10–5, Sun. 11–4; tours Christmas holidays–Jan., daily at 10:30.*

★ ㉗ **Cape Kidnappers** was named by Captain James Cook after local Maori tried to kidnap the servant of Cook's Tahitian interpreter. The cape is the site of a large **gannet colony.** The gannet is a large white seabird with black-tipped flight feathers, a golden crown, and wings that can reach a span of 6 ft. When the birds find a shoal of fish, they fold their wings and plunge straight into the sea at tremendous speed. Their migratory pattern ranges from western Australia to the Chatham Islands, about 800 km (500 mi) east of Christchurch, but they generally nest only on remote islands. The colony at Cape Kidnappers is believed to be the only mainland gannet sanctuary in existence. Between October and March, about 15,000 gannets build their nests here, hatch their young, and prepare them for their long migratory flight.

You can walk to the sanctuary along the beach from Clifton, which is about 24 km (15 mi) south of Napier, but not at high tide. The 8-km (5-mi) walk must begin no earlier than three hours after the high tide mark, and the return journey must begin no later than four hours before the next high tide. Tidal information is available at Clifton and at Napier Visitor Information Centre. A rest hut with refreshments is available near the colony.

Because of these tidal restrictions, one easy way to get to the colony is to take a **Gannet Beach Adventures** (☎ 06/875–0898) tractor-trailer, which is pulled along the beach starting from Clifton Reserve, Clifton Beach. Tractors depart approximately two hours before low tide, and the trip ($22) takes 4–4½ hours. If tides prevent the trip along the beach, the only other access is across private farmland. **Gannet Safaris** (☎ 06/ 875–0888) runs a four-wheel-drive bus to Cape Kidnappers from Summerlee Station, just past Te Awanga. A minimum of four is required for this tour ($38 each), which takes three hours. Advance booking is essential for all gannet colony tours.

㉘ **Hastings** is Napier's twin city in Hawke's Bay, and it is worth at least driving through on your way to or from the wineries—it's just 18 km (11 mi) south of Napier, down Highway 2. True, the town doesn't have the same concentrated interest of Napier, but buildings in the center exhibit similar art deco flourishes—the 1931 earthquake did a lot of damage here too. Where Hastings stands out is in its Spanish Mission buildings, a style borrowed from California, which produced such beauties as the **Municipal Theater** (⊠ Hastings St.) and the **Westermans Building** (⊠ Russell St.). Out of town, 3 km (2 mi) to the southeast, the village of Havelock North provides access to **Te Mata Peak**, a famed local viewpoint where it's possible to gaze right across the plains to Napier and the rumpled hills behind. The summit is a 15-minute (signposted) drive from Havelock North.

More of Hawke's Bay's wineries are sited closer to Hastings than Napier, particularly **Vidal Estate Winery** (⊠ 913 St. Aubyn St. E, Hastings, ☎ 06/876–8105), a sister winery of Esk Valley Estate that consistently produces some of New Zealand's finest reds—and has a pleasant restaurant, and **Huthlee Estate Winery** (⊠ 84 Montana Rd., Bridge Pa, ☎ 𝖥𝖠𝖷 06/879–6234), a family-owned vineyard and winery specializing in reds.

Stonecroft is best known for a rare and expensive syrah, but Dr. Alan Limmer also produces startlingly good gewürztraminer and top-class chardonnay and sauvignon blanc. The vineyard's stony soil reflects the rays of the sun onto the ripening grapes, which is one of the reasons Alan has had such success with syrah—most parts of the country are too cool for it to ripen. It also explains why he has been able to produce a big, inky zinfandel. It's only in experimental quantities so far, but he loves talking about it. ⊠ *Mere Rd., Hastings, ☎ 06/879–9610. ☉ Sat. 11–5, Sun. 11–4.*

Dining and Lodging

$$$–$$$$ ✕ **Sileni Estates.** The impressive space-age Sileni Estates Winery building houses two restaurants, with both kitchens under the control of local culinary hero, Vicki Bruhns-Bolderson. At the more casual, seven-day-a-week **Mesa**, crab and blue nose (a local fish) cakes top an asparagus salad, and duck leg is roasted and served with a duck liver *croûte* (pastry), caramelized red onion tart, and a vinaigrette based on the winery's own cabernet. From Wednesday to Saturday nights, **RD One** offers the best of the bay's produce prepared in innovative ways—think of grilled, braised quail served with roasted golden bell peppers, or cervena, with wild boar bacon and mushroom-flavored polenta. The wine list isn't selfish—owner Graeme Avery also runs an importing company, so the options cover the world. ⊠ *2016 Maraekakaho Rd, Bridge Pa, Hastings, ☎ 06/879–8768. AE, DC, MC, V.*

$$–$$$ ✕ **Corn Exchange.** Big and bustling, this eatery was once a storehouse for local produce. A wood-fired pizza oven, moved here from Auckland's Cin Cin, dominates the kitchen. Beyond pizza, try the likes of oven-roasted lamb on a honeyed pumpkin cake or cervena (venison) with a bourbon-based reduction sauce. Choose local labels or wine from outside the region. ⊠ *118 Maraekakohoe Rd., Hastings, ☎ 06/870–8333. AE, DC, MC, V.*

$$ ✕ **Brookfields Winery Restaurant.** Run in cooperation with the winery, this pleasant spot offers a splendid selection of Jenny Parton's modern Asian-influenced dishes that taste perfect alongside a glass of Brookfields wine. Try a seared salmon fillet with lime chilli aioli and *salade niçoise* at lunch, or lamb rump atop fig and orange couscous at night. ⊠ *Brookfields Rd., Meeanee,* ☎ *06/834–4615. AE, DC, MC, V. No dinner Sun.–Tues.*

$$ ✕ **Rose & Shamrock.** The developers of this Irish pub were so keen on authenticity, they sent their architect on a three-week tour of Ireland. The result is like a transplant from Dublin. Beers, wines, and spirits mix with old-fashioned but honest pub fare like grilled beef sirloin, or a generous platter of seafood, much of it battered and deep-fried. Hints of restaurant style creep in with dishes like crumbed chicken breasts with apricot sauce. ⊠ *Napier Rd., Havelock North,* ☎ *06/877–2999. AE, DC, MC, V.*

$$ ✕ **Te Awa Farm Winery & Restaurant.** The Farm features the considerable talents of Rick Rutledge-Manning, a peripatetic chef who set up some of the best restaurants in the country before settling in the bay. Now, he's cooking up a storm and giving free rein to his second great passion—matching food and wine (the first is golf). The Farm's French-trained wine maker, Jenny Dobson, is delighted to have him in town, and the two have a lot of fun matching flavors on the menu. Think about confit of duck in vanilla essence partnered by gamay, or salmon encased in butter pastry, set under a warm salad of potatoes with a chardonnay dressing, and served with the same Longlands Chardonnay alongside. After lunch, pop over and try the wines at expat Australian John Hancock's impressive nearby **Trinity Hill** winery. ⊠ *2375 State Hwy. 50, Hastings,* ☎ *06/879–7602. AE, DC, MC, V.*

$$$$ ✕⊡ **Mangapapa Lodge.** The beautifully restored Mangapapa Lodge
★ was once the home of the Wattie family, which started a fruit-picking business that is now one of New Zealand's giants. Each room is styled and furnished according to a particular country—the Austrian room, for example, has a large four-poster bed decorated with Austrian folk art. Owners Guenter and Shirley Engels are wine and food enthusiasts, and dinners at the lodge are open to house guests and casual diners who eat outside under parasols on hot days. Chef Kim Fell moved to the bay from Wellington's trendy Fog City Restaurant, and is enjoying the move back to a more classical style. Produce is seasonal and, where possible, local; the bread is always homemade and the cheeses served are from New Zealand. ⊠ *466 Napier Rd., Havelock North,* ☎ *06/878–3234,* ℻ *06/878–1214. 9 rooms. Restaurant, bar, pool, sauna, spa, tennis court, croquet, bicycles. AE, DC, MC, V.*

$$$ ⊡ **Hawthorne Country Lodge.** In a former life Jeanette Kelly was the
★ Auckland-based publicist for Taupo's Huka Lodge, so she knows a thing or two about the hospitality business. She and husband Peter restored this charming Edwardian house and planted its extensive gardens, which are just right for a game of croquet. The individually decorated rooms all have private verandas and fine linen. A hearty breakfast featuring local produce (including coffee from Peter's own coffee roasting company) is included in the tariff: eat it communally at the dining room table or in your room. Dinners can also be arranged with local wine makers. The house is 6 km (4 mi) south of Hastings. ⊠ *420 State Hwy. 2, Hastings South,* ☎ *06/878–0035,* ℻ *06/878–0035. 5 rooms. AE, MC, V. BP.* ✒

Shopping

Napier's Art Deco Trust maintains an **Art Deco Shop** in town, selling some unique gifts, from handcrafted jewelry, T-shirts, and ceramics to wine glasses, books, posters, and cards. ⊠ *163 Tennyson St.,* ☎ *06/835–0022.*

Napier and Hawke's Bay A to Z

Arriving and Departing

BY BUS

Newmans and **InterCity** (☎ 09/913–6100) operate daily bus services between Napier and Auckland, Taupo, Rotorua, and Wellington. There are also frequent local services between Napier and Hastings. For tickets and information, go to the Napier Visitor Information Centre (☞ *below*).

BY CAR

The main route between Napier and the north is Highway 5. Driving time from Taupo is two hours, five hours if you're coming straight from Auckland. Highway 2 is the main route heading south. Driving time to Wellington is five hours.

BY PLANE

Air New Zealand (☎ 0800/737–000) has several flights daily between Napier and Auckland, Wellington, and Christchurch. The airport is 5 km (3 mi) north of Napier, from which shuttle taxis run into town.

BY TRAIN

Tranz Rail's *Bay Express* (☎ 0800/802–802) leaves Napier at 2:05 daily for Wellington (passing through Hastings at 2:29), arriving in the capital at 7:36 PM. It leaves Wellington for Napier at 8 AM, arriving Napier at 1:20. If you are traveling to South Island, you will probably have to overnight in Wellington before joining the Cook Strait ferry. Bookings can be made for both the train and the ferry at the Napier Visitor Information Centre (☞ *below*).

Contacts and Resources

EMERGENCIES

Dial 111 for **fire, police, and ambulance** services.

GUIDED TOURS

The **Art Deco Trust** has a couple of excellent and informative guided walking tours of Napier. A one-hour walk starts daily at 10 AM from the Napier Visitor Information Centre (☞ *below*); a longer afternoon walk, starting at the Art Deco Shop (☞ Shopping, *above*), takes 2½ hours and includes slide and video presentations. Or take the Trust's self-guided Art Deco Walk; leaflets ($2) are available at its shop or at the visitor center. ⊠ *Art Deco Shop, 163 Tennyson St.* ☜ *10 AM tour $7, 2 PM tour $10.* ✆ *Oct.–June, daily at 10 and 2; July–Sept., Wed. and weekends at 2.*

Bay Tours has a four-hour tour of area wineries. It offers a chance to sample some of the boutique wines unavailable to independent travelers, and lunch at one of the winery restaurants is usually available too (at your own cost). ⊠ *Napier Visitor Information Centre, Marine Parade,* ☎ *06/843–6953.* ☜ *$35.* ✆ *Daily at 1.*

VISITOR INFORMATION

Hastings Visitor Information Centre. ⊠ *Russell St. N, Hastings,* ☎ *06/873–5526.* ✆ *Weekdays 8:30–5, weekends 10–3.*

GISBORNE AND EASTLAND

Traveling to Eastland takes you well away from the tourist track in North Island. For some people, that is reason enough to make the trip. Once here, you will find rugged coastline, accessible beaches, dense forests, gentle nature trails, and small, predominantly Maori communities. Eastland provides one of the closest links with the nation's earliest past. Kaiti Beach, near the city of Gisborne, is where the *waka* (long canoe) *Horouta* landed, and nearby Titirangi was named by the first Maori settlers in remembrance of their mountain in Hawaiki, their Polynesian island of origin. Kaiti Beach is also where Captain Cook set foot in 1769—the first European landing in New Zealand.

Gisborne's warm climate and fertile soil make the region one of New Zealand's most successful wine areas. Often overshadowed by Hawke's Bay (and its formidable PR machine), Gisborne has 7,000 acres under vine, and it is the country's largest supplier of chardonnay grapes. It has in fact been dubbed the chardonnay capital of New Zealand, which makes that the variety to concentrate on if you go tasting.

Gisborne

② *210 km (130 mi) northeast of Napier, 500 km (310 mi) southeast of Auckland.*

The Maori name for the Gisborne district is Tairawhiti (tye-ra-*fee*-tee)—the coast upon which the sun shines across the water. Indeed, as the easternmost city in New Zealand, Gisborne is the first in the world to see the new day's sunrise, a fact that made it the focus of world-wide millennium celebrations at dawn on January 1, 2000, when thousands gathered here to see the sun come up. Although the city (population 30,000) is hardly large, you will need a day or so to get around town properly. Most of the historical sights and other attractions are too spread out to explore them all by foot, and you'll need a car to get into the spectacular countryside nearby.

The **Museum and Arts Centre,** with its Maori and Pakeha (European) artifacts and an extensive photographic collection, provides a good introduction to the region's Maori and colonial history. A maritime gallery covers seafaring matters, and there are changing exhibits of local and national artists' work. Outside the museum, the colonial-style **Wyllie Cottage,** built in 1872, is the oldest building in town. ⊠ *18 Stout St.,* ☎ *06/867–3832.* ☞ *Free.* ⊙ *Weekdays 10–4, weekends 1:30–4.*

Cook Landing Site National Historic Reserve has deep historical significance for New Zealanders, but not so much to keep an international visitor amused. At Kaiti Beach, across the river southeast of the city center, it is marked by a statue of Captain James Cook, who first set foot on New Zealand soil here on October 9, 1769. The beach itself, at low tide, attracts interesting bird life. ⊠ *Esplanade on south end of Turanganui River.*

The **Titirangi Domain** on Kaiti Hill has excellent views of Gisborne, Poverty Bay, and the surrounding rural areas. Titirangi was the site of an extensive *pa* (fortified village), the origins of which can be traced back at least 24 Maori generations. The **Titirangi Recreational Reserve,** part of the Domain, is a pleasant place for a picnic or a walk among native trees. The Domain is south of Turanganui River. Pass the harbor and turn right onto Esplanade, then left onto Crawford Road, right onto Queens Drive, and follow it to several lookout points in the Domain.

Te Poho o Rawiri Meeting House is one of the largest Maori marae in New Zealand, and the interior has excellent traditional carving. On the side of the hill stands the Toko Toro Tapu Church. Ask permission to explore both sites from the **Gisborne-Eastland Visitor Information Centre** (☞ Contacts and Resources *in* Gisborne and Eastland A to Z, *below*) in town. ⊠ *Kaiti Hill,* ☎ 06/868–5364. ➲ *Small donation suggested.*

Matawhero Wines is a Gisborne original—both in style and longevity. Gewürztraminer is a specialty for owner Denis Irwin, but you can also taste chenin blanc, chardonnay, cabernet-merlot blends, and pinot noir, often from earlier vintages. The vineyard is southwest of Gisborne; follow State Highway 35 out of town. ⊠ *Riverpoint Rd., Gisborne,* ☎ 06/868–8366. ☉ *Mon.–Sat. 11–4.*

Millton Vineyard has an attractive garden area, making it a logical place to sit with a picnic lunch and sip some barrel-fermented chardonnay. The award-winning Opou Riesling is also recommended. James and Annie Millton grow their grapes organically and biodynamically, following the precepts of philosopher Rudolf Steiner. ⊠ *Papatu Rd., Manutuke, Gisborne,* ☎ 06/862–8680, ℻ 06/862–8869. ☉ *Summer, daily 10–5; winter, by appointment.*

OFF THE
BEATEN PATH

EASTWOODHILL ARBORETUM – Inspired not by the native trees of New Zealand but by English gardens, William Douglas Cook returned home from a trip to England in 1910 and began planting 160 acres. Only first-rate material was collected for the plantings, and the result today is a stunning collection of over 500 genera of trees from around the world. Eastwoodhill is a place of seasonal change seldom seen in New Zealand. In spring and summer daffodils mass yellow, magnolias bloom in clouds of pink and white, and cherries, crab apples, wisteria, and azalea all add to the spectacle. In autumn and winter leaves of yellow, rust, and scarlet cover the ground. The main tracks in the park can be walked in about 45 minutes. Maps and self-guided tour booklets are available. Drive west from Gisborne center on Highway 2 toward Napier and turn at the rotary into the Ngatapa-Rere Road before leaving town. Follow it 35 km (22 mi) to the arboretum. ⊠ *Ngatapa-Rere Rd.,* ☎ 06/863–9800. ➲ *$5.* ☉ *Daily 9–5.*

Dining and Lodging

$$$ ✕ **Café Villagio.** This casual and relaxed café-restaurant in a converted house is a Gisborne favorite. The menu style covers most of the bases—Caesar salad, risotto with chorizo, roast pork with *hoisin* (Chinese sweet sauce) or coated in Indian tandoori spices. The wine list is extensive and service is country-style cheerful. ⊠ *M57 Ballance St.,* ☎ 06/868–1611, ℻ 06/868–6855. *AE, DC, MC, V. Licensed and BYOB. No dinner Sun.–Tues.; May–Aug., no lunch Sat.–Mon.*

$$$ ✕ **Young Nick's on the Beach.** Known for years as Pete's on the Beach, this Gisborne institution has been completely renovated by new owners. A giant 3-D replica of the *Endeavour,* the ship in which Captain Cook "discovered" New Zealand, dominates one wall, and a relief head of his cabin boy, Young Nick—reputed to be the first on board to spot land—keeps an eye on proceedings. There's a reasonable emphasis on seafood, but not as much as you'd expect from the location. Start with Greenshell mussels, steamed open in coconut cream and white wine, and move onto the catch-of-the-day, oven-baked with chive and garlic mashed potatoes, pesto-roasted eggplant, and a scallop and prawn

skewer. Yep—servings are generous! The best tables are against the windows, overlooking the Pacific, or—if it's not windy—on the deck. ⊠ *Marine Parade, Medway Beach,* ☎ *06/867–5861. AE, DC, MC, V. No lunch weekdays.*

$$–$$$ ✕ **Wharf Café Bar Restaurant.** Built in a former storage shed on the Gisborne wharf, this brash, noisy eatery is operated by the former owners of Villagio. Open from 9 AM every day, Wharf offers food that leans to the Mediterranean, but has its own style. For brunch, think seared salmon with spinach and poached eggs on English muffins, or *bruschetta* (garlic bread) topped with tomato, fresh basil, and mozzarella. At night, get more serious over seared tuna with wasabi dressing, or beef tenderloin with a blue cheese and peppercorn sauce. The wine list has a good representation of local producers, along with an array of other New Zealand labels and a few imports. ⊠ *60 The Esplanade,* ☎ *06/868–4876. AE, DC, MC, V.*

$ ✕ **Verve Café.** This funky little midtown coffee bar is a popular stop for backpackers from around the world. The decor is eclectic, the reading matter interesting, and the food honest and generous. The kitchen smokes fish to order, and uses it in combos like smoked salmon on a potato cake with homemade mustard mayo, grapes, blue cheese, and baby-leaf salad. Breakfasts are hearty. The cakes are suitably decadent and, best of all, the coffee is terrific. If the bush has got you starved for technology, sip one while you surf the net. ⊠ *121 Gladstone Rd., Gisborne,* ☎ *06/868–9095. AE, DC, MC, V. BYOB. No dinner Sun.*

$$$$ ✕🏠 **Katoa Country Lodge.** The gardens and tree-lined lake by this country home are the first things to impress. The next is the hospitality of hosts Zona and Charles Averill, which a quick glance at the visitors' book will confirm. You can join the Averills for dinner (most choose to) or eat alone—either way this is a great place to relax and sample New Zealand wine and delicious country cuisine. Wineries are easy to get to, and farm walks, cross-country horse riding, even expeditions to see freshwater eels are among the lodge's farm-related activities. Evenings you can relax in the sitting room—and contemplate, if not play, the Mason and Hamlin organ. Furniture and fittings in the rooms tend to wear classic British creams, greens, and burgundies. Rates include meals, predinner drinks, and wine at dinner. The lodge is 17 km (11 mi) west of Gisborne. ⊠ *Taurau Valley Rd., Manutuke,* ☎ *06/862– 8764,* FAX *06/862–8786. 6 rooms. Pool. MC, V.*

$$$–$$$$ ✕🏠 **Acton Estate.** Lisa and Andrew Tauber's transformation of Acton into one of the finest boutique lodges in the country included finding its dining room table—once in residence at Lupbrook Hall in England—at a Sydney auction house and rescuing a writing desk and chair for one room from a schooner built in 1902. Rooms vary in size and price; two have private bathrooms down the hall. There is a charming cottage at the back of the main house; the Grand Master Room has a French cherry-wood bed covered in luxurious Italian linen. Hosts James (who doubles as chef) and Jenni Reddington add their friendly and efficient touches. Even though the four-course evening meal is not included in the tariff (breakfast *is*), Acton is still priced below other comparable lodges around the country. ⊠ *577 Back Ormond Rd., Gisborne,* ☎ *06/867–9999,* FAX *06/867–1116. 6 rooms. Dining room, tennis court, billiards. AE, DC, MC, V. BP.*

$$ ✕🏠 **Waiatai Valley Farmstays.** Sophia Ross's Cordon Bleu training makes Waiatai stand apart from the usual Kiwi homestay. She can deliver anything from Thai red curry chicken to lamb shanks Romarin over to the two farm cottages across the road from where she lives with her farmer husband, John. If you want to sample local seafood, or bantam eggs from the farm, just ask. Rooms have large windows looking out to the farm, wooden bedsteads with white bedspreads, wooden chests

of drawers, wardrobe space, and kitchen facilities—plain, perhaps, but with fantastic sunrises and sunsets. This is a working farm, so sheep come right up to the balcony. Local bird life abounds, and trout fishing and bushwalks are all easily accessible. Lunch and dinner are available for an additional cost. The farm is an hour southwest of Gisborne, or just 10 minutes from Wairoa town. ✉ *Pirinoa Station, 418 Waiatai Valley Rd., R.D. 6, Wairoa,* ☎ *06/837–7552,* 🖷 *06/837–7409. 2 cottages (1 with kitchen). No credit cards. BP.*

$$$ 🛏 **Tunanui Station Cottages.** Tunanui Station is a 3,000-acre sheep and cattle station, and the road here from Gisborne (an hour to the north) winds through Eastland's hill country before it takes you past some of the most spectacular coastal views in the country. Hosts Leslie and Ray Thompson provide accommodation in either a 90-year-old restored cottage or a farmhouse. The cottage has more historic charm, including a lovely kauri table in the hallway made by a local craftsman and rimu tongue-and-groove flooring. The farmhouse has more room and better views over the Mahia peninsula. Both have kitchen facilities, so bring food for cooking on-site. You can also arrange to have breakfast ($12) and dinner ($40) at the owners' nearby home. Ray Thompson will take experienced horseback riders out onto the station to see the farm at work. ✉ *1001 Tunanui Rd., Opoutama, Mahia,* ☎ *06/837–5790,* 🖷 *06/837–5797. 3-bedroom cottage, 4-bedroom farmhouse. Dining room, kitchenettes. No credit cards.*

Outdoor Activities and Sports

FISHING

Albacore, yellowfin tuna, mako sharks, and marlin are all prized catches off the East Cape from January to April. Fishing operators include **Tolaga Bay East Cape Charters** (☎ 06/862–6715), in Tolaga Bay, just north of Gisborne, whose skipper, Bert Lee, has had more than 35 years' experience in recreational fishing. **Surfit Boat Charters** (☎ 06/867–2970) is based in Gisborne. Fishing trips start at $90 per person.

JET BOATING

Motu River Jet Boat Tours (☎ 07/315–8107), based in Opotiki—147 km (92 mi) from Gisborne—combines the thrills and spills of speeding along the river with the opportunity to learn about the ecology and history of the region. The trip lasts about two hours and costs $85. **Eastland Jet Boats** (☎ 06/868–4454) operates out of Gisborne itself, and provides transfers to the start of their exciting trips.

Gisborne–Opotiki Loop

Soak in the beauty and remoteness of Eastland driving the loop between Gisborne and Opotiki, the northwest anchor of the East Cape. Rolling green hills drop into wide crescent beaches or rock-strewn coves. Small towns appear here and there along the route, only to fade into the surrounding landscape. It is one of the country's ultimate roads less traveled. Some scenic highlights are **Anaura Bay,** with rocky headlands, a long beach favored by surfers, and offshore islands; it is between **Tolaga Bay** and **Tokomaru Bay,** two former shipping towns. Tolaga Bay has an incredibly long wharf stretching over a beach into the sea, and Cooks Cove Walkway is a pleasant amble (two-hour round-trip) through the countryside past a rock arch. In **Tikitiki** farther up the coast, an Anglican Church is full of carved Maori panels and beams. Tikitiki has a gas station.

East of the small town of **Te Araroa,** which has the oldest *pohutukawa* (po-hoo-too-*ka*-wa) tree in the country, the coast is about as remote as you could imagine. At the tip of the cape (21 km, or 13 mi, from Te Araroa), the **East Cape Lighthouse** and fantastic views are a long steep climb from the beach. **Hicks Bay** has another long beach. Back toward Opotiki, **Whanarua** (fahn-ah-*roo*-ah) **Bay** is one of the most beautiful on the East Cape, with isolated beaches ideal for a picnic and a swim. Farther on, there is an intricately carved Maori marae (meetinghouse) called Tukaki in **Te Kaha.**

If you plan to take your time along the way, inquire at the **Gisborne–Eastland Visitor Information Centre** (☞ Contacts and Resources *in* Gisborne and Eastland A to Z, *below*) about lodging. There are motel accommodations at various points on the cape, and some superbly sited motor camps (☞ Motor Camps *in* Lodging *in* Smart Travel Tips A to Z) and backpackers' lodges, though you'll need to be well stocked with foodstuffs before you set off. Driving time on the loop—about 330 km (205 mi)—is about five hours without stops. You can, of course, drive the loop the other way—from Opotiki around the cape to Gisborne: to get to Opotiki from the north, take Highway 2 from Tauranga and the Bay of Plenty.

Te Urewera National Park

③⓪ *163 km (101 mi) west of Gisborne.*

Te Urewera National Park is a vast, remote region of forests and lakes straddling the Huiarau Range. The park's outstanding feature is the glorious **Lake Waikaremoana** (sea of rippling waters), a forest-girded lake with good swimming, boating, and fishing. The lake is circled by a 50-km (31-mi) walking track; the three- to four-day walk is popular, and in the summer months the lakeside tramping huts are often heavily used. For information about this route, call in at the **Department of Conservation Visitor Centre** (☎ 06/837–3803) at Aniwaniwa, on the eastern arm of Lake Waikaremoana. You'll be able to pick up walking leaflets and maps, and ask advice about the many other shorter walks in the park, like that to the **Aniwaniwa Falls** (30 minutes roundtrip) or to **Lake Waikareiti** (five–six hours round-trip). The motor camp on the lakeshore, not far from the visitor center, has cabins, chalets, and motel units. In summer a launch operates sightseeing and fishing trips from the motor camp. Access to the park is from Wairoa, 100 km (62 mi) southwest of Gisborne down Highway 2. It's then another 63 km (39 mi) from Wairoa along Highway 38 to Lake Waikaremoana.

Gisborne and Eastland A to Z

Arriving and Departing

BY BUS

There's one bus service a day to Gisborne with **Newmans and InterCity** (☎ 09/913–6100) from either Auckland, via Rotorua, or from Wellington, via Napier.

BY CAR

Gisborne is a long way from almost anywhere, though the coastal and bush scenery along the way makes the drive wholly worthwhile. The most direct route from the north is to follow State Highway 2 around the Bay of Plenty (☞ Chapter 1) to Opotiki, Eastland's northern gateway, then continue to Gisborne through the Waioeka Gorge Scenic Reserve. The drive from Auckland to Gisborne takes seven hours. South from Gisborne, you will pass through Wairoa, about 90 minutes away, before passing Napier, Hawke's Bay, and Wairarapa on the way to Wellington, about 7½ hours by car.

BY PLANE
Air New Zealand Link (☎ 0800/737–000) flies daily to Gisborne from Auckland and Wellington.

Contacts and Resources

EMERGENCIES
Dial 111 for **fire, police, and ambulance** services.

VISITOR INFORMATION
The **Gisborne–Eastland Visitor Information Centre** is easily identifiable by the Canadian totem pole next door. ⊠ *209 Grey St., Gisborne,* ☎ *06/868–6139,* 𝖥𝖠𝖷 *06/868–6138.* ⊙ *Daily 9–5:30.*

NEW PLYMOUTH AND TARANAKI

On a clear winter day, with a cover of snow, Mt. Taranaki (its Maori name; Mt. Egmont is its English moniker) towers above its flat rural surroundings and seems to draw the sky right down to the sea. No less astonishing in other seasons, the solitary peak is similar in appearance to Japan's Mt. Fuji. It is the icon of the Taranaki region, and the province has shaped itself around the mountain. Northeast of Taranaki, the provincial seat of New Plymouth huddles between the monolith and a rugged coastline, and smaller towns dot the road that circles the mountain's base. For visitors, the Taranaki mountain and the national park that surrounds it, known as Egmont National Park, is often the center of attention. You can hike up it and around it, ski on it (for a short period), stay the night on it, and dine at restaurants on its flanks.

The Taranaki region is one of the most successful agricultural areas in the country because of layers of volcanic ash that have created superb free-draining topsoil, and a mountainous coastal position that ensures abundant rainfall. What serves farmers serves gardeners as well. Some of the country's most magnificent gardens grow in the rich local soil, and the annual Rhododendron Festival held late in the year celebrates the area's horticultural excellence.

Taranaki has plenty of other ground-level delights, too. By the water's edge—along the so-called Surf Highway (Highway 45)—you can surf, swim, and fish, and several museums delve into Taranaki history, which is particularly rich on the subject of the Maori. You could take in most of the area in a couple of days, but that will keep you on the run. Just getting from place to place around the mountain takes time. Most people use New Plymouth as a base, though Stratford also has comfortable accommodations, and there are B&Bs, motels, and motor camps spread throughout the region.

The weather is constantly in flux—locals say that if you can't see Mt. Taranaki it's raining, and if you can it's going to rain. Day in and day out, this meteorological mix makes for stunning contrasts of sun and clouds on and around the mountain.

New Plymouth

③① *375 km (235 mi) south of Auckland, 190 km (120 mi) southwest of Waitomo, 163 (102 mi) northwest of Wanganui.*

New Plymouth is a center both for one of New Zealand's most productive dairy regions and the nation's gas and oil industries. This natural wealth means that even when New Zealand's economy is in hard times, the people of New Plymouth retain a sense of optimism. Prior to the arrival of Europeans in 1841, several Maori pa (fortified villages) were in the vicinity. In the mid-1800s, Maori-European land disputes racked Taranaki, and open war broke out in New Plymouth in 1860. Formal peace between the government and Maori was made in 1881, after which New Plymouth began to form its current identity. Today's city is second-best to its surroundings, but its few surviving colonial buildings and serene parkland are well worth half a day's exploration. The cafés and stores along the main drag, Devon Street (East and West), provide as cosmopolitan an experience as you'll find this far west.

The jewels of New Plymouth are most definitely **Pukekura Park** and the connected **Brooklands Park**, whose valley lawns, lakes, groves, and woodland lend real character to the city. Pukekura has water running throughout, and it's a real pleasure to hire a rowboat (from near the lakeside teahouse) and explore the small islands and nooks and crannies of the main lake. The park also has a fernery—caverns carved out of the hillside that connect through fern-cloaked tunnels—and botanical display houses, whose flowering plant collections are some of the most extensive in the country.

Brooklands was once a great estate, laid out in 1843 around the house of Captain Henry King, New Plymouth's first magistrate. During the land wars of the 1860s local Maori burned down the manor house, and the brick fireplace is all that remains of it, standing alone in the sweeping lawns among trees. Today, Brooklands is best known for its amazing variety of trees, mostly planted in the second half of the 19th century. There are giant copper beeches, pines, walnuts, and oaks, and the Monterey pine, magnolia *soulangeana*, ginkgo, and native *karaka* and *kohekohe* are all the largest of their kind in New Zealand. Take a walk along the outskirts of the park on tracks leading through native, subtropical bush. This area has been relatively untouched for the last few thousand years, and 1,500-year-old trees are not uncommon. A *puriri* tree near the Somerset Street entrance—one of 20 in the park—is believed to be more than 2,000 years old.

For a reminder of colonial days, visit Brookland's former hospital, the **Gables**, built in 1847, which now serves as an art gallery and medical museum. The adjacent zoo is an old-fashioned example of how to keep birds and animals, but it is still a favorite of children. Brooklands has a rhododendron dell and a stadium used for a variety of entertainment throughout the year. ⊠ *Park entrances on Brooklands Park Ave. and Liardet, Somerset, and Rogan Sts.,* ☎ *06/759-6060.* ☜ *Free.* ☉ *Daily dawn–dusk; teahouse July–May, Wed.–Mon. dawn–dusk; display houses daily 8–4; tours by appointment.*

Taranaki Museum, founded in 1847, is the second oldest in New Zealand. The museum cares for a large number of *Taonga* (Maori treasures) that are associated with various *iwi* (tribes). Also of interest is a diverse collection of colonial items, many of which date from the earliest years of European settlement. ⊠ *Ariki and Egmont Sts.,* ☎ *06/758-9583.* ☜ *Free.* ☉ *Weekdays 10:30–4:30, weekends 1–5.*

The Queen Elizabeth II National Trust is a publicly funded organization established to conserve privately held native landscapes. The two New Zealand gardens in the trust are in Taranaki: in New Plymouth, **Tupare,** and south of the mountain in Kaponga, **Hollard Gardens** (☞ Egmont National Park, *below*).

Complete with Tudor-style houses, Tupare is truly an English-style garden. Built in 1927, the estate of Sir Russell and Lady Matthews sits on a steep hillside that plunges down to the rushing Waiwhakaiho (why-fah-kye-ho) River. Russell Matthews, a road-building contractor, cleverly enlisted his crew during the off-season to build the impressive terraces, garden walls, and pools that define Tupare. Many varieties of maple trees have been planted, along with a grand tulip tree, cherries and magnolias, and a stand of native rimu pine. There are numerous rhododendrons and azaleas, to be expected in Taranaki, with underplantings of hellebores, daffodils, and bluebells, creating a glorious floral vision in spring. Tupare is also noted for its autumnal foliage display. ⊠ *487 Mangorei Rd.,* ☎ *06/758–6480.* ☜ *$5.* ☉ *Sept.–Mar., daily 9–5; Apr.–Aug., by appointment only. Some paths may be closed in winter for maintenance.*

On the western outskirts of New Plymouth, the world-renowned
★ **Pukeiti Rhododendron Trust** scenically spreads over 900 acres of lush native rain forest adjacent to Egmont National Park on the northwest slope of the mountain. The Pukeiti (poo-kay-*ee*-tee) collection of 2,500 hybrid and species rhododendrons is the largest in New Zealand. Many of these varieties were first grown here, like the giant winter-blooming *R. protistum var. giganteum* Pukeiti, collected from seed in 1953 and now standing 15 ft tall—or the beautiful Lemon Lodge and Spring Honey hybrids that bloom in spring. Kyawi, a large red rhodie, is the very last to bloom, in April (autumn). Rhododendrons aside, there are many other rare and special plants to enjoy at Pukeiti. All winter long the Himalayan daphnes fragrance the pathways. Spring- to summer-growing candelabra primroses can reach up to 4 ft, and for a month around Christmas spectacular 8-ft Himalayan *cardiocrinum* lilies bear heavenly scented 12-inch white trumpet flowers. Even if you're not an avid gardener, walking the paths that wind throughout the vast gardens and surrounding native bush is a delight. This is a wonderful bird habitat, so keep your eyes and ears open for them, too. Pukeiti is 20 km (12½ mi) southwest of New Plymouth center. ⊠ *2290 Carrington Rd.,* ☎ *06/752–4141,* 𝔽𝔸𝕏 *06/752–4151.* ☜ *$6.* ☉ *Oct.–Mar., daily 9–5; Apr.–Sept., daily 10–3.*

To get a shadowy feeling for part of the Maori past in New Plymouth, pay a visit to **Koru Pa,** the former stronghold of the Nga Mahanga a Tairi *hapu* (subtribe) of the Taranaki iwi. The bush has taken it back in large measure, but you can still make out the main defensive ditch and stonewalled terraces that drop a considerable way from the highest part of the pa, where chiefs lived, down to the Oakura River. Part of the reserve has a picnic site. Take Highway 45 southwest out of New Plymouth to the beach suburb of Oakura, 17 km (10 mi) away, and turn left onto Wairau Road. Take it to Surrey Hills Road, where another left will take you to the pa (fortified village) site.

OFF THE
BEATEN PATH

TARANAKI-WAITOMO – Mt. Taranaki is an ever-receding presence in your rear-view mirror as you head northeast up the Taranaki coast from New Plymouth on Highway 3. The highway provides the most direct route to Waitomo Caves and Hamilton, turning inland at Awakino, 90 km (56 mi) from New Plymouth. The Awakino Gorge, between Mahoenui and the coast, is breathtaking. Sheep have worn trails that seem to hang on the sides of precipitous green hills that are broken here and there with marvelous limestone outcrops. From Awakino, you could be in Waitomo within the hour if you stick to the main highway, but a far more enjoyable route is to follow the minor road north, at the turnoff just beyond Awakino. This runs for 58 km (36 mi) to Marokopa (☞ Waitomo Caves *in* the Waikato and Waitomo, *above*). It's a gravel road for the most part but a reasonable trip provided you take care. The drive is through attractive sheep country, passing through the Manganui Gorge, and with a possible 4-km (2½-mi) detour down the Waikawau Road to the stunningly isolated Waikawau Beach. The sweep of black sand here, backed by high cliffs, is reached through a hand-dug drover's tunnel.

ONE LAST TRAVEL TIP:

Pack an easy way to reach the world.

123 456 7891 2345
J.D. SMITH

Wherever you travel, the MCI WorldCom Card℠ is the easiest way to stay in touch. You can use it to call to and from more than 125 countries worldwide. And you can earn bonus miles every time you use your card. So go ahead, travel the world. MCI WorldCom℠ makes it even more rewarding. For additional access codes, visit **www.wcom.com/worldphone.**

MCI WORLDCOM.

EASY TO CALL WORLDWIDE

1. Just dial the WorldPhone® access number of the country you're calling from.

2. Dial or give the operator your MCI WorldCom Card number.

3. Dial or give the number you're calling.

Aruba (A) ⊹	800-888-8
Australia ◆	1-800-881-100
Bahamas ⊹	1-800-888-8000
Barbados (A) ⊹	1-800-888-8000
Bermuda ⊹	1-800-888-8000
British Virgin Islands (A) ⊹	1-800-888-8000
Canada	1-800-888-8000
Costa Rica (A) ◆	0800-012-2222
New Zealand	000-912
Puerto Rico	1-800-888-8000
United States	1-800-888-8000
U.S. Virgin Islands	1-800-888-8000

(A) Calls back to U.S. only. ⊹ Limited availability. ◆ Public phones may require deposit of coin or phone card for dial tone.

EARN FREQUENT FLIER MILES

AmericanAirlines®
AAdvantage®

CHINA AIRLINES

▲ Delta Air Lines
SkyMiles®

TWA®

/// UNITED
Mileage Plus®

≡ U.S. AIRWAYS
DIVIDEND MILES

Bureau de change

Cambio

外国為替

In this city, you can find money on almost any street.

NO-FEE FOREIGN EXCHANGE

The Chase Manhattan Bank has over 80 convenient
locations near New York City destinations such as:
    Times Square
    Rockefeller Center
    Empire State Building
    2 World Trade Center
    United Nations Plaza
Exchange any of 75 foreign currencies

◑ CHASE

THE RIGHT RELATIONSHIP IS EVERYTHING.®

Total driving time from Awakino to Marokopa, including a picnic stop, is around three hours, plus another hour from Marokopa to Waitomo.

Dining and Lodging

$$–$$$ ✕ **André L'Escargot Restaurant and Bar.** Considered by both locals and visitors to be the finest restaurant in New Plymouth, L'Escargot focuses on classic southern French preparations, serving lighter worldbeat dishes as well. Dine inside New Plymouth's oldest commercial building on such delights as lamb racks stuffed with beets and mashed zucchini, or go traditional with osso buco or *pissaladière,* a southern French tart of onions, eggplant, bell pepper, olives, and anchovies. Desserts look to Europe for their inspiration. ⊠ *37–43 Brougham St.,* ☎ *06/758–4812. AE, DC, MC, V.*

$$–$$$ ✕ **Steps Restaurant.** The thoroughly pleasant old-house atmosphere
★ in this cozy 30-seater will get you out of the travel-meal rut while you're in the Taranaki region. Lunches are thoroughly relaxed, with downhome, friendly service and a mixture of classical and mod dishes that use mostly local produce. Evenings are more upscale, the welcome is just as genuine, and you can tuck into the likes of freshly caught fish on ratatouille with saffron beurre blanc, or the restaurant's wonderful seafood bisque. The wine list is well priced. In fine weather, ask for a table in the courtyard. ⊠ *37 Gover St., New Plymouth,* ☎ *06/758–3393. AE, DC, MC, V. Licensed and BYOB. Closed Sun.–Mon. No lunch Sat.*

$–$$ ✕ **Macfarlane's Caffe.** One of the new generation of New Zealand restaurants—friendly, ambitious, casual, and looking around the world for influences—Macfarlane's does its best to liven up the dining scene in the town of Inglewood, midway between New Plymouth and Stratford. Traditional farm-style breakfasts, lunches of Caesar salad or attractively assembled sandwiches, and dinner entrées like pork fillet on chunky potatoes with wok-fried vegetables, are persuasively prepared and pleasantly delivered. New Zealand wine and beer are in abundance. ⊠ *Kelly and Matai Sts., Inglewood,* ☎ *06/756–6665. AE, DC, MC, V.*

$$–$$$ 🛏 **Henwood House.** This century-old B&B occupies a homestead that has been completely refurbished and refined by architect Graeme Axten and his wife, Lynne. The two play the role of charming hosts to the likes of the British high commissioner in New Zealand (who recommends the place, if you'd like to know), but the rates make Henwood House accessible not only to heads of state. There is a variety of rooms, including one with a balcony and fireplace. The property is 6 km (4 mi) from town, and it is extremely peaceful. Breakfast is served in the country-style kitchen each morning, and you'll find it easy to relax in the rather grand guest lounge evenings. ⊠ *314 Henwood Rd, New Plymouth,* ☎ 𝙵𝙰𝚇 *06/755–1212. 5 rooms, 3 with bath. AE, MC, V. BP.*

$$ 🛏 **Devon Hotel.** This salmon-pink hotel is easy to find, just a short drive (or 20-minute walk) north of the city center. The smaller economy rooms don't enjoy a lot of space, but do look over a pretty internal courtyard; the larger, regular rooms are better equipped (with refrigerators and minibars) and have either sea or mountain views, though those at the front face on to a busy main road. Hotel guests may use facilities at a nearby health club. ⊠ *390 Devon St. E,* ☎ *06/759–9099,* 𝙵𝙰𝚇 *06/758–2229. 100 rooms. Restaurant, bar, pool. AE, DC, MC, V.*

Outdoor Activities and Sports

BEACHES

Some of the coastal waters can be quite wild, so it's wise to swim at patrolled beaches. **Fitzroy Beach** has lifeguards in summer and is easily accessible from New Plymouth. **East End Beach** also has lifeguards.

Ngamotu Beach, along Ocean View Parade, is calm and suitable for young children. And not for nothing is the road around the coast between New Plymouth and Hawera known as the **Surf Highway**—virtually any beach en route has consistently good waves. Fitzroy and East End are both popular with surfers, as are **Back Beach** and **Bell Block,** though the favored surf beach by those in-the-know is that at **Oakura,** 17 km (10 mi) southwest of town.

BOATING

Happy Chaddy's Charters' launch starts with the guide announcing, "Hold on to your knickers, because we're about to take off"—then the old English lifeboat rocks back and forth in its shed (with you onboard), slides down its rails, and hits the sea with a spray of water. The trip lasts an hour, during which time you'll see seals and get a close-up view of the Sugar Loaf Islands just offshore from New Plymouth. ⊠ *Ocean View Parade, New Plymouth,* ☎ *06/758–9133.* ☜ *$20, chartered fishing trip $10 per person per hr (minimum 8 people).*

Egmont National Park

🕸 *North Egmont Visitor Centre 26 km (16 mi) south of New Plymouth; Dawson Falls Visitor Centre 68 km (42 mi) southwest of New Plymouth*

Stately **Mt. Taranaki** rises 8,309 ft right out of the sea, and if you spend any more than a few hours in the vicinity, it is difficult not to be drawn toward it. The lower reaches are cloaked in magical subtropical forests; above the tree line lower vegetation allows you to look out over the paddocks and seascape below. The mountain is surrounded, and protected, by **Egmont National Park,** which wraps itself in a circle around the flanks of Taranaki. The three main roads to the mountain turn off State Highway 3 and are all well signposted. The first, as you drive south from New Plymouth, is Egmont Road and leads to the **North Egmont Visitor Centre** (⊠ Egmont Rd., ☎ 06/756–0990), where it's worth dropping in to learn something about the mountain and its lush vegetation. The second road up the mountain (Pembroke Rd.) takes you to the Mountain House and, a little farther on, to **Stratford Plateau,** the mountain's ski slope, from which there are some stunning views. The third road (Manaia Rd.) leads to the southernmost **Dawson Falls Visitor Centre** (⊠ Manaia Rd., ☎ 025/430–248).

There are signposted local walks of varying difficulty from each of the three main mountain areas. For just a taste of the scenery, the best short walks are from the Dawson Falls Visitor Centre, where there are five popular routes—taking 1–2½ hours—including the forest tramp (one-hour round-trip) to the 50-ft-high **Dawson Falls** themselves. Ascents to the summit of Mt. Taranaki are also achieved relatively easily in summer, from either Dawson Falls or North Egmont visitor centers, and take anything from seven to 10 hours round-trip. You must be properly equipped and let the visitor centers know in advance of your intentions. If you are really serious about getting out and striding, consider taking from three to five days to walk around the entire mountain. The circuit is well signposted, and there are accommodation huts at one-day intervals along the way, the cost for which is usually $10 for adults per night. There are also budget bunkhouses ($15 per night) at Dawson Falls and North Egmont. Advance bookings for all hiking accommodation is essential; contact the visitor centers.

★ Surrounded by dairy farms, **Hollard Gardens,** near the southern entrance to Egmont National Park, was conceived in 1927 when Bernard and Rose Hollard sectioned off a piece of their land and started building the impressive collection of plants now under the care of the Queen

Elizabeth II National Trust. The 14-acre garden was created in two stages: the old garden, dating from 1927, is a woodland area with narrow, winding paths, intensely planted with rhododendrons, azaleas, camellias, and other related plants. The broad lawns, paths, and mixed borders of the new garden, established in 1982, contain a comprehensive blend of exotics and natives. Brochures at the information shelter detail two self-guided walking tours and help locate some of the treasures.

The main season for flowering is from September through March. Hollard Gardens are 8 km (5 mi) south of Dawson Falls. ⊠ *Upper Manaia Rd. off Opunake Rd., Kaponga,* ☏ *06/764–6544.* ⌨ *$5.* ☉ *Sept.– Mar., daily 9–5; Apr.–Aug., by appointment only.*

Dining and Lodging

$$$ ✕⛺ **Dawson Falls Lodge.** The most delightful accommodation in the region, with a touch of eccentricity, Dawson Falls has been styled on a Swiss alpine lodge. Each room has its own character and touches, with carved, painted headboards on the beds and wood paneling throughout, and the lodge is decorated with skis and other alpine collectibles. Breakfast and dinner are served in the restaurant. During the evening enjoy hearty home-cooked fare, such as medallion of beef with a rosemary jus or oven-baked chicken with an herb crust. The lodge stands on the south side of Mt. Taranaki (23 km/14 mi from Stratford), about halfway up and very near the visitor center. Request a room with a view up the mountain. ⊠ *Manaia Rd. off Opunake Rd., Dawson Falls,* ☏ ⟨FAX⟩ *06/765–5457. 11 rooms. Restaurant, bar, lounge. AE, DC, MC, V.*

$$ ✕⛺ **Mountain House Motor Lodge.** The best lodging on the east side of Mt. Taranaki is the wonderfully sited Mountain House. Trails from the building ascend the lower reaches of the mountain; in winter a T-bar lift from the lodge takes you to the base of the ski slopes. Hosts Keith and Bertha (*ber*-ta) Anderson preside over a series of simple motel-style rooms, six of which stand apart from the main building and are equipped with kitchenettes. What really makes Mountain House stand out is the restaurant, where meals are a marriage of Bertha Anderson's Swiss upbringing and delicious New Zealand produce. Seasonal whitebait fritters make great starters and entrées may include roast lamb, lean venison with a pepper wine sauce, or even kangaroo fillet. Apple strudel and cream is a scrumptious way to wrap up the alpine meal. ⊠ *Pembroke Rd., Stratford,* ☏ ⟨FAX⟩ *06/765–6100. 10 rooms. Restaurant, bar, kitchenettes (some), sauna. AE, DC, MC, V.* ❧

$$ ⛺ **Anderson's Alpine Residence.** The latest venture for the Anderson's (☞ *above*) is this smart but cozy B&B lodge, 5 km (3 mi) back down the road from the Mountain House. Just three rooms are available, including the deluxe Top Room which has glorious mountain views from a separate lounge area. The lodge sits in its own native bush and has a log staircase, wood-burning fire, and wooden deck; the walls are decorated with Keith Anderson's paintings of Taranaki. Dinner can be arranged at the Mountain House. ⊠ *922 Pembroke Rd., Stratford,* ☏ *06/765–6620,* ⟨FAX⟩ *06/765–6100. 3 rooms. AE, DC, MC, V. CP.* ❧

Stratford

③③ *41 km (27 mi) southeast of New Plymouth.*

Stratford is the main town on the eastern side of Mt. Taranaki, and the principal supply base for the mountain. It's fairly unremarkable, but as it sits at the junction of Highways 3 and 43 you're more than likely to pass through at some stage during any exploration of Taranaki. Its shops and food stores will give you a local sense of New Zealand's agricultural life and in the valley to the east are some of the country's most interesting private gardens.

Of all the gardens in New Zealand, the one you'll most likely want to
★ return to is **Aramaunga** (path between the mountains), whether to see the garden itself or Gwyn Masters, its presiding sage and sprightly creator. A garden is surely a reflection of its maker, and Mrs. Masters has over the last 50 years transformed a farm paddock into a garden with a personality to match her own. Most visitors comment on the wisteria, from the century-old specimen on the front of the cottage to other wisteria that's been encouraged to climb into the treetops along with various clematis species to throw bursts of color where it is least expected.

Garden beds are filled with masses of color and form that mix beautifully: rhododendrons (ask to see the true red Gwynneth Masters hybrid that she developed from seed), azalea mollis, magnolias, cherries, and Japanese maples, along with interesting pottery and herbaceous plants that include lots of self-seeded columbine. Bridges crossing a flower-ringed pond connect with woodland on the opposite shore, where there's a glorious view back across the water, gardens, and cottage. Aramaunga is open to the public by appointment; there is a small entry fee. ☒ *669 Beaconsfield Rd., Stratford,* ☎ *06/765–7600.*

OFF THE BEATEN PATH	**STRATFORD–TAUMARUNUI** – Highway 43, heading northeast from Stratford, gives a real glimpse of the rural heart of New Zealand, winding through high farmland on the way to Taumarunui (the northern access point for the Wanganui river region). It's 145 km (90 mi), a three- to four-hour trip, nearly all on a paved, though narrow, road: fill up with gas in Stratford before you set off. Highlights on the way include the Kaieto Café, a scenically sited rest stop halfway along, on top of the Tahora saddle; and, starting just after Tahora, the dramatic, lush Tangarakau Gorge. The gorge is the only gravel section of the road—21 km (12 mi) of slow driving.

Lodging

$$ 🏠 **Te Popo.** Tucked away on a back road northeast of Stratford, this peaceful, Spanish-style homestead is set in 6 acres of lovingly tended gardens. Tuis, wood pigeons, bellbirds, and fantails visit the gardens year-round; and you can see glowworms at dusk. Rooms have plenty of natural light, and the colorful furnishings work well with the outside surroundings. Rates include breakfast, served in a sunny conservatory; dinner is available by separate arrangement. Te Popo is a 15-minute drive from Stratford town on good country roads. You can visit the gardens separately (October–April, Thursday–Sunday 10–5; $3), but it's well worth staying the night. ☒ *636 Stanley Rd., Midhirst, R.D. 24, Stratford,* ☎ 🖷 *06/762–8775. 3 rooms. MC, V. BP.*

Hawera

③④ *29 km (18 mi) south of Stratford.*

An undistinguished farming and local service center, Hawera doesn't grab the attention of passersby save for its one unique museum attraction.

The **Tawhiti Museum** is a labor of love for Nigel Ogle, who bought an old cheese factory in 1975 and proceeded to fill it up with life-size figures from Taranaki's past. He creates the fiberglass figures from molds of local people, giving them a far more lifelike look than those in other museums. You may get a chance to watch Nigel at work, or discuss regional history with him. On the first Sunday of each month, the museum's Tawhiti Bush Railway springs into life, rattling through a variety of outdoor displays that highlight the historical logging operations in Taranaki. Take Onhangai Road southeast out of Normanby, or Tawhiti Road northeast out of Hawera, and continue 4 km (2½ mi) to the museum. ✉ *401 Ohangai Rd., Hawera,* ☎ *06/278–6837.* ✉ *$5.* ⊙ *Sept.–Dec. and Feb.–May, Fri.–Mon. 10–4; Jan., daily 10–4; June–Aug., Sun. 10–4.*

Just up the road from the Tawhiti Museum, the astonishing **Turuturumokai Pa** is one of the most impressive Maori citadels in the province. Defense ditches and walls ring the former village, and the top is pocked with storage pits. ✉ *Turuturu Rd. near Ohangai Rd., Hawera.* ✉ *Free.* ⊙ *Dawn–dusk.*

New Plymouth and Taranaki A to Z

Arriving and Departing

BY BUS

New Plymouth is served daily by **Newmans** and **InterCity** (☎ 09/913–6100) buses from Auckland, via Hamilton, and Wellington, via Wanganui, Hawera, and Stratford. Buses arrive at and depart from the New Plymouth Travel Centre (☎ 06/759–9039) on Queen Street. There is no public transportation to Mt. Taranaki, though there are private shuttlebus services to destinations like North Egmont Visitor Centre (☞ *below*) or Stratford Mountain House—call the Travel Centre for details.

BY CAR

New Plymouth looks well out of the way on the map, but it is only 4½ hours from Auckland, and 6 hours from Wellington. From the north, head to Te Kuiti near Waitomo caves, then simply continue on State Highway 3. Leaving Taranaki heading south, take State Highway 3 to the next main center, Wanganui. Staying on Highway 3, keep traveling to Sanson, where you have the option of heading east—still on Highway 3—through Palmerston North, the Manawatu Gorge, and on to the Wairarapa region; or following State Highway 1 down the West Coast to Wellington.

BY PLANE

Air New Zealand (☎ 0800/737–000) operates flights seven times daily between Auckland and New Plymouth and five times daily into Wellington.

Contacts and Resources

EMERGENCIES

Dial 111 for **fire, police, and ambulance** services.

GUIDED TOURS

Taranaki Scenic Flights' most popular tour is to the snowcapped summit of Mt. Taranaki and over Egmont National Park. You can also take a trip along the coastline, around the city, or out to the Maui offshore gas field. ✉ *New Plymouth Airport,* ☎ *06/755–0500.*

VISITOR INFORMATION

Dawson Falls Visitor Centre. ✉ *Manaia Rd., Dawson Falls,* ☎ *025/430–248.* ⊙ *Mid-Nov.–Feb., daily 9–4:30; Mar.–mid-Nov., Wed–Sun. 9–4:30.*

New Plymouth Information Centre. ✉ *Leach and Liardet Sts., New Plymouth,* ☎ *06/759–6080.* ⊙ *Weekdays 8:30–5, weekends 10–3.*

North Egmont Visitor Centre. ✉ *Egmont Rd., Egmont Village,* ☎ *06/756–0990.* ⊙ *Oct.–Mar., daily 9–4; Apr.–Sept., Wed.–Sun. 9–4.*

Stratford Information Centre. ✉ *Broadway South and Miranda St., Stratford,* ☎ *06/765–6708.* ⊙ *Weekdays 8:30–5, weekends 10–3:30.*

WANGANUI AND THE WHANGANUI RIVER

The attractive river town of Wanganui marks the starting-point of one of the North Island's most distinctive, yet unsung, journeys—following the historic trail that lies along the slow-moving Whanganui River, the longest navigable waterway in the country (as opposed to the Waikato, which is the longest river). You'll need to put aside time to make the trip, since this is not country you can rush through, especially if you plan to kayak in, or tramp around, the middle section of the river, which is encompassed by the isolated Whanganui National Park. Three days gives you enough leeway to see the best of the river and park, though even with just a day to spare you can visit the historic settlements along the meandering Whanganui River Road, which winds alongside the river from Wanganui.

Note: The town is Wanganui, and the river, region, and national park are Whanganui (with an "h") The difference is the result of an ongoing debate over Maori and European influence in the region. Just to confuse the issue further, both are pronounced the same—local Maori don't pronounce "wh" as "fa," as is the case elsewhere in New Zealand.

Wanganui

㉟ *163 km (102 mi) southeast of New Plymouth, 193 km (121 mi) north of Wellington, 225 km (141 mi) southwest of Taupo.*

Local Maori trace their occupation of the land around the Whanganui River back as far as the 10th century AD. With the European settlement of the garrison town of Wanganui in 1840, and subsequent appropriation of much of the land, conflict was inevitable. Land rights have always been an issue here, though today's town is making a determined effort to put past troubles behind it. Set on the banks of the Whanganui River, the compact town center shows off a series of revitalized streets and heritage buildings that hark back to colonial times and trading days. A stroll along Victoria Avenue, with its Victorian gaslights, wrought-iron seats, and avenue of palm and plane trees, gives you a pretty good idea of the whole. In summer (December–March), a profusion of hanging baskets and window boxes enhance its appeal.

For an overview of the Maori history, drop into the **Whanganui Regional Museum,** by Queens Park, which contains some wonderful *waka* (canoes), as well as Maori carvings, decorative ornaments, cloaks of kiwi feathers, greenstone clubs, tools, bone flutes, and ceremonial portraits. The museum also re-creates the 19th-century town in a series of traditional shop windows, filled with relics and curios. ✉ *Watt St.,* ☎ *06/345–7443.* ✆ *$2.* ☉ *Mon.–Sat. 10–4:30, Sun. 1–4.*

For a taste of the old days on the river, catch a ride on the restored paddle steamer, the **Waimarie,** built in 1899. This worked the river for 50 years before sinking in 1952, but painstaking restoration has made the craft shine like new. Two-hour cruises offer a stately ride up the Whanganui River from Wanganui—just don't wear anything white, as the coal-burning steamer throws out flecks of soot. ✉ *Whanganui River Boat Centre, Taupo Quay,* ☎ *06/347–1863.* ✆ *$25.* ☉ *Jan.–Mar., cruises available daily; call for schedule at other times.*

Dining and Lodging

$–$$ ✕ **Amadeus Riverbank Café.** If you don't feel right unless you've had bacon and eggs for breakfast, this is the place for you. Amadeus boasts great views, and the food is predictable, but very reasonable. It's mostly served buffet style through the day, and includes a range of salads, nachos, pizzas, and the like, with the occasional innovation, like Chinese chicken on baby greens. ⊠ *Suite 6, 69 Taupo Quay,* ☎ *06/345-1538. MC, V. Licensed and BYOB. No dinner Sun.–Tues.*

$–$$ ✕ **Victoria's Restaurant, Bar & Grill.** Brushed apricot walls and green carpet give this friendly eatery a summery feel, which is appropriate for the food served here. Victoria's has two personalities—café fare includes chicken and cranberry *panini* (sandwiches), and pink-cooked lamb on focaccia, or you can get serious with best-sellers like lamb rump stuffed with bacon and pumpkin, served on slivers of kumara with a mint bordelaise sauce, or salmon poached in white wine with couscous on the side. ⊠ *13 Victoria St.,* ☎ *06/347-7007. AE, DC, MC, V. Licensed and BYOB. No lunch Sat.–Mon., no dinner Sun.–Mon.*

$–$$ ✕ **Zanzibar.** Sunny colors indoors and lots of plants in the courtyard make this well-regarded restaurant a pleasant place to sit in any weather. The dishes on the extensive menu are a mixture of classical and modern, and in full main-course size, they're very generous. Beef tenderloin sitting on mushroom risotto, accompanied by a crispy duxelles parcel and drizzled with red wine sauce is typical. ⊠ *Victoria Court, 92 Victoria Ave.,* ☎ *06/345-5900. AE, MC, V. Licensed and BYOB. No lunch Sat.*

$$$ ✕🏨 **Rutland Arms.** This renovated Victorian inn in the center of Wanganui is the top choice in town, with just eight guest rooms upstairs making the most of the spacious interior. The rooms have comfortable beds, repro period furniture, and bright bathrooms; downstairs, the bar has character with a traditional English look and a wide choice of imported beers. You can eat here, surrounded by the horse brasses and other agricultural paraphernalia, or in the sunny courtyard. A daily fish choice, Kiwi lamb, steaks, and venison are always on the menu, finished with well-judged sauces or glazes. ⊠ *Victoria Ave. and Ridgeway St.,* ☎ *06/347-7677,* ℻ *06/347-7345. 8 rooms. Restaurant, bar. AE, DC, MC, V. BP.* ⊛

$$ 🏨 **Arles Homestay.** Edwardian elegance on the river is how best to sum up this delightful out-of-town homestay. Surrounded by 2 acres of gardens, and with its high ceilings, rimu paneling, kauri-built staircase, and library, there's a stately air to the property. Still, you'll receive an honest Kiwi welcome from hosts Margaret and Peter McAra. Floral wallpaper and carpets and a vine-hung conservatory echo the lush garden outside; rooms are spacious and quiet (the only TV is downstairs) and open on to a shared balcony with river views. A country breakfast is served in the dining room, and includes home-baked bread and muffins. ⊠ *50 Riverbank Rd., Wanganui,* ☎ *06/343-6557. 4 rooms, 1 self-catering 2-room apartment. Pool, library. MC, V. BP.*

The Whanganui River

The town of Wanganui sits at the southern end of the Whanganui River, whose source lies 329 km (206 mi) north on the flanks of Mt. Tongariro. Between the two are 239 rapids, several sheer-sided gorges, isolated lowland forest scenery, rolling farmland, and a whole series of historic sites and Maori communities that preserve the ways of New Zealand's early river life. Most visitors planning on seeing the river by kayak do so from the northern town of Taumarunui, 170 km (106 mi) north of Wanganui along Highway 4, or from Whakahoro, a put-in point 60 km (38 mi) to the south of Taumarunui. Local tour operators (☞ Canoeing and Kayaking, *below*) can arrange one- to five-day river trips downstream to Pipiriki, gateway community to Whanganui National Park.

An alternative for those with less time, or less inclination to travel by kayak, is to concentrate on the southern section of the river by following the **Whanganui River Road** from Wanganui town. Built in 1934 to provide access to communities that had been somewhat isolated since the ending of regular riverboat services, the road runs for 79 km (49 mi) north, as far as Pipiriki. You can drive this yourself. It's a narrow backcountry road, unpaved in stretches, though perfectly doable with care. But many choose instead to take the early morning Rural Mail bus (☞ Wanganui and the Whanganui River A to Z, *below*), which gets you to Pipiriki and back in a day and allows sightseeing stops on the outward and return journeys. You'll see the remains of giant, fossilized oyster shells at **Oyster Cliffs** (28 km/17 mi from Wanganui). You'll next arrive at the tidy Maori village of **Koriniti** (47 km/29 mi), with its well-kept ceremonial buildings and small Anglican church. The restored **Kawana Flour Mill** (56 km/35 mi) and colonial miller's cottage is always open, if you'd like a glimpse of bygone rural life. At the farming settlement of **Ranana** (60 km/37 mi), a Roman Catholic church from the 1890s is still used today. And there is the larger St. Joseph's Church and Catholic Mission at pretty **Hiruharama** (66 km/41 mi), better known locally as Jerusalem. Drive up the track to see the carved Maori altar inside the church. Finally, at **Pipiriki** (79 km/49 mi) it's possible to arrange jet-boat tours, short canoe trips, and overnight stays at some of the idiosyncratic lodges and farm stays in the area.

Dining and Lodging

$-$$$　✕🅜 **The Flying Fox.** This is probably the most unique overnight ex-
★　perience you'll have in New Zealand. For a start, access is by Flying Fox—a simple aerial cable car to the uninitiated—which deposits you high above the west bank of the Whanganui River in a grove of apple and walnut trees. Accommodation is in one of two highly individual cottages—think Gilligan's Island meets Swiss Family Robinson—fashioned from rescued materials but comfortably appointed. Wooden walls are lined with burlap or plastered pueblo-style and the decor includes rug-covered brick floors, tie-dye throws, carved screens, wood-burning stoves, wind chimes, baskets, and collectibles. Each cottage sleeps two to four people. Outhouse toilet and hot-water showers are bush-style, as is the outdoor, wood-fired clawfoot tub, sitting in a rustic dell. Annette, one of the friendly owners, dishes up tasty, mostly organic, modern New Zealand cuisine, using homegrown ingredients—avocados from her own trees, smoked eel from the river, seasonal produce, and homemade ice cream, bread, and muffins. The price includes dinner and breakfast, though both cottages are self-catering for a lower rate. The Flying Fox can also arrange half-day kayak trips downriver to Omaka hill farm, as well as horseback riding, jet-boat rides, and other activities. ⊠ *The Flying Fox, Whanganui River Rd., Koriniti,* 🕾 ᴘᴀx *06/342–8160. 2 cottages. MC, V. MAP.* ◈

Outdoor Activities and Sports

CANOEING AND KAYAKING

The main season for Whanganui River trips is between October and Easter, with the busiest period being in the summer holidays from Christmas through January. Transport is either in open, two-seater, Canadian-style canoes or in kayaks, with options ranging from one-day picnic trips to five-day camping expeditions. Operators can supply all equipment, transfers, and the necessary campsite passes; and trips can either be guided and catered, or independently undertaken (you supply your own food). Your first call should be to one of the operators to discuss itineraries. No experience is necessary, and the Whanganui is considered a safe river—it's definitely not "white-water" adventure. Prices vary wildly, according to the length and style of the trip, but you can expect to pay from around $40 for a simple one-day trip, around $400 for a fully inclusive three-day trip, and up to $700 for five days on the river. Recommended operators include: **Canoe Safaris** (☎ 06/385–9237), **Plateau Adventure Guides** (☎ 07/892–2740), **Rivercity Tours** (☎ 06/344–2554), **Wades Landing Outdoors** (☎ 07/895–5995), and **Whanganui River Adventures** (☎ 07/333–7099).

Wanganui and the Whanganui River A to Z

Arriving and Departing

BY BUS

InterCity and **Newmans** buses (☎ 09/913–6100, 04/472–5111 in Wellington) have four or five daily services between Wellington and Wanganui. There's also daily service to Wanganui from New Plymouth.

Rivercity Tours (☎ 06/344–2554) operates the Rural Mail bus service on weekdays, leaving Wanganui at 7:30 AM and arriving in Pipiriki around 11:30 AM. The bus returns to Wanganui that afternoon; bring your own picnic lunch; tea and coffee is supplied. The cost is $25 per person round-trip.

BY CAR

Wanganui is three hours' drive from Wellington; take Highway 1 north to Sanson and Highway 3 west from there. The Whanganui River Road is a minor route—you can expect it to take two hours to drive from Wanganui to Pipiriki, longer if you stop to sightsee on the way. To reach the kayak starting points, take Highway 4 north from Wanganui; it's a three-hour drive to Taumarunui, via Raetihi. A minor road connects Pipiriki to Raetihi, so you could always drive north up the Whanganui River Road, cut east along the minor road to Raetihi, and then make a quick return down Highway 4 to Wanganui.

Contacts and Resources

GUIDED TOURS

In Pipiriki, call ahead to ensure a space on the popular jet-boat tour to the **Bridge to Nowhere,** a concrete bridge across the lush Mangaparua Gorge that is the only surviving remnant of a pioneering settlement abandoned in 1942. The four-hour tour includes a speedy ride up- and downriver (complete with spins and turns), an easy 40-minute bushwalk to the bridge, and entertaining tales of local life. Bring your own picnic. Cost is $70 per person. ✉ *Bridge to Nowhere Jet Boat Tours, Whanganui River Rd.,* ☎ *06/385–4128.*

Wairua Hikoi Tours (☎ 06/345–3485) offers one-day guided kayak journeys with a Maori slant. Local guides share their experiences of river life and customs. You'll spend around five hours on the river, departing from Hiruharama (Jerusalem); cost is $75 per person.

VISITOR INFORMATION

Wanganui Visitor Information Centre. ✉ *101 Guyton St.,* ☎ *06/349–0508.* ☉ *Weekdays 8:30–5, weekends 10–2.*

WELLINGTON

New Zealand's capital city is indeed named for the then-duke of Wellington, ultimate conqueror of Napoléon at Waterloo in 1815. And it was English pioneers, having purchased land from the New Zealand Company, who settled here. In 1840, shortly after the signing of the Treaty of Waitangi, Auckland was chosen as the site for the national capital. But prosperous and influential South Island gold miners waged a campaign for a more central capital, and by 1865 they managed to have the seat of government moved to Wellington.

This city of 407,000, squeezed against the sea by peaks that rear up nearly 3,000 ft, works its way up the surrounding hills from the western shores of Port Nicholson. Behind the city, suburbs full of quaint timber houses hunker on the sides of precipitous slopes. The air currents funneled through Cook Strait, the 17-km-wide (11-mi-wide) channel separating North and South islands, give the city a feisty climate. Windy Wellington is a nickname that springs readily to the lips of most New Zealanders who don't live here. Although the city's reputation for climatic vigor is exaggerated, it's no accident that one of its landmarks is an experimental, wind-powered generator that overlooks the suburb of Brooklyn.

Most of the city sights are contained within the tightly packed downtown area, though even with just a couple of days you'll also get a feel for the very different suburbs. Thorndon, north of the business and parliamentary district, is the oldest part of the city and retains many historic wooden houses (including the childhood home of author Katherine Mansfield). Across the harbor, to the south, Oriental Bay features a lovely promenade, a small beach, and a fine run of art deco buildings and apartments; and behind, in Mount Victoria, timber houses dot the wooded heights that climb to the city's best lookout point.

Exploring Wellington

A Good Walk

Wellington is an easy city to get around on foot, although some of its tangles of streets can get confusing. The following walking tour includes city views, formal gardens, literary history, some fine examples of 19th-century architecture, and the seat of government. It ends right in the heart of downtown Wellington with a visit to the city's two major museum collections.

Begin at the **Kelburn Cable Car** ㊱ terminus in Cable Car Lane off Lambton Quay, opposite Grey Street. Taking the cable car is a good way to get up high to see the city's layout—and end up walking down many of the hills instead of up them.

Leave the Kelburn Terminal and take the Northern Walkway, following the arrow that points to St. Mary Street. This path skirts the edge of the **Wellington Botanic Garden** ㊲ with city views on one side and the domes of the Dominion Observatory on the other. As you round this hilltop, you'll see an immense green hill with transmission towers on top; this is Tinakori Hill, known to the Maoris as Ahumairangi— "sloping down from the sky." Continue along the path, which becomes quite steep as it plunges toward the **Lady Norwood Rose Garden** ㊳, with more than 100 rose cultivars spilling out their blossoms and fragrance between November and the end of April. There's a tearoom by the rose garden hothouse, always a nice place to take a break.

Tear yourself away from the roses and walk to the right around the enclosed Anderson Park, following the sign to Bolton Street Memorial Park, site of the city's historic cemeteries. At the end of this short road, detour to the monument on the right. The **John Seddon Memorial** ㊴ is dedicated to the remarkable early 20th-century prime minister. Close to the memorial a track zigzags down the hill beneath a stand of pohutukawa trees. At the bottom, cross Bowen Street, walk downhill, take the path to your left, and climb narrow old **Ascot Street** ㊵, with its wonderful old city cottages.

Turn right into **Tinakori Road** ㊶. Another fact of early life in Wellington is illustrated by No. 306, the pasta shop. Pressed for want of level ground, the citizens of early Wellington tended to build tall, narrow houses. This example—one room wide and five stories high—took things to extremes. Just below the house, make a short detour to see the three superbly kept timber houses side by side in Upton Terrace. Behind a green fence a few steps farther down Tinakori Road is Premier House, the official residence of the prime minister.

Continue down a relatively drab part of Tinakori Road to No. 25, just beyond the Hobson Street Bridge. This is the **Katherine Mansfield House** ㊷, where the celebrated writer was born (as Kathleen Beauchamp) and lived the first five years of her life.

Turning back along Tinakori Road to the Hobson Street overpass, and on the far side of the motorway, turn right to walk through the elms of Katherine Mansfield Memorial Park. Turn left around the rather stern compound of the U.S. Embassy, and walk down Murphy Street, which becomes Mulgrave Street, to **Old St. Paul's Cathedral** ㊸, one of the country's wooden Gothic Revival gems. Continue down Mulgrave Street and turn right at Archives House into Aitken Street. The modern building on the right is the **National Library** ㊹, housing the nation's largest collection of books. Cross Molesworth Street and walk through the gate to the various **Parliament Buildings** ㊺ on the far side. Left of Parliament House, the **Executive Office Building** ㊻, alias the Beehive, is the strange-looking office space for government officials. Walk down the hill from the Beehive to the tremendous wooden **Original Government Buildings** ㊼.

The wide street curving behind the bronze lions is Lambton Quay. As its name suggests, this was once Wellington's waterfront. All the land between your feet and the present-day shoreline has been reclaimed, and brass markers at intervals on the sidewalk show just how much of downtown Wellington stands on reclaimed land. From this point, the shops of the city center are within easy walking distance along Lambton Quay, and if you cut off to the left down Brandon or Panama streets you'll reach Customhouse Quay and the present-day harborside. At Queens Wharf, the **Museum of Wellington, City and Sea** ㊽ occupies a former warehouse. Walk along and around the wharf—past happening bar-restaurants like Shed Five and Dockside—and up the steps into Frank Kitts Park, site of many an outdoor concert. Your route continues through the small park, down around the rowing club basin, and across the wooden bridge into **Civic Square** ㊾, an expanse containing the library, town hall, City Gallery, cafés, and some thought-provoking public sculpture. From the bridge, you'll have glimpsed the imposing (and locally unloved) shell of the national museum, **Te Papa– Museum of New Zealand** ㊿; reach it on foot by following Cable Street from Jervois Quay, which is the main road in front of Civic Square.

Timing

You could briskly walk the route outlined above in four hours, stopping to take in the views and glancing at the most important monuments and buildings. But this sort of timing—half a day—wouldn't give you the opportunity to tour the parliament buildings or scour the main museums. In a seven-hour day, incorporating lunch downtown, you could hope to walk the tour and visit Te Papa—the one must-see—though really Wellington deserves two days. In this case, do the cable car, Botanic Gardens, and parliament area on one day; and save downtown, shops, and museums for day two.

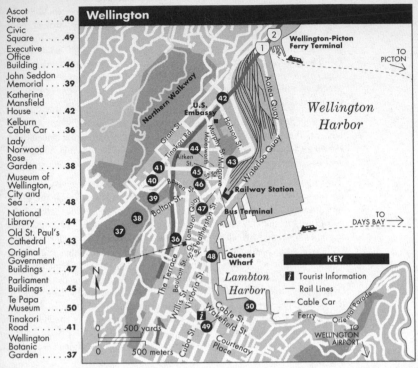

Wellington

Sights to See

40 Ascot Street. The tiny, doll-like cottages along Ascot were built in the 1870s, and this remains the finest example of a 19th-century streetscape in Wellington. There is a bench at the top end of the street that has been thoughtfully provided in the shady courtyard if you need to catch your breath. ⊠ *Off Glenmore St. and Tinakori Rd. northeast of Wellington Botanic Garden.*

Bolton Street Memorial Park. Soon after its foundation in 1840, the new city needed a cemetery. Burials until 1892 were conducted on this site (now a landscaped park) and divided into Anglican, Roman Catholic, and Jewish plots. The surviving gravestones, now mottled with aged and entwined by roses and shrubs, provide a snapshot of early colonial life and death. ⊠ *Bolton St. northeast of Wellington Botanic Garden.*

★ City Gallery. Whether it's the latest exhibition of New Zealand's avant-garde artists, an international collection visiting the gallery, the Open City film series, or just the gallery's café, there are plenty of reasons to put Wellington's eyes-and-ears-on-the-arts into your schedule. It is an excellent representation of New Zealand's thoughtful, contemporary cultural set—something that you won't see much of in the countryside. The gallery has no permanent collection, so everything here is transitory. You may be in town when a show of local painters is on the walls or a Diego Rivera and Frieda Kahlo retrospective. The film series plays everything from John Huston to New Zealand documentaries scored with music played by the National Symphony Orchestra. ⊠ *Civic Sq., Wakefield St.,* ☎ *04/801–3952.* ⊡ *Free to New Zealand exhibits, otherwise $4–10, depending on the exhibit.* ☺ *Daily 11–5.* ⊛

49 Civic Square. Wellington's modernistic Civic Square is the most visible symbol of the cultural vitality of Wellington. Reminiscent of an Italian piazza, it is a delightful sanctuary from the traffic, with its outdoor cafés, benches, lawns, and harbor viewpoints. The ☞ **City Gallery,** perhaps the nation's finest art space, the library, and the concert venue town hall are all just steps apart. Architect Ian Athfield's steel *nikau* palms are a marvel, and Maori artist Para Matchitt contributed the impressionistic sculptures flanking the wide wooden bridge that connects the square to the harbor. ⊠ *Wakefield, Victoria, and Harris Sts.*

46 Executive Office Building. It would be difficult to imagine a more complete contrast in architectural styles than that of the Parliament House and the Executive Office Building. Known for obvious reasons as the Beehive, it contains the offices of government ministers and their staffs. ⊠ *Molesworth St.*

39 John Seddon Memorial. This monument is dedicated to the colorful and popular liberal politician who served as prime minister from 1893 to 1906. Under Seddon's leadership, New Zealand became the first country to give women voting rights and to pay its citizens an old-age pension. ⊠ *Bolton Street Memorial Park, northeast end of Wellington Botanic Garden.*

42 Katherine Mansfield House. Here at 25 Tinakori Road the writer, née Kathleen Beauchamp, came into the world (1888) and lived the first five years of her life. Mansfield left to pursue her career in the wider world of Europe when she was 20, but many of her short stories are set in Wellington. A year before her death in 1923, she wrote, "New Zealand is in my very bones. What wouldn't I give to have a look at it!" The house, which has been restored as a typical Victorian family home, contains furnishings, photographs, videos, and tapes that elucidate Mansfield's life and times. ⊠ *25 Tinakori Rd., Thorndon,* ☎ *04/473–7268.* ▦ *$5.* ☉ *Daily 10–4.*

36 Kelburn Cable Car. The Swiss-built funicular railway makes a short but sharp climb to Kelburn Terminal, from which there are great views across parks and city buildings to Port Nicholson. Sit on the left side during the six-minute journey for the best scenery. At the top, the Skyline Cafe (daily 8–4) has more great views from its picture windows and terrace. ⊠ *280 Lambton Quay, at Grey St.; and Upland Rd., Kelburn,* ☎ *04/ 472–2199.* ▦ *$1.50 one way, $2.50 round-trip.* ☉ *Departures about every 10 mins, weekdays 7 AM–10 PM, weekends 9 AM–10 PM.*

★ **38 Lady Norwood Rose Garden.** On a fine summer day you couldn't find a better place to go for a sniff and a smile. The rose garden is in fact the most popular part of the ☞ **Wellington Botanic Garden.** Situated on a plateau, the formal circular layout consists of 106 beds, each planted with a single variety of modern and traditional shrubs. Climbing roses cover a brick-and-timber colonnade on the perimeter. Adjacent to the rose beds, the Begonia House conservatory is filled with tender plants and has a teahouse serving light meals. ⊠ *North end of Wellington Botanic Garden, Tinakori Rd. (for parking lot),* ☎ *04/801–3071.* ▦ *Donation requested.* ☉ *Begonia House daily 10–4, main gardens open sunrise–sunset.*

★ **48 Museum of Wellington, City and Sea.** Housed in the refurbished 1892 Bond Store (where goods were stored until duty was paid), this excellent museum explores the experience of the original Maori tribes who fished the harbor shores and of the Europeans who settled here in 1840. Three floors of well-presented exhibits include displays about life, leisure, work, crime, and education in 19th-century Wellington; coverage of the city's precarious position on a geological fault line; and a history of Cook Strait crossings to the South Island, which incorporates a short film about the *Wahine,* the interisland ferry that foundered in the harbor in 1968, with the loss of 51 lives. ⊠ *The Bond Store, Queens Wharf,* ☎ *04/472–8904.* ▣ *$5.* ☉ *Daily 9:30–5:30.* ☙

㊹ National Library. This modern building houses the nation's largest collection of books, as well as the remarkable Alexander Turnbull Library. The latter contains an extensive Pacific history section, including accounts of every important European voyage of discovery since Magellan. A collection of sketches of New Zealand made by early visitors is displayed in changing exhibitions. ⊠ *Molesworth and Aitken Sts.,* ☎ *04/474–3000.* ▣ *Free.* ☉ *Weekdays 9–5, Sat. 9–1.*

㊸ Old St. Paul's Cathedral. Consecrated in 1866, the church is a splendid example of the English Gothic Revival style executed in wood. Even the trusses supporting the roof transcend their mundane function with splendid craftsmanship. The hexagonal oak pulpit was a gift from the widow of Prime Minister Richard Seddon, in memory of her husband. ⊠ *Mulgrave St., Thorndon,* ☎ *04/473–6722.* ▣ *Free.* ☉ *Mon.–Sat. 10–5.*

㊼ Original Government Buildings. This second-largest wooden structure in the world is now home to Victoria University's law faculty. It's an extraordinary conceit—built in 1876 and designed to look like stone, it was instead entirely fashioned from kauri timber. Inside are historic exhibits about the building and a Department of Conservation (DOC) information center, though it's the exterior that most captivates. ⊠ *15 Lambton Quay,* ☎ *04/472–7356.* ▣ *Free.* ☉ *Weekdays 9–4:30, weekends 10–3.*

㊺ Parliament Buildings. Following a $150-million renovation program, the three structures that comprise the Parliament Buildings are open for public tours. The eye-catching pink Gothic Revival structure is the **Parliamentary Library,** a soaring, graceful building compared with the ponderous gray bulk of the **Parliament House** next door. Tours of the buildings explain the parliamentary process in detail. The **Debating Chamber,** where legislation is presented, debated, and voted on, is a copy of that in the British Houses of Parliament at Westminster, right down to the Speaker's mace and the dispatch boxes. There's fine Maori artwork in the **Maori Affairs Select Committee Room,** at the front of Parliament House; and your tour may even step into the Executive Office Building, known popularly as the **Beehive.** ⊠ *Molesworth St.,* ☎ *04/471–9999.* ▣ *Free.* ☉ *Tours depart on the hr weekdays 10– 4, Sat. 10–3, Sun. 1–3.*

Premier House. The official residence of New Zealand's Prime Minister was a simple cottage when first erected in 1843, though it's increased in size and grandeur somewhat since then. Prime Ministers remained in residence until 1935, when the new Labour government, caught up in its reforming zeal, turned it into a dental clinic. The house had fallen into disrepair by the early 1990s. Since then renovations have restored it to its proper status—and allowed the Prime Minister of the day to move back in. The house isn't open to the public. ⊠ *Tinakori Rd.*

★ ☺ **㊿ Te Papa–Museum of New Zealand.** Opened early in 1998, this museum quickly exceeded all expectations by attracting more visitors—250,000 in its first month—than anything else in New Zealand. This is partly because of the lack of modern, interactive museums elsewhere in the country, but also because Te Papa is such a good introduction to the country's people, cultures, landforms, flora, and fauna—with exhibits that make you feel an earthquake by standing in a house that rocks and shakes, or that take you into a marae (Maori meetinghouse) where a *powhiri* (Maori greeting involving song and speeches) welcomes you. You can also explore an outdoor forest area with moa (the extinct, ostrichlike native bird) bones and glowworms or delve into the stories of New Zealand's early European migrants. In the Time Warp area, a sort-of theme park where most activities have additional fees, you can simulate a bungy jump, a trip back to the ancient Gondwanaland supercontinent, or leap three generations ahead to Wellington in 2055. Four discovery centers allow children to weave, hear storytelling, and learn a bit of Maori through song. Eateries in the complex come with an impeccable pedigree, having been set up by a team of top chefs. ⊠ *Cable St., Wellington,* ☏ *04/381–7000.* 💷 *Free, some exhibits cost up to $8.* ⊙ *Daily 10–6 (Thurs. to 9 PM).* 🐾

❹ Tinakori Road. The lack of suitable local stone combined with the collapse of most of Wellington's brick buildings in the earthquake of 1848 ensured the almost exclusive use of timber for building here in the second half of the 19th century. Most carpenters of the period had learned their skills as cabinetmakers and shipwrights in Europe, and the sturdy houses in this street are a tribute to their craftsmanship. Two notables are the tall and narrow No. 306 and ☞ **Premier House** just up the road from 306. From the Botanic Garden, follow Glenmore Road northeast until it turns into Tinakori Road around ☞ **Ascot Street.**

★ ❸ Wellington Botanic Garden. In the hills overlooking downtown, this urban delight has scenery as varied as its terrain. Woodland gardens under native and exotic trees fill the valleys, water-loving plants line a pond and mountain streams, dry, craggy slopes are studded with succulents and rock-loving plants, and lawns spread over flatter sections with beds of bright seasonal bulbs and annuals. The lovely ☞ **Lady Norwood Rose Garden** is in the northeast part of the garden. **Carter Observatory and Planetarium,** the only one of its kind in New Zealand, has public displays and programs, including evening telescope viewings, which are great opportunities for those from the northern hemisphere to learn about the southern night sky. If you don't want to walk the hill up to the garden, the ☞ **Kelburn Cable Car** can take you. Or take the No. 12 bus (direction: Karori) from Lambton Quay to the main (Glenmore Street) entrance. ⊠ *Tinakori Rd. for parking lot; main entrances on Upland Rd. (for cable car) and Glenmore St.,* ☏ *04/801–3071 gardens, 04/472–8167 observatory and planetarium.* 💷 *Main gardens free, Carter observatory and planetarium $7 and $10.* ⊙ *Main gardens, daily sunrise–sunset; observatory and planetarium weekdays 10–5, weekends noon–5, plus Tues., Thurs., and Sat. 6:30 PM–10:30 PM.*

Around Wellington

★ Moss Green Garden. Set in the steep, bush-clad hills along the Akatarawa River, Moss Green makes for a superb day trip from the capital for serious gardeners and those venturing off the beaten path. Some 9 ft of rain fall here annually, and the land and vegetation have evolved to flourish under these conditions, as have Bob and Jo Munro. With great horticultural skill and intelligence, they plant accordingly, boldly using indigenous plants and unusual exotics from the Himalayas, North America, and Europe. The Munros have also placed copper sentinels, stone tables and chairs, and large ceramic vessels throughout the garden—pieces that they created in their other lives as nonhorticultural artists. These are every bit as intriguing as the garden itself.

There are two approaches to the garden, both via Akatarawa Road an hour north of Wellington: from the east follow Highway 2 from the city to Upper Hutt, where Akatarawa Road climbs into the valley to Moss Green. There are wonderful old trestle bridges as you near the garden. From the west take Akatarawa Road from Highway 1 in Waikanae. You'll climb it over the pass, dropping down to the garden from above. This approach is not for the faint of heart, as it may be the narrowest, most precipitous road on North Island—watch closely for oncoming cars. Visitors are welcome to picnic on the grounds. ✉ *2420 Akatarawa Rd., Upper Hutt,* ☎ *04/526–7531.* ⛱ *$5.* ☉ *Aug.– Apr., Wed.–Mon. 10–5; June and July, by appointment.*

★ **Otari Native Botanic Garden.** Anyone with even the slightest interest in native New Zealand flora should pick up picnic provisions and spend an afternoon at Otari, just outside the city. Devoted to gathering and preserving indigenous plants, Otari's collection is the largest of its kind. With clearly marked bushwalks and landscape demonstration gardens, it aims to educate the public and thereby ensure the survival of New Zealand's unique and diverse plant life. While in the garden, you'll learn to dissect the forest, from the various *blechnum* ferns underfoot to the tallest trees towering overhead—the rimu, *kahikatea* (ka-hee-ka-tee-ah), and northern *rata*—and everything in between. An aerial walkway has been added, crossing the bush high above the ground to offer an unusual vantage point over the gardens. Look and listen for the native birds that flock to this haven: the bellbird (*korimako*), gray duck (*parera*), fantail (*piwakawaka*), New Zealand wood pigeon (*kereru*), silvereye (*tauhou*), and tui, among others. Cultivated borders highlight everything from Wellington coast plants to grasses and alpine rock garden plants. Take the No. 14 Wilton bus from downtown (20 minutes). ✉ *Wilton Rd., Wilton,* ☎ *04/475–3245.* ⛱ *Free.* ☉ *Daily dawn–dusk.*

Southward Museum. This is in fact the largest collection of vintage and veteran cars in the southern hemisphere, with more than 250 vehicles, among them Bugattis; a Hispano-Suiza; one of only 17 Davis three-wheelers ever made; a De Lorean; a gull-wing 1955 Mercedes 300SL; gangster Micky Cohen's armor-plated 1950 Cadillac; and a Cadillac once owned by Marlene Dietrich. The motorcycle collection, which has a number of early Harley-Davidsons and Indians, a Brough Superior, and a Vincent V-twin, is almost as impressive. The museum is just off Highway 1, a 45-minute drive north of Wellington. ✉ *Otaihanga Rd., Paraparaumu,* ☎ *04/297–1221.* ⛱ *$5.* ☉ *Daily 9–4:30.*

Dining

$$$$ ✕ **Logan Brown.** This temple to gastronomy in a former bank building won oohs and ahs for its opulent decor before the food earned its own reputation. You'll be offered starters like *paua* (black abalone) ravioli with fresh lime, basil, and coriander beurre blanc, or sweetbreads with chickpea cumin puree and paprika salsa. Recent main courses have included grilled rare tuna with olive tapenade, and panfried goat cheese and potato terrine with wild mushrooms. The wine list includes many rare imports, plus the very best from New Zealand, and the separate bar stays open long into the night. ✉ *Cuba St. at Vivian St.,* ☎ *04/ 801–5114. AE, DC, MC, V. No lunch weekends.*

$$$–$$$$ ✕ **Icon.** Peter Thornley is one of New Zealand's most innovative chefs, and he's won a stack of international awards with creations like roasted scallops on fennel puree, ravioli of prawns on lava-seared seaweed, and braised monkfish wrapped in prosciutto. The decor is clean-cut and welcoming, and staff members are friendly and knowledgeable. And because of the museum, Icon often stays open on public holidays when other restaurants are shut. ✉ *Te Papa–Museum of New Zealand, Cable St.,* ☎ *04/801–5300. AE, DC, MC, V.*

$$$ ✕ **Boulcott Street Bistro.** Serious foodies flock to this long-established bistro in a historic house for its modern interpretations of French country classics. Owner/chef Chris Green contributes to the Air New Zealand menu and is in great demand for "great chefs" dinners around the country, where various star chefs cook a course each. The kitchen style leans to French provincial, but Asian influences appear in dishes like a crayfish, crab, and pork spring roll with soy and oyster aioli and wasabi mayo. Duck leg fritters dabbed with mango chutney are popular, as are pork cutlets with a cider and pepper glaze. Chris's braised lamb shank with mashed potato and minted peas is a Wellington institution. ⊠ *99 Boulcott St.,* ☎ *04/499–4199. Reservations not accepted for dinner. AE, DC, MC, V. No lunch weekends.*

$$$ ✕ **Brasserie Flipp.** Style, polish, and subdued lighting make Flipp a fash-
★ ionable choice among Wellington's sophisticates. Chef Martin Bosley's sensibly innovative recent starters include a timbale of tuna and citrus-cured salmon, and veal sweetbreads with potato gnocchi, mushrooms, and watercress. Hearty eaters love tucking into a roasted, stuffed chicken leg with blood sausage, and the traditional Kiwi beer-battered fish-and-chips have a loyal following. The wine list has a good selection of New Zealand wine and token bottles from just about everywhere else. ⊠ *RSA Bldg., 103 Ghunzee St.,* ☎ *04/385–9493. AE, DC, MC, V. Closed Sun. No lunch Sat.*

$$$ ✕ **François.** If you need a French fix, take a taxi to this cozy suburban eatery. You'll think you're in a Paris bistro—bare walls except for ornately framed mirrors, a menu written in French, and serving staff who are passionate about the dishes they bring to the table. Choose from such authentic delights as rib steak with red wine sauce, confit of duck, and even a warm salad of *whitloof* (Belgian chicory) and duck giblets. The wine list carries a mix of French and New Zealand labels. ⊠ *10A Murphy St., Thorndon,* ☎ *04/499–5252. AE, DC, MC, V. Closed Sun. No lunch weekends. No dinner Mon.*

$$$ ✕ **Il Casino.** Owner Remiro Bresolin has been awarded a Hall of Fame award by his peers for his huge contribution to the Wellington restaurant scene. The food is Northern Italian and quite authentic. Chef Franco Zanotto makes most of the pasta himself, and uses quality ingredients for his always-flavorsome sauces. Rack of lamb is served with a roasted pear and grappa sauce and calamari is thinly sliced and deep-fried. The wine list reads like the efforts of the New Zealand–Italy friendship society, and the service is correct in the old-fashioned way, with a dash of Kiwi friendliness. ⊠ *108 Tory St.,* ☎ *04/385–7496. AE, DC, MC, V.*

$$$ ✕ **Petit Lyon.** This Wellington institution has withstood a change of
★ address and the loss of one of the founding partners but still remains synonymous with good eating. The decor is summery at the front, moody and romantic at the back. The kitchen avoids the conventional. Prepare to wrap your taste buds around combos like wild venison with spiced dates, grilled quail with mushrooms, or a breast of corn-fed chicken with plum sauce, spinach, and crayfish. The wine list is wide-ranging, and includes several New Zealand classics from earlier vintages—at prices that reflect their rarity. ⊠ *270 Willis St.,* ☎ *04/384–9402. AE, DC, MC, V. Closed Sun. No lunch Sat.*

$$$ ✕ **Roxburgh Bistro.** The considerable skills of chef-owner Mark Limacher
★ ensure that this cozy, bustling bistro has remained one of the city's hot spots for many a year. The menu usually includes a couple of well-prepared offal dishes—rabbit livers with French mustard cream was one recent offering. Vegetarians rave about dishes like warm eggplant and mozzarella terrine with roasted red peppers, olives, and couscous, while carnivores can savor a classic steak tartare. Commendably, individual local cheeses are offered rather than the ubiquitous mixed-cheese board. The wine list is serious and well priced. ⊠ *18 Marjoribanks St.,* ☎ *04/385–7577. AE, DC, MC, V. Closed Sun.–Mon. No lunch Sat.*

$$$ ✕ **White House.** Chef Paul Hoather's cooking gets the vote from a num-
★ ber of Wellington foodies as the best in town. The restaurant occupies a cute cottage that dates from the 1870s, but the food is pure new millennium. Try the three-cheese soufflé with pesto, and move on to cer-

FISH, FRUIT, AND MEAT: NEW ZEALAND'S BOUNTY

A POETIC GOURMET ONCE called New Zealand "the little green garden at the bottom of the world." It's a good description. Vegetables, fruit, and animals thrive in this Pacific paradise's temperate climate.

Internationally, the country's early food fame was earned for its butter and lamb, but these two staples have now been joined by a large number of other edibles. The hairy brown fruit known in most countries as a kiwi, but in New Zealand as a kiwifruit (or, more recently, by the export marketing name zespri) has been a huge worldwide success.

Though many countries have incorporated dishes enjoyed by their original inhabitants into their everyday cuisine, there's not a lot of Maori influence on mainstream New Zealand cuisine. The best-known Maori meal is a hangi, which involves cooking the food over heated stones buried in the earth. It's a method that doesn't translate easily to a European-style kitchen, though a few chic restaurants try to approximate it. One native vegetable, considered sacred to the Maori, is a common sight on most New Zealanders' tables: the kumara, New Zealand's own sweet potato. It's eaten boiled, baked, or mashed, or whipped into elaborate concoctions by fine Kiwi chefs. Look for kumara rösti, a sweet-potato fritter, in top urban restaurants.

At the bottom of the South Island and on Stewart Island, you might be offered muttonbird, also known as titi, which was eaten by local Maori for centuries and is eaten by local New Zealanders of all stripes today. It's a young seabird, cured for eating, and is salty and extremely fatty—definitely an acquired taste.

Meat cuts in New Zealand follow both American and European traditions. One exclusively local meat is cervena, the registered name for farmed venison. Not all restaurants use the term, so it pays to ask. Occasionally, the venison listed will be wild and will have a gamier flavor.

Several unique species of shellfish are caught around the coast. Pipi and tuatua are both similar to clams, but you are unlikely to come across another near-relation, the toheroa, in your restaurant travels. Dwindling stocks mean harvesting has been largely banned for some years, and looks to remain so far into the future.

The registered name for the New Zealand farmed mussel is the Greenshell mussel. It is larger than its North American counterparts and is slightly sweet and succulent. Oysters are available in several species. Those from Bluff are considered the best, although Nelson Bay's come a close second. Rock oysters are rare. Most common are the Pacifics, which are sometimes (but not always) watery and insipid.

Whitebait, the juvenile of several fish species, are much smaller than their European equivalents. They are eaten whole, usually mixed into an omelet-like fritter. Another local delicacy from the sea is the roe of the kina, or sea egg, which is similar to a sea urchin. You'll see it for sale at roadside stalls, and occasionally in innovative restaurants.

When you're visiting restaurants, be aware that many vegetables have two names, used interchangeably. Eggplants are often called aubergines here, and zucchini are also known as courgettes. The vegetable Americans know as a bell pepper is a capsicum in New Zealand.

Finally, if you're looking to to start a good-natured argument with a Kiwi, suggest that it was the Australians who invented that cream-topped, fruit-and-meringue concoction, the Pavlova. Though it's known for sure to be named for Russian ballerina Anna Pavlova, the question of where it originated is the source of constant trans-Tasman Sea rivalry.

vena (venison) steaks arranged over what the menu calls an "orgy"(!) of mushrooms. A fixed-price menu is available, and recommended for tables of 12 or more. ⌧ *270 Willis St.,* ☎ *04/385–8555. AE, DC, MC, V. Closed Sun. No lunch Sat.*

$$–$$$ ✕ **Castro's.** It's been a butcher's shop and a delicatessen—now it's a contemporary Kiwi café with a pretty serious kitchen. Yellowfin tuna is roasted and served with green tea noodles; salmon is oven-baked after being brushed with miso and lime. Vegetarians are well catered to with the likes of grilled snake beans (a fibrous Chinese bean) with forest mushrooms, aioli, and pecorino. Castro's also puts more thought into its soups than most places around town. If the paddle crab and bell pepper combo is listed, don't miss it. Paddle crab is a local delicacy, and it's delicious. Lunch may be served for groups on request. ⌧ *12 Marjoribanks St.,* ☎ *04/384–8733. AE, DC, MC, V. No lunch.*

$$–$$$ ✕ **Dockside and Shed Five.** These separate restaurants are listed together because they are both in a redeveloped waterfront warehouse—and both specialize in seafood. Look for the likes of grilled salmon fillet with buckwheat noodles and a ginger-and-mint salad at Shed Five, and grilled grouper fillet with green olive tapenade and warm scallopini (disc-shape zucchini) and red onion salad at Dockside. ⌧ *Dockside: Shed 3, Queens Wharf, Jervois Quay,* ☎ *04/499–9900. AE, DC, MC, V.* ⌧ *Shed Five: Shed Five, Queens Wharf, Jervois Quay,* ☎ *04/499–9069. AE, DC, MC, V.*

$$–$$$ ✕ **Fog City Restaurant.** A roaring fire keeps this suburban restaurant warm on colder evenings, and a broad view of chef Steve Morris's kitchen team in action provides the predinner entertainment. Dine on eclectic food like a salmon fillet topped with scallop mousse, served with a sauce based on olives and oranges, or go for the Asian-influenced poached chicken on Szechuan pickled cucumber. Service is friendly and knowledgeable. ⌧ *Marsden Village, 153 Karori Rd., Karori,* ☎ *04/476–8100. AE, DC, MC, V. Closed Sun.–Mon. No lunch.*

$$–$$$ ✕ **Serrano's.** Serrano's is where the city's chefs like to eat—and that's always a good sign. Influences from France, Italy, and Asia can be tasted in this seafood-focused cuisine. Chef Sue Bowen crusts cubes of bean curd with black pepper and serves them with steamed vegetables, or drizzles watercress cream sauce spiked with strips of bacon over salmon steaks. The seafood platter is a popular choice, and carnivores are catered to with innovative treatments of beef and lamb. If you love chocolate, leave room for the appropriately named Chocolate Decadence. ⌧ *105 Vivian St.,* ☎ *04/384–6466. AE, DC, MC, V. Closed Sun.–Mon. No lunch.*

$$–$$$ ✕ **Two Rooms.** Brother-and-sister team Dolly and Jonathon England raised a few eyebrows when they opened their simply decorated restaurant in a rather run-down suburban shopping center, but their mix of traditional European dishes, like French onion soup and country-style terrines, have attracted hungry hordes since day one. Italy also features strongly on the regularly changing menu, but here, too, the dishes are more likely to conjure up the past than blaze new trails. Dated? Perhaps, but sometimes we need reminding about just how good those old favorites were. The wine list covers the world. ⌧ *382 Broadway Ave., Strathmore,* ☎ *04/388–8428. AE, DC, MC, V. Closed Sun.–Mon. No lunch.*

$–$$ ✕ **Café L'Affaré.** This open-fronted, bustling café is based around a coffee-roasting operation, where customers can see (and smell!) the beans undergoing their metamorphosis. The dark-timbered interior is traditional; the open-plan kitchen decidedly modern. Nearly everything served is made on the premises, including a range of delicious breads. A rug-covered children's area is well stocked with toys and other means of keeping the little ones happy while Mom and Dad enjoy their cappuccinos. The all-day breakfast is hugely popular, but more serious diners can opt for the likes of a classic Caesar salad, fettuccine with smoked salmon and dill, or grilled chilli squid. ✉ *27 College St.,* ☎ *04/385–9748. AE, MC, V. Closed Sun.*

$–$$ ✕ **The Malthouse.** Tired of wine? This comfy, wood-paneled bar and restaurant has 30 beers on tap, many naturally brewed by micro-breweries around the country. Choose your mood—eat outdoors on the balcony, inside in the lounge, or split the difference in the conservatory. As befits the resident beverage, the food is honest, hearty (think Greenshell mussels in broth, beer-battered fish, and fries), and well priced. ✉ *47 Willis St.,* ☎ *04/473–0731. AE, DC, MC, V. Closed Sun.*

$–$$ ✕ **Vista.** With a view over Oriental Bay to the city center, this bright and breezy café is a pleasant place to while away an hour or two. Sit outside on sunny days, inside if it's overcast, or back in the bar area at night. Choose from light but tasty snacks, or more serious offerings like gnocchi, which has a huge Wellington following, or Caesar salad with either pancetta or house-smoked salmon. Breakfast? It's on all day—think about toasted pumpkin and corn muffins with avocado, roasted tomatoes, ricotta, and chilli jam. ✉ *106 Oriental Parade,* ☎ *04/385–7724. AE, DC, MC, V. Closed Mon., June–Aug.*

$ ✕ **Dixon Street Gourmet Deli.** This city-center delicatessen stocks a fine
★ range of taste treats. There are homemade breads and bagels, an international choice of meats, cheeses, pickles, preserves, and chocolates, plus local smoked fish, Greenshell mussels—everything you need for a superior picnic. If you prefer to dine in, you can do that, too—the deli has a licensed café attached. Staff members delight in steering visitors towards the city's best sights. ✉ *45–47 Dixon St.,* ☎ *04/384–2436. AE, DC, MC, V.*

$ ✕ **The Lido.** This busy corner café across from the tourist information center is a fun, funky place that turns out an ever-changing selection of inspired savory and sweet muffins, pasta dishes, vegetarian food, and yummy desserts—at breakfast, lunch, and dinner. It regularly stays open way past midnight, and you can sit indoors or out when weather permits. ✉ *Victoria and Wakefield Sts.,* ☎ *04/499–6666. Reservations not accepted. AE, DC, MC, V.*

Lodging

$$$$ ⊞ **Parkroyal Wellington.** The Parkroyal claims the mantle of best
★ hotel in Wellington, and its young staff works hard to make you feel right at home. Distinctive color tones throughout—soft yellows, rich blues—are matched by blond wood furnishings and prolific displays of New Zealand artwork. Some guest rooms have a queen-size bed and brown marble bathroom, others have a king-size bed and corner-style bath with jets. And all come with working desk, bathrobes, hair dryer, and ironing board. A ninth-floor club lounge (open to all guests) serves Continental breakfast and all-day coffee and snacks, with views over the harbor. Or there's sustenance in the ground-floor Chameleon café-bar, a contemporary power-breakfast meeting place that's popular with the locals. ✉ *Featherston and Grey Sts.,* ☎ *04/472–2722,* ☏ *04/472–4724. 232 rooms. 2 bars, café, in-room data ports, indoor pool, sauna, exercise room, laundry service. AE, DC, MC, V.*

$$$–$$$$ ⊞ **City Life Wellington.** This contemporary all-suite hotel has an excellent location, right in the middle of the city. And if you can snag a suite at a weekend or special summer rate, you've got one of the best-value lodgings in town. Guests have a wide selection of studios and spacious one-, two-, and three-bedroom suites with cream-and-white carpets and walls enlivened by Asian-style area rugs. Facilities are similar in all suites and include self-catering kitchens, washers and dryers, and dishwashers (though the rooms are also serviced). Despite the location, you don't get street noise in the rooms. Breakfast is only included in the special weekend rate. ⊠ *300 Lambton Quay, The Terrace,* ☏ *04/472–8588 or 0800/368–888,* FAX *04/473–8588. 65 suites. In-room data ports, in-room VCRs, kitchenettes, exercise room. AE, DC, MC, V.* ✺

$$$ ⊞ **Dunrobin House.** Carol and John Sutherland's elegant, turn-of-the-last-century villa sits in the heart of the Mount Victoria suburb, just 10 minutes' walk uphill from the Courtenay Place restaurant zone. This house of high ceilings, polished rimu-wood doors and staircase, and restored tiled fireplaces has two double rooms available. The largest has a separate dressing room (with a single bed, allowing this to sleep three), and both have cotton bed linen, cane chairs, and a complimentary decanter of port. Breakfast is served in the dining room, or in the farmhouse-style kitchen, which opens on to a pretty courtyard. ⊠ *89 Austin St., at Derby St., Mt. Victoria,* ☏ *04/385–0335,* FAX *04/385–0336. 2 rooms. MC, V. BP.*

$$$ ⊞ **Eight Parliament Street.** Walk through the door of this traditional wooden house, just five minutes from the Parliament Buildings, and you're transported into contemporary B&B lodgings of a decidedly superior, stylish nature. Brightly colored linen, funky sculpted mirrors, vases of dried flowers, and commissioned New Zealand artwork offset the cool cream drapes and cord carpeting. Small, but charming, bathrooms are spic-and-span, and there's a washer and dryer for guests' use. Breakfast might be smoked salmon and scrambled eggs, or fresh fruit, yogurt, and espresso, and there are tables outside in the sheltered courtyard, where the only sounds to be heard are the crickets and birds. ⊠ *8 Parliament St., off Hill St., Thorndon,* ☏ *04/499–0808,* FAX *04/ 479–6705. 3 rooms, 1 with bath. MC, V. BP.* ✺

$$$ ⊞ **Shepherds Arms Hotel.** New Zealand's oldest hotel, the Shepherds Arms has been refurbished to close to its original state. Four-poster beds, deep-blue carpets, and burgundy curtains all add to the charm of the hotel. Its only failing is that in keeping with the time it was first built, the rooms are fairly small (especially the three single rooms, which share a bathroom). Head down to the bar after five and mix with locals as they come in for a drink after a busy day at the office. Old photos on the wall show what Wellington looked like in the hotel's early days. The Shepherds Arms is extremely popular, especially on weeknights, so reserve well in advance. By Wellington standards it is a bit out of town—about four minutes' walk to the Parliament Buildings and about 10 to the main shopping district. ⊠ *285 Tinakori Rd., Thorndon,* ☏ *04/472–1320,* FAX *04/472–0523. 12 rooms, 9 with bath. Restaurant, bar. AE, DC, MC, V.*

$$–$$$ ⊞ **Halswell Lodge.** For restaurant, theater, and cinema going, you can't beat the location, right by the eastern end of Courtenay Place. And you'll find it hard to beat the prices, too, at this lodge with a room for every budget. Standard hotel rooms at the front of the building are small and functional. Motel units, studios or two-bedrooms, are set farther back, each with kitchenette. Three of these have jet baths. Finally, there's the newly restored 1920s' villa at the rear of the property; its six superior rooms come with cane chairs, burnished wood decor, antique wardrobes, and restored fireplaces. Guests here can use the villa kitchen to prepare light meals. ⊠ *21 Kent Terr.,* ☏ *04/385–0196,* FAX *04/385–0503. 25 rooms, 11 motel units. Coin laundry. AE, DC, MC, V.* ✺

$$ ⊞ **Tinakori Lodge.** In a historic suburb overlooking the city, this Victorian villa offers atmospheric B&B accommodations in tranquil surroundings. The rooms (which can sleep up to three) are simply furnished but feature comfortable beds. It's the public areas that most impress, especially a bright conservatory and small garden at the rear, facing a bush reserve. A buffet breakfast is laid out each morning, and the own-

ers are extremely friendly and helpful. The city center is a 10-minute
walk away. Children are accommodated by arrangement. ✉ *182
Tinakori Rd., Thorndon,* ☎ *04/473–3478,* FAX *04/472–5554. 9 rooms,
5 with bath. AE, DC, MC, V. BP.*

Nightlife and the Arts

For a current listing of cultural events in Wellington, check the *City
Voice, Capital Times,* the *Dominion,* and the *Evening Post.* The free
booklet *Wellington What's On* (available from the Visitor Information
Centre, ☞ Wellington A to Z, *below*) also has seasonal listings of cultural events. **Ticketek** (☎ 04/384–3840) sells tickets for local performances.

The Arts

The major arts event in town is the **New Zealand International Festival,** held in March every two years (in even-numbered years) at venues
across the city. This attracts a huge array of international talent in the
fields of music, drama, dance, the visual arts, and media. Advance information and a festival program is available from the Festival Office
(☎ 04/473–0149).

Wellington is the home of the **New Zealand Ballet Company,** the **National Opera of New Zealand,** and the **New Zealand Symphony Orchestra.** The main venues for the performing arts are the **Michael
Fowler Centre** and **Town Hall** (✉ Civic Sq., Wakefield St., ☎ 04/801–
4242) for theater and music both classical and contemporary, and the
St. James Theatre (✉ 77–83 Courtenay Pl., ☎ 04/802–4060) and the
Opera House (✉ 111–113 Manners St., ☎ 04/384–3840) for drama,
ballet, and opera.

The **Circa Theatre** is a good bet to catch contemporary New Zealand
works. ✉ *1 Taranaki St.,* ☎ *04/801–7992.*

The **Downstage Theatre** holds frequent performances of stage classics,
contemporary drama, comedy, and dance. ✉ *Hannah Playhouse,
Courtenay Pl. and Cambridge Terr.,* ☎ *04/801–6946.*

Nightlife

Wellington's after-dark scene splits between several main areas. The
funky cafés of Cuba Street stay open most of the night for pre- and
post-bar and club coffees; some put on regular gigs too. Courtenay Place
is where most of the drinking action is, with a selection of brash Irish
pubs, sports bars, grand salons, and upscale establishments. In the downtown business district—between Lambton Quay and Manners Street—
a couple of brewpubs and a few taverns cater to the after-work mob.
Down by the harbor, a flashy crowd hangs out in several warehouse-
style bars, which absolutely rock weekends.

Downtown, make an early start at the **Arizona Bar** (✉ Grey and Featherston Sts., ☎ 04/495–7867), a Western theme bar on the ground floor
of the Parkroyal Hotel. The **Malthouse** (✉ 47 Willis St., ☎ 04/499–
4355), upstairs in a renovated historic building, brews its own beers
and has conservatory-style seating looking down on the street. At the
Loaded Hog (✉ 14–18 Bond St., ☎ 04/472–9160) you get microbrewed
beers, live music several nights a week, and an outdoor deck.

Courtenay Place has two great Irish bars, both of which have regular
traditional music gigs: **Molly Malone's** (✉ Taranaki St. and Courtenay Pl., ☎ 04/384–2896) is big, with the bonus of an upstairs bar with
an outdoor deck for watching the crowds; **Kitty O'Shea's** (✉ 28
Courtenay Pl., ☎ 04/384–7392) is an intimate choice.

The well-lived-in **Grand** (✉ 69–71 Courtenay Pl., ☎ 04/80–7800), once a brewery and then a distillery, has exposed brick walls, timber floors, and four levels with everything from a 400-person main bar to a garden bar to a 10-table poolroom. **CO2** (✉ 28 Blair St., ☎ 04/38–1064) is smallish and, true to its name, serves only sparkling wine.

On the waterfront, the two big draws are the bars at **Shed Five** and **Dockside** (☞ Dining, *above*). In good weather, everyone spills outside for the best close-up harbor views in Wellington. Later on, move across to **Chicago** (✉ Jervois Quay, ☎ 04/473–4900) on Queens Wharf, a spacious sports bar that sees boisterous post-game parties, live bands, dancing, and late-night pool sessions.

The best place to catch local rock music is **Bar Bodega** (✉ 286 Willis St., ☎ 04/384–8212). Touring acts most often play the **James Cabaret** (✉ 5 Hania St., ☎ 04/937–7397).

Shopping

Department Store
Kirkcaldie & Stains. ✉ *165–177 Lambton Quay,* ☎ *04/472–5899.* ◷ *Mon.–Thurs. 9–5:30, Fri. 9–7, Sat. 10–4:30, Sun. 11–3.*

Districts
The main **downtown shopping area,** for department stores, clothes, shoes, books, outdoor gear, and souvenirs, is the so-called Golden Mile—from Lambton Quay, up Willis, Victoria, and Manners streets. The principal shopping center is **Harbour City** on Lambton Quay, though there are also varied store outlets in **Capital On The Quay,** a mall on Lambton Quay, and **The Old Bank Arcade** (corner of Lambton Quay and Customhouse Quay). For ethnic gift stores, boutiques, secondhand shops, and crafts, visit trendy **Cuba Street.**

Markets
The **Wellington Market** (✉ Taranaki and Cable Sts., ☎ 04/801–8991) is the place to find souvenirs, New Zealand crafts, and collectibles, and also has a great Asian food court. It's open Friday–Sunday 10–5:30. **James Smiths Corner** (✉ 55 Cuba St., ☎ 04/801–8812) has a second-floor market area selling ethnic crafts, jewelry, and gifts; downstairs are more mainstream stores and a food court. It's open daily 9–5.

Specialty Stores
BOOKS AND MAPS
Arty Bee's Books is a friendly store for secondhand books and sheet music has a book-exchange service too. ✉ *17 Courtenay Pl.,* ☎ *04/ 385–1819.* ◷ *Mon.–Sat. 9:30–6, Sun. 11–5.* **Parson's Books & Music** is not the largest bookstore in town, but it's one of the most intriguing—strong on New Zealand writing and travel, and also featuring comprehensive classical recordings, and a small upper-floor café. ✉ *126 Lambton Quay,* ☎ *04/472–4587.* ◷ *Mon.–Sat. 9:30–5:30.*

OUTDOOR CLOTHES AND EQUIPMENT
Wellington is a fine place to stock up on camping supplies before hitting the great outdoors. If you can't find what you need at **Kathmandu** (✉ 34 Manners St., ☎ 04/801–8755), **Mainly Tramping** (✉ 39 Mercer St., ☎ 04/473–5353), or **Ski & Camping Great Outdoors Centre** (✉ 181 Wakefield St., ☎ 04/801–8704), it probably doesn't exist.

SOUVENIRS
Sommerfields is is a great shop for New Zealand–made crafts. ✉ *296 Lambton Quay,* ☎ *04/499–4847.* ◷ *Weekdays 9:30–5:30, Sat. 9:30–1.*

Wellington A to Z

Arriving and Departing

BY BUS

InterCity and **Newmans** buses (☎ 04/472–5111) arrive at and depart from Wellington Railway Station. There are daily departures to all major North Island destinations, and connections with InterIslander and Lynx sailings to Picton (on South Island).

BY CAR

The main access to the city is via the Wellington Urban Motorway, which starts just after the merging of Highways 1 and 2, a few miles north of the city center. The motorway links the city center with all towns and cities to the north.

BY FERRY

The **InterIslander** (☎ 0800/802–802) runs vehicle and passenger ferries between Wellington and the South Island port of Picton. The standard one-way adult fare is $46, though economy and saver fares are often available if booked in advance and bring the price down to between $23 and $39. The fare for a medium-size sedan is between $116 and $165 depending on the time of year. Most rental agencies have North Island–South Island transfer programs for their vehicles: leave one car off in Wellington and pick another one up in Picton on the same contract. It is common practice, quickly and easily done. The crossing takes about three hours and can be very rough. There are up to five departures in each direction every day, and bookings should be made in advance, particularly during holiday periods.

The fast **Lynx** ferry service (☎ 0800/802–802) between Wellington and Picton takes an hour and 45 minutes. There are three daily departures (at 8 AM, 1:30 PM, and 6:30 PM), but the service only operates between December and April. Fares vary, with the standard one-way adult ticket costing between $30 and $59. Taking a medium-size sedan costs between $95 and $190. Economy and special saver tickets are often available.

The InterIslander and Lynx terminal is about 3 km (2 mi) from the city. A free bus leaves Platform 9 at the Wellington Railway Station for the ferry terminal 40 minutes before sailings.

BY PLANE

Wellington International Airport lies about 8 km (5 mi) from the city. **Super Shuttle** (☎ 04/387–8787) operates a 10-seater bus between the airport and any address in the city ($10 for one person, $13 for two). The bus meets all incoming flights; tickets are available from the driver.

International carriers serving Wellington are **Air New Zealand** (☎ 0800/737–000) and **Qantas** (☎ 0800/808–767). Domestic carriers, with services across the country, include **Air New Zealand** and **Ansett** (☎ 04/471–1146).

BY TRAIN

The terminal for all TranzRail train services is **Wellington Railway Station** (☎ 04/498–3000) on Bunny Street, 1½ km (about 1 mi) from the city center.

TranzMetro (☎ 04/801–7000) operates electric suburban train services to Wellington from the Hutt Valley, Palmerston North, and Masterton.

Getting Around
BY BICYCLE

If the sun is shining and the wind is still, a bicycle is an ideal way to explore the city and its surrounding bays. **Penny Farthing Cycles** (⊠ 89 Courtenay Pl., ☎ 04/385–2772) rents out mountain bikes for $25 per day or $140 per week, including helmets.

BY BUS

Wellington's bus and trolley-bus network is operated by several companies, though it's easy to find out information on routes and fares by calling the public transport information service known as **Ridewell** (☎ 04/801–7000; ☉ Mon.–Sat. 7:30 AM–8:30 PM, Sun. 9–3). The main terminals for services are at the railway station and from Courtenay Place. The City Circular Bus departs every 10 minutes on a circular loop through the center passing all the main sights and attractions. For all trips in the inner city, the fare is $1. **STARpass** tickets ($7) allow a day's unlimited travel on all buses; a **Two-Hour Ticket** ($4), purchased from the driver, lets you board as many buses as you wish within two hours. For maps and timetables, go to the visitor information center (⊠ Victoria and Wakefield Sts.), the railway station (⊠ Bunny St.), or the Wellington Regional Council Centre (⊠ 142–146 Wakefield St.).

BY TAXI

Wellington is only a small city, but a taxi ride can save your legs on the long haul around the harbor or up the steep hills to Kelburn and the Botanic Gardens. Most city rides cost under $6. There are taxis outside the railway station, as well as on Dixon Street and along Courtenay Place and Lambton Quay.

Contacts and Resources
CAR RENTAL

Avis, Budget, and Hertz have offices at Wellington airport (☞ Car Rental *in* Smart Travel Tips A to Z). But you'll often find cheaper rates at one of several local agencies; contact details and more information from the Wellington Visitor Information Centre (☞ *below*).

EMBASSIES AND HIGH COMMISSIONS

Australian High Commission. ⊠ *72–78 Hobson St., Thorndon,* ☎ *04/ 473–6411.* ☉ *Weekdays 8:45–12:15.*

British High Commission. ⊠ *44 Hill St., Thorndon,* ☎ *04/472–6049.* ☉ *Weekdays 9:30–noon and 2–3:30.*

Canadian High Commission. ⊠ *61 Molesworth St., Thorndon,* ☎ *04/ 473–9577.* ☉ *Weekdays 8:30–4:30.*

United States Embassy. ⊠ *29 Fitzherbert Terr., Thorndon,* ☎ *04/472– 2068.* ☉ *Weekdays 10–noon and 2–4.*

EMERGENCIES

Dial 111 for **fire, police, or ambulance** services.

Wellington Hospital. ⊠ *Riddiford St., Newtown,* ☎ *04/385–5999.*

After-Hours Medical Centre. ⊠ *17 Adelaide Rd., Newtown,* ☎ *04/384– 4944.* ☉ *24 hrs.*

GUIDED TOURS

Wally Hammond, a tour operator with a great anecdotal knowledge and a fund of stories about the city, offers a 2½-hour minibus tour of the city and Marine Drive. This can be combined with a half-day Kapiti Coast Tour, during which Southward Car Museum is visited. Tours depart from Travel World, Mercer, and Victoria streets at 10 and 2. Passengers can be picked up at their city hotels at no extra cost. ☎ *04/472–0869.* ☒ *City tour $25, combined tour $70.*

Westpac Trust Ferry, a commuter service between the city and Days Bay, on the east side of Port Nicholson, is one of the best-value tours in the city. On the way to Days Bay you can stop at Somes Island, formerly a quarantine station that is an unusual picnic spot on a summer afternoon. Days Bay itself has a seaside village atmosphere, local crafts shops, and great views of Wellington. Weekdays the catamaran departs from Queens Wharf at 6, 7:15, 8:20, noon, 2, 4:15, 5:30, and 6:30; weekends at 10:15, noon, 2, 3:45, and 5. The direct trip takes 25 minutes. ⊠ *Queens Wharf,* ☎ *04/499–1273.* ➨ *Round-trip to Days Bay $14, to Somes Island $16.*

TRAVEL AGENCIES

American Express Travel Service. ⊠ *Level 7, Greenock House, 39 The Terrace,* ☎ *04/471–5560.*
Thomas Cook. ⊠ *108 Lambton Quay,* ☎ *04/473–5167.*

VISITOR INFORMATION

Wellington Visitor Information Centre. ⊠ *Civic Administration Bldg., Victoria and Wakefield Sts.,* ☎ *04/801–4000.* ☉ *Weekdays 8:30–5:30, weekends 9:30–4:30.*

THE WAIRARAPA

Wellington residents call the Rimutaka Range to the north of the city "the Hill," and for years it has been both a physical and psychological barrier that has allowed the Wairarapa region to develop at its own pace, in its own style. The hill has also kept tour buses away, and as a result landscapes such as the Pinnacles—cliff faces carved by the wind into shapes reminiscent of a cathedral—are uncrowded and easy to reach. There are great hikes and walks in the area. Times are changing quickly, however. An expanding wine trail in the southern Wairarapa is drawing visitors in increasing numbers, as well as city dwellers who want to move into the region for a lifestyle change. Meanwhile, the Wairarapa is still a place to discover, a delightful side trip from Wellington, and a destination in its own right.

Martinborough

⑤ *70 km (44 mi) north of Wellington.*

Martinborough is the hub of the Wairarapa's wine industry, and as a result this small town is attracting interest from developers keen to cash in on growing tourist numbers. So far changes have been tasteful, with people refurbishing historic places and opening their homes as B&Bs. The town gets its name from founder John Martin, who planned the streets in a Union Jack pattern stretching out from a square that remains the center of activity. Most restaurants and shops are on or close to the square.

Local records indicate that grapes have been raised in the region since the turn of the last century. The present industry only dates from 1979, and the popularity of Martinborough wine has grown tremendously since the mid- to late 1980s. That said, many local producers have small outputs, which means that some local varieties can be scarce everywhere but here, and prices tend to be higher than in other New Zealand wine regions. A number of the wineries are within a 10-minute walk of town, and there is a wine-trail horse-carriage tour as well. As in Hawke's Bay, red grape varieties seem to have the best go in the area's soil, with pinot noir being the most exceptional. Keep in mind that from year to year,

Greater Wellington and Wairarapa

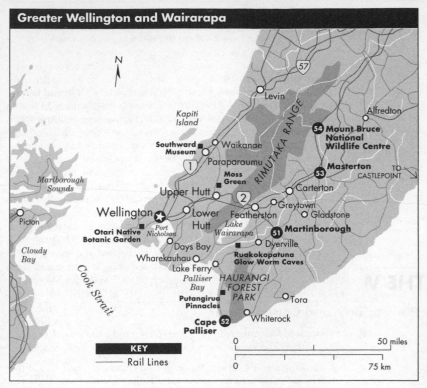

any given winery's varieties may change depending on grape quality. Here is a short list of the best of the region's wineries:

Dry River (⊠ Puruatanga Rd., ☎ 06/306–9388) is undoubtedly the country's hottest small (read: tiny) producer. Neil and Dawn McCallum's ultra-selectively produced vintages sell out immediately on release. Bringing home a bottle of their gewürztraminer or pinot noir would be a coup. Call ahead for an appointment. **Ata Rangi Vineyard** (⊠ Puruatanga Rd., ☎ 06/306–9570) makes exceptional chardonnay, pinot noir, and Célèbre (a cabernet-merlot-shiraz blend), again in small quantities. Tastings are held October–April, daily 11–5. **Martinborough Vineyard** (⊠ Princess St., ☎ 06/306–9955), open daily 11–5, is a larger but equally fine regional winery—actually the first to convince the world of the Wairarapa's pinot noir potential. Martinborough's chardonnay is also exceptional. **Palliser Estate** (⊠ Kitchener St., ☎ 06/ 306–9019) has come out with some of the best local whites. The sauvignon blanc and late-harvest riesling are both distinguished by their intense flavors. Palliser is open daily 10–6.

OFF THE BEATEN PATH

RUAKOKOPATUNA GLOWWORM CAVES – The glowworm display here is not quite as impressive as the one at Waitomo in the King Country, but the sense of adventure is much greater—nobody will tell you to duck when you're approaching a low-hanging rock, so be careful. You'll walk right through a cave following a freshwater stream: expect to get wet feet, and take a flashlight. Once you have found a cluster of glowworms, turn your flashlight off for the best display, then switch it on again as you walk deeper into the cave. And keep in mind that as you stay in the cave longer, your eyes will adjust to the darkness, allowing you to see more lights. Take Lake Ferry Road southwest from Martinborough 7 km (4½ mi), turn left on Dyerville Road, and drive another 8 km (5 mi) to a sign for the caves. Entrance is free, and it is best to call ahead for permission before you go as the caves are on private property. ☎ 06/306-9393.

Dining and Lodging

$$$$ X☷ **Martinborough Hotel.** This restored wooden 1890s hotel, with an
★   internal courtyard filled with flowers, has the best location in town, right on Martinborough's square. Built in colonial style refurbishment has enhanced its historic qualities. Rooms are each decorated uniquely with elegant drapes, area rugs, and a mix of antique and contemporary furnishings, such as four-poster beds and writing tables. Some bathrooms have clawfoot tubs. Upstairs rooms in the main building open onto the veranda, and garden rooms look out on to roses and lavender bushes. In the attractive, wood-floored Martinborough Bistrot on site, appetizers might include seasonal whitebait fritters served with lemon and dill mayonnaise, or shucked Marlborough oysters with a red wine and shallot vinegar. The kitchen has a way with even humble steak and salmon: try the fillet steak, barbecued and served with a Stilton and olive polenta, or an herb-crusted salmon with seared scallops and creamed spinach. ⊠ *The Square,* ☎ 06/306-9350, ℻ 06/306-9345. *16 rooms. Restaurant, 2 bars. AE, DC, MC, V. BP.* ✎

Palliser Bay and Cape Palliser

52 *Southwest of Martinborough: 25 km (16 mi) to Lake Ferry, 40 km (25 mi) to Putangirua Pinnacles, 60 km (37 mi) to Cape Palliser.*

For the Wairarapa's most remote, blustery scenery—and to see the North Island's southernmost point, Cape Palliser—you need to make the drive southwest from Martinborough. It's 25 km (16 mi) through rolling sheep country to the coast at the little settlement of **Lake Ferry** on Palliser Bay. The lake in question, called Onoke, is a salt lagoon formed by the long sand bank here. Vacation homes, fishing spots, and remarkable sunsets over the bay bring in the weekend Wellingtonian crowd.

Just before Lake Ferry, turn left (coming from Martinborough) at the sign for "Cape Palliser" and drive another 15 km (9 mi) around Palliser Bay to Te Kopi, where the **Putangirua Pinnacles Scenic Reserve** is protected from the hordes by its relative isolation. The spectacular rocks have been formed over the last 120,000 years as rains have washed away an ancient gravel deposit, and pinnacles and towers now soar hundreds of feet into the air on both sides of a stony riverbank. An hour-long round-trip walk from the parking area takes you along the riverbank and close up to the base of the pinnacles. If you're feeling adventurous, there is a three- to four-hour bushwalk involving some steep climbs and wonderful vistas of the coast—as far off as South Island on a clear day. The Pinnacles are an hour's drive from Martinborough.

The road to Cape Palliser deteriorates after the Pinnacles and is unpaved in places. It's a dramatic, bleak ride, though not particularly hard, provided you take care. After 20 km (12 mi), the road ends at **Cape Palliser** itself, where 250 wooden steps climb up to the candy-striped lighthouse. The views from here, up and down the wild coastline, are terrific. Below the lighthouse, splashing in the surf and basking on the rocks, are members of the North Island's only resident **fur seal colony**. You'll be able to get pretty close for photos, but not too close—these are wild animals and fiercely protective of their young. Best advice: don't get between seals and pups, or seals and the ocean.

Dining and Lodging

$$$$ ✕🍴 **Wharekauhau.** This Edwardian-style homestead set on a 5,000-
★ acre working sheep station is luxury lashed by nature. On a hot summer afternoon this is one of the most peaceful places on earth; on a
windy, wet morning it's like something out of *Wuthering Heights.* The
public areas are in the homestead, which retains the feeling of a family lodge, and guest rooms are fashioned after staff quarters, with a
style and comfort that no farmworker, of course, ever had. Each room
has a king-size bed, a small patio, and an open fireplace. On the farm
you can take in the workings of the sheep station and walk around the
gloriously remote coastline. Trout fishing is also an option, as are
tours to the seal colony at Palliser Bay. Rates include breakfast, dinner, and predinner drinks, and seasonally changing menus highlight the
best of local produce—especially lamb and fish—accompanied by fine
Martinborough wines. Vineyard visits can be arranged. The homestead
is 40 minutes' drive south of Featherston on the rugged coast at the
northern end of Palliser Bay; from Featherston, take the minor road
along the west side of Lake Wairarapa. ⊠ *Western Lake Rd., Palliser
Bay, R.D. 3, Featherston,* ☎ *06/307–7581,* 🖷 *06/307–7799. 12 rooms.
Tennis courts, fishing. AE, DC, MC, V. MAP.* ✎

$ ✕🍴 **Lake Ferry Hotel.** The southernmost hotel in the North Island is
a simple pub with no-frills rooms, but the location more than makes
up for any lack of city style. Four of the rooms open on to a veranda
for lake and ocean views—take drinks on the deck as the sun sets and
then tuck into a hearty steak or locally caught fish-and-chip dinner at
very reasonable prices. The locals make the pub very much their own,
but the hotel sees a fair amount of weekend getaways from Wellington. Ask about the local fishing, said to be very good from the sand-
bank opposite the hotel. ⊠ *Lake Ferry,* ☎ *06/307–7831,* 🖷 *06/307–
7868. 8 rooms, 4 with bath. Restaurant. BP. MC, V.*

Masterton

㊾ *40 km (25 mi) northeast of Martinborough, 230 km (144 mi) southwest of Napier.*

Masterton is Wairarapa's major population center, but—in common
with the other towns strung out along Highway 2 from Wellington,
like Featherston, Greytown, and Carterton—you will find little of interest beyond its suitability as an exploring base. Visitors are best advised to make for the coast, an hour's drive east of Masterton through
lovely hill country, where **Castlepoint** is perhaps the most spectacular
site on the entire Wairarapa coast. Here, Castle Rock rises a sheer 500
ft out of the sea; below, in **Deliverance Cove,** seals sometimes play. There's
a fantastic walk to the peninsula lighthouse, and surfers rate highly the
beach break at Deliverance Cove. There's a beachside motor camp and
a couple of small motels at Castlepoint.

There are enjoyable bushwalks in beautiful forests laced with streams
at **Tararua Forest Park,** which also has picnic facilities. The Mt.
Holdsworth area at the east end of the park is particularly popular for
tramping. To get there turn off State Highway 2 onto Norfolk Road,
2 km (1 mi) south of Masterton.

Shopping

For a unique souvenir, visit the **Paua Shell Factory and Shop** (⊠ 54
Kent St., Carterton, ☎ 06/379–6777), 15 km (9 mi) south of Masterton. Paua (abalone) has been collected by the Maori for food since ancient times. The rainbow-color shell interiors are highly prized (used

by the Maori to represent eyes in their statues), and here are polished
and processed, then turned into jewelry and other gifts.

Mount Bruce National Wildlife Centre

54 *30 km (19 mi) north of Masterton.*

★ The **Mount Bruce National Wildlife Centre** makes a fine introduction
to the country's wildlife, particularly its endangered bird species. An
easy-to-walk trail (one-hr round-trip) through the bush takes you past
aviaries containing rare, endangered, or vulnerable birds, including the
takahe (a flightless bird thought to be extinct until it was rediscovered
in 1948), *kokako,* saddleback, and stitchbird. The real highlight,
though, is the nocturnal habitat containing foraging kiwis, the country's symbol, which are endearing little bundles of energy. It takes a
while for your eyes to adjust to the artificial gloom, but it's worth the
wait. Don't miss the eel feeding (daily at 1:30 PM) when the reserve's
stream writhes with the New Zealand long-finned eel. A tearoom
serves toasted sandwiches and snacks. ⊠ *State Hwy. 2, 30 km (19 mi)*
north of Masterton, ☎ *06/375–8004.* ⌑ *$8.* ⊙ *Daily 9:30–4.* ⊛

The Wairarapa A to Z

Arriving and Departing

BY CAR

A car is essential for getting around the Wairarapa. State Highway 2
runs through the region from north and south, between Napier and
Wellington. From Wellington you'll drive through Upper Hutt, over
the Rimutaka Range, then into the gateway town of Featherston.
Highway 53 will take you to Martinborough; turn southwest here on
Lake Ferry Road for Lake Ferry and Cape Palliser. Masterton is farther north along State Highway 2. The journey from Wellington to Martinborough takes 1½ hours; Masterton is another half hour. From
Napier, Masterton is about three hours.

Contacts and Resources

GUIDED TOURS

The **Horse and Carriage Establishment** runs tours around the vineyards.
The cost is $40 per person for a two-hour tour; advance booking is
essential. The company also has twilight carriage drives, mystery tours,
and horse and carriage hire for any specific journey. ⊠ *Martinborough,*
☎ *025/477–852.*

VISITOR INFORMATION

Tourism Wairarapa. ⊠ *5 Dixon St., Masterton,* ☎ *06/378–7373.* ⊙
Weekdays 8:30–5:30, weekends 9–4.
Martinborough Visitor Information Centre. ⊠ *Kitchener and Broadway*
Sts., Martinborough, ☎ *06/306–9043.* ⊙ *Daily 10–4.*

3 UPPER SOUTH ISLAND

Natural wonders never cease—not on South Island. Nor do the opportunities for adventure: sea-kayaking, glacier hiking, trekking, fishing, mountain biking, rafting, and rock climbing. If you'd rather kick back while you feast your senses, you can fly over brilliant glaciers and snowy peaks, watch whales from on deck, or taste some of the regions's delicious wines. Add New Zealand hospitality, and you can't go wrong.

HE CLOSE PASSAGE across Cook Strait separates North Island from South Island, but the difference between the two is far greater than the distance suggests. Whether you're seeing South Island from aboard a ferry as it noses through the rocky entrance to Marlborough Sounds or through the window of a plane bound for Christchurch, the immediate impression is that the landscape has turned feral: the mellow, green beauty of North Island has given way to jagged snow-capped mountains and rivers that charge down from the heights and sprawl across vast, rocky shingle beds. South Island has been carved by ice and water, a process still rapidly occurring. Locals will tell you that you haven't seen rain until you've been drenched by a storm on the West Coast, where annual precipitation is ambitiously measured in meters.

The top half of South Island is a fair introduction to the contrasts of New Zealand's less populated island. The Marlborough Province occupies the northeast corner, where the inlets of Marlborough Sounds flow around verdant peninsulas and sandy coves. Marlborough is now the largest wine-growing region in New Zealand, with more than 7,200 acres of vineyards. Predominant varieties grown are sauvignon blanc, chardonnay, riesling, pinot noir, pinot gris, cabernet sauvignon, and merlot. An abundance of other fruit is grown in the area as well. Marlborough is relatively dry, beautifully sunny, and in summer the inland plains look something like the American West, with mountains rising out of grassy flats. Throughout Upper South Island, you'll notice commercial foresting of the hills—Californian *Pinus radiata* (Monterey pine) mature rapidly in New Zealand soil. Their 25-year harvest cycle is one of the shortest in the world, a fact duly noted by Japanese lumber concerns.

The northwest corner of the island, the Nelson region, is a sporting paradise with a mild climate that allows a year-round array of outdoor activities. Sun-drenched Nelson is the area's gateway, a lively town with fine restaurants and a vibrant network of artists and craftspeople who produce an abundance of wares. To the west of the city, Abel Tasman National Park, like the Marlborough Sounds across the island, is ringed with spectacular coastal waters—of a nearly indescribable blue—studded with rock outcrops guarding coves and sands that are sea-kayakers', trekkers', beachcombers', and sunbathers' dreams. The area is literally surrounded by great national parks and hiking tracks (trails), such as Kahurangi National Park, Nelson Lakes National Park, and the Heaphy Track, one of the world's great walks.

After the gentler climate of Marlborough and Nelson, the wild grandeur of the West Coast comes as a surprise. This is Mother Nature with her hair down, flaying the coastline with huge seas and drenching rains and littering its beaches with evocative pieces of bleached driftwood. When it rains, you'll feel like you're inside a fishbowl; then the sun bursts out, and you'd swear you're in paradise. It's a country that has created a special breed of people, and the rough-hewn and powerfully independent locals—known to the rest of the country as coasters—occupy a special place in New Zealand folklore.

These three regions, which ring the north and west coasts of South Island, offer an immense variety of scenery, from the siren seascapes of Marlborough Sounds and rocky Kaikoura, to the mellow river valleys of Golden Bay and Abel Tasman National Park, to the West Coast's colliding rain forests and glaciers, where the Southern Alps soar to 12,000 ft within 32 km (20 mi) of the shore.

Note: For more information on bicycling, fishing, hiking, and sea-kayaking in Upper South Island, *see* Chapter 5.

Pleasures and Pastimes

Dining

The top of the South Island is where you'll find some of the country's best seafood, fruit, and wine. In Marlborough check out at least one winery restaurant—there's no better way to ensure that your meal suits what you're drinking. The region is famous for sauvignon blanc, but also produces excellent chardonnay and riesling, and good pinot noir. Salmon and Greenshell mussels are both farmed in the pristine Marlborough Sounds, and local crops—besides grapes—include cherries (delicious!), wasabi, and garlic. In Kaikoura try crayfish. The region is named after the delicacy (*kai* means food in Maori, *koura* means lobster), and you'll find it not only in restaurants, but occasionally sold in makeshift vans or roadside sheds. On the West Coast, try whitebait fritters—a sort of omelet starring masses of baby fish, called *inanga* by Maori. One warning: restaurants and cafés around the glaciers can be quick to close their doors at night. Be there by 8:30, or you might go hungry.

For price category information, *see* the chart *under* Dining *in* Smart Travel Tips A to Z.

Lodging

North Islanders might disagree, but you may find New Zealand's friendliest people in the rural areas of South Island. And the best way to get to know them is to stay with them. Bed-and-breakfasts, farm stays, and homestays, all a variation on the same theme, abound in South Island in some spectacular coastal or mountain settings. Your hosts will feed you great breakfasts and help with advice on where to eat and what to do locally. Other choices include luxury lodges and hotels, or standard, inexpensive motel rooms—there are plenty of the latter.

For price category information, *see* the chart *under* Lodging *in* Smart Travel Tips A to Z.

Mountains and Glaciers

South Island is piled high with mountains. The massive Southern Alps mountain chain virtually slices the island lengthwise, and many outlying ranges spring up farther north. Most of the mountains are easily accessible. You can walk on and around them, ski, or catch a helicopter to land on a glacier and tramp around. Much of the skiing in the upper half of South Island is reasonably challenging for intermediate skiers—the more advanced should look farther south.

Trekking and climbing are as challenging as you care to make them. Department of Conservation tracks and huts are spread around the region, and you can get details on hundreds of hikes from department offices or information centers. Even if you just want to take a casual, scenic walk, the opportunities are endless. In some places, such as the Kaikoura Coastal Track, pioneering farmers have banded together to create farm-to-farm hiking trails. These take you through otherwise inaccessible mountains, bush, and coastal areas.

Wildlife and Wilderness

The West Coast is the habitat for some very interesting creatures. South by Lake Moeraki, New Zealand fur seals and fiordland crested penguins are abundant, and bird life up and down the coast is fascinating. On the other side of the island, the Kaikoura Coast is still a sleepy and uncrowded region where you can get as close to whales, dolphins, and seals as is possible in a wild setting.

South Island's West Coast has a rugged beauty that can be inviting in one instance and almost threatening the next. You can wake up to the sun shining off tall, snowcapped mountains, then a couple of hours later the mist and rain can swirl around the peaks and give them an entirely different complexion. Because of changing conditions, check local conditions before you head into some of the world's most dramatic mountain, bush, and coastal scenery.

Wine

It took only a couple of decades for Marlborough to establish itself as one of the world's great wine-making regions. The local sunny-day–cool-night climate mean grapes come off the vines plump with flavor, and that translates into wines with aromas that positively burst out of the glass. It's an exciting feistiness that some American connoisseurs consider too unbridled—but the wine is delicious, and you should seriously consider bringing a few bottles home. At any of the smaller wineries, it's quite likely you'll share your first taste of their labors with the wine makers themselves.

Exploring Upper South Island

Most people come to Marlborough and Nelson on the ferry to Picton, the northern entrance to South Island. From here the choices open up before you. In four days you can see much of the northernmost part of the island. To undertake a walk on the Queen Charlotte, Abel Tasman, or Heaphy tracks, you'll need more time. For the West Coast three days is a bare minimum—it takes a half day just to get there.

Great Itineraries

Numbers in the text correspond to numbers in the margin and on the Upper South Island map.

IF YOU HAVE 2 DAYS

Spend a day touring the wineries in and around ⌘ **Blenheim** ④. On the second day head down to ⌘ **Kaikoura** ⑤, stopping at the Awatere Valley Gardens or Winterhome on the way. Alternately, you could head straight from the ferry to ⌘ **Nelson** ⑥, taking the first day in town and the second in ⌘ **Abel Tasman National Park** ⑰, or the second visiting Nelson's wineries while following one of its unique arts-and-crafts or heritage trails.

IF YOU HAVE 4 DAYS

With four days you confront the kind of conundrum that makes trip planning for South Island difficult: you can see the top of the island: relaxing ⌘ **Nelson** ⑥, the wineries of ⌘ **Blenheim** ④, the beautiful beaches and forests of ⌘ **Abel Tasman National Park** ⑰ (perhaps all four days hiking one of Abel Tasman's tracks or the Queen Charlotte Track in the Marlborough Sounds). Or you can head straight for four days with the coastal rock formations, glaciers, and wildlife of the West Coast.

IF YOU HAVE 7 DAYS

You *could* try to cover three of the major areas in this chapter—Marlborough, Nelson, and the West Coast, or Marlborough, Nelson, and Kaikoura, but allowing three or four days each for two areas is a better plan. Spend a day or two at the wineries, a day or two on the Marlborough Sounds sea-kayaking or walking, perhaps swinging through **Havelock** ③ on the way to or from the beautiful Kenepuru and Pelorus sounds, and then head to ⌘ **Nelson** ⑥ or the West Coast.

Or spend the first three days in and around Nelson, looking at arts and crafts, following a heritage trail, tasting wine, and taking in ⌘ **Abel Tasman National Park** ⑰ and **Golden Bay–Takaka** ⑱ area, then head

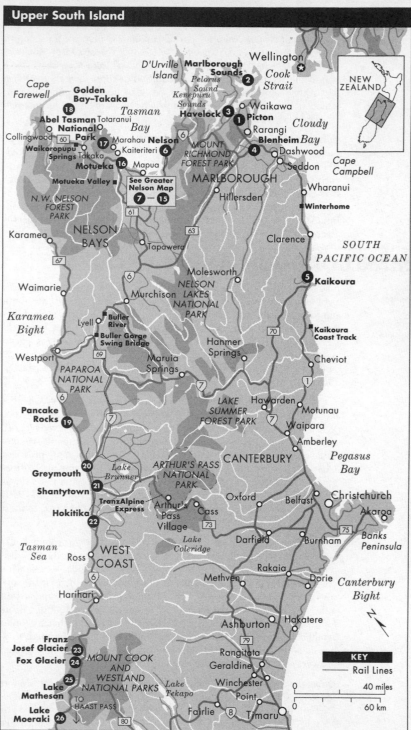

NEW ZEALAND

Cape Farewell

D'Urville Island

Marlborough Sounds ②

Wellington

Cook Strait

Pelorus Sound

Golden Bay-Takaka ⑱

Kenepuru Sounds

Waikawa

Havelock ③

Picton ①

Abel Tasman National Park ⑰

Totaranui

Tasman Bay

Rarangi

Cloudy Bay

Collingwood

Marahau

Nelson ⑥

Blenheim ④

Dashwood

Waikoropupu Springs

Takaka

Kaiteriteri

MOUNT RICHMOND FOREST PARK

Seddon

Motueka ⑯

Mapua

MARLBOROUGH

Wharanui

Motueka Valley ■

See Greater Nelson Map ⑦ — ⑮

Hillersden

Winterhome ■

N.W. NELSON FOREST PARK

NELSON BAYS

Tapawera

SOUTH PACIFIC OCEAN

Karamea

Clarence

Waimarie

Molesworth

NELSON LAKES NATIONAL PARK

⑤ Kaikoura

Karamea Bight

Murchison

Lyell

Buller River

Buller Gorge Swing Bridge

Hanmer Springs

Kaikoura Coast Track ■

Westport

PAPAROA NATIONAL PARK

Maruia Springs

Cheviot

Pancake Rocks ⑲

LAKE SUMMER FOREST PARK

Hawarden

Motunau

Greymouth ⑳

Lake Brunner

Waipara

Shantytown ㉑

ARTHUR'S PASS NATIONAL PARK

Amberley

Pegasus Bay

Hokitika

TranzAlpine Express

Arthur's Pass Village

Cass

Oxford

Belfast

Christchurch

㉒

Lake Coleridge

73

Darfield

Burnham

Akaroa

Tasman Sea

Ross

WEST COAST

75

Banks Peninsula

Rakaia

Harihari

Methven

Dorie

Canterbury Bight

Hakatere

Ashburton

Franz Josef Glacier ㉓

Fox Glacier ㉔

MOUNT COOK AND WESTLAND NATIONAL PARKS

79

Rangitata

Geraldine

Lake Matheson ㉕

Lake Tekapo

Winchester

Point

Lake Moeraki ㉖

TO HAAST PASS

80

Fairlie

⑧

Timaru

to the West Coast. On the way down, stop at the town of Punakaiki for the coastal phenomenon called **Pancake Rocks** ⑲. You could overnight at ⊡ **Greymouth** ⑳ or ⊡ **Hokitika** ㉒ before continuing to Westland National Park to get yourself on the ⊡ **Franz Josef Glacier** ㉓ or ⊡ **Fox Glacier** ㉔. If the wildlife around ⊡ **Lake Moeraki** ㉖ lures you to the West Coast, plan to spend two or three days there after a day at the glaciers. Leave the West Coast by heading south to Haast, which also has great beaches, then driving to Wanaka or Queenstown via the Haast Pass.

When to Tour Upper South Island

Nelson and Marlborough are pleasant year-round, but beach activities are best from December to mid-April. Between December and early February is the busiest time on walking tracks, with New Zealanders setting out on their own vacations. Snow covers the mountains from June through October, which is a beautiful sight from seaside Kaikoura. The pleasures of winter weather around the West Coast glaciers—clear skies and no snow at sea level—are so far a well-kept local secret.

MARLBOROUGH AND KAIKOURA

By Stu Freeman, Stephen Wolf, and Mere Wetere

The Marlborough Sounds were originally settled by seafaring Maori people, who in their day kept to the coastal areas, living off the abundant fruits of the sea. It's no wonder they didn't venture inland, because these coastal areas are spectacular. The Maori named the area Te Tau Ihu O Te Waka a Maui (the prow of Maui's canoe), as legend has it that from his canoe Maui fished up North Island with the jawbone of a whale. Consequently North Island is called Te Ika a Maui—the fish of Maui.

Captain James Cook met the Maori settlers around 1770, when he stopped in the sounds to repair his ships and take on fresh provisions. Whalers later set up shop in Queen Charlotte Sound, but it wasn't until the 1840s that *Pakeha* (Europeans) came to the Wairau and Awatere valleys around Blenheim. Thirty years later, the unwittingly prescient Charles Empson and David Herd began planting red muscatel grapes among local sheep and grain farms. Their modest viticultural torch was rekindled in the next century by the Freeth family, and by the 1940s Marlborough wineries were producing port, sherry, and Madeira most successfully.

At the same time, commercial wineries were growing up around Auckland and Hawke's Bay. But the volume of their grape production didn't meet their needs. In the mid-1970s New Zealand's largest wine company, Montana, planted vines in Marlborough to increase the supply of New Zealand grapes. Other vintners followed suit, and within a decade today's major players—like Hunter's, whose founder, Ernie Hunter, almost single-handedly launched the Marlborough name—had established the region's international reputation. Marlborough now boasts New Zealand's single largest area under vine, and many local growers sell grapes to wine makers outside the area.

Down the coast from Blenheim, Kaikoura is another area that the Maori settled, the predominant tribe being Ngai Tahu. True to their seafaring heritage, they are active in today's whale-watching interests. As of March 1998, Ngai Tahu is one of the first major Maori tribes to receive compensation from the New Zealand government—to the tune of $170 million—along with an apology for unjust confiscation of their lands, forests, and fishing areas. The tribe has extensive interests in tourism, fishing, and horticulture. Kaikoura's name denotes its original significance for the Maori—"to eat crayfish." These clean-tasting, clawless lobsters are a delight, and there are no better reasons to come to Kaikoura than to eat *kaikoura* and to take in the refreshing ocean air.

Picton

❶ *29 km (18 mi) north of Blenheim, 110 km (69 mi) east of Nelson.*

The maritime township of Picton lies at the head of Queen Charlotte Sound and is the arrival point for ferries from North Island, as well as a growing number of international cruise ships. It plays a major role in providing services and transport by water taxi to a multitude of remote communities in the area of islands, peninsulas, and waterways that makes up the Marlborough Sounds Maritime Park. With such an expansive watery environment, it is not surprising that Picton is a yachting mecca and has two sizable marinas, at Picton Harbour and at the adjacent Waikawa Bay. Along with the port of Havelock, these make up the second-largest marina complex in New Zealand.

There's plenty to do in the township, with craft markets during summer, historical sights to see, and walking tracks to scenic lookouts over the sounds. The township wraps around the harbor and is easy to traverse on foot. It has a good number of restaurants—seafood gets top billing—within easy reach of relatively reasonable inns.

❷ Picton is the base for cruising in the **Marlborough Sounds,** the labyrinth of waterways that was formed when the rising sea invaded a series of river valleys at the northern tip of the South Island. Backed by forested hills that at times rise almost vertically from the water, the sounds are a wild, majestic place edged with tiny beaches and rocky coves and studded with islands where such native wildlife as gannets and the primitive tuatara lizard have remained undisturbed by introduced species. Maori legend says the sounds were formed when a great warrior and navigator called Kupe fought with a giant octopus. Its thrashings separated the surrounding mountains, and its tentacles became parts of the sunken valleys. These waterways are the country's second favorite for boating after the Bay of Islands (☞ Chapter 1), but for their isolation and rugged grandeur they are in a class of their own.

Much of the area around Picton is a national park, and it has changed little since Captain Cook found refuge here in the 1770s. There are rudimentary roads on the long fingers of land jutting into the sounds, but the most convenient access is invariably by water. One of the best ways to discover the area is by hitching a ride in Havelock aboard the Pelorus Mail Boat, *Adventurer,* which delivers mail and supplies to outlying settlements scattered around Pelorus Sound (☞ Guided Tours *in* Marlborough and Kaikoura A to Z, *below*).

To get your feet on the ground in and around the sounds, you can take any number of hikes on the **Queen Charlotte Track.** Starting northwest of Picton, the trail stretches 67 km (42 mi) south to north, playing hide-and-seek with the sounds along the way. Tramp through lush native forests filled with bird life, and stop here and there for a swim or to pick up shells on the shore. Unlike along tracks such as the Abel Tasman in Golden Bay, there are no Department of Conservation huts to stay in, just a few points on the way for camping. There are other types of accommodation on the walk, however, from backpacking options to lodges, resorts, and homestays (☞ Dining and Lodging, *below*). Boats such as the *Cougar Line* can drop you off at various places for one-to four-day walks (guided or unguided), or you can kayak parts of it (☞ Guided Tours *in* Marlborough and Kaikoura A to Z, *below*).

For local and Queen Charlotte Track information, contact the **Picton Visitor Information Centre** (⊠ Picton Foreshore, ☎ 03/573–7477, ℻ 03/573–5021).

Dining and Lodging

$$$ ✕ **Marlborough Terranean.** Murals, murals, murals—they're all around you at this Mediterranean-leaning restaurant. Longtime owners Lothar and Tracy Greiner put the place on the market some time ago, but present indications are that they'll be around for a while yet. Whatever happens, the many regulars are likely to insist the menu remains pretty much unchanged. Seafood chowder is always a good bet, as is carpaccio of sliced raw beef fillet with extra-virgin olive oil, lemon juice, and Parmesan. Another Italian classic, saltimbocca—a schnitzel of milk-fed veal (hard to find in New Zealand) topped with smoked ham in white wine, cream, and sage sauce—is a big seller, and there are usually at least three preparations of fresh Marlborough fish. The decisions continue on the dessert list, with a choice of five accompaniments for homemade chocolate mousse—oh joy! ⊠ *31 High St.,* ☎ *03/573–7122. AE, DC, MC, V.*

$ ✕ **Expresso House.** This sunny, friendly spot has rapidly established a reputation for quality and excellent value. Open sandwiches like spicy chicken on rye bread with lemon-caper sauce, regularly changing soups (try any with Thai flavors—the kitchen makes them from scratch), and salad bowls that might include smoked salmon or chicken *satay* (grilled skewers) rule the day. At night the place takes on a bistro ambience, and the menu changes accordingly with dishes like oven-baked local salmon with dill cream sauce, or heartier options like venison Bolognese, and Dutch sausage with *kumara* (sweet potato) mash. Pasta lovers will find plenty of satisfaction here, and there's a good selection of local wines. Save room for the homemade desserts. ⊠ *58 Auckland St.,* ☎ *03/573–7112. MC, V. Licensed and BYOB. Closed Wed.*

$$$$ ✕🏨 **Craglee Lodge.** On a hillside overlooking the emerald waters of
★   the Bay of Many Coves, this three-level complex is a perfect place to unwind. It's swathed in *punga* (tree ferns) and native bush and serenaded by bellbirds and *tuis*. Marilyn and Gary Lowe serve healthy fare from the sea and the region's produce, and serve some outstanding local wines. All the comfortable, contemporary rooms open onto balconies and look over the bay. The two well-maintained tracks from the lodge are worth climbing for two reasons: the stunning views from Kenepuru Saddle and Marilyn's great packed lunch. Sea kayaks, fishing gear, and sailing dinghies are available and fishing trips can be arranged (your catch could be smoked on-site at the end of the day). Take a 45-minute *Cougar Line* water taxi ride, possibly accompanied by dolphins, to get to this remote spot. Rates include three meals. ⊠ *Bay of Many Coves, Queen Charlotte Sound, Private Bag 407, Picton,* ☎ *03/579–9223,* ℻ *03/579–9923. 5 rooms, 2 with bath. Restaurant, lounge, outdoor hot tub, boating, fishing. AE, DC, MC, V.* ✑

$$ ✕🏨 **Punga Cove Resort.** This sanctuary in the Queen Charlotte Sound was carved out of the bush. From its crossroads on the Queen Charlotte Track there are serene vistas of Camp Bay and Endeavour Inlet. The A-frame chalets tucked into the bush, some with cooking facilities, are sunny retreats at a reasonable rate. More luxurious options are the large, tastefully decorated self-contained chalets; each comes with two bedrooms with king-size beds, as well as a barbecue, whirlpool, and ample wraparound decking. If you only want to come for an evening meal, you can dine indoors or out on local fare such as grilled scallops and lime skewers or sugar-cured venison racks with grilled kumara layered in a robust port and prune jus. You can rent kayaks and dinghies on site, fishing trips can be arranged, and there is a small grocery market. Access is quickest by the *Cougar Line* water taxi, 45 minutes from

Picton. Otherwise, a two-hour-plus drive winds along Queen Charlotte Sound Drive to the turnoff at Link Water, where you come through the spectacular scenery of the Kenepuru Sound via some 15 km (10 mi) of gravel road—this is wonderfully off the beaten path. ⊠ *Punga Cove, Endeavour Inlet, Queen Charlotte Sound, Rural Bag 408, Picton,* ☎ *03/579–8561 or 0800/809–697,* FAX *03/579–8080. 2 luxury chalets, 11 smaller chalets. Restaurant, bar, pool. AE, DC, MC, V.* ✍

$$ 🏠 **House of Glenora.** One of Picton's oldest houses, built in the 1860s for the town's first magistrate, is a stylish combination of homestay, weaving school, and gallery, in which you'll find exquisite examples of owner Birgite Armstrong's natural fiber garments. This gracious, smoke-free home, with a large, sunny veranda overlooking sprawling gardens and views toward the harbor, has all but one of its five rooms upstairs. They're spacious and inviting, each with its own stylish color theme. Native woods such as kauri and rimu have been used extensively in restoring Glenora. Breakfast, which is Swedish smorgasbord style with a Kiwi twist, is included in the rates. ⊠ *22 Broadway, Picton,* ☎ *03/573–6966,* FAX *03/573–7735. 5 rooms, 3 with bath. Lounge, shop. MC, V. BP.* ✍

$$ 🏠 **Ocean Ridge Homestay and Bed & Breakfast.** Overlooking Ocean
★ Bay, 32 km (20 mi) south of Picton on the Port Underwood Road, is a piece of paradise. In 1840 this coast was one of the busiest whaling areas in the South Pacific. Standing on the decks of this modern seaside retreat, you can look along the rugged coastline and imagine the many coves teaming with whaling ships and Maori *waka* (canoes). These days you're more likely to see mussel farms, fur seals, penguins, and dolphins. Orca are even known to visit en route to Kaikoura. Ken and Sarah Roush, the American couple who came upon this site just before their ferry was to have departed, have built the contemporary lodge with an eye to comfort and lovely views. Each of the three suites has sea views and there is an upstairs lounge, dining area, and fully equipped kitchen for guests. Sarah provides dinner and drinks for guests for $30 by arrangement. Be sure to check out the on-site pewter studio and gallery. Because the Port Underwood Road is partially unpaved, allow 45 minutes' traveling time either from Blenheim, turning off at Tuamarina, or from Picton via Waikawa Bay. ⊠ *Port Underwood Rd., Ocean Bay, Private Bag, Blenheim,* ☎ *03/579–9474,* FAX *03/579–9474. 3 rooms. Outdoor hot tub, beach, hiking. MC, V. BP.* ✍

En Route To take the long way to Blenheim (☞ *below*), **Port Underwood Road** is yet another unbelievably scenic road in a country full of unbelievably scenic roads. There are picnic areas north of Waikawa before you reach the eastern coastal bays, and a couple more near Rarangi. Get on Waikawa Road north out of Picton and continue through the town of Waikawa, then turn south at Opihi Bay. You could also pick up the road driving north out of Rarangi.

Heading west out of Picton toward the town of Havelock (☞ *below*), **Queen Charlotte Drive** rises spectacularly along the edge of Queen Charlotte Sound. It cuts across the base of the peninsula that separates this from Pelorus Sound, then drops into a coastal plain before coming to Havelock. Beyond town the road winds through forested river valleys before it rounds the eastern side of Tasman Bay and reaches Nelson. To start the drive from the InterIslander ferry terminal in Picton, turn right after leaving the parking lot and follow the signs.

About a third of the way to Havelock, **Governor's Bay** is a gorgeous spot for a picnic, a stroll along the forested shore, or a swim in season. Watch for seabirds, and, if the sun is dipping in and out of the clouds, the changes in the colors of the bay.

Havelock

❸ *35 km (22 mi) west of Picton.*

Arguably the Greenshell mussel capital of the world, Havelock is at the head of the **Kenepuru and Pelorus sounds,** and trips around the sounds on the Pelorus Mail Boat, *Adventurer,* depart here. Locals will forgive you for thinking you've seen what the Marlborough Sounds are all about after crossing from North Island to South Island on the ferry—that's just a foretaste of better things to come. Small, seaside Havelock (pop. 400) is good to potter around in, looking at crafts and tucking into some of those mussels.

Dining

$ ✕ **Mussel Boys Restaurant.** Outside, giant fiberglass mussels are playing rugby on the roof. Inside, mussels (real ones!) are served two ways—steamed for three minutes in the whole shell (steamers) and on the half shell (flats). Delicately enhancing the mussel's flavor is a choice of light sauces with which the mussels are steamed, then topped: a sauce of white wine, garlic, and fresh herbs; or coconut, chilli, and coriander; or even basil, parsley, and pesto with tomato and Parmesan cheese. Sauvignon blanc from nearby Marlborough is a perfect partner for almost any dish on the menu. So delighted was one visitor that he remarked, "When are you coming to San Francisco?" ✉ *73 Main Rd., Havelock,* ☎ *03/574–2824. AE, DC, MC, V. Closes earlier winter months.*

Blenheim

❹ *29 km (18 mi) south of Picton, 120 km (73 mi) southeast of Nelson, 129 km (80 mi) north of Kaikoura.*

Most people come to Blenheim (pronounced *blennum* by the locals) for one reason—wine. Most years, Marlborough boasts the highest total sunshine hours in New Zealand, and this daytime warmth combines with crisp, cool nights to give local grapes a long, slow ripening period. The smooth river pebbles that cover the best vineyards are a bonus—they reflect heat onto the ripening bunches. All these factors together create grapes with audacious flavors. Whites reign supreme. Cabernet sauvignon has mostly been pulled out following disappointing results, but recent examples of pinot noir have been pretty impressive.

In 1973 the Montana company paid two Californian wine authorities to investigate local grape-growing potential. Both were impressed with what they found. It was the locals who were skeptical—until they tasted the first wines produced.

There is no reason to race around to all the wineries here—if you do, chances are good that your taste buds won't serve you very well by the time you get to the 39th tasting room. Those mentioned below are among the country's notables, but you won't go wrong if you stop at any of the vineyards around Blenheim. More than half of the wine bottled here is exported, particularly to the United Kingdom, although a few forward-thinkers are targeting the United States. If you've never tried a Marlborough wine, you have some great discoveries ahead of you.

The streets where most wineries are located are arranged more or less in a grid, which makes getting around relatively straightforward. Pick up a map of the Marlborough wine region at the **Blenheim Visitor Information Centre** (✉ The Forum, Queen St., ☎ 03/578–9904) in the Forum on Queen Street in the center of Blenheim.

NEW ZEALAND WINES

NEW ZEALAND WINE is on a roll. Eight times in the last 10 years this tiny country has taken the sauvignon blanc trophy at London's annual International Wine and Spirits Competition, along with three trophies for pinot noir and one for chardonnay. Similar accolades are being won all over the world, yet just decades ago wines that could be offered with pride to overseas guests could be counted on the fingers of one hand—in fact, the knuckle of one finger would have done it.

There are more than 300 wineries here, but only four produce more than 2 million liters. Because even the largest companies are small by international standards, management remains close to the wine-making process—with outstanding results. Passion for the product is evident in all the country's wineries, regardless of their size.

The country's long, narrow shape means that there are major differences between the grape-growing regions. This geographic diversity means that most of Europe's great grapes have found a second home somewhere in the country.

- Sauvignon blanc, particularly from Marlborough, is the export star. Early versions were fiercely aromatic, reminiscent of cut grass or green peppers, but later models have tropical fruit characters more like passion fruit and pineapple.

- Chardonnay grows well all over the country. Left to its own devices, it has a citric, melonlike flavor, but wine makers love to work their magic on it. Barrel fermentation adds a graininess, and wood-aging gives it spiciness and, sometimes, a hint of vanilla.

- Riesling is a gentle variety, with a floral, lightly scented bouquet and fruity taste. Most local versions have at least a touch of sweetness.

- Gewürztraminer is the most distinctive grape variety of them all, with a super-spicy bouquet reminiscent of litchis and cloves. Many of the best Kiwi examples come from Gisborne, but a couple of exceptional versions have come out of Hawke's Bay and Martinborough.

- Originally from Alsace, pinot gris is an up-and-coming variety in New Zealand. At its best, it produces wine with delightfully grainy character and loads of honest flavor.

- Many people believe New Zealand sparkling wine will be the country's next big export success story. Most local examples are made from Marlborough grapes, and it is this province that has been chosen by the international Champagne house involved in local sparkling wine production, Deutz.

- In the red corner, cabernet sauvignon is well suited to warmer parts of New Zealand. Most years, it performs best in Hawke's Bay and on Waiheke Island, in Auckland's Hauraki Gulf, but when conditions are right, good examples have also come from West Auckland, and as far south as Nelson. It is often blended with merlot and cabernet franc.

- Merlot was first used in blends, to fill what was seen as a "flavor hole" in the mid-palate of Kiwi cabernet. Now more and more wine makers are bottling it on its own. It has leather-coffee-tobacco undertones that are often summed up as "British gentleman's club."

- Notoriously difficult to grow, pinot noir has become the ultimate challenge for many wine makers. It seems to behave best in the Wairarapa and Central Otago, but good examples have also been made in Canterbury, Waipara, Marlborough, and Hawke's Bay. It has characters variously described as being like strawberries, cherries, and mushrooms.

Cloudy Bay Vineyards. From the start, Kevin Judd has produced first-class sauvignon blanc, and an equally impressive chardonnay was added to the portfolio soon afterward. That was the intention of Australia's Cape Mentelle Vineyards when they got Cloudy Bay up and running in 1985. The winery's sauvignon blanc is very fine and the only New Zealand wine many overseas visitors have heard of. A smidgen of oak-matured *sémillon* in the blend helps give it a crisp but beautifully balanced flavor profile. Drink it young. The chardonnay is more complex, and better suited to two or three years in the cellar and to drinking with more flavorful food—smoked salmon, for example. For many people, however, the star act is Pelorus, a classy sparkling wine with loads of creamy, savory, crisp flavors. ⊠ *Jackson's Rd., Blenheim,* ☎ *03/572–8914,* ℻ *03/572–8065.* ⊙ *Daily 10–4:30; tours by appointment.*

Allan Scott Wines. Allan Scott helped establish the big-selling Stoneleigh label for Corbans, the country's second-biggest wine company, before launching his own company in 1990. Now he makes well-respected sauvignon blanc, chardonnay, and riesling. The tasting room is adjacent to a pleasant indoor-outdoor restaurant. ⊠ *Jackson's Rd., R.D. 3, Blenheim,* ☎ *03/572–9054,* ℻ *03/572–9053.* ⊙ *Daily 9:30–5. Oct.–Mar., restaurant daily.*

Corbans Marlborough Winery. The Stoneleigh label is the one to look for at Corbans; it's one of the company's best-known export names, so you might have already tasted it at home. Most of the wines in the extensive local range are likely to be available for tasting, and many of them will have picked up awards in New Zealand and overseas. ⊠ *Jackson's Rd., Blenheim,* ☎ *03/572–8198,* ℻ *03/572–8199.* ⊙ *Daily 10–4; tours by appointment.*

Hunter's Wines. Expatriate Irishman Ernie Hunter's marketing skills thrust Marlborough into the international spotlight, and the company he founded continues to be a leader. Tragically, he died in a car accident at the age of 37. Energetic Jane Hunter, his wife, took the reins and has masterfully shaped Hunter's reputation—which should be no surprise, since she has a long family history of wine making. Expect consistently strong sauvignon blanc—the oak-aged version is particularly good—tangy and delightfully herbal. Chardonnay will have very subtle oak flavors and intense fruit. The winery has an attached restaurant that has proved variable over the years, but can be very good. (☞ Dining and Lodging, *below*). ⊠ *Rapaura Rd., Blenheim,* ☎ *03/572–8489,* ℻ *03/572–8457.* ⊙ *Mon.–Sat. 9:30–4:30, Sun. 10–4.*

Gillan Estate Wines. Entrepreneurial Blenheim residents Toni and Terry Gillan have launched a shopping center, a hotel, and this well-regarded wine company since they moved to town a few years ago. *Méthode champenoise* sparkling wine is their specialty, but their wine maker, Sam Weaver, also crafts very good sauvignon blanc and enjoyable chardonnay and merlot. The wine is made under contract off-site, but the pleasant tasting room is well worth visiting, not least for the tasty tapas prepared to partner the wine. ⊠ *Rapaura Rd., Blenheim,* ☎ *03/ 572–9979,* ℻ *03/572–9980.* ⊙ *Summer 10:30–4:30, winter by appointment.*

Wairau River Wines. Phil and Chris Rose were the first contract grape growers in Marlborough. Now they produce a small range of wines under their own label. The tasting room is made from mud bricks; it also serves as a restaurant, concentrating on local produce. Try the multi-award-winning sauvignon blanc, then move on to the elegant chardonnay and, if it's available, the startlingly good, sweet riesling, made in some years from grapes infected with the mold the French call the "noble rot." ⊠ *Rapaura Rd. and State Hwy. 6, Blenheim,* ☎ *03/572–9800,* FAX *03/572–9885.* ⊙ *Daily 10–5.*

Vavasour Wines. An almost instant hit among Marlborough's mid-1980s start-ups, the small, extremely conscientious wine-making operation at Vavasour produces sensitively balanced whites and reds. Based on the quality of a given year's harvest, grapes will be used either for Reserve vintages available in limited quantities or the medium-price-range Dashwood label. Vavasour is in its own microclimate, in the Awatere Valley south of Blenheim. The viticulturist and wine maker focus on the finesse of smaller grape yields. You won't taste as many varieties here, but what you taste will be interesting and very well crafted. ⊠ *Redwood Pass Rd., Awatere Valley, 20 km (12 mi) south of Blenheim,* ☎ *03/575–7481,* FAX *03/575–7240.* ⊙ *Oct.–Mar., daily 10–4; Apr.–Sept., Mon.–Sat. 10–4; tours by appointment.*

Awatere Valley Gardens. Spend an afternoon strolling in two delightful gardens, a short drive south of Blenheim. Both have splendid herbaceous borders, as well as their own individual characteristics. At **Alton Downs,** take in the results of Alistair and Gaye Elliot's love of heritage roses, such as the French Alberic Babier, propagated around 1850, and their 200-ft oak walk. Carolyn and Joe Ferraby's **Barewood** has beautiful terraced borders—blooming pink, blue, apricot, and white—surrounding their century-old cottage. A sizable *potager* (kitchen garden) filled with ornamental vegetables and herbs is hedged with hornbeam. A 100-year-old cob house on the property was the original home of Mr. Ferraby's ancestors. Carolyn now uses it as a shop, where she sells plants and garden accessories. ⊠ *Alton Downs, Awatere Valley Rd., 5 km (3 mi) west of State Hwy. 1,* ☎ *03/575–7414,* FAX *03/575–7111.* ⊠ *Barewood, Marama Rd., outside Seddon, 18 km (11 mi) west of State Hwy. 1,* ☎ *03/575–7432,* FAX *03/575–7436.* 🎫 *$4 per garden.* ⊙ *By appointment.*

Winterhome. Susan Macfarlane is on the mark when she says that there is no other garden in New Zealand quite like hers. The dry limestone soil and an abundance of sunshine lends a Mediterranean air to this land. And it is with a strong sense of design and drama that Susan and her husband, Richard, have moved beyond the cottage-garden phenomenon so popular today. Winterhome is a study in the rules of traditional garden design and structure. Straight lines and geometric patterns provide clear boundaries for the plantings. The palette is restrained, and the effect is unified and rhythmic. A large, sunken garden is hedged with dwarf boxwood and filled solely with fragrant, white Margaret Merril roses. A broad pathway takes you past sweeps of lavender boldly punctuated by evergreen spires. High brick walls enclose spaces and provide a sense of intimacy and safety. Benches are exactly where you want them: in a cool spot at the end of a long pathway or overlooking the Pacific. The views are lovely here and made more enticing because they've been framed with aesthetic control, be it with greenery or the span of an arched gateway. Be sure to stop in for a fabulous meal at the MacFarlane's nearby restaurant, the **Store** (☞ Dining and Lodging, *below*). Winterhome is south of Blenheim en route to Kaikoura. ⊠ *State Hwy. 1, Kekerengu,* ☎ *03/575–8674,* FAX *03/575–8620.* 🎫 *Small entry fee.* ⊙ *Late Oct.–Easter, daily 10–4.*

Dining and Lodging

$$$ ✕ **Bacchus.** Marcel Rood has cooked at Michelin-starred restaurants in Europe and done the rounds of top kitchens in New Zealand. Now he's settled in wine country—and loving it. His restaurant has a romantic and sumptuous feel, with rich burgundy walls and lots of velvet. A fountain (of Bacchus—who else?) occupies center stage, and an open fire keeps things cozy in winter. The food is traditional and flavorsome, and Marcel makes good use of New Zealand produce in dishes like bacon-wrapped beef fillet on kumara mash. Vegetarians will be happy with the smoked cheddar and Brie torte, dabbed with cranberry relish. ⊠ *3 Main St.,* ☎ *03/578–8099. AE, DC, MC, V. No lunch.*

$$$ ✕ **d'Urville Wine Bar and Brasserie.** On the ground floor of Hotel d'Urville (☞ *below*), this long, narrow restaurant serves everything from a cup of coffee to a delightful dinner featuring local produce. The setting is unusual and tasteful, and the food generally very good. Check out the seafood chowder if it's on—it's chock-full of piscatorial goodies. The kitchen treats scallops well, and is equally skilled with mussels from the nearby sounds. On one recent visit, they were steamed open in herb-laced white wine and served with black beans and chilli. Delicious! ⊠ *52 Queen St.,* ☎ *03/577–9945. AE, DC, MC, V. No breakfast or lunch weekends.*

$$$ ✕ **Rocco's.** Regular Marlborough visitors will be sad to learn that this rambling restaurant's ebullient founder, Piero Rocco, has sold the restaurant to a couple of fellow Italians he met many years ago when they all dug hydro tunnels for a living. The food is much the same, which is to say hearty and generous, but the crazy fun quota has gone down a little. Like Piero, the new owners make their own pasta, and they're particularly proud of their grilled scampi with garlic and parsley butter (Piero left them the recipe). The wine list reads like a Who's Who of Marlborough labels, and includes a few earlier vintages. ⊠ *5 Dodson St.,* ☎ *03/578–6940. AE, DC, MC, V.*

$$–$$$ ✕ **Bellafico Caffé & Wine Bar.** Brunch, lunch, dinner, or a snack in between—this pleasant spot does them all. Start the day with fresh fruit on crunchy granola, or savory waffles with sliced banana, maple syrup, and crispy bacon. Later, choose a pizza—with chorizo, olives, tomato, and basil, for one—or share a meze platter with smoked beef, gherkins, tapenade, pickles, and cheese. The kitchen uses wild venison whenever it can get it, which makes a nice change from all that *cervena* (farmed venison), and if you're a serious meat lover, you can follow that with sautéed pork medallions on a bed of red cabbage with orange and walnut marmalade. Noncarnivore? Vegetarians are treated well with dishes like vegetable curry (famous locally) and pumpkin ravioli with a creamy mushroom sauce. ⊠ *17 Maxwell Rd.,* ☎ *03/577–6072. AE, DC, MC, V.*

$$–$$$ ✕ **The Store.** Susan and Richard Macfarlane of **Winterhome** (☞ *above*)
★ have branched out and built a one-stop store and café below their gardens at Kekerengu, on the main highway between Blenheim and Kaikoura. This new venture has gotten a lot of recognition: New Zealand food and wine writer Michael Guy says, "The Store at Kekerengu is the most talked about café in New Zealand." No wonder. Its dramatic setting at the edge of the Pacific Ocean—which is literally pounding at your feet—makes it a great place to relish cooked crayfish and a glass of wine or to stop for a light lunch or dinner. ⊠ *State Hwy. 1, Kekerengu,* ☎ *03/575–8600,* 𝔽𝔸𝕏 *03/575–8620. MC, V.*

$–$$$ ✕ **Paysanne.** This bright and breezy central restaurant is a popular meeting place for Blenheimites. The food is modern New Zealand café style, which means you can choose from a simple snack to a full-blown, three-course extravaganza. Gourmet pizzas, cooked in a wood-fired oven, have a big local following—tandoori chicken is the biggest-selling topping—and generous bowls of pasta also sell well. At night, look for the likes of pumpkin, sage, and feta hotcakes, or Moroccan-spiced salmon, panfried and served on rice with a citrus relish. ⊠ *The Forum, Market Place,* ☎ *03/577–6278. AE, DC, MC, V. No lunch Sun.*

$$ ✕ **Hunter's Vineyard Restaurant.** Dining at a vineyard is a great way
★ to appreciate how seriously the best New Zealand wine makers have
food in mind when they create their wine. Local produce is the star at
this pleasant indoor-outdoor eatery. Marlborough Greenshell mus-
sels, steamed open in Hunter's Riesling with wild thyme and garlic and
finished with cream, are a great match for a glass of that same ries-
ling; blue cod is panfried and topped with hollandaise sauce enlivened
with chunks of house-smoked salmon. Dishes like double-braised lamb
shanks with rosemary-tossed potatoes may tempt you to try one of the
Hunter's reds. They're leaner and greener than North Island examples,
but they go well with the local food. ✉ *Rapaura Rd.,* ☏ *03/572–8803.
AE, DC, MC, V.*

$ ✕ **Paddy Barry's Bar and Restaurant.** Locals come here for a chat and
a beer, and the menu is casual, straightforward, and very well priced.
In other words, it's a good place to come down from traveler's stom-
ach and overenthusiastic gourmandizing—a local peril. A plate of bat-
tered and fried seafood is very reasonable, and a pleasure alongside a
well-poured Guinness. You'll find Guinness *in* the food, too, in the form
of a beef 'n' Guinness hot pot, one of three or more likely to be on
offer. ✉ *51 Scott St.,* ☏ *03/578–7470. AE, DC, MC, V.*

$$$$ ✕⌕ **Timara Lodge.** Taking a relaxing stroll around the well-tended gar-
★ dens, rowing about the lodge's pond, enjoying a drink inside in the li-
brary, or tasting some of the finest meals in the country along with
appropriate glasses of local wine around a magnificent oak table—Timara
Lodge offers one of the most luxurious experiences on South Island.
Built in 1923 as a rural getaway, the lodge is a marvel of craftsman-
ship and beautiful use of native timber. In rooms, bedsteads swollen
with comfortable linens stand alongside well-chosen antiques. Down-
stairs, beautifully constructed rooms and furnishings speak of the quiet
elegance of times past. Jeremy and Suzie Jones preside over the lodge,
with Jeremy turning out masterful dishes that focus on the freshness
of local ingredients: fruits and greens, scallops (with roe in season),
salmon, venison, or tender racks of lamb. Wine tours, trout fishing,
sea-kayaking, golf, skiing, even whale-watching (an hour and a half
away in Kaikoura) can be arranged for you. The per-person price in-
cludes breakfast, dinner, and cocktails. ✉ *Dog Point Rd., R.D. 2,
Blenheim,* ☏ *03/572–8276,* ⅎ *03/572–9191. 4 rooms. AE, DC, MC,
V. MAP.* ✇

$$$ ✕⌕ **The Marlborough.** The art deco–inspired furnishings throughout
this attractive, contemporary luxury hotel are enhanced by a color scheme
that seems to emulate the region's ripening produce, its brilliant sun,
and the blue-green waters of the Marlborough Sounds. Standard rooms
have queen-size beds; deluxe rooms and suites have high rimu wood
ceilings and super-king-size beds. Suites also have whirlpool baths. The
hotel has one of the largest collections of contemporary New Zealand
art and a fine restaurant. It is on the edge of town, opposite the Wairau
River on the road to Nelson. ✉ *20 Nelson St., Blenheim,* ☏ *03/577–
7333,* ⅎ *03/577–7337. 22 deluxe rooms, 2 standard rooms, 4 suites.
Restaurant, bar. AE, DC, MC, V.* ✇

$$$$ ⌕ **Hotel d'Urville.** Every room is unique in this modern boutique hotel
★ in the old Public Trust building. You could choose the Raja Room, where
silk saris are draped over the main bed and there are various brass ornaments and a carved Javanese day bed; or the room with an African
theme; or the sensory trip of the Color Room. One room matches the
overall travel theme of the hotel and is based on the exploits of Du-
mont d'Urville, who made voyages to the Pacific and the Antarctic in
the 1820s and 1830s. Six of the rooms come only with showers. The
hotel is built around the Public Trust's original vault, which now serves
as a public area for guests. The hotel also has a very good restaurant

(☞ *above*). ✉ *52 Queen St., Blenheim,* ☎ *03/577–9945,* FAX *03/577–9946. 9 rooms. Restaurant, bar. AE, DC, MC, V.* 🐾

$$$–$$$$ 🏠 **Le Grys Vineyard Homestay.** If wine has brought you to Marlborough, consider starting the day in your own cottage in the heart of a
★ vineyard. Waterfall Lodge is a self-contained mud-block cottage with a brook running past, literally surrounded by the Le Grys vineyard's sauvignon blanc, pinot noir, merlot, and chardonnay grapes. The main bedroom has a canopied queen-size bed, and you don't even have to leave the cottage for breakfast, as it arrives in a basket at the front door. You can also stay in the spacious ranch-style homestead, with its wraparound verandas and sophisticated touches, with hosts John and Jennifer Joslin, who built the house and cottage. Their first Le Grys Sauvignon Blanc was bottled in 1996; now they produce a small portfolio that has a loyal following and has won many prestigious awards. Rates include breakfast, and the hosts can arrange trout fishing, horse trekking, boating on the sounds, and scenic flights. The homestay is 12 km (7 mi) west of Blenheim in Renwick; two minutes west of the town you'll see Conders Bend Road on the left. ✉ *Conders Bend Rd., Renwick,* ☎ *03/572–9490,* FAX *03/572–9491. 1 room, 1 cottage. MC, V.* 🐾

Fishing

For information on stream fishing in the Nelson Lakes district and deep-sea fishing out of Picton, *see* Chapter 5.

Kaikoura

❺ *129 km (81 mi) south of Blenheim, 182 km (114 mi) north of Christchurch.*

The town of Kaikoura sits on a rocky protrusion on the east coast, backed by an impressive mountainous upthrust. There is plenty of local crayfish to be had at roadside stalls, which is an excellent reason to come here, but an even better one is sighting the sperm whales that frequent the coast in greater numbers than anywhere else on earth. The sperm whale, the largest toothed mammal, can reach a length of 60 ft and a weight of 70 tons. The reason for the whales' concentration in this area is the abundance of squid—among other species, the giant squid of seafaring lore—which is their main food. Scientists speculate that the whales use a form of sonar to find the squid, which they then bombard with deep, powerful sound waves generated in the massive cavities in the fronts of their heads. Their hunting is all the more remarkable considering that much of it is done at great depths, in darkness. The whales' food source swims in the trench just off the continental shelf, barely a kilometer (½ mi) off Kaikoura. You are most likely to see the whales between October and August.

Fyffe House is Kaikoura's oldest surviving building, erected soon after Robert Fyffe's whaling station was established in 1842. Built on whalebone piles, the house provides a look at what life was like when people aimed at whales with harpoons rather than cameras. ✉ *62 Avoca St., Kaikoura,* ☎ *03/319–5835.* 🎟 *$3.50.* ☉ *Daily 10–5.*

The Kaikoura Peninsula has two **walks**—not to be confused with the Kaikoura Coast Track (☞ Outdoor Activities and Sports, *below*)—that are particularly worthwhile, considering the town's spectacular coastal scenery: the cliff-top walk, from which you can look over seal colonies, and the longer shoreline walk that takes you much closer to the colonies. Consult the information center about tides to avoid getting flooded out of certain parts of the walks. ✉ *Walks start at the end of Fyffe Quay.*

On the first Saturday of October the town celebrates its annual **Seafest**, during which the best of this coastal area's food, wine, and beer are served up while top New Zealand entertainers perform on an outdoor stage. Tickets are available from the **Kaikoura Information and Tourism Centre** (☞ Visitor Information *in* Marlborough and Kaikoura A to Z, *below*).

Dining and Lodging

$$$ ✕ **White Morph Restaurant.** Set in what was once the first bank of Kaikoura, White Morph has historic elegance. Locally made gilded mirrors and marine art adorn the walls, but the best scenes are the seaside views from the front windows. Crayfish features strongly on the menu (there's a whole one on the seafood platter), but there are lots of alternatives. Pepper steak, *tagine* of lamb, and Thai chicken salad have all proved popular in recent months, and there's always at least one vegetarian dish. ⊠ *92–94 the Esplanade,* ☎ *03/319–5676. AE, DC, MC, V.*

$$ ✕ **The Craypot.** This casual and modern café relies strongly, as the name suggests, on the local delicacy. Crayfish isn't cheap, but this kitchen sure knows how to prepare it. Other types of seafood also figure large on the menu, and if you feel like a change you can choose from several variations on the steak, chicken, and lamb themes. Homemade desserts are worth leaving room for. In summer there is outdoor dining; in winter an open fire roars at night. ⊠ *70 West End Rd.,* ☎ *03/ 319–6027. AE, DC, MC, V.*

$ ✕ **Hislops Café.** Homey and wholesome Hislops is a few minutes' drive north of town and well worth the trip, especially when the sun happens to be streaming in the windows. In the morning you'll find tasty eggs and bacon, and a real treat in the freshly baked whole-grain bread served with marmalade or honey. There are also tasty muffins, both sweet and savory. Lunches and dinners are all based on organic whole foods used with imagination and style. On fine days eat outside on the veranda. Open all day, every day. ⊠ *Main Hwy.,* ☎ *03/319– 6971. AE, DC, MC, V.*

$$ ▥ **Old Convent.** Some old habits are hard to shake. At this 1912 former French convent, it's still possible to imagine an austere cluster of robed nuns rustling silently about their day. French architect and chef Marc Launay and wife Wendy have infused a warm and welcoming touch, adding creature comforts that the convent's former residents would have eschewed, while preserving essential aspects of the convent. They've cleverly combined what must have been small adjoining studies and meditation rooms for the nuns. The two large queen bedrooms have great views of the Kaikoura Ranges. The guest lounge used to be a chapel and still has its cathedral ceiling, and there is an ornate wrought-iron stairwell that winds down from the chapel to a reception area. The heart of this sprawling bed-and-breakfast is the French restaurant where many guests get together around large rimu wooden tables in the morning or during dinner. The restaurant is for guests only. Rates include breakfast; dinner is from $45 per person. The convent is a few minutes' drive out of town. ⊠ *Mt. Fyffe Rd.,* ☎ *03/319–6603 or 0800/365–603,* 𝔽𝔸𝕏 *03/319–6660. 17 rooms, 15 with bath. Restaurant, croquet, bicycles. BP. AE, MC, V.* ❧

$$ ▥ **White Morph Motor Inn.** A waterfront view is hard to ignore in most places—even more so on the rugged coast of Kaikoura. This contemporary motel-style inn is in a great spot just opposite the beach, and its two foremost suites get the best views of the sea. Of the 19 self-contained units, 12 are studios, 4 are luxury suites with king-size beds and double whirlpool baths, and 3 others are two-bedroom apartments with lounges and kitchens downstairs, two bedrooms upstairs. Upstairs rooms have decks from which you can enjoy views of the magnificent Kaikoura Ranges, and downstairs units have courtyards. You can

book local activities from here, and the inn's restaurant (☞ *above*) is in a historic building next door. ✉ *92–94 the Esplanade,* ☎ *03/319–5014,* 🖷 *03/319–5015. 12 rooms, 4 suites, 3 apartments. AE, DC, MC, V.* ✨

$ 　🖭 **Beachfront Bed and Breakfast.** The big attraction here is the beach-
★ 　side location and the sea views—which are best in upstairs rooms. Sit on the balcony and enjoy crayfish and a bottle of wine while you take in the sea air. It's that feeling of contentment that enticed owner Glynn Beets, after being away from New Zealand for 20 years, to fall in love with the top end of South Island. Glynn also loves cooking and hap-pily prepares breakfast to suit your preferences. All rooms are spacious and comfortable, though one double's private bathroom is separate from the room. In part because of reasonable prices, this is always the first bed-and-breakfast in town to sell out—phone well ahead to book a room. ✉ *78 the Esplanade,* ☎ *03/319–5890,* 🖷 *03/319–5895. 4 rooms. MC, V.* ✨

Outdoor Activities and Sports

Whale-watching and swimming with dolphins or seals are both extremely popular in December and January, so either avoid Kaikoura at those times or book well in advance. To keep your feet on terra firma, the three-day Kaikoura Coast Track is a great way to see a spectacular mix of rugged coastline, pioneering farms, and mountain scenery.

HIKING

Kaikoura Coast Track. The descendants of two Scottish pioneering families—the Caverhills and Macfarlanes, who settled the huge 57,000-acre Hawkswood Range in 1860—have opened up their farms and homes to travelers. This three-day walk combines uncrowded hik-ing—10 people at a time maximum—and farm hospitality. Take binoc-ulars to search out sea life like whales and dolphins.

Warm, clean cottages with kitchens and hot baths or showers are at the end of each day's hike. You can arrange a meal with your hosts on weekdays or buy fresh farm produce to prepare yourself. Breakfast and lunches are also available. The first night is at Hawkswood in the his-toric sheep station setting of the **Staging Post,** where host J. D. Mac-farlane has a passion for Shakespeare and old stagecoaches. Accommodations are in rustic mud-brick or log cabins. A challenging five- to six-hour walk the next day will take you to **Ngaroma,** Heather and Bruce Macfarlane's 3,000-acre sheep and cattle farm. The Loft has a large lounge with a log fire and rooms that each sleep up to four peo-ple. The next day's hike is along the beach, passing an ancient buried forest before heading across farmland to an area of regenerating bush. Around the dinner table at **Medina,** where you'll spend the third night in either Te Whare or the Garden Cottage (better for couples), you might meet David Handyside's father, Miles, who settled the 1,600-acre sheep and cattle farm in 1945. The final day, a demanding four- to five-hour walk, takes you over the 2,000-ft-plus Mt. Wilson, with its breathtaking views of the Waiau River and the Kaikoura Ranges.

The fee for walking the track is $110 per person, and a guided walk can be arranged. If you opt to have all meals included and need bed-ding, the total cost is $81 per day. Bookings are essential. The track is a ¾-hour drive south of Kaikoura and a 1½-hour drive north of Christchurch on State Highway 1. Shuttles or buses can drop you at the gate. ✉ *Medina, R.D. Parnassus, North Canterbury,* ☎ *03/319–2715,* 🖷 *03/319–2724.* ☉ *Oct.–Apr.* ✨

Top Spot Seal Swims (☎ 03/319–5540) has two trips daily November–April, $40 per person. **Graeme's Seal Swims** (☎ 03/319–6812, ✆), a shore-based operation, has three trips daily November–April, $40 per person. **Dolphin Mary Charters** (☎ 03/319–6777, ✆) has dolphin swims at 6 AM, 9 AM, and 12:30 PM from October to April. The cost is $85 per person.

WHALE-WATCHING

Whale Watch™ Kaikoura Ltd. Whale Watch is owned by the Ngai Tahu *iwi* (tribe). Since arriving in the Kaikoura area in AD 850, Ngai Tahu, the predominant South Island Maori iwi, claims to have lived and worked based on a philosophy of sustainable management and sensible use of natural resources. Having worked these waters since 1987, Whale Watch skippers can recognize individual whales and adjust operations, such as the boat's proximity to the whale, accordingly. Allow 3½ hours for the whole experience, 2½ hours on the water.

Book in advance: 7 to 10 days November–April, 3 to 4 days at other times. Trips depend on the weather, and should you miss seeing a whale, which is rare, you will get up to an 80% refund of your fare. Take motion-sickness pills if you suspect you'll need them: even in calm weather, the sea around Kaikoura often has a sizable swell. ⊠ *Whaleway Station, Box 89, Kaikoura,* ☎ *03/319–6767 or 0800/655–121,* FAX *03/319–6545.* 🖬 *$95. AE, DC, MC, V.* ✆

Wings Over Whales. If you'd rather get above the action, take a 30-minute whale-spotting flight. Your aircraft, a nine-seater Islander or a 14-seater GAF Nomad N24A, will be smoothly and skillfully piloted to circle above, affording a bird's-eye view of the giant sperm whales' immensity. While searching for other whales' telltale water spouts, pilot and copilot provide informative commentary on the creatures' habits. The trick is to stay glued to your window—which isn't hard because at least half the time, with the plane banked in an almost perpetual circle, gravity ensures that your face is just about stuck to it. ⊠ *Peketa Airfield, State Hwy. 1, Kaikoura,* ☎ *03/319–6580 or 0800/226–269,* FAX *03/319–6668.* 🖬 *$95. AE, DC, MC, V.*

By dint of interactive digital imagery—to wit a photo of you superimposed onto a whale's tail—**Whale Watch Photography** prints clever color photos and postcards. It takes about five minutes to shoot and process the photos. ⊠ *The Whaleway Station, Box 89, Kaikoura,* ☎ *0800/655–121 or ext. 823.*

Marlborough and Kaikoura A to Z

Arriving and Departing

BY BUS

InterCity (☎ 03/577–2890) runs service between Christchurch and Kaikoura, Picton, and Blenheim.

BY FERRY

InterIsland Line (☎ 0800/802–802 ✆) runs vehicle and passenger ferries between Wellington and Picton. The one-way adult fare ranges from $23 to $46 depending on the time of year. The fare for a medium-size sedan ranges from $116 to $165. The crossing takes about three hours and can be very rough. InterIsland's slightly more expensive fast ferry the *Lynx* does the journey in half the time when it runs from early December until late April. There are at least two departures in each direction every day, and bookings should be made in advance, particularly during holiday periods. The one-way adult fare ranges from $30 to $59 and the fare for a medium-size sedan ranges from $95 to $190, again depending on time of travel. The ferry docks in Picton at the town wharf.

BY PLANE

The very scenic flight from Wellington to Picton takes about a half hour. **Air New Zealand Link** (☎ 04/474–8950) has 10 departures to and from Wellington daily. From Wellington, **Soundsair** (☎ 03/573–6184, 04/801–0111, or 0800/505–005) also flies to Picton ($50).

Getting Around

BY BOAT

See Guided Tours, *below.*

BY CAR

Blenheim is a 25-minute drive from the ferry terminal in Picton and just less than a two-hour drive from Nelson to the west and Kaikoura to the south.

Contacts and Resources

CAR RENTAL

Most rental agencies have North Island–South Island transfer programs for their vehicles: leave one car off in Wellington and pick another one up in Picton on the same contract. It is common practice, quickly and easily done. If you initiate a rental in Picton, the following agencies are represented at the ferry terminal: **Avis** (☎ 03/573–6363), **Budget** (☎ 03/573–6081), and **Hertz** (☎ 03/573–7224).

EMERGENCIES

Dial 111 for **fire, police, or ambulance** services.

GUIDED TOURS

Action in Marlborough. To see the glorious Marlborough Sounds, try a two- or four-day fully catered and guided inn-to-inn walk on the Queen Charlotte Track. The four-day walk includes all land and water transport, comfortable accommodations in three Sounds Resorts—Punga Cove Resort (☞ Picton Dining and Lodging, *above*), Furneaux Lodge, and the Portage. Experienced guides ensure that you are well informed on the area's rich natural and human history. Advance bookings are essential. The company also takes four-day hikes into the gorgeous Nelson Lakes area. ✉ *67 George St., Blenheim,* ☎ FAX *03/578–4531 or 0800/266–266.* ▣ *4 days $849.* ✎

The Pelorus Mail Boat, **Adventurer,** a small launch that makes a day-long trip ferrying mail and supplies around Pelorus Sound, is one of the best ways to discover the waterway and meet its residents. The boat leaves from Havelock, west of Picton, Tuesday, Thursday, and Friday at 9:30 AM and returns in the late afternoon. ✉ *For reservations,* ☞ *Beachcomber Cruises, below. You can also make bookings at the Havelock Outdoor Centre,* ✉ *65A Main Rd., Havelock,* ☎ FAX *03/574–2114.* ▣ *$70.*

Beachcomber Cruises can take you to and from any point on the Queen Charlotte Walkway for one-day or longer unguided walks. Boats depart at 10:15 and 2:15 and charge around $32. ✉ *Beachcomber Pier, Town Wharf, Box 12, Picton,* ☎ *03/573–6175,* FAX *03/573–6176.*

The **Cougar Line** runs scheduled trips through the Queen Charlotte Sounds four times daily, dropping passengers (sightseers included) at accommodations, private homes, or other points. A Queen Charlotte drop-off and pickup service costs $48 for multiday hikes, $43 for day hikes that end at Furneaux Lodge. Water taxi service to area lodges costs from $15 to $45, depending on distances. ✉ *Picton Wharf,* ☎ *03/573–7925 or 0800/504–090,* FAX *03/573–7926.* ✎

Marlborough Sounds Adventure Company has one- and four-day guided kayak tours of the sounds, as well as kayak rentals for experienced paddlers. The cost is $80 for a one-day guided tour, and $475 for a three-day guided tour, including water transportation, food, and camping equipment. A kayak rental costs $40 per person per day. The company also guides trampers on the Queen Charlotte Walkway on three-day ($600) or four-day ($845) trips. ⊠ *The Waterfront, London Quay, Picton,* ☎ *03/573–6078,* 🅵🅰🆇 *03/573–8827.* 🕸

Mussel Farm Cruises will take you into the largely untouched Kenepuru and Pelorus sounds, which are part of the labyrinth of waterways comprising the Marlborough Sounds. The world's largest production of Greenshell mussels is done in the sounds, and guide Ed Knowles runs a daily four-hour cruise to visit farms where the mussels are at varying stages of development. You can even get in and swim with them. The 40-ft MV *Mavis* is a 1919 kauri-wood launch. ⊠ *Havelock Outdoor Centre, 65a Main Rd., Havelock,* ☎ 🅵🅰🆇 *03/574–2114.* 🖃 *$45.*

The Sounds Connection is a family-run tour company that offers half-day and full-day fishing trips. It also has daily scheduled wine tours and private charter wine tours. ⊠ *10 London Quay, Picton,* ☎ *03/573–8843,* 🅵🅰🆇 *03/573–7726.* 🕸

VISITOR INFORMATION

Blenheim Visitor Information Centre. ⊠ *The Forum, Queen St.,* ☎ *03/578–9904,* 🅵🅰🆇 *03/578–6084.* ☉ *Daily 8:30–5:30.* 🕸
Kaikoura Information and Tourism Centre. ⊠ *West End,* ☎ *03/319–5641,* 🅵🅰🆇 *03/319–6819.* ☉ *Daily 9–5.* 🕸
Picton Visitor Information Centre. ⊠ *Picton Foreshore,* ☎ *03/573–7477,* 🅵🅰🆇 *03/573–5021.* ☉ *Daily 8:30–5.*

NELSON AND THE NORTHWEST

Set on the broad curve of its bay with views of the Tasman Mountains on the far side, and with a sunny and agreeable climate, Nelson makes a strong case for itself as one of the top areas in New Zealand for year-round adventure. To the west, the sandy crescents of Abel Tasman National Park and Golden Bay beckon with their seaside charms. To the south, mellow river valleys and the peaks and glacial lakes of Nelson Lakes National Park are a pristine wonderland for hiking, mountaineering, and cross-country skiing. Beyond those geographic splendors, Nelson has more hours of sunlight than any major city in the country. New Zealanders are well aware of these attractions, and in December and January the city is swamped with vacationers. Apart from this brief burst of activity, you can expect to have the roads and beaches mostly to yourself.

Nelson

❻ *116 km (73 mi) west of Blenheim.*

Relaxed, hospitable, and easy to explore on foot, Nelson has a way of making you feel like you should stay longer, no matter how long you're here. Local craftspeople weave wool into clothing and blankets and make pots and jewelry that fill up shops throughout the area. You can make your way around the mostly two-story town in a day, poking into shops and stopping at cafés, but two days is a practical minimum, especially if you need a respite in the midst of a busy itinerary. Use Nelson as a base for a variety of activities within an hour's drive of the town itself.

To get your bearings in town, the **Visitor Information Centre** is on the corner of Trafalgar and Halifax streets. The heart of town is farther up Trafalgar Street, between two parallel roads, Bridge Street and Hardy Street. These areas are fringed with shops, some of them with walk-through access back on to Trafalgar Street. A Saturday crafts market is held at the Montgomery parking lot. There are a few shops in Nile Street and Selwyn Place, but the majority are in Trafalgar, Hardy, and Bridge streets. For a dose of greenery, the **Queens Gardens** are on Bridge Street between Collingwood and Tasman.

Suter Art Gallery exhibits both historical and contemporary art. It is the easiest way to see work from an area that has long attracted painters, potters, woodworkers, and other artists. Many of them come for the scenery, the lifestyle, and the clay and, as a result, Nelson is considered the ceramics center of New Zealand. In recent years the gallery has increased its emphasis on painting and sculpture. Exhibits change every three or four weeks. ⊠ *Queens Gardens, Bridge St.,* ☎ *03/548–4699,* 🖷 *03/548–1236.* 🖾 *$2.* ☉ *Daily 10:30–4:30.*

Nelson's iffy architectural "highlight" is **Christ Church Cathedral,** which sits on a hilltop surrounded by gardens. Work on the church began in 1925 and dragged on for the next 40 years. During construction the design was altered to withstand earthquakes, and despite its promising location at the end of Trafalgar Street, it looks like a building designed by a committee. ⊠ *Cathedral Square.* 🖾 *Free, tower $4.*

Dining and Lodging

$$–$$$ ✗ **Appelman's.** Long established as one of Nelson's best restaurants, Appelman's startled the locals by moving to the suburb of Richmond, 20 minutes away, early in 1997. John Appelman is a skilled cook and loves working with local seafood, but the food can be variable if he's not in the kitchen when you visit. Look for Golden Bay whelks and crabs, Nelson Bay scallops, and Motueka crabs, usually prepared in traditional ways and always flavorsome. ⊠ *294 Queen St., Richmond,* ☎ *03/544–0610. AE, DC, MC, V. No lunch.*

$$–$$$ ✗ **The Boat Shed.** The name is no flight of marketing fancy—this is a genuine boat shed, jutting into the bay. Chef Luke McCann has a nice Asian-influenced touch. Crabs from nearby Golden Bay are cooked, Singapore style, with coriander, coconut cream, and heaps of chilli. Available medium, hot, or extra-hot, the resulting dish is a local legend. Crayfish from holding tanks can be simply steamed, or smeared with herb butter and grilled, and carnivores are catered to with a couple of imaginative beef or lamb dishes. ⊠ *350 Wakefield Quay,* ☎ *03/546–9783. AE, DC, MC, V. Licensed and BYOB.*

$–$$ ✗ **Broccoli Row.** This friendly, self-styled fish and vegetarian restau-
★ rant is highly regarded for its presentation and innovative cooking. The small menu caters to varied appetites with dishes such as grilled scallops with rosemary, salmon fillet stuffed with ratatouille, asparagus and Brie tart with tomato-basil sauce, a tapas platter, Caesar salad, and seafood chowder with garlic focaccia. The Mediterranean-style courtyard is the place to eat when the sun is shining. ⊠ *5 Buxton Sq.,* ☎ *03/548–9621. AE, DC, MC, V. Closed Sun.*

$–$$ ✗ **Italian Gourmet.** The impressively fully laden antipasto cabinet is the big feature of this contemporary bistro. All that colorful food stands out well against the white walls, made to look even whiter by halogen lighting. Touches of walnut timber act as a contrast. Sit indoors or out, and choose Mediterranean delights like a salad of seared baby octopus and tomato, or poached chicken with marinated carrots and capers. If you prefer to order from the menu, the pastas and pizzas cover most Italian provinces with flair. Call ahead for hours open. ⊠ *195 Hardy St.,* ☎ *03/545–6220. MC, V.*

$$$ ⊞ **Cambria House.** Built for a sea captain, this 1860 house has been
★ sympathetically modernized to offer bed-and-breakfast accommodations with personality and a dash of luxury. The furnishings mix antiques with modern fabrics. The home still has its original kauri doors that have been accented by the addition of recycled rimu paneling and furniture. Each bedroom has an en-suite bathroom with shower; two have a shower and separate bathtub. The house is in a quiet street within easy walking distance of the center of Nelson. ⊠ *7 Cambria St.,* ☎ *03/548–4681,* FAX *03/546–6649. 7 rooms. MC, V. BP.*

$$$ ⊞ **Cathedral Inn.** Abandoning the corporate world didn't require a second thought for hosts and seasoned travelers Peter and Lesley Cavanagh, who enjoy nothing better than meeting with fellow globe-trotters. Their luxurious lodge, a transformed 1878 deanery, appears almost Mediterranean from the outside—the front courtyard has turquoise and terra-cotta colors—but inside you'll find solid colonial-style furniture made from native rimu and kauri wood, as well as wrought-iron and brass bedsteads. Breakfast in the large drawing room around the recycled *matai* wood table is a gracious affair. The inn is a short walk through Christ Church Cathedral's garden to shops and restaurants. ⊠ *369 Trafalgar St.,* ☎ *03/548–7369,* FAX *03/548–0369. 7 rooms. AE, DC, MC, V.* ☙

$$$ ⊞ **A Little Manor.** This little historic A-frame home, on land first surveyed in 1864, seems to defy the modern-day neighborhood around it. Owners, Angela Higgins and Christopher Geen, have furnished the cottage with antiques and have retained the original clawfoot bath and open fire. The decor combines indigenous timbers, such as rimu, kauri, and matai, with luxurious furnishings and modern appliances. The sunny upper deck and lower garden are well secluded. There is a kitchenette, a pantry full of goodies (such as homemade jams and sauces), a dining area, reading room, and two guest lounges. Everything you need for breakfast is provided and included in the rate. Best of all, you're just a short walk to cafés and restaurants, and surrounded by art galleries and pottery studios. ⊠ *12 Nile St. W,* ☎ *03/545–1411,* FAX *03/ 545–1417. 2 rooms without bath. Kitchenette. AE, DC, MC, V.*

$$$ ⊞ **Mapledurham.** This colonial-style homestead in the nearby town of
★ Richmond, presided over by Deborah and Giles Grigg, is as friendly and comfortable a place as you'll find in the Nelson area. The hosts are ever ready with suggestions about local activities and restaurants, and the garden around the house and fresh flowers in your room make it a pleasant place to come to at the end of the day. Take advantage of the private trellised courtyard covered in vines at the back of the garden or the shade of the home's spacious veranda. Incredible full breakfasts make for a lavish start in the morning. ⊠ *8 Edward St., Richmond,* ☎ FAX *03/544–4210. 3 rooms. MC, V. BP.* ☙

$$ ⊞ **Aloha Lodge.** A stone's throw from Tahunanui Beach, this modern B&B has luxury accommodations at a reasonable price. The design of the lodge is Asian, even in its garden—landscaped using the principles of the Chinese design philosophy *feng shui.* An ample breakfast is served in the outer courtyard or the spacious dining room. Hosts John and Linda Bergman are always willing to help out with information on the area's activities and sights. Aloha Lodge is in Tahunanui, about a five-minute drive from Nelson via Haven Road. ⊠ *19 Beach Rd., Tahunanui,* ☎ *03/546–4000,* FAX *03/546–4420. 17 rooms, 4 suites. AE, DC, MC, V.*

Outdoor Activities and Sports

There is hiking and sea-kayaking aplenty in the glorious coastal Abel Tasman National Park west of Nelson (☞ Abel Tasman National Park, *below*). For information on stream fishing in the Nelson Lakes district, *see* Chapter 5.

Shopping

There are artist's studios and crafts shops in various parts of town, and a stroll will take you past many of them. Throughout the region there are more than 300 full-time artists who work in many media: ceramics, glassblowing, wood turning, fiber, sculpture, and painting. Not surprisingly there are 16 arts-and-crafts trails to follow, for which there is a brochure at the information center. There is also a colorful Saturday- and Sunday-morning crafts market. If you are going to be in town in September, call ahead to find out when the **Montana New Zealand Wearable Art Awards** will be held. At this extravaganza—the brainchild of Nelson resident Susie Moncrieff—entries from around the world can be outrageous and sometimes quite inspired.

Gael Montgomerie Fine Woodturning. Just a short way out of the center of town you'll meet a woman whose passion for her craft is captured in every wood grain of her meticulously honed and oiled work. Check out her ornamental or practical—but never plain—kitchenware. ⊠ *117 Nile St.,* ☎ FAX *03/546–6576.*

Hoglund Art Glass Blowing Studio. From the collectible family of penguins to the bold and innovative large platters and vases, the Hoglund touch is unmistakable. Ola and Marie Hoglunds' clean designs show the influence of their native Scandinavia, but are also in keeping with a growing trend in Pacific-style art—with bold colors and inspiration from New Zealand's environment. Hoglund art glass is now exported to the United States and these artisans were chosen to design and create a gift to mark President Bill Clinton's visit in 1999. ⊠ *Lansdowne Rd., Richmond,* ☎ *03/544–6500.* ☉ *Daily 9–5.*

Jens Hansen Workshop. Hansen's skilled craftspeople create thoughtfully designed, well-made gold and silver jewelry. Contemporary pieces are handmade at the workshop-showroom, and many are set with precious stones or *pounamu* (jade) from the West Coast of the South Island. Jens passed away in August 1999 but his son, Thorkild Hansen, continues in his father's footsteps. ⊠ *320 Trafalgar Sq.,* ☎ *03/548–0640.*

South Street Gallery. This 19th-century, two-story cottage houses a gallery that is literally overflowing with ceramic art, sculpture, and housewares. The labors of some 25 of New Zealand's notable artisans—all from Nelson—are featured here. Look out for work by Christine Boswjik or Katie Gold, both local women who are making an international name with their highly collectible work. ⊠ *10 Nile St. W,* ☎ *03/548–8117.* ☉ *Daily 9–5.*

Around Nelson

❼ The **Nelson Provincial Museum** is on the grounds of **Isel Park** and has a small but outstanding collection of Maori carvings. The museum also has a number of artifacts relating to the so-called Maungatapu murders, grisly goldfields killings committed near Nelson in 1866.

Isel House, near the Nelson Provincial Museum, was built for Thomas Marsden, one of the region's prosperous pioneers. It was Marsden who laid out the magnificent gardens surrounding the house, which include a towering California redwood and a 140-ft Monterey pine. The house itself contains the Marsden family's impressive porcelain and furniture.

To get to the Isel Park from Nelson, follow Rutherford Street out of town—the street was named for the eminent nuclear physicist Ernest Rutherford, who was born and raised nearby. On the outskirts of the city, take the right fork onto Waimea Road and continue as it becomes Main Road. Turn left into Marsden Road, where a sign points to the

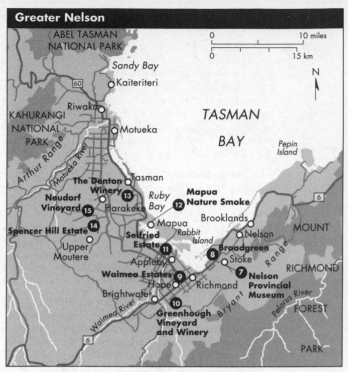

Greater Nelson

park. ✉ *Isel Park, Stoke, 7 km (4½ mi) south of Nelson,* ☎ *03/547–9740.* ✆ *Isel Park $2, Isel House $2.50.* ⊙ *Isel Park Tues.–Fri. 10–4, weekends 2–5; Isel House Sept.–May, weekends 2–4.*

⑧ Broadgreen is a fine example of a Victorian cob house. Cob houses, made from straw and horsehair bonded together with mud and clay, are commonly found in the southern English county of Devon, where many of Nelson's pioneers originated. The house is furnished as it might have been in the 1850s, with patchwork quilts and kauri furniture. ✉ *276 Nayland Rd., Stoke,* ☎ *03/546–0283.* ✆ *$2.* ⊙ *Nov.–Apr., Tues.–Fri. 10:30–4:30, weekends 1:30–4:30; May–Oct., Wed. and weekends 2–4:30.*

⑨ Waimea Estates is one of the newer names on the Nelson scene, but it's making big waves. The owners used to own orchards, but they're enjoying the move to wine. The range includes chardonnay, riesling, and—unusual in this region—a couple of variations on the cabernet sauvignon and merlot themes. A café next to the tasting room serves interesting and flavorsome dishes, mostly using local produce. ✉ *22 Appleby Hwy., Appleby,* ☎ *03/544–4963,* 🖷 *03/544–6385.* ⊙ *Café open daily, wine tastings by appointment.*

⑩ Andrew Greenhough and Jennifer Wheeler's **Greenhough Vineyard and Winery** in the optimistically named suburb of Hope has established a big reputation for quality in a short time. Andrew is somewhat reserved, Jennifer more outgoing—but both are passionate about their product. Sauvignon blanc, chardonnay, pinot noir, and the occasional supersweet dessert wine are all worth trying. ✉ *Patons Rd., Hope,* ☎ *03/542–3462,* 🖷 *03/542–3462.* ⊙ *Daily 1–5.*

⑪ Seifried Estate is a 15-minute drive from Nelson's main center, on the way to Motueka. Hermann Seifried produces fine sauvignon blanc, chardonnay, and especially riesling. A large, sunny restaurant is next door to the tasting room. ✉ *Redwood Rd., Appleby,* ☎ *03/544–5599,* FAX *03/544–5522.* ⊘ *Daily 10–5.*

★ ⑫ It might be hard to resist stopping at **Mapua Nature Smoke,** operated by Vivienne and Tom Fox, who buy their fish right off local boats, fillet it, marinate it according to a secret recipe, smoke it—and offer samples. Especially if you're headed south, you won't find a better lunch along the way than a slab of smoked snapper or albacore tuna with a loaf of crusty bread from the bakery in Motueka and apples from one of the roadside orchard stalls. Mapua Nature Smoke is in Mapua Port on the wharf in a blue corrugated-iron building. ✉ *Mapua Wharf,* ☎ *03/540–2280.* ⊘ *Daily 9–5:30; extended hrs in summer.*

⑬ The **Denton Winery** is spectacularly sited on a hilltop offering commanding views of the surrounding countryside. Richard Denton gave up a pressure career in the computer industry to grow grapes and make wine. Now he and his wife, Alex, an artist, run this pleasant winery and café, and produce a range of wines that get better with every vintage. Syrah is one unusual variety that has won praise from visitors. More in tune with the area are chardonnay, pinot noir, and sauvignon blanc. ✉ *Awa Awa Rd. off Marriages Rd., Upper Moutere,* ☎ *03/540–3555,* FAX *03/540–3555.* ⊘ *Daily 11–6.*

⑭ Expatriate Californian Philip Jones doesn't follow established flavor patterns at his equipment-crammed **Spencer Hill Estate.** His best wines have great flavor concentration, and many have won major awards. Some experimental styles are less successful, but they're always interesting—and Philip loves to talk about them. Spencer Hill is the top label, used for the home-vineyard product. Tasman Bay wines are made from other grapes, not always from the Nelson region. Try chardonnay, sémillon, sauvignon blanc, and merlot. ✉ *Best Rd., Upper Moutere,* ☎ *03/543–2031,* FAX *03/543–2031.* ⊘ *Tastings daily 12–4 in summer, sales only 8–4 other seasons.*

⑮ Despite its tiny size, **Neudorf Vineyard** has established an international reputation for chardonnay, but riesling, sauvignon blanc, and pinot noir are also highly regarded. Owners Tim and Judy Finn are enthusiastic about their region's attributes and will talk at length about local food and wine. Platters of bread and cheese are available at the cellar door. The top wines wear the Moutere designation on the label. ✉ *Neudorf Rd., Upper Moutere,* ☎ *03/543–2643,* FAX *03/543–2955.* ⊘ *Sept.–May, daily 10–5.*

En Route West of Mapua, on the way to Motueka, Highway 60 loops around quiet little sea coves that, for all but the warmest months of the year, mirror the snow-frosted peaks on the far shore. The tall vines along the roadside are hops, used in the making of beer.

Motueka

⑯ *50 km (31 mi) west of Nelson.*

Motueka (mo-too-*eh*-ka) is an agricultural center—tobacco, hops, kiwi fruit, and apples are among its staples. South of town, the Motueka River valley is known for trout fishing, rafting, and its sporting lodges. About 15 km (9 mi) northeast of town on the edge of the national park, **Kaiteriteri Beach** is one of New Zealand's best-known beaches, famous for its golden sand and great for a swim.

Dining and Lodging

$$$ ✕ **Doone Cottage.** This serene 100-year-old country homestay is set
★ in a pretty part of the Motueka River valley, within easy reach of five trout streams. Hosts Stan and Glen Davenport are a relaxed, hospitable

couple who have lived in this valley for many years. Rooms are comfortable and crowded with family memorabilia. Dinners are likely to feature organically grown vegetables, fruit, and local meat. Children are not accommodated. Doone Cottage is a 20-minute drive from Motueka. ✉ *R.D. 1, Motueka,* ☎ FAX *03/526–8740. 3 rooms with en suite. MC, V.* ⬙

$$$$ 🏨 **Motueka River Lodge.** One of New Zealand's exclusive retreats, this lodge offers tranquillity, marvelous scenery, and a superb standard of comfort. Owned and operated by former Londoner, adman, and publisher Mick Mason and Cordon Bleu–trained Fiona Mason, the lodge is on 80 acres of the Motueka Valley bordering the Motueka River, with magnificent mountain views. The interior of the rustic house is accented with antiques collected around the world. You can hike and raft nearby, but the lodge's specialty is fishing, especially dry fly-fishing for brown trout in the wild river country. The activities are restricted outside the October–April fishing season. Rates include all meals. ✉ *Motueka Valley Rd., Motueka,* ☎ FAX *03/526–8668. 5 rooms. Dining room, hot tub, tennis court, fishing. AE, DC, MC, V. FAP.* ⬙

Outdoor Activities and Sports

Rapid River Adventure Rafting has rafting trips down the Gowan or Buller rivers (both Grade 3–4). Choose from a half-day ($79), full-day ($105), or two-day trip ($165). ✉ *Box 996, Nelson,* ☎ *03/545–0332,* FAX *03/545–7076.*

Ultimate Descents Rafting Adventure Company. Don Allardice, one of New Zealand's leading white-water adventurers, along with Deane Parker, guide on the Buller (Grade 3–4) or the Karamea (Grade 5) rivers. Choose from half-day ($95), full-day ($125), or a variety of multiday trips. ✉ *51 Fairfax St., Murchison,* ☎ *03/523–9899 or 0800/748–377,* FAX *03/523–9811.* ⬙

En Route   If you don't head out to Abel Tasman National Park and Golden Bay and are headed toward the West Coast, turn south onto Highway 61 at the Rothmans Clock Tower in Motueka, following the sign to Murchison. The road snakes through **Motueka Valley** alongside the Motueka River, which is edged with poplars and yellow gorse, with the green valley walls pressing close alongside. If this river could talk, it would probably scream, "Trout!" After the town of Tapawera, turn south on State Highway 6 and continue to the West Coast.

Abel Tasman National Park

⓱ *77 km (48 mi) northwest of Motueka, 110 km (69 mi) northwest of Nelson.*

Beyond the town of Motueka, Highway 60 passes close to Kaiteriteri Beach, then turns inland to skirt **Abel Tasman National Park.** Its coastline is a succession of idyllic beaches backed by a rugged hinterland of native beech forests, granite gorges, and waterfalls. The cove and inlets at **Anchorage,** to mention one part of the park, are spectacular.

Abel Tasman has a number of walking trails, from both Totaranui at its north end and Marahau in the south. The most popular is the two- to three-day **Coastal Track,** open year-round. Launches from **Abel Tasman National Park Enterprises** (☞ Hiking, *below*) will drop off and pick up hikers from several points along the track. A popular way to explore the clear waters and rock-strewn coastline is by sea kayak (☞ Sea-Kayaking, *below*). The main accommodations base for the national park is **Motueka River Lodge** (☞ Motueka Dining and Lodging, *above*) and Abel Tasman Marahau Lodge (☞ Dining and Lodging, *below*).

Dining and Lodging

$$ ✕☷ **Awaroa Lodge & Cafe.** Relax in an idyllic part of the spectacular Abel Tasman National Park—Awaroa Bay—surrounded by native bush, just two minutes' walk to the beach. You can choose from standard doubles with shared facilities or fully self-contained chalets. Much of the wood used to build and to finish the interiors has been recycled from the local bush, and the modern furniture suits the setting. The attached restaurant, with its chunky wooden furnishings and open adobe fireplace, serves hearty vegetarian fare (and some meat) with most produce grown organically on the property. Access is only by boat. Contact **Aqua Taxis** (☎ 03/527–8083), which leaves from Marahau daily or fly direct from Nelson with **Tasman Bay Aviation** (☎ 03/547–2378). ✉ *Awaroa Bay, Abel Tasman National Park, Motueka,* ☎ *03/528–8758,* ☎ *03/528–6561. 14 rooms, 8 with bath. Restaurant. AE, MC, V.*✆

$$ ☷ **Abel Tasman Marahau Lodge.** With Abel Tasman National Park 200 yards in one direction and the Marahau beach 200 yards in the other, this location is hard to resist. The boutique lodge has spacious fully self-contained chalets, clustered in groups of two or four with native gardens between them. Units are finished in natural wood and have high cathedral ceilings, clean-lined wooden furniture, New Zealand wool carpets, queen- or king-size beds, and balconies from which to take in the park's natural beauty. The lodge has a communal kitchen, and staff can give information about and make reservations for sea-kayaking, water-taxis, and hiking options. ✉ *Marahau, R.D. 2, Motueka,* ☎ *03/527–8250,* ☎ *03/ 527–8258. 8 rooms. Outdoor hot tub, sauna. DC, MC, V.*✆

Outdoor Activities and Sports

HIKING

Bushwalk in the park on your own—it's called freedom walking—or opt for a guided walk. The **Department of Conservation Field Centre** (✉ 62 Commercial St., Takaka, ☎ 03/525–8026) provides trail maps.

Abel Tasman National Park Enterprises are the original operators of day excursions ($15–$85) to the Abel Tasman National Park. It offers bushwalks, trips to beaches, launch cruises, and sea-kayaking. It also runs three- and five-day hiking or hiking-kayaking treks around the park (☞ Guided Tours *in* Nelson and the Northwest A to Z, *below*). ✉ *265 High St., Motueka,* ☎ *03/528–7801 or 800/223–582.* ✆

SEA-KAYAKING

Ocean River Adventure Company has a variety of guided sea-kayaking trips in Abel Tasman National Park, lasting from one to five days. Guided trips cost from $92 per person per day, "freedom" rentals from $95 per person with a two-day minimum rental. ✉ *Marahau, R.D. 2, Motueka,* ☎ *03/527–8266,* ☎ *03/527–8006.* ✆

The Sea Kayak Company offers a range of guided kayaking options through the pristine waters of the Abel Tasman National Park to beaches and campsites often inaccessible to hikers. If you want to kayak on your own, a minimum of two days is required; be prepared for a two- to three-hour comprehensive safety briefing and weather appraisal. "Freedom" rental costs $90 per person for two days. The guided options range from a three-hour Twilight Tour ($45) to the five-day kayaking-hiking Explorer's Journey ($550). Ask about the Magical Moonlight tour. ✉ *506 High St., Motueka,* ☎ *03/528–7251 or 0508/252–925,* ☎ *03/528–7221.* ✆

Golden Bay–Takaka

⑱ *55 km (35 mi) northwest of Motueka, 110 km (70 mi) west of Nelson.*

The gorgeous stretch of coastline that begins at the town of Takaka is known, deservedly, as **Golden Bay.** Alternating sandy and rocky shores curve up to the sands of Farewell Spit, the arcing prong that encloses the bay. Dutch navigator Abel Tasman anchored here briefly just a few days before Christmas 1642. His visit ended abruptly when four of his crew were killed by the then-resident Maori *iwi* (tribe), Ngati Tumata Kokiri. Bitterly disappointed, Tasman named the place Moordenaers, or Murderers' Bay, and sailed away without ever setting foot on New Zealand soil. If you have time to explore it, Golden Bay is a delight— a sunny, 40-km (25-mi) crescent with a relaxed crew of locals who firmly believe they live in paradise.

Eight kilometers (5 miles) west of Takaka is **Waikoropupu Springs,** known as Pupu Springs. This is the largest spring system in New Zealand, and clear cold water bubbles into the Waikoropupu Valley after traveling underground from its source at the nearby Takaka River. Dated tourist brochures still available in the area show people swimming in the springs, but this is now frowned upon—alas—because of the impact it has on the delicate flora within the springs. It's best to leave the bathing suit in the car and take a leisurely stroll around the valley on the 90-minute Pupu Walkway. Take your time and go quietly—the better to spot *tuis,* bellbirds, wood pigeons, and other bird life.

Less well known but no less fascinating is the **Labyrinth,** a system of twisting tunnels and gullies carved into the rocks by long-receded river systems. The phenomenon went unnoticed for years and until recently was simply part of grazing land. Now the delightfully eccentric and totally enthusiastic Dave Whittaker has proclaimed himself to be "keeper of the rocks" and has opened the place to the public. You will find rocks shaped like crocodiles and other reptiles, plus a natural maze. Dave has hidden a few gnomes and other fairy-tale creatures around the park, which is great for kids. A troll bridge, an Asian garden, and a picnic site are other features. ⊠ *Off Abel Tasman Dr.,* ☎ *03/525–8434.* ☞ *$5.* ☉ *12:30–5.*

Lodging

$$$ ⊞ **Westhaven Retreat.** If it's remote luxury you're after, this peninsula retreat is for you. It's set on 800 acres of regenerating native forest surrounded by the Tasman Sea, the Westhaven Entrance, and the Whanganui Inlet. Austrian-born Bruno and Monika Stompe literally carved the accommodations out of the environment (access roads into the property and throughout were built by Bruno, once a successful industrial engineer). Rooms in the main house feature rimu wood panelling and neutral colors. Large windows in the dining area provide gorgeous views. The separate cottage is modern, roomy, and bright. It's also well-stocked with beverages, snacks, and toiletries. With at least 40 km (25 mi) of gravel road between you and the nearest store, your hosts make sure you're well provided for! On-site you'll find a menagerie of farm animals, including more than 20 gentle llamas, who will be as intrigued with you as you are with them. The $35 European-style dinner includes wine, and lunch can be arranged. If you're not used to gravel roads, inquire about helicopter access or about being picked up at Nelson Airport, Motueka, or Takaka. ⊠ *Te Hapu Rd., Collingwood,* ☎ *03/524–8354,* ℻ *03/524–8354. 3 rooms, 1 cottage. Hiking, beaches. AE, DC, MC, V. BP.* ❧

$$ ⊞ **Anatoki Lodge.** This spacious, contemporary motel is close to Takaka center. Owners Marilyn and Gary McClintock can help point out the main attractions and best places to eat in the area. The lodge has spacious studios and one- and two-bedroom units; each opens out to a private patio and grass courtyard. A cooked or Continental breakfast can be delivered to your room. ✉ *87 Commercial St.,* ☎ *03/525–8047,* FAX *03/525–8433. 5 studios, 4 one-bedrooms, 1 two-bedroom. Indoor pool. AE, DC, MC, V. BP.*

Outdoor Activities and Sports

BEACHES

Golden Bay has miles of swimming beaches. **Paton's Rock** is one of the best near Takaka. Check the tides before taking the 10-minute drive from town, as swimming is best with a full tide. Farther out, less suitable for swimming but spectacular for its coastal landscapes, is **Wharariki Beach.** You'll find massive sand dunes, and among these you're likely to come across fur seals sunbathing. They are, of course, wild seals, and if you get too close to them, they might charge or even bite. Keep a 15-ft distance. To get here, drive past Collingwood and follow the signs. Go as far as the road will take you, then walk over farmland on a well-defined track for 20 minutes.

FISHING

For information on deep-sea fishing in Golden Bay out of Takaka, *see* Chapter 5.

HIKING

The wild **Kahurangi National Park** has a diversity of walks and treks. This vast patch of land includes in its compass great fern-clad forests, rivers, rolling hills, snowcapped mountains, and beaches pounded by West Coast surf. The most famous walk is the **Heaphy Track.** It is known primarily as a "free walk"—a slight misnomer in that trekkers need to pay a nominal fee to camp or use huts ($15–$18) during the four- to six-day experience. It is best to purchase these tickets in advance from information centers at Nelson, Motueka, or Takaka. Tickets in hand, all you really need to do is get to the track and start walking toward Karamea on the West Coast. Huts along the way have gas cooking and heating facilities, water, and toilets. You'll need to carry your own food and bedding. And be prepared for weather of all kinds at all times of year—bring rain gear and warm clothing even in summer (and insect repellent for the sand flies!). The east entrance to the park is 35 km (23 mi) west of Takaka, south of the town of Collingwood.

The **Department of Conservation Golden Bay Area Office** (✉ 62 Commercial St., Takaka, ☎ 03/525–8026) provides local trail maps.

If you'd like some expert company on hikes around the national park, **Kahurangi Guided Walks** (☎ 03/525–7177, 🐾) runs easy one-day treks (from $65) on routes known to locals but virtually untouched by visitors. One goes to a remote historic hut, known as Chaffey Cottage, where a couple lived for 40 years. A more strenuous, three-day walk ($255) goes to the rarely visited Boulder Lake. You can also choose a five-day hike on the Heaphy Track ($720).

Kahurangi National Park Bus Services (☎ 03/525–9434, FAX 03/525–9430, 🐾) offer transport to the track from Takaka on demand for $100 (drop-off and pickup). They also provide general charter services and scheduled services between Golden Bay, Abel Tasman, and Nelson. From Nelson, **Intercity** runs buses at 7:30 AM each day. ☎ *03/548–1538.* 🚌 *$31.*

HORSE TREKKING

Cape Farewell Horse Treks has a range of treks, from trips around a farm yard for kids to overnighters down the West Coast. The sturdy, hand-picked standard Thoroughbred horses know exactly where they're going—even if you don't. For great views of Farewell Spit, ask about the Pillar Point Light trek. Book ahead in summer. ✉ *Wharariki Beach Rd., Puponga,* ☎ *03/524–8031.*

Nelson and the Northwest A to Z

Arriving and Departing

BY BUS

InterCity (reservations from Nelson, ☎ 03/548–1538) buses are readily available to Nelson from the ferry terminal in Picton. From Nelson, InterCity runs the length of both the west and east coasts daily.

BY CAR

Nelson is about a two-hour drive from the ferry in Picton. The distance is 145 km (90 mi), but the winding roads don't allow for fast open-road driving.

From Nelson, Highway 6 runs southwest to the West Coast, down the coast to the glaciers, then over the Haast Pass to Wanaka and Queenstown. If you're going to the West Coast, allow at least seven hours for the 458-km (284-mi) journey from Nelson to Franz Josef. The same applies if you plan to drive from Nelson to Christchurch, 424 km (265 mi) to the southeast, whether you drive through the mountains of Nelson Lakes National Park or through Blenheim and Kaikoura down the coast.

BY PLANE

Air New Zealand (☎ 03/546–9300) and **Ansett New Zealand** (☎ 03/547–7560) link Nelson with Christchurch, Queenstown, Dunedin, the West Coast town of Hokitika, and all major cities on North Island. **Nelson Airport** is 10 km (6 mi) south of the city. **Super Shuttle** (☎ 03/547–5782) buses meet all incoming flights; the cost is $8 to the city for one passenger, $5 each for two. Taxi fare is about $14.

Contacts and Resources

CAR RENTAL

Avis (✉ Nelson Airport, ☎ 03/547–2727), **Budget** (✉ Nelson Airport, ☎ 03/547–9586), and **Hertz** (✉ Nelson Airport, ☎ 03/547–2299).

EMERGENCIES

Dial 111 for **fire, police, or ambulance** services.

GUIDED TOURS

Abel Tasman National Park Enterprises guide day trips and three- and five-day treks in the beautiful coastal park. Spend nights in comfortable lodges and eat well, without having to carry a big pack. The rates for a five-day kayaking and hiking trip or five-day guided walk are from $1,080, depending on the season; the three-day kayaking and hiking trip or three-day guided walk start at $720. ✉ 265 High St., Motueka, ☎ 03/528–7801 or 0800/223–582, FAX 03/528–6087. ⊛

Bay Tours Nelson runs daily tours of wine trails, half- and full-day arts-and-crafts tours, and scenic adventure tours by arrangement. Trips include the city and its immediate district, and also go farther afield to Motueka and Kaiteriteri Beach and south to Nelson Lakes National Park. ✉ 48 Brougham St., Nelson, ☎ 03/545–7114 or 0800/229–868, FAX 03/545–7119.

The **Scenic Mail Run** is a five-hour tour aboard the bus that delivers the mail and supplies to isolated farming communities around Cape Farewell, and Westhaven Inlet at the tip of Golden Bay. The tour includes a picnic lunch at any number of scenic points. The eight-seater bus departs from the Collingwood post office on Golden Bay. ✉ Collingwood Bus Services, Collingwood, ☎ 03/524–8188, FAX 03/524–8091. ⊠ $35. ⊘ Weekdays 10:30.

VISITOR INFORMATION
Golden Bay Visitor Information Centre. ✉ *Willow St.,* ☎ *03/525–9136.* ⊘ *Daily 9–5.*
Motueka Visitor Information Centre. ✉ *Wallace St.,* ☎ *03/528–6543,* FAX *03/528–6563.* ⊘ *Daily 8–7.*
Nelson Visitor Information Centre. ✉ *Trafalgar and Halifax Sts.,* ☎ *03/548–2304.* ⊘ *Daily 8:30–5:30.* 🐚

THE WEST COAST

Southwest of Nelson, the wild West Coast region is a land unto itself. The mystical Pancake Rocks and blowholes around Punakaiki (poon-ah-*kye*-kee) set the scene for the rugged, sometimes forlorn landscape to the south. Early *pakeha* (European) settlers lived a hardscrabble life, digging for gold and farming where they could, constantly washed by the Wet Coast rains. The towns along the way don't have much of interest in their own right, but they are good bases from which to explore the coast, mountains, lakes, and forests of the region.

At the glacier towns of Franz Josef and Fox, the unique combination of soaring mountains and voluminous precipitation means that the massive valleys of ice descend straight into rain forests—interestingly enough, a combination also found on the southwest coast of South America. South of the glaciers, the road follows the seacoast, where fur seals and fiordland crested penguins inhabit fantastical beaches and forests. On sunny days the Tasman Sea along the stretch between Lake Moeraki and Haast takes on a transcendent shade of blue.

For all its beauty, this is not the most hospitable of New Zealand's provinces. The people are friendly and welcoming, but the landscape and weather can make things difficult if you don't have an adventurous streak. Locals pride themselves on their ability to coexist with the wild, primeval landscape on their doorstep. Be prepared for rain, fog, and cold nights, all of which can get your spirits down. The meteorological mix can, unfortunately, mean that the glacier flight that you planned at Franz Josef or Fox won't fly the day that you're there. If you do end up here on a rainy day, keep in mind that you might wake up the next morning to have brilliant sunshine lighting up the region's glorious scenery.

If you're driving to the West Coast from Nelson or Motueka, Highway 6, beyond Murchison, parallels the broad **Buller River** as it carves a deep gorge from the jagged mountain peaks. Nineteen kilometers (12 miles) south of Murchison, the **Newtown Hotel,** no longer licensed, teeters on the brink of the gorge, surrounded by a wild junkyard of obsolete farm machinery. The Buller once carried a fabulous cargo of gold, but you'll have to use your imagination to reconstruct the days when places such as Lyell, 34 km (21 mi) past Murchison, were bustling mining towns. Not far from here is New Zealand's longest swaying footbridge, the **Buller Gorge Swing Bridge. Hawk's Crag,** where the highway passes beneath a rock overhang with the river wheeling alongside, is the scenic climax of the trip along the Buller. Before the town of Westport, turn left to continue along Highway 6.

Punakaiki

269 km (168 mi) southeast of Nelson.

Punakaiki is just a small collection of shops at first glance. In fact, the big attraction is not the town. From the visitor center, an easy 10-minute walk leads to a fantastic maze of limestone rocks stacked high above the sea. These are the surreal **Pancake Rocks,** the outstanding feature of the surrounding **Paparoa National Park** (☎ 03/731–1895, FAX 03/731–1888). At high tide, a blowhole spouts a thundering geyser of spray. Aoraki (Mt. Cook) is sometimes visible to the south.

Greymouth

㉟ *44 km (28 mi) south of Punakaiki.*

The town of Greymouth (said like the anatomical feature) is aptly named—at first take it's a rather dispirited strip of motels and industrial buildings. But the **Jade Boulder Gallery** is a great place to pick up a distinctive souvenir. The gallery exhibits the work of Ian Boustridge, one of the country's most accomplished sculptors of greenstone, the jade that is highly prized by the Maori. You're in a Ngai Tahu iwi (tribe) area and as part of the tribe's 1997 Treaty of Waitangi settlement, the government recognized Ngai Tahu as having sole rights to collect and sell the precious jade in its natural form. Earrings start at about $10, and sculpture can cost anything up to $35,000. You'll find that the stone can manifest itself in a number of colors, including deep blues, rusts, even creams, depending on what minerals and conditions have worked their magic. ✉ *1 Guiness St.,* ☎ *03/768–0700.* ⊙ *Summer, weekdays 8:30 AM–9 PM, weekends 9–9; winter, weekdays 8:30–5, weekends 9–5.*

㉑ On the southern outskirts of Greymouth, **Shantytown** is a lively reenactment of a gold-mining town of the 1880s. Except for the church and the town hall, most of the buildings are replicas, but the gold diggings are authentic and fascinating. Displays include a water jet for blasting the gold-bearing quartz from the hillside, water sluices, and a stamper—battery-powered by a 30-ft waterwheel—for crushing the ore. You can pan for gold—there's even a good chance of striking "color." ✉ *Rutherglen,* ☎ *03/762–6634,* FAX *03/762–6649.* ☞ *$13 with gold panning, $10.50 without.* ⊙ *Daily 8:30–5.* 🕾

Dining and Lodging

$$$$ ✕🏨 **Lake Brunner Sporting Lodge.** Set on the southern shore of Lake
★ Brunner, a 40-minute drive southeast of Greymouth, this sprawling lodge, first established in 1868, has excellent fishing, a variety of activities, and a high level of comfort at a price that is relatively low by the standards of New Zealand's elite lodges. Rooms are large and well equipped, with the emphasis on comfort rather than opulence. The best rooms are at the front of the villa, overlooking the lake. The lodge is known for its clear-water stalking, since brown trout can be easily seen in the clear waters of the surrounding rivers. Fly-fishing is the primary method used but good spin fishing is also available at certain times of the year, and the lodge follows a catch-and-release policy. Hiking, boating, mountain biking, bird-watching, and nature tours are also available—the lodge is surrounded by untouched forests. If you get the chance, walk through the Carew Reserve at the back of the lodge with hostess Marian van der Goes. Her knowledge of the rain forest will open your eyes to things you would otherwise miss, such as native orchids nestled in the boughs of high branches. The Lodge's kitchen features seasonal and fresh local meat and produce. Mains might include a roasted venison with merlot sauce served with honeyed wild rice and glazed green beans, or a marinated and roasted rack of lamb with red pepper sauce. Rates include all meals. ✉ *Mitchells, R.D. 1, Kumara, Westland,* ☎ FAX *03/738–0163. 11 en-suite rooms. Dining room, fishing, mountain bikes, library. FAP. AE, DC, MC, V. Closed Aug.–Sept. FAP.* 🕾

$$ 🏨 **Rosewood.** This superior, centrally located B&B in a restored 1920s home is a great base for further exploration of the area. Your hosts, Margaret Smith and Ian Wooster, know the region well and offer guided trips with customized itineraries, including exploring nearby ancient rain forests. ⊠ *20 High St., Greymouth,* ☎ *03/768–4674,* ℻ *03/768–4694. 5 rooms. Laundry service. MC, V. BP.* ⊛

Hokitika

㉒ *41 km (26 mi) south of Greymouth.*

Hokitika won't exactly wow you, but if you're finding the drive down to the glaciers a bit long, it is a convenient stopover for the night. There are crafts shops in town if you have time for browsing, or a few local bushwalks, and the beach is littered with some very interesting driftwood. If you happen to get into town in the middle of a rainstorm, it might seem bleak.

One annual Hokitika event worth stopping for is the **Wildfoods Festival,** where you'll find a plethora of gourmet bushtucker (food from the bush) from the West Coast's natural food sources. Bite into such delectables as *huhu* grubs (they look like large maggots), worm sushi, whitebait patties (far more mainstream), and snail caviar, and wash it all down with gorse wine, moonshine, or Monteith's bitter beer. The mid-March fest attracts crowds of up to 13,500, four times the local population. Entertainment includes lively performances by members of the Hokitika Live Poets Society at the tree stump by Billy Tea Hut (where else). It can get rowdy at night at the barn dance, which seems to spill through the town. Of course, a good dump of West Coast rain will quiet things down—until the next year. Take your gum boots.

Lodging

$–$$ ⌂ **Teichelmann's Central Bed & Breakfast.** Named for Ebenezer Teichelmann, the surgeon-mountaineer-conservationist who built the original part of the house, this is the most comfortable place in town. It's been a bed-and-breakfast for 25 years, and its genteel atmosphere has a lot to do with hosts Norm Duncan and Lorraine Johnston, who are happy to make suggestions for local activities. Furnishings are a combination of antique and country-cottage style, using plenty of native wood. At breakfast, serve yourself fruit and cereals from the Southland beech-wood sideboard. And the rimu bookcase is full of literature about the area. ⊠ *20 Hamilton St.,* ☎ *03/755–8232,* ℻ *03/755–8239. 6 rooms, 4 rooms with bath. AE, MC, V. BP.* ⊛

Franz Josef and Fox Glaciers

㉓ ㉔ *Franz Josef is 146 km (91 mi) south of Hokitika; Fox is 24 km (15 mi) south of Franz Josef.*

The north end of **Westland National Park** begins at the Franz Josef glacier field. These glaciers—New Zealanders say "glassy-urs"—are formed by the massive precipitation of the West Coast— up to 300 inches per annum—which descends as snow on the névé, or head, of the glacier. The snow is compressed into ice, which actually flows downhill under its own weight. There are more than 60 glaciers in the park; the most famous and accessible are at Franz Josef and Fox. The glacier at **Fox** is slightly larger and longer than that at Franz Josef, but you'll miss nothing important if you see only one. Both glaciers have separate townships, and if you are spending the night, **Franz Josef** is marginally preferable. There are parking areas outside the towns of Franz Josef and Fox from which you can walk about 30 minutes to reach the glaciers' terminal faces. Both parking lots are sometimes terrorized by keas (*kee-ahs*)—mountain parrots—which specialize in destroying the rubber molding around car windows. Keas are harmless to humans, and a coating of insect repellent around the window frames should safeguard your vehicle.

Trails from the parking lots wind across the rocky valley floor to the glacier faces, where a tormented vocabulary of squeaks, creaks, groans, and gurgles can be heard as the glacier creeps down the mountainside at an average rate of up to 3 ft per day. Care must be taken here, since rocks and chunks of ice frequently drop from the melting face.

These being New Zealand glaciers, there is much to do besides admire them. You can fly over them in helicopters or planes and land on the stable névé, or hike on them with guides. Remember that these structures are dynamic and always in motion—an ice cave that was visible yesterday might today be smashed under tons of ice that used to be just uphill of it. Likewise some of the fascinating formations that you see on the surface of the glacier were fairly recently at the very bottom of it higher up in the valley. It pays not to be in or on anything that is about to collapse, and guides know where to avoid such dangers.

For the most part, flights are best made early in the morning, when visibility tends to be clearest. Seasonal variables around the glaciers are a surprising thing. Summer is, of course, warmer and by far the busiest season. But there is a lot more rain and fog that can scuttle "flight-seeing" and hiking plans. Winter is in fact a well-kept secret in these parts. In winter, snow doesn't fall at sea level in Franz Josef or Fox. Skies are clearer, which means fewer canceled flights and glacier hikes and more of the dazzling sunshine that makes views of the mountains so spectacular.

㉕ Outside the town of Fox Glacier, **Lake Matheson** has one of the country's most famous views. A walking trail winds along the lakeshore, and the snowcapped peaks of Aoraki and Mt. Tasman are reflected in the water. Allow at least an hour for the complete walk from town to the "view of views." The best time is early morning, before the mirrorlike reflections are fractured by the wind. From town, turn and walk toward the sea where a sign points to Gillespies Beach, then turn right again to reach the lake.

Dining and Lodging

$$ ✕ **Blue Ice Café.** You'll welcome an alternative both in cuisine and decor to the steak-and-chips joints so common on the West Coast. Along with pizza and a light menu of salads, lasagna, and the like, you'll find Greenshell mussels, pork ribs, rack of lamb, and cervena (farmed venison). Coffee and desserts such as hot kumara custard pudding or fudge cake are delicious. With a 2 AM license, Blue Ice buzzes long into the night in the tourist season. ⊠ *South end of Main Rd., Franz Josef,* ☎ *03/752–0707. MC, V. No lunch.*

$$$ ✕▥ **Franz Josef Glacier Hotels.** The largest hotel in the glacier region, this motel-style complex at the north end of Franz Josef village offers rooms a cut above the average in size and furnishings. Be sure to ask for a room with glacier views—particularly stunning as the sun rises over the Southern Alps and lights up the glaciers. Larger suites with upgraded facilities are also available, and the hotel has a choice of three restaurants, none of which serve lunch. ⊠ *State Hwy. 6, Franz Josef,* ☎ *03/752–0729 or 0800/228–228,* ℻ *03/752–0709. 177 rooms. 3 restaurants, 3 bars, 2 hot tubs, coin laundry. AE, DC, MC, V.* 🐾

Outdoor Activities and Sports

FISHING

For information on fishing around Franz Josef and Fox, *see* Chapter 5.

ON AND ABOVE THE GLACIERS

The walks to the glacier heads mentioned above are the easiest and most basic way of seeing the glaciers. But joining a guided walk and getting up close to the glaciers' ice formations—the shapes created by the glaciers' movement and the streams of water running through them—is unforgettable.

Flying over the glaciers is also quite thrilling, and that thrill comes at considerable expense. The ultimate combination is to fly by fixed-wing plane or helicopter to the top or middle of the glacier and get out and walk on it. Fixed-wing landings on the snow atop the ice fields are fabulously scenic, but you have only 10 minutes out of the plane. Helihikes give you the most time on the ice, two to three hours of snaking up and down right in the middle of a stable part of the glacier. If you've never flown in a helicopter, the experience can be nearly heart-stopping. It is exactly what you'd imagine flying on a magic carpet would be like, the way the pull of the rotors lifts you up and into the glacial valleys. As you make your way to a landing spot, the pilot banks the helicopter so that the only things between you and the mass of ice below you are a sheet of glass and centrifugal force. It's a wild ride.

Alpine Guides Fox Glacier has half- or full-day guided walks on Fox Glacier, the only safe way to experience the ethereal beauty of the ice caves, pinnacles, and crevasses on top of the glaciers. The 3½- to 4-hour walk travels about 2 km (1 mi) up the glacier. The climb requires some fitness. Arguably the best option is to heli-hike, combining a helicopter flight onto and off Fox Glacier and walking for two hours on the ice with a guide. Or try the full-day ice-climbing excursion with mountaineering equipment provided. ⊠ *Box 38, Fox Glacier,* ☎ *03/751–0825,* ℻ *03/751–0857.* ⊑ *½-day $39, full-day $65, heli-hikes $170, ice climbing $150.* ☉ *Tours daily at 9:30 and 2.* ⊛

The **Helicopter Line** operates several scenic flights over the glaciers from heliports at Franz Josef and Fox. The shortest is the 20-minute flight over Franz Josef Glacier ($135 per person); the longest is a 40-minute flight that includes a landing on the head of the glacier and a circuit of Aoraki and Mt. Tasman ($260). Two-and-a-half-hour heli-hikes are yet another option ($190). ⊠ *Main St., Box 45, Franz Josef,* ☎ *03/752–0767 or 0800/807–767,* ℻ *03/752–0769. AE, DC, MC, V.* ⊛

Mount Cook Lines Ski Plane has fixed-wing ski planes that fly over the glaciers. Landings amid craggy peaks in the high-altitude ski slopes are otherworldly. The 40-minute ($190) and one-hour ($250) flights both cover Fox and Franz Josef glaciers; the longer one includes a circuit of Aoraki and lands on Tasman Glacier. ⊠ *Franz Josef,* ☎ *03/752–0714 or 0800/800–737 for Franz Josef; 0800/800–702 for Fox. AE, DC, MC, V.*

Lake Moeraki

㉖ *90 km (56 mi) south of Fox Glacier, 30 km (19 mi) north of Haast.*

Lake Moeraki itself sits in the midst of Westland National Park. There isn't a town here; it's the site of a thoughtfully designed wilderness lodge (☞ Dining and Lodging, *below*). The immediate area's public access is **Monro Beach.** The 45-minute walk to the beach takes you through spectacular, fern-filled native forest to a truly remarkable beach: rock clusters jut out of incredibly blue waters, and rivers and streams flow over the sand into the Tasman Sea. You might arrive at a time when spunky little fiordland crested penguins are in transit from the sea to their stream- or hillside nests. Early morning and late afternoon are good but not sure bets to find them.

Two kilometers (1 mile) south of the trail entrance on the beach is a seal colony, which you will smell before you see it. If you venture that way, be sure to keep about 16½ ft away from the seals (the legal distance), and don't block their path to the sea. A spooked seal will bowl you over on its lurch for the water and may even bite, so be extremely respectful of their space. Sculpted dark gray rocks also litter the beach to the south, and seals like to lie behind and among them, so look carefully before you cross in front of these rocks.

Monro Beach is an utter dream, not least if you collect driftwood or rocks. On the road 2 km (1 mi) or so south of it, there is a lookout over the rock stacks at **Knights Point.** Farther south still, between Moeraki and Haast, the walkways and beach at **Ship Creek** are another stop for ferny forests and rugged coastline. Sand flies here can be voracious. Bring insect repellent and hope for a windy day!

Dining and Lodging

$$$$ ✕🖼 **Wilderness Lodge Lake Moeraki.** Dr. Gerry McSweeney, a lead-
★ ing voice in New Zealand's conservation movement, runs this lodge with the intention of demonstrating that tourism is an economic alternative to logging in the forests of South Westland. The lodge has a splendid setting, along a river flowing out of the lake, north of the town of Haast. Fiordland crested penguins—the rarest on earth—nest along streams and on hills above the beach. On-staff naturalists will take you to see fur seals and, if he's around, the giant elephant seal whom they call Humphrey. They will also take you along while they feed local eels in the morning. Canoes and kayaks are available for paddling the lake, and forest trails from the lodge, some of which lead to the beach, echo with the sound of rushing streams and birdcalls. There are also glowworm and night-sky walks, on which guides point out the enchanting constellations of the southern hemisphere. After all your outdoors activities, you'll eat local produce and drink New Zealand wine at dinner. Rates include full breakfast and dinner, two short guided nature activities, and the use of canoes and mountain bikes. Longer guided hikes, fishing guides, lunch, and dinner drinks come at extra charge. ✉ *Private Bag, Hokitika,* ☎ *03/750–0881,* ℻ *03/750–0882. 18 rooms, 4 superior suites. Beach, boating, fishing, laundry service. AE, DC, MC, V.* 🐾

Fishing

For information on deep-sea fishing out of Haast, *see* Chapter 5.

West Coast A to Z

Arriving and Departing

BY BUS

InterCity buses run the length of the West Coast daily; reservate at **Franz Josef** (☎ 03/752–0164), **Greymouth** (☎ 03/768–5101), and **Nelson** (☎ 03/548–1538).

BY CAR

The north end of the West Coast is roughly a four-hour drive from Nelson on Highway 6, or a five- to six-hour drive over Arthur's Pass on Highway 7 from Christchurch, the very top of which is harrowing to say the least. Hokitika and Greymouth are about 256 km (166 mi) from Christchurch.

To continue south out of the region, beyond Lake Moeraki, take Highway 6 along the south coast to Haast, where it turns inland to Wanaka and Queenstown. The driving time between Moeraki and Wanaka is about five hours.

BY TRAIN

The West Coast in general is poorly served by the rail network, but one glowing exception is the **TranzAlpine Express** (☎ 800/802–802), which ranks as one of the world's great rail journeys. This passenger train crosses the Southern Alps between Christchurch and Greymouth, winding through beech forests and mountains that are covered by snow for most of the year. The bridges and tunnels along this line, including the 8-km (5-mi) Otira Tunnel, represent a prodigious feat of engineering. The train is modern and comfortable, with panoramic windows as well as dining and bar service. The train departs Christchurch daily at 9 AM and arrives in Greymouth at 1:25 PM; the return train departs Greymouth at 2:25 PM and arrives at Christchurch at 6:35 PM. The one-way fare is $76, round-trip $99.

Contacts and Resources

EMERGENCIES

Dial 111 for **fire, police, or ambulance** services.

VISITOR INFORMATION

Franz Josef Glacier Visitor Information Centre. ⊠ *State Hwy. 6, Franz Josef,* ☎ *03/752–0796.* ☉ *Summer, daily 8:30–6; winter, daily 8:30–5.* ☜

Greymouth Information Centre. ⊠ *Mackay and Herbert Sts., Greymouth,* ☎ *03/768–5101.* ☉ *Weekdays 9–5:30, weekends 10–4.* ☜

4 CHRISTCHURCH AND LOWER SOUTH ISLAND

This is it—picture-postcard New Zealand, where the country's tallest mountains are reflected in crystal-clear lakes and sheer rock faces tower above the fjords. The choice of activity is yours. You can enjoy some of the world's most dramatic views in complete peace and quiet or leap—literally, if you'd like—from one adrenaline rush to the next.

AS THE KEA FLIES, it's only 130 km (80 mi) from the eastern shores of South Island to its highest peak, 12,283-ft Aoraki (Mt. Cook). As many as 60 glaciers of varying size are locked in the Southern Alps, slowly grinding their way down to lower altitudes, where they melt into running rivers of uncanny blue-green hues. Aoraki National Park is a UNESCO World Heritage Area, and the alpine region around it contains the Tasman Glacier, New Zealand's longest.

The wide-open Canterbury Plains separate the mountains from the ocean. This is some of New Zealand's finest pastureland, and the higher reaches of the Canterbury are sheep station territory, where life and lore mingle in South Island's cowboy country. This is the territory where young Samuel Butler dreamed up the satirical *Erewhon*—the word is an anagram of "nowhere." The station he lived on is now on a horse-trekking route.

Trekking is one of the things that Southland does best. The southwest corner of the island, where glaciers over millennia have cut the Alps into stone walls dropping sheer into fjords, is laced with walking tracks that take you into the heart of wild Fiordland National Park. The Milford Track is the best known—it has been called the finest walk in the world since a headline to that effect appeared in the London *Spectator* in 1908. If you're not keen on walking all the way to the Milford Sound, drive in and hop on a boat and take in the sights and sounds from on deck.

Christchurch was built on the fortunes made from the Canterbury region's sheep runs. People call it the most English city outside England and indeed Christchurch was founded in 1850 by the Canterbury Association, a group of leading British churchmen, politicians, and peers who envisioned a settlement that would serve as a model of industry and ideals, governed by the principles of the Anglican faith. Whatever the historical reasons, the earthy gentility of Christchurch makes it a pleasant foil for the wilds of South Island.

Gold, on the other hand, fueled Dunedin's glory days. Following the Central Otago strike of 1861 thousands of tons of gold were shipped out of the city's port, but not before some of it went into building some of New Zealand's finest buildings in the city. Southwest of Dunedin, hanging off the bottom of South Island, Stewart Island is a study in remoteness. Commercial fishing settlements give way to bushland that the kiwi bird—so rare elsewhere in the country—still haunts. Expansive views across the Foveaux Strait from time to time alight with the *aurora australis*, the spectacular southern hemisphere equivalent of the northern lights.

South Island is without doubt the wilder of the country's two largest islands. Beyond the well-defined tourist routes, its beech forests, lakes, trout streams, and mountain trails are a paradise for hikers, anglers, and anyone who enjoys a good dose of fresh air.

Note: For more information on bicycling, cross-country skiing, fishing, hiking, horse trekking, rafting, and sailing in lower South Island, *see* Chapter 5.

Pleasures and Pastimes

Bungy Jumping

Don't worry, New Zealanders aren't going to pressure you into jumping off a bridge with an elastic cord tied to your ankles. But if you have an overwhelming desire to bungy (the Kiwi spelling for bungee), this is the place to do it. The cost of the jump usually includes a "been there–done that" T-shirt and even a video of your daredevil act.

Dining

Christchurch has a fairly wide range of eateries, from cosmopolitan restaurants to earthy vegetarian cafés. The region has a thriving wine industry, as does the Waipara district.

The small fishing town of Bluff is known for two reasons in New Zealand—it is the southernmost tip of the South Island, and it gives its name to an oyster. The Bluff oyster is one of the country's great delicacies, so pick up a dozen fresh ones from a fish shop if you can, or try them in a restaurant. As for Dunedin and Queenstown, you'll find a good variety of restaurants because of the former's student population and the latter's influx of international visitors.

Hiking

South Island's southwestern wilderness areas are the stuff of legendary tramping. The Milford Track, the Kepler, the Routeburn, the Hollyford—it doesn't get any better than these. The variety on these treks is astonishing; you'll see mountains, fjords, waterfalls, and rain forests.

Lodging

No matter where you stay in Christchurch, you're sure to find some of the best lodging in New Zealand, from luxury hotels and lodges to very fine B&Bs. The rest of lower South Island is blessed with great views; you'll almost always be able to find a place to stay overlooking a lake, river, or mountainous landscape. If you can forego luxury, basic but comfortable cabins can often be found in the most beautiful places. Farm stays are often set on lush green grasslands with snow-capped mountains as a backdrop.

Skiing

South Island's best-known ski areas are here. Use Wanaka as a base for Treble Cone and Cadrona, or Queenstown as a base for Coronet Peak and the Remarkables. For the biggest thrill, go heli-skiing in areas otherwise unreachable.

Exploring Christchurch and Lower South Island

Great Itineraries

Touring the lower half of South Island requires making difficult choices. Do you want to walk the Milford Track, or does the remote Stewart Island appeal more? Will you go away disappointed if you miss Queenstown, the adventure capital, or would you just as soon station yourself in the snowy reaches of Aoraki? The Otago Peninsula has its own spectacular scenery, interesting wildlife, and the charming city of Dunedin. The scenic coastal highway from Dunedin to Invercargill presents the exciting and wild Catlins coast to explore. And then there is Christchurch and side trips from the city to the precipitous Banks Peninsula.

To literally see it all would take a good three weeks, if you intend to do it justice and stay sane. Short of that, treat each of these areas as two- to three-day segments, mix them up to suit your fancy, and take into account travel time of three to five hours between each.

Numbers in the text correspond to points of interest on the Canterbury Region and the Southern Alps; Christchurch; and Southland, Otago, and Stewart Island maps.

IF YOU HAVE 3 DAYS

Spend the first or last day in ⊞ **Christchurch** ①–⑬, strolling through the beautiful **Christchurch Botanic Gardens** ⑤, poking around the **Arts Centre** ⑧, perhaps heading out to **Mona Vale** ⑪ for afternoon tea. Then choose whether to fly to ⊞ **Aoraki** ㉒, to ⊞ **Queenstown** ㉕, or to ⊞ **Stewart Island** ㉟–㊱ for two days. If you pick Aoraki, explore some of South Canterbury one day, making sure to stop at ⊞ **Lake Tekapo** ⑲, and take in the view from inside the **Church of the Good Shepherd** ⑳. You could spend the night here or on Mt. Cook. On the next day take a flight over the mountain or onto the **Tasman Glacier** ㉓, followed by a walk into the Hooker Valley or up Mt. Sebastopol.

IF YOU HAVE 5 DAYS

Spend two days in ⊞ **Christchurch** ①–⑬, using the second to see the **International Antarctic Centre** ⑩ or ride the **Christchurch Gondola** ⑫. You could otherwise take the whole day and go to the town of ⊞ **Akaroa** ⑭ on the Banks Peninsula, drive up the summit of the volcanic dome, then take a road down to one of the bays on the other side of the peninsula. On the third day fly to ⊞ **Queenstown** ㉕. Depending on how active you are, you could easily spend three days here throwing yourself off a bridge, heli-skiing, jet-boat riding, white-water rafting, and taking a steamer trip on Lake Wakatipu. Leave some time to relax and take in the stunning views from the **Skyline Gondola** ㉖ as well. On the fourth day head to **Milford Sound** ㉚ to take in the amazing spectacle of sheer cliffs, deep water, and dense native bush. You could spend an adventurous day in ⊞ **Wanaka** ㉔, stopping in at Stuart Landsborough's Puzzling World, or getting familiar with this gorgeous alpine area by kayaking, rafting, or skydiving. From here you could easily tack on a trip to the stunning West Coast (☞ Chapter 3), driving over the scenic Haast Pass to get there.

IF YOU HAVE 8 DAYS

With eight days you have the luxury of taking your time. You could spend four of them on the Milford or Kepler tracks, a couple more in ⊞ **Wanaka** ㉔ and ⊞ **Queenstown** ㉕, plus a couple more in ⊞ **Christchurch** ①–⑬ or **Dunedin** ㉛. Or you could feel like you're skirting the edge of the earth by driving to Dunedin to explore the fascinating Otago Peninsula and view its wildlife, **Larnach Castle** ㉜, and **Taiaroa Head** ㉝, then continuing south along the rugged coast to **Invercargill** ㉞ and on to the southernmost **Stewart Island** ㉟–㊱, where you can spend three or four days doing some serious bushwalking and looking for kiwi birds in the wild. You could combine two or three days in Christchurch with two or three in Dunedin and the same on Stewart Island. Or just go alpine and spend all of your time around Aoraki, Wanaka, and Queenstown.

When to Tour Christchurch and Lower South Island

Because of the Alps, this is the part of New Zealand that gets cold with a capital C in winter, so if you're coming for warm weather stay away between May and September. For skiing, snowboarding, and other winter sports, this is *the* time to come. From July through September you can be assured of snow around Queenstown and Wanaka, where the ski scene is pretty lively. In the height of summer—from December into February—popular places like Queenstown can get so crowded that they lose the relaxed, laid-back atmosphere New Zealand is famous for. If you hold off until April or May, leaves turn yellow and red, and the nearby mountains have a smattering of early season snow. You'll have the Alps more to yourself, and some lodgings offer bargains.

The Canterbury Region and the Southern Alps

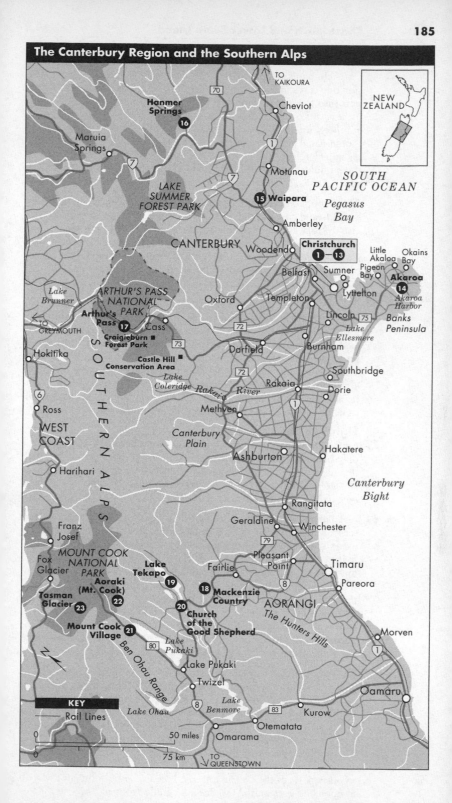

NEW ZEALAND

TO KAIKOURA

Cheviot

Hanmer Springs 16

Maruia Springs

70

SOUTH PACIFIC OCEAN

7

7

Motunau

LAKE SUMMER FOREST PARK

15 Waipara

1

Pegasus Bay

Amberley

CANTERBURY

Woodend

Christchurch 1 — 13

Little Akaloa

Okains Bay

Lake Brunner

ARTHUR'S PASS NATIONAL PARK

Belfast

Sumner

Pigeon Bay

Akaroa 14

Arthur's Pass 17

Cass

Oxford

Templeton

Lyttelton

Akaroa Harbor

TO GREYMOUTH

Craigieburn Forest Park

73

Lincoln

75

Banks Peninsula

Hokitika

Castle Hill Conservation Area

Darfield

72

Lake Ellesmere

Burnham

6

SOUTHERN

Lake Coleridge

Rakaia River

Rakaia

Southbridge

Ross

WEST COAST

Methven

Dorie

ALPS

Canterbury Plain

72

1

Harihari

Ashburton

Hakatere

Canterbury Bight

Rangitata

Franz Josef

MOUNT COOK NATIONAL PARK

Lake Tekapo 19

Geraldine

Winchester

79

Fox Glacier

Aoraki (Mt. Cook) 22

18 Mackenzie Country

Pleasant Point

Fairlie

AORANGI

Timaru

Tasman Glacier 23

20

8

Pareora

Mount Cook Village 21

Church of the Good Shepherd

The Hunters Hills

Ben Ohau Range

80

Lake Pukaki

Lake Pukaki

Morven

1

Twizel

8

Lake Benmore

83

Kurow

Oamaru

Lake Ohau

Omarama

Otematata

KEY

Rail Lines

0   50 miles
0   75 km

TO QUEENSTOWN

CHRISTCHURCH

Christchurch is something of a paradox—a city under the grand delusion that it is somewhere in southern England. The drive from the airport into town takes you through pristine suburbs of houses lapped by seas of flowers and past playing fields where children flail at one another's legs with hockey sticks. The heart of this pancake-flat city is dominated by church spires; its streets are named Durham, Gloucester, and Hereford; and instead of the usual wild New Zealand torrents, there bubbles, between banks lined with willows and oaks, the narrow Avon River, suitable only for punting.

With a population approaching 300,000, Christchurch is the largest South Island city and the only one with an international airport. It is also the forward supply depot for the main U.S. Antarctic base at McMurdo Sound, and if you come in by plane, you are likely to see the giant U.S. Air Force transport planes of Operation Deep Freeze parked on the tarmac at Christchurch International Airport.

Exploring Christchurch

The inner city is compact and so easy to explore by foot that there is little need to follow a preset walking tour. Just pick a sight or two, like Cathedral Square or the Arts Centre, and set out—you won't have very far to go. Outside the city boundaries, there are a number of special-interest museums and activities about 20 minutes away by car. There are also side trips from Christchurch into the Canterbury Plains countryside and to the Akaroa Peninsula, the remnant of an ancient volcanic dome whose steep, grassy walls drop to the sea.

Sights to See

❹ Antigua Boatshed. Built for the Christchurch Boating Club, this is the only boat shed that remains of the half dozen that once stood along the Avon. Canoes may be rented for short river trips. ✉ *Rolleston Ave.,* ☎ *03/366–5885.* ⌑ *Canoe $6 per hr, rowboat $20 per hr.* ☉ *Summer, daily 7–5:30; winter, daily 10–4.*

★ **❽ Arts Centre.** Why Canterbury University gave up its former quarters seems a mystery. The collection of Gothic Revival stone buildings it used to inhabit represents some of New Zealand's finest architecture. In the college days of Ernest Rutherford (1871–1937), the university's most illustrious pupil, classes were held in what is now the Arts Centre. Just past the information desk inside you'll find "Rutherford's Den," the modest stone chamber where the eminent physicist conducted experiments in what was then a new field, radioactivity. It was Rutherford who first succeeded in splitting the atom, a crucial step in the harnessing of atomic power. In 1908 Rutherford's work earned him the Nobel prize—not for physics but for chemistry.

The Arts Centre houses more than 40 speciality shops and studios, as well as art galleries, theaters, and cinemas. It is also an excellent place to stop for food, coffee, or a glass of wine if you are walking from the Cathedral Square to the Canterbury Museum—there are three cafés and a wine bar. There is also a **Saturday and Sunday Market,** where you'll find jewelry, prints, bric-a-brac, and handmade clothing and crafts. This market is a seeding ground for talented artisans: many former stall holders are now resident in the Centre or running successful businesses in other parts of the city or country. Free live entertainment kicks off at noon and goes until 2 PM. For a $5 guided tour of the center led by the "town crier"—Hear ye, hear ye—you should meet at the clock tower at 11 AM weekdays. ✉ *Worcester St. between Montreal St. and Rolle-*

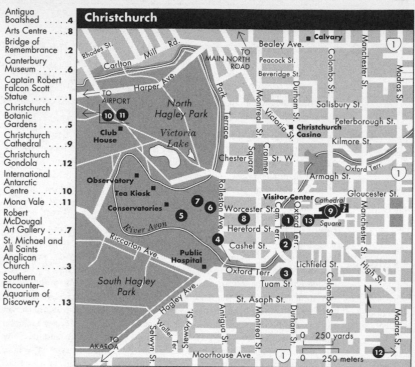

Christchurch

Antigua
Boatshed 4

Arts Centre 8

Bridge of
Remembrance . .2

Canterbury
Museum 6

Captain Robert
Falcon Scott
Statue 1

Christchurch
Botanic
Gardens 5

Christchurch
Cathedral 9

Christchurch
Gondola 12

International
Antarctic
Centre 10

Mona Vale . . .11

Robert
McDougal
Art Gallery 7

St. Michael and
All Saints
Anglican
Church 3

Southern
Encounter—
Aquarium of
Discovery 13

ston Ave., ☎ 03/366–0989. ☉ *Shops and galleries daily 10–4:30, with
extended hrs in the summer. Tours by arrangement (☎ 03/366–0980).*

NEED A
BREAK?

The Arts Centre has four eateries in its stone buildings and quadrangles.
Housed in a mock-Tudor building, **Dux de Lux** (☎ 03/366–6919) is a
sprawling, upbeat, popular cafeteria-style restaurant. The blackboard
menu offers vegetarian items and seafood: quiches, crepes, sandwiches,
breads and dips, pizzas, and a range of crisp salads. The courtyard is
a great spot on a sunny day, especially with a beer from the brewery next
door. And at night the brewery bustles with twenty- and thirtysomethings.
The **Boulevard Bakehouse** is great for coffee and a sweet. There is another
café half a block down from the Bakehouse, and **Annies Restaurant and
Wine Bar** (✉ 41 Hereford St., ☎ 03/366–6919) is the most refined of
the four, a very pleasant place to taste New Zealand wine alongside
bistro fare. All but the wine bar have outdoor seating in season.

---

② **Bridge of Remembrance.** Arching over the Avon, this bridge was built
in memory of the soldiers who crossed the river here from King Edward Barracks, just down Cashel Street, on their way to the battlefields
of Europe during World War I. ✉ *Avon River at Cashel St.*

 ⑥ **Canterbury Museum.** When this museum was founded in 1867, its trading power with national and international museums was in moa bones.
These Jurassic birds roamed the plains of Canterbury and are believed
to have been hunted to extinction by early Maori settlers. The museum
still houses one of the largest collections of artifacts from the moa hunting period. You'll also find a reconstruction of an early Christchurch
streetscape and a natural history discovery center that's great for kids.
The Hall of Antarctic Discovery charts the links between the city and
the U.S. bases on the frozen continent from the days of Captain Scott;
Christchurch is still used as a forward supply depot for U.S. Antarc-

tic bases. ⊠ *Rolleston Ave. and Worcester St.,* ☎ *03/366–8379.* 🖼 *Donation requested.* ⊙ *Daily 9–5:30.*

❶ Captain Robert Falcon Scott statue. "Scott of the Antarctic" (1868–1912), who visited Christchurch on his two Antarctic expeditions, is just across Worcester Street from the information center. The statue was sculpted by his widow, Kathleen Lady Kennett, and inscribed with his last words, written as he and his party lay dying in a blizzard on their return journey from the South Pole. ⊠ *Worcester Blvd. and Oxford Terr.*

★ **❺ Christchurch Botanic Gardens.** Your introduction to the garden will probably begin just beyond the ☞ **Robert McDougal Art Gallery** at the remarkable 310-ft herbaceous border, which should clue you in to the scale of things to come. These superb gardens are known for the magnificent trees that were planted in the 19th century. Many are the largest specimens found in the country—or even in their native lands. Pick up the Historic Tree Walk brochure for a self-guided Who's Who tour of the tree world. There are a number of specialty gardens as well. In spring spend time in the woodlands, in the rock garden, or at the primrose garden. In summer the rose garden is a display of every conceivable way to grow these beauties, and the annual plantings and water garden call out for attention now as well. In autumn that magnificent perennial border and the herb garden continue to amaze. And as the weather cools, the hips of species roses begin to redden, putting on yet another display. Spend time in the conservatories to discover tropical plants, cacti, and ferns on days when you'd rather not be outside. Any time of the year, be sure to go to the New Zealand plants area, where you can see plant life that you won't find in other countries. A small information center has displays, books, and plant information. ⊠ *Rolleston Ave.,* ☎ *03/366–1701.* 🖼 *Free.* ⊙ *Daily 7 AM–dusk, conservatories daily 10:15–4.*

❾ Christchurch Cathedral. The city's dominating landmark was begun in 1864, 14 years after the arrival of the Canterbury Pilgrims, but it wasn't consecrated until 1904. Carvings inside commemorate the work of the Anglican missionaries, including Tamihana Te Rauparaha, the son of a fierce and, for the settlers, troublesome Maori chief. Free guided tours begin daily at 11 and 2. For a view across the city to the Southern Alps, climb the 133 steps to the top of the bell tower. The cathedral is known for its boys' choir, which can be heard singing evensong at 4:30 on Friday, except during school holidays. It is in **Cathedral Square,** the city's focal point, which functions as a bus terminal and a venue for an arts-and-crafts market, food stalls, and street musicians.

If it's close to 1 PM when you emerge from the cathedral, look for the bearded gentleman with long hair, who's easy to spot because of the crowd that instantly forms around him. This is the **Wizard,** who offers funny and irreverent dissertations on just about any controversial subject—especially religion, politics, sex, and women's issues. Originally a free-lance soapbox orator, the Wizard (whose real name is Ian Channel) became so popular that he is now employed by the city council—one of his frequent targets. Don't be too disappointed if he's not around; his appearances have become less frequent in recent years, and he doesn't come out in winter, between May and October. ⊠ *Cathedral Sq.* 🖼 *Tower $3.* ⊙ *Daily 8:30 AM–9 PM.*

⓬ Christchurch Gondola. East of the city in the Port Hills, the gondola is the best vantage point from which to overlook Christchurch, the Canterbury Plains, and Lyttleton Harbour. At the top, you can wander through the **Time Tunnel,** which gives a brief history of the region and finishes with an audiovisual about present-day Canterbury. Best of all, sit with a glass of local wine at the Summit Cafe Brasserie and watch the sunset. Remember to ride the tram with your back to the mountain for the best views. If you don't have a car, free shuttles leave daily from the visitor center every two hours from 10 to 4. ⊠ *10 Bridle Path Rd., Heathcote,* ☎ *03/384–0700.* ☞ *$12, $9 after 5 PM.* ☉ *Sun.–Thurs. 10–8, Fri.–Sat. 10–9.* ☜

⑩ **International Antarctic Centre.** Ever since Scott wintered his dogs at nearby Quail Island in preparation for his ill-fated South Pole expedition of 1912, Christchurch has maintained a close connection with the frozen continent. Dedicated to the past, present, and future of Antarctic exploration, this complex includes intriguing interactive displays, in which you can feel firsthand the –5°C Antarctic conditions, for example, as well as photographs and exhibits showing the sophisticated clothing and hardware that modern-day scientists use to carry out their work at the Antarctic bases. The audiovisual show is superb. Added in late 1999 is the opportunity to ride the actual tracked vehicle used by the U.S. and New Zealand Antarctic programs—called the Hagglund. After touring the working Antarctic Campus, where scientists and support staff prepare to travel to Antarctica, you can take a 45-minute tour-ride in the all-terrain Hagglund on a specially designed adventure course. It departs every day on the hour at the front of the complex. The exhibition is within walking distance of the airport—you can also catch a free shuttle from there—and about a 20-minute drive from central Christchurch. There is also a café and bar and an Antarctic shop with a variety of mementos to take home. ⊠ *Orchard Rd.,* ☎ *03/358–9896.* ☞ *$16, $20 Hagglund tour-ride, $32 both.* ☉ *Oct.–Mar., daily 9–8; Apr.–Sept., daily 9–5:30.*

⑪ **Mona Vale.** One of Christchurch's great historic homesteads, the turn-of-the-last-century, riverside Mona Vale makes for a lovely outing from the city. Come for lunch or Devonshire tea and make believe that your estate lies along the Avon as you stroll under the stately trees and through the well-tended fuchsia, dahlia, herb, and iris gardens. Stop to smell the many roses, then move on to the fernery and lily pond. If the mood really takes you, go for a punt ride (a gondola-like boat) and contemplate your travels from the water. ⊠ *63 Fendalton Rd., 2 km (1 mi) from city center,* ☎ *03/348–9659 or 03/348–9666.* ☞ *Free.* ☉ *Grounds Oct.–Mar., daily 8–7:30; Apr.–Sept., daily 8:30–5:30; tea Sun.–Fri. at 10 AM and 3; smorgasbord lunch Sun. (reservations essential).*

⑦ **Robert McDougal Art Gallery.** You're likely to see some of the city's more innovative shows here, along with works by 19th-century New Zealand artists and an international collection of painting and sculpture, including two Rodins. The gallery is behind the Christchurch Museum next to the Botanic Gardens. ⊠ *Rolleston Ave.,* ☎ *03/365–0915.* ☞ *Free.* ☉ *Daily 10–4:30.*

③ **St. Michael and All Saints Anglican Church.** St. Michael's dates from the city's earliest days. The first settlers sent out by Christchurch's founding Canterbury Association were known as the Canterbury Pilgrims, and their churches were focal points for the whole community. Built in 1872, the white-timber St. Michael's is an outstanding building. One of the bells in the wooden belfry came from England aboard one of four ships that carried the Canterbury Pilgrims. ⊠ *Oxford Terr. and Durham St.* ☉ *Daily noon–2.*

⑬ **Southern Encounter–Aquarium of Discovery.** Fish and divers in the heart of Christchurch? This giant aquarium has an enormous variety of New Zealand fish species—from rocky tidal-pool creatures to those from lakes, rivers, and the briny deep. In some displays you can actually touch the critters—if you want to. Watch divers feed giant eels or carpet sharks, cod, skates, and other rarely seen deep-water fish. There's also an historic gold-mining town and a fishing lodge where you can learn fly tying from an expert. ✉ *Cathedral Sq.*, ☎ *03/377–3474*, 📠 *03/377–9196.* ✉ *$12.50.* ☉ *Summer, daily 9–7; winter, daily 10–6.*

OFF THE BEATEN PATH	**GETHSEMANE GARDENS –** Set high overlooking Pegasus Bay in suburban Sumner, Gethsemane isn't quite like your local garden center back home. It is, as you might guess from the name, a born-again Christian garden, and the benefit the plants receive from the tonic of spirituality seems clear. The nursery, with its extensive display gardens, has the largest, most colorful disease- and pest-free plants around. As you approach, take note of the 90-ft-long fence work that spells GETHSEMANE. Inside, four meticulous knot gardens form a Star of David, Star of Bethlehem, and two parallel Jerusalem crosses. The Rosery is filled with fragrant old-fashioned roses and more lettering: the path work spells JESUS. The potager, an ornamental vegetable garden, has as its centerpiece a life-size pietà covered by a trellised structure supporting a forbidding crown-of-thorns plant. The plant people among you may be too amazed by the lushness of the gardens to notice any symbolism. Perhaps, then, you should end your visit to Gethsemane at the small chapel, where you can pray to have plants of your own like these. The garden is a 20-minute drive east of central Christchurch along Ferry Road. It's just before the township of Sumner. ✉ *33 Revelation Dr., at top of Clifton Terr., Sumner*, ☎ *03/326–5848.* ✉ *$5.* ☉ *Daily 9–5.*

Dining

$$$–$$$$ ✕ **Pescatore.** In the small but perfectly formed George Hotel, Pescatore enjoys good views over picturesque Hagley Park, and offers fare like Moreton Bay bugs (Australian shellfish that look like a cross between a crab and a prawn) on mango mash, or *poussin* (baby chicken) stuffed with seasoned polenta, served over a tart of stewed leeks. Red meat lovers can try beef fillet with wild mushroom ravioli and a classic wine reduction sauce. The wine list is extensive. ✉ *The George, 50 Park Terr.*, ☎ *03/371–0257. AE, DC, MC, V. No lunch.*

$$$–$$$$ ✕ **Sign of the Takahe.** Located in a castlelike building with a great view from some tables, this stately restaurant is a Christchurch institution. With dining becoming an ever more relaxed affair, it's not as popular as it used to be, but it's still the place for people with something to celebrate. Make up an occasion and be spoiled with dishes like charred venison layered with wild mushroom duxelles on *pommes Anna* (potato pie). It's not all traditional—one recent menu matched scallops with blood pudding, a decidedly new millennium idea. Between courses, admire the heraldic display—it's the southern hemisphere's largest. ✉ *200 Hackthorne Rd., Cashmere Hills*, ☎ *03/332–4052. AE, DC, MC, V.*

$$$ ✕ **Cook'n with Gas.** This place was hot from the moment the kitchen team—mostly refugees from fine-dining establishments—first lit up the stoves. The surroundings are funky and the food sensibly innovative. Dishes like vanilla-seared prawns with saffron mousse, and braised rabbit flavored with thyme keep the locals happy and drag in quite a few out-of-town foodies. The wine list focuses on New Zealand and Australia, but includes a few bottles from farther afield. ✉ *23 Worcester Blvd.*, ☎ *03/377–9166. AE, DC, MC, V. Closed Sun. No lunch.*

$$$ ✕ **Le Bon Bolli.** Phillip Kraal's eccentrically decorated eatery—think ancient Rome crossed with Provence—tries to be all things to all foodies and comes close to succeeding, thanks to a clear style division between the downstairs brasserie and the more upmarket upstairs restaurant. Offal is a feature of both spaces—this is the only place in the country you can order testicles—and slow-cooked braises are popular in winter. Spanish paella is a downstairs star; upstairs, try braised ox cheeks with field mushrooms and oxtail dumplings. The wine list is more than 100 bottles strong, with 60-plus available by the glass. It's open for breakfast on weekends. ✉ *Montreal and Worcester Sts.,* ☎ *03/374–9035. AE, DC, MC, V.*

$$$ ✕ **Pedro's.** New Zealand's only Spanish restaurant has had a loyal following for two decades, and the menu hasn't changed a lot in all that time. Not that it has needed to—two favorites with the many regulars are *huevos a la flamenca*—which combines eggs with chilli-hot chorizo—and a whole roasted shoulder of baby lamb (for which you have to be seriously hungry!). The wine list is not particularly wide-ranging, but you can certainly find something suitable. The decor is woody, simple, and, like the food, probably hasn't changed much since the doors were opened for the first time. ✉ *143 Worcester St.,* ☎ *03/379–7668. AE, DC, MC, V.*

$$$ ✕ **Saggio di Vino.** As the name suggests, wine is the raison d'être for this long-established Christchurch café. The extensive list includes around 150 library choices, both local and imported. The menu isn't large, but it features classics like carpaccio, a warm quail salad, and fettuccine with pesto. Daily specials take advantage of seasonal produce. Staff members are adept as recommending wine by the glass, half bottles, or full bottles to accompany specific dishes. ✉ *185 Victoria St.,* ☎ *03/379–4006. AE, DC, MC, V. No lunch Sat.*

$$–$$$ ✕ **50 on Park** Don't miss the breakfasts at this light and airy streetside restaurant in the George Hotel—they're legendary. Start with the likes of black rice pudding with coconut milk, or baked semolina with char-grilled grapefruit and spiced rhubarb compote. Move on to chive waffles with roasted tomatoes and smoked bacon, or house-smoked salmon on English muffins with béarnaise sauce. Later in the day you can choose from dishes like lime-scented scallops and scampi, or roasted *cervena* (farmed venison) with broad bean mash. ✉ *The George, 50 Park Terr.,* ☎ *03/371–0250. AE, DC, MC, V.*

$$–$$$ ✕ **Sala Sala.** Generally considered to be Christchurch's top Japanese restaurant, Sala Sala is well regarded for its wine-and-food–matching abilities. Diners can choose from sushi, *teppan yaki* (show time at the table), or traditional set meals. The latter gives the chefs the opportunity to demonstrate their considerable skills. You might not recognize all the ingredients, but you can rest assured they will be fresh and delicious. The wine list is reasonably extensive, and the staff knowledgeable. ✉ *184–186 Oxford Terr.,* ☎ *03/366–6755. AE, DC, MC, V. No lunch.*

$–$$$ ✕ **Barringtons Big Steak Pub.** Serious carnivores will be supremely happy in the old-English, woody surroundings of this fun-time steak house. As the name suggests, the meaty meals are massive—some of the steaks weigh in at more than a kilogram (that's around 2 pounds)! Beef reins supreme, but ostrich, venison, and other red meat is featured. For those with smaller appetites, there is a big range of snacks and light meals for under $10, and a few chicken and seafood options. The preparations are mostly predictable, but the kitchen team knows the basics—especially when they're handling steak. ✉ *256 Barrington St.,* ☎ *03/ 337–5192. AE, DC, MC, V.*

$$ ✕ **The Cocoa Club.** This quirkily decorated restaurant (painted brick, antique tiles, brightly colored artwork) has had several rave reviews in prominent publications, which means it might be hard to find a table some nights. Chef Tony Astle has cooked at a couple of Michelin-starred spots in Europe, and specializes in unusual combinations—fish crackling with shrimp paste and sweet pork relish, salmon with artichokes and fennel. That sort of innovation sounds expensive, but the prices

are, in fact, pretty reasonable. ⊠ *705 Gloucestor St.,* ☎ *03/381–2496. AE, MC, V. Licensed and BYOB. Closed Sun.–Mon. No lunch.*

$$ ✕ **Zydeco.** Cajun fans suffering chilli withdrawal will find a pretty good facsimile of what they're used to at this long-established central city eatery. The 'gator on one wall and accordions on another set the scene for a menu chock-full of New Orleans classics like gumbo, jambalaya, and prawns (okay, they're not crawfish, but they're close) with andouille sausage. ⊠ *113 Manchester St.,* ☎ *03/365–4556. AE, DC, MC, V. Licensed and BYOB.*

$–$$ ✕ **Espresso 124.** This bright and breezy restaurant is a good bet for
★ mid-morning coffee or midnight snacks—it has a high-energy atmosphere generated by the stylish crowd that frequents it. Simplicity is the key on a menu that features thin-crust pizza, char-grilled steak, lamb shank, and seafood. The river and the heart of the city are both close. Part of the operation is a lunchtime deli, with inexpensive sandwiches, focaccia, pasta, and savory pies. Dine indoors or out. ⊠ *124 Oxford Terr.,* ☎ *03/365–0547. AE, DC, MC, V.*

$ ✕ **Main Street Café and Bar.** If you lived in Christchurch and liked hearty
★ vegetarian cooking, you'd probably end up at this bohemian storefront haunt once a week with a good friend. Pumpkin and *kumara* (native sweet potato) balls with peanut sauce are rich and yummy, and daily soups or a choice of three mixed salads with a piece of homemade bread will help you get out of a vacation-food rut. Espresso is great, and desserts are phenomenally delicious. Main Street is open for all meals (counter service only), and there's plenty of seating at old wooden tables in a few rooms downstairs, upstairs, and outside. The bar next door has a selection of beers from around the world. ⊠ *840 Colombo St., at Salisbury St.,* ☎ *03/365–0421. AE, DC, MC, V.*

Lodging

$$$$ ▥ **Bangor Country Estate.** Don't be in a hurry when you stay with Cliff
★ and Biba Baker at their historic 1854 colonial mansion. Just coming up the long, meandering, tree-lined drive will take you back to the era of opulence that this lodge recaptures. The grand entranceway with its sweeping staircase, the stately dining room, and the reception floor to the suites are filled with antiques and fine art from around the globe. The six individual suites, two of which are detached from the main house, are each a study in elegance. The J. Hamilton Suite, for example, has a huge mahogany bed, love seat, and clawfoot marble tub. The steep rates include full breakfast, predinner drinks, and a marvelous five-course dinner. The estate is 25 minutes from Christchurch International Airport and 5 minutes from the rural township of Darfield, just south of Christchurch. Pickup from the airport can be arranged. ⊠ *Bangor Rd., Darfield,* ☎ *03/318–7588,* ℻ *03/318–8485. 6 suites. Dining room, lounge, pool, library. AE, DC, MC, V. MAP.* ☙

$$$$ ▥ **Charlotte Jane.** Go on spoil yourself and let hosts Moira and
★ Siegfried Lindlbauer do the same at this magnificent 1891 villa, once a girls' school and now a luxurious boutique hotel. Inside and out, the centrally located house speaks for itself—a stunning Victorian veranda, a stained-glassed window above the entrance depicting the *Charlotte Rose* (one of the first four ships to bring settlers to Christchurch in 1850), crystal chandeliers from Austria, a native kauri and *rimu* wood staircase, ivory damask curtains, English-tile bathrooms, a rimu-paneled dining room, and period furniture throughout the 10 beautiful guest rooms. Suites have large whirlpool baths, and the Honeymoon Suite has a great hand-carved Elizabethan mahogany four-poster bed. Just across the courtyard is a new addition to the complex—a gracious, converted 1930s town house and atrium. It houses the Alexander Lawrence

Restaurant, a dome-ceiling bar, painstakingly lined with rimu, as well as two more luxury suites upstairs. French head chef Phillipe Meyer enhances the region's best offerings with European flair and Siegfried keeps a selective wine cellar. Delicious gourmet breakfasts are included in the tariff. ✉ *110 Papanui Rd.,* ☎ *03/355–1028,* FAX *03/355–8882. 12 rooms. Restaurant, bar, in-room VCRs, no-smoking rooms, laundry service. AE, DC, MC, V.*

$$$$ 🏨 **The George.** The adage that great things come in small packages
★ holds true for the George. General manager Mark Dakin has paid scrupulous attention to detail, providing all the luxury facilities and pampering one expects in a large complex. What's remarkable is that the hotel also succeeds in making you feel at home. The spacious guest rooms are modern, with a crisp, monochromatic color scheme that is woven through everything, from the bedside notepads to the beautiful range of bathroom products. The luxury executive suites each have a separate lounge area, a whirlpool bath, and complimentary sherry and port. Wherever you turn, you'll find exquisite touches: the magnificent, brass handles on the entrance door, selected pieces of modernistic local art work, the verdigris brass bannister, the cherry-wood parquet floors in the foyer. Adjacent to the Avon River and Hagley Park, it's just a short walk to the Arts Centre and downtown shopping. The two on-site restaurants, 50 on the Park and Pescatore (☞ Dining, *above*), are topflight eateries. ✉ *50 Park Terr.,* ☎ *03/379–4560,* FAX *03/366–6747. 57 rooms. 2 restaurants, massage, tennis court, health club, coin laundry, laundry service, free parking. AE, DC, MC, V.* 📵

$$$$ 🏨 **Millennium.** The fabulously located Millennium is a stylish complex with an interesting mix of European and Asian touches in the public areas. In the rooms Italian lamps stand beside Asian ginger jars, and the designer has chosen strong classical blues and golds, with sophisticated results. Millennium has two top-class restaurants, Restaurant Piko Piko and the Millennium Lounge and Mezzanine. The former is elegantly decorated with polished jarrah timber floors and shutters, marble columns, and bronze sculptures, and the latter provides you with a magnificent view over the heart of Christchurch. Outdoor dining allows you to experience the Cathedral Square's colorful ambience, night and day. ✉ *14 Cathedral Sq.,* ☎ *03/365–1111 or 800/35–8888,* FAX *03/365–7676. 179 rooms. 2 restaurants, bar, café, sauna, health club, business services, valet parking. AE, DC, MC, V.*

$$$$ 🏨 **Parkroyal Christchurch.** This plush hotel is set in a prime location overlooking Victoria Square and the river. The rooms are large and luxurious, colored in rich tones of burgundy, gold, and blue. In summer the best views are from rooms overlooking Victoria Square, but in the winter popularity switches to those with views of the snowcapped Alps to the west. The hotel is especially well equipped with restaurants and bars. A pianist plays in the glass-roof atrium—the heart of this hotel—at lunch or in the evening. The Canterbury Tales restaurant, which specializes in innovative New Zealand cookery, and the Japanese restaurant, Yamagen, which has teppan yaki and traditional fare, are among the city's finest. ✉ *Kilmore and Durham Sts.,* ☎ *03/365–7799,* FAX *03/365–0082. 298 rooms. 3 restaurants, 3 bars, sauna, exercise room, bicycles, car rental. AE, DC, MC, V.*

$$$$ 🏨 **The Weston House** This fine, neo-Georgian building, registered by the New Zealand Historic Places Trust, was built in the early 1920s for a prominent Christchurch lawyer named George Weston. Your hosts Stephanie and Len May have fully restored and refurbished the house, combining elegant, old-world style with all the modern amenities. It's an intimate lodging with two spacious suites, private access, a guest lounge, dining area, and a secluded garden where you can take break-

fast or just relax. ⊠ *62 Park Terr.,* ☎ *03/366–0234,* FAX *03/366–5454. 2 suites. AE, DC, MC, V. BP.*

$$$ 🏨 **Centra.** A contemporary hotel where business travelers, vacationers, and conference delegates converge, the Centra has some of the most interesting rooms and suites in town. In this converted bank building, guests stay in what once were offices—rooms' shapes and sizes are anything but standard. Decor is sophisticated; suites with muted green and gold soft furnishings and modern rimu wood furniture come with black marble bathrooms. Ceiling-to-floor windows afford panoramic views of the cityscape. Situated in the central business district, it's just a minute or two on foot from Cathedral Square and close to Victoria Square. The Streetside Bar is arguably the best place in Christchurch to have a gin and tonic, to watch Christchurch's working population go by on a weekday, or to mix with them in the evening. The European-style brasserie is also a popular dining spot. ⊠ *Cashel and High Sts.,* ☎ *03/365–8888,* FAX *03/365–8822. 199 rooms, 2 suites. Restaurant, bar, health club, business services. AE, DC, MC, V.* ✍

$$$ 🏨 **The Chateau on the Park.** One of the older Christchurch hotels, this
★ French-chateau–style property is beautifully set. It's surrounded by 5 acres of delightful, landscaped gardens and adjacent to Hagley Park. The main building has an indoor water garden that wraps around the main entrance and foyer. Rooms are spacious and the service is gracious and attentive. The Camelot Restaurant has a medieval atmosphere and fine dining; the Garden Court Brasserie serves a sumptuous breakfast and offers the option to dine alfresco; and the Den Bar is straight out of old England. ⊠ *189 Deans Ave.,* ☎ *03/348–8999,* FAX *03/348– 8990. 190 rooms, 6 suites. 2 restaurants, bar, pool. AE, DC, MC, V.* ✍

$$$ 🏨 **Riverview Lodge & Churchill Suites.** This grand Edwardian house
★ overlooking the Avon is one of the finest bed-and-breakfasts in Christchurch. With native timber in details throughout the house—such as solid kauri stairs and doors—it offers superbly comfortable, historic accommodations and a tasty breakfast at reasonable cost. All rooms are upstairs, and the three front rooms provide great views of the river. The Turret Room has a charming alcove from which to enjoy the view while snuggled in the antique chaise lounge. In an adjacent two-story, Edwardian town house are two spacious suites, each with a lounge and kitchen. The lower-floor suite has one bedroom and French doors that open out to a secluded garden. The upper floor has two bedrooms. Ernst Wipperfuerth is an amiable host; don't hesitate to ask him about dining or exploring suggestions. Children are accommodated by prior arrangement. The city center is a pleasant (and safe at night) 15-minute walk along the river, which allows you to leave the car behind. ⊠ *361 Cambridge Terr.,* ☎ *03/365–2860,* FAX *03/365– 2845., 4 rooms, 2 suites. Boating, bicycles. MC, V. BP.* ✍

$$ 🏨 **Turret House.** Built in 1905 as a family home for a retired farmer, this lodge has comfortable, well-maintained rooms and a friendly atmosphere that makes it another standout among Christchurch's B&B accommodations. All rooms are furnished differently, and prices vary accordingly. For a couple, the medium-size rooms offer a good combination of space and value. Current managers Patrick and Justine Dougherty are retired farmers from Central Otago. If you happen to be interested in rugby, the couple are both keen on the sport—and happy to fill you in on the latest. Despite its location close to a major intersection, noise is not a problem. ⊠ *435 Durham St.,* ☎ *03/365– 5601. 8 rooms. AE, DC, MC, V. BP.*

Nightlife

Christchurch's after-dark action has picked up over the years, so you don't have to go to sleep as soon as the sun goes down. The 24-hour **Christchurch Casino** has blackjack, roulette, baccarat, gaming machines, and other ways to try your luck. Dress is smart-casual or better, and you will be turned away at the door if you arrive in jeans. ⊠ *30 Victoria St.,* ☎ *03/365–9999.* ⊙ *Daily.*

For dancing and dining into the wee hours, your best bet is to head to the myriad bars and cafés along the popular **Oxford Terrace strip** by the Avon River. Many of the venues spill out onto the footpath, where you'll also find alfresco dining areas. The **Coyote** (⊠ 126 Oxford Terr., ☎ 03/366–6055) serves good food during the day and then transforms into one of the city's popular bars, with partying 'til the break of dawn.

For some natural suds in the city center try the **Loaded Hog** bar and restaurant (⊠ Manchester and Cashel Sts., ☎ 03/366–6674). This brewery produces excellent, 100% naturally brewed beers like Hogs Dark and Hogs Gold. Check out the amusing caricatures of pop culture icons. If you just want to kick back over a coffee or delicious New Zealand wine while watching Christchurch go by at night, try **Bar Santé in the Square** (⊠ 14 Cathedral Sq., ☎ 03/365–1111).

The Bard (⊠ Oxford Terr. and Gloucester St., ☎ 03/377–1493) is said to be Christchurch's only authentic English pub with live entertainment, English ales on tap, and hearty pub meals.

Outdoor Activities and Sports

Bicycling
Pacific Cycle Tours has a seven-day, 386-km (241-mi, some of it off-road) escorted bicycle tour from Christchurch. You'll ride over Arthur's Pass on the TranzAlpine Express, then cycle up the West Coast (☞ Chapter 3), over to Kaikoura, and back down to Christchurch. Mountain bikes, the train trip, midrange accommodations, and breakfast and lunch are included, as is a backup bus. ⊠ *17 Trent St., Christchurch,* ☎ *03/389–0583,* ℻ *03/389–0498.* ⬛ *$1,575.*

Fishing
For information on trout and salmon fishing in Rakaia in the Canterbury region, *see* Chapter 5.

Horse Trekking
Around Christchurch, the Canterbury Plains and encircling mountain ranges provide a dramatic setting for riding. *See* Chapter 5 for operators and trip information.

Shopping

The best **Arts Centre** shopping is at the **Saturday and Sunday Market**, which has various Kiwi goods, including handmade sweaters and woolens, that you might want to take home with you. Inside the Arts Centre buildings, the **Galleria** consists of a dozen shops and studios for artisans and crafts workers, from potters to weavers to some very good jewelry makers. The quality of work varies considerably from shop to shop, but this is one of the few places where many crafts workers are represented under one roof. Most shops, including a bookstore, are open from 10 to 4; some are closed weekends. Most do not take credit cards. ⊠ *Worcester St.,* ☎ *03/379–7573.*

Kathmandu sells a complete and colorful range of outdoor gear and maps. ⊠ *110 Lichfield St.,* ☎ *03/366–7148.*

Christchurch has an excellent range of organic food shops, including **Organics Organics** (⊠ 425 Cashel St., ☎ 03/381–1122). **Piko Wholefoods** (⊠ Kilmore and Barbadoes St., ☎ 03/366–8116) is another good place for wholesome eats.

Riccarton Mall is South Island's largest shopping mall. It has more than 90 stores. ⊠ *129 Riccarton Rd.,* ☎ *03/348–4119.*

Untouched World is an offbeat store that brings together all that's hip and natural in New Zealand. Apart from its own line of stylish, outdoorsy clothing, you'll find New Zealand artwork, handcrafted jewelry, organic produce, aromatherapy and essential oils, natural skin-care products, and great gift ideas. The attached restaurant serves organic food, wine, and beer. ⊠ *155 Roydale Ave.,* ☎ *03/357–9399.* ❧

Christchurch A to Z

Arriving and Departing

BY BUS AND TRAIN

InterCity (☎ 03/377–0951) operates a daily bus service between Christchurch and Dunedin, Mount Cook Village, Nelson, and Queenstown. InterCity also operates a daily **TranzAlpine Express** train to Arthur's Pass Village and Greymouth, departing at 9 AM. The **Coast to Coast Shuttle** (☎ 0800/800–847) is a bus that goes to Arthur's Pass Village and Greymouth from Christchurch.

BY CAR

Highway 1 links Christchurch with Kaikoura and Blenheim in the north and Dunedin in the south. Driving time for the 330-km (205-mi) journey between Christchurch and Mount Cook Village is five hours and between Christchurch and Dunedin, 5½ hours. Driving time for the 192-km (119 mi) journey from Christchurch to Kaikoura is three hours.

BY PLANE

Ansett New Zealand (☎ 03/371–1146) and **Air New Zealand** (☎ 03/379–5200) link Christchurch with cities on both North and South islands. **Air New Zealand** also flies from Christchurch to Queenstown, Aoraki, and Te Anau. **Christchurch Airport** is 10 km (6 mi) northwest of the city. **Super Shuttle** buses (☎ 03/365–5655) meet all incoming flights and charge between $5 and $10 per passenger to city hotels, depending on the number of people traveling. **CANRIDE** buses operate between the airport and Cathedral Square from 6 AM to 11 PM daily. The fare is $2.70. A **taxi** to the city costs about $20.

Getting Around

The city of Christchurch is flat and compact, and the best way to explore it is on foot.

BY BICYCLE

Trailblazers (⊠ 96 Worcester St., ☎ 03/366–6033) rents out mountain bikes for $25 per day. The shop is open weekdays 9–5:30 and weekends 10–4.

BY BUS OR TRAM

The historical **Christchurch Tramway** (☎ 03/366–7830) serves as an attraction in its own right and doubles as a way to get around when those feet tire. A city circuit takes in Cathedral Square, Worcester Boulevard, Rolleston Avenue, Armagh Street, and New Regent Street. It stops close to all major attractions, including the Arts Centre, Botanic Gardens, and Canterbury Museum. But you'll never have to get off: the air-conditioned, Christchurch Tramway Restaurant serves all meals. A one-hour ticket costs $6, a full-day pass costs $7. There's no need to use the confusing bus system unless you are actually heading out of town.

Contacts and Resources

Dial 111 for **fire, police, or ambulance** services.

Canterbury Leisure Tours (✉ ☎ 03/377–5566 or 0800/484–485, ✍) offers day tours to Kaikoura, Hanmer Springs, Akaroa, Arthur's Pass, and Aoraki (Mt. Cook). It also offers a range of half-day tours and activities, including wine trails, night tours, sheep-farm visits, and horse-trekking, jet boating, and golfing excursions.

Anne and Brian Lucas' **Canterbury Trails, Ltd.** run day tours from Christchurch to Akaroa (which can include farm visits and harbor cruises), Arthur's Pass National Park, and Hanmer Springs. Generous lunches come with New Zealand wine; prices range from $320 to $375 per couple. There are also nine-day wilderness-and-luxury-lodge trips for $3,930 per person. ✉ *5 Dannys La., Cashmere, Christchurch,* ☎ *03/337–1185,* FAX *03/337–5085.*

Guided walking tours ($8) of the city depart daily at 9:45 and 12:45 from the Christchurch–Canterbury Visitor Information Centre (☞ Visitor Information, *below*) and depart at 10 and 1 from the red-and-black kiosk in Cathedral Square. The tours take about two hours.

Taking the **High Country Explorer** is definitely one of the best and most action-packed ways of getting into the Canterbury Plains, the Southern Alps, and experiencing the world-famous TranzAlpine train journey. The full-day trip takes you on a one-hour bus trip, a 15-km (9-mi) jet-boat cruise, and a 65-km (40-mi) four-wheel-drive safari, before setting you on the TranzAlpine back to Christchurch. The tour includes morning tea at a riverside lodge and lunch at Flock Hill Lodge—situated on the 35,000-acre Flock Hill farm. Pickup from your accommodations is at 9 AM. The scenery is spectacular, the boat ride a thrill, and your safari guide will discuss the region's human and natural history, flora and fauna, and geography and geology with ease. After the two-hour train trip back to Christchurch railway station, a coach or shuttle will take you to your accommodations around 6:45. A full-day trip is $259 per person. A half-day trip (8 AM–1:30 PM), which does not include the TranzAlpine trip, is $169 per person. ✉ *6 Fraser Pl., Rangiora,* ☎ *03/377–1391,* FAX *03/313–6494.* ✍

Jack Treagar, great-great-grandson of early settler Thomas Jackson Hughes—who arrived in Lyttelton in 1848, provides a personal historic tour of Christchurch. It covers Lyttelton, Sumner, and the Canterbury Provincial Council buildings and takes just over three hours. The tour includes an elegant morning tea and entry to the Timeball Station at Lyttelton. ☎ *03/322–7844 or 021/320–951.* ✍ *$53.*

Punting on the Avon is perfectly suited to the pace of Christchurch. You can hire punts with expert boatmen at the Worcester Street Bridge, near the corner of Oxford Terrace, daily from 10 to 6 in summer and from 10 to 4 the rest of the year. A 20-minute trip costs $10.

Christchurch–Canterbury Visitor Information Centre. ✉ *Chief Post Office Building, Cathedral Sq.,* ☎ *03/379–9629.* ☉ *Weekdays 8:30–5, weekends 8:30–4.*

SIDE TRIPS FROM CHRISTCHURCH

If you have more than a day or two to spend in the Christchurch area, head out to the countryside for a change of pace. The Banks Peninsula, east of the city, features a wonderful coastline. Looking north, consider stopping in Waipara and its wineries if you're en route to or from Kaikoura. Hanmer Springs' thermal baths are good for a relaxing soak. Plan an entire day for any of these side trips.

Akaroa and the Banks Peninsula

⑭ *82 km (50 mi) east of Christchurch.*

Bearing the shape of a long-dormant volcanic cone, the Banks Peninsula—that nub that juts into the Pacific southeast of Christchurch—has a coastline indented with small bays, where sheep graze almost to the water's edge. It's best known for the town of Akaroa, which was chosen as the site for a French colony in 1838. The first French settlers arrived in 1840 only to find that the British had already established sovereignty over New Zealand by the Treaty of Waitangi. Less than 10 years later, the French abandoned their attempt at colonization, but the settlers remained and gradually intermarried with the local English community. Apart from the street names and a few surnames, there is little sign of a French connection anymore, but the village has a splendid setting, and on a sunny day it makes a marvelous trip from Christchurch. A half day will get you to and from Akaroa, including a drive up to the edge of the former volcanic dome, but take a full day if you want to do other exploring of the peninsula. The main route to Akaroa is Highway 75, which leaves the southwest corner of Christchurch as Lincoln Road. The 82-km (50-mi) drive takes about 90 minutes. If you'd rather not drive, the **Akaroa Shuttle** (☎ 0800/500–929) runs between the Christchurch–Canterbury Visitor Information Centre and Akaroa. Buses depart daily from Christchurch in summer (December–April) at 9, 10, and 4. They depart from the Akaroa Information Centre (✉ Rues Lavaud and Balguerie, ☎ 03/377–1755) at 8:30, 2:15, and 4:30. In winter (May–November), the shuttle departs Christchurch daily at 10 and leaves from Akaroa at 4, but there are often extra scheduled trips that vary—check the latest timetables. The cost is $15 one way or $25 round-trip.

The best way to get the feel of Akaroa is to stroll along the waterfront from the lighthouse to Jubilee Park. The focus of historic interest is the **Akaroa Museum,** which has a display of Maori greenstones and embroidery and dolls dating from the days of the French settlement. The museum includes Langlois-Eteveneaux House, the two-room cottage of an early French settler, which bears the imprint of his homeland in its architecture. ✉ *Rues Lavaud and Balguerie,* ☎ *03/304–7614.* 🎟 *$2.50.* ☉ *Daily 10:30–4:30.*

The picture-book **Church of St. Patrick,** near the Akaroa museum, was built in 1864 to replace two previous Catholic churches—the first destroyed by a fire, the second by a storm. ✉ *Rue Pompallier.* ☉ *Daily 8–5.*

The contrast of the rim of the old volcanic cone and the coves below is striking. An afternoon drive to the summit, around it, and then a drop into one of the coves leaves you with a feeling like you've found your own corner of the world. At **Okains Bay,** a small settlement lies at the bottom of Okains Bay road, which winds down from the summit and ends at a beach sheltered by tall headlands. There's a cave in the rocks on the right and a path above it that leads to the remnants of a pier, now just a cluster of tilting pilings in the water. A stream lets out into the bay on the left side of the beach. Sheep paddocks rise a couple of hundred feet on either side of the sand, cradling it in green. There's a small general store that doubles as a post office back in the village, as well as a tiny old church to poke your head into if you're curious.

Another way to get to the feel of the peninsula is to have an afternoon cold one with locals at **Hilltop Tavern.** ⊠ *Hwy. 75 at Summit Rd., Akaroa,* ☎ *03/325–1005*

Dining and Lodging

In Akaroa, eat at **L'hotel** (⊠ 72 Church St., ☎ 03/304–7559), where the ambience is old-world and the food a mix of traditional and contemporary. **Cafe De La Mer** (⊠ 71 Beach Rd., ☎ 03/304–7656) specializes in superb French-influenced seafood cuisine. Nearby, **French Farm** (⊠ 12 Winery Rd. ☎ 03/304–5784) is a vineyard with an attached restaurant.

$$$ 🏠 **Oinako Lodge.** Surrounded by a garden and greenery, a five-minute walk from the town and harbor of Akaroa, this charming Victorian manor house still has its original ornamented plaster ceilings and marble fireplaces. It's due for some refurbishment, but its original grandeur is still plainly evident. You'll find fresh flowers in the spacious and pleasantly decorated rooms. ⊠ *99 Beach Rd., Akaroa,* ☎ *03/304–8787. 6 rooms. Dining room, lounge. AE, DC, MC, V. BP.* 🐾

Outdoor Activities and Sports

The 35-km (22-mi) **Banks Peninsula Track** crosses beautiful coastal terrain. From Akaroa you hike over headlands, and past several bays, waterfalls, and seal and penguin colonies, and you might see Hector's dolphins at sea. Two-day ($70) and four-day ($140) tramps are available between October 1 and April 27. Overnight in cabins with fully equipped kitchens, which you might share with other hikers. Rates include lodging, transport from Akaroa to the first hut, landowners' fees, and a booklet describing the features of the track. No fear of overcrowding here—the track is limited to accommodate 12 people at a time and booking well ahead is essential. ⊠ *Box 50, Akaroa,* ☎ *03/ 304–7612.*

Waipara

⑮ *57 km (35 mi) north of Christchurch.*

The attractive rural township of Waipara is about 45 minutes north of Christchurch heading toward Kaikoura. The area was once renowned for its profusion of moa (an enormous, extinct, flightless bird) bones. It used to be dotted with swamps—perhaps the reason the Maori named it Waipara, meaning "muddy water"—into which hundreds of moa tumbled over the centuries. That same geological history has given Waipara a different soil type from the rest of Canterbury and Waipara is consequently one of the country's most exciting wine-making regions.

Waipara is a departure point for the **Weka Pass Railway,** which drives through farmlands and interesting rock formations in a train pulled by a vintage locomotive. It runs the first and third Sunday of each month and public holidays. The morning trip is 11:30 AM to 1:45 PM and the afternoon trip departs at 2 PM, returning as 4 PM. ⊠ *McKenzies Rd.,* ☎ *03/389–4078.* 🎫 *$12.*

Dining and Lodging

A handful of Waipara's 15 or so wineries operate pleasant restaurants as well. Prices at most establishments range from $10 to 15 for a two-person platter of wine-friendly snacks, up to the mid-$20s for a serious main course. The following restaurants all accept major credit cards. The huge, cathedral-like **Canterbury House Winery** (⊠ 780 Glasnevin

Rd., Amberly, ☎ 03/314–6900) is probably the most serious in the area, offering indoor-outdoor dining and well-prepared local produce. At nearby **Waipara Springs Winery** (✉ 409 Omihi Rd., State Highway 1, Waipara, ☎ 𝔽𝔸𝕏 03/314–6777) you'll be able to sample riesling, sauvignon blanc, chardonnay, cabernet sauvignon, and pinot noir before or after lunch. At family-run **Pegasus Bay** (✉ Stockgrove Rd., Waipara, ☎ 𝔽𝔸𝕏 03/314–6869) you can wash down restaurant manager Edward Donaldson's food with wines made by his brother, Matthew, and his partner, Lynette Hudson. This winery probably enjoys the region's best reputation. Pick up a list of the region's other wineries at any of the three.

$$ ✕ **Norwester Café & Bar.** Cultured dining in rural places is one of life's great pleasures. Try an ostrich-egg frittata, an Italian omelet filled with kumara, spinach, and spring onions, served with a tomato and rocket (arugula) salad for brunch or lunch. After 5 PM you can order the fish of the day, panfried and served with grilled bananas, coriander, and lime salsa and steamed jasmine rice. A great complement is Waipara Springs' Riesling. Norwester is in the nearby town of Ambersly, on the way to Waipara from Christchurch. ✉ *95 Main North Rd., Amberley,* ☎ *03/314–9411. AE, DC, MC, V.*

$$$$ 🏠 **Mountford Vineyard.** At this stylish, country boutique lodge you can
★   settle into the Canterbury Plains amid the chardonnay and pinot noir grapes of a working vineyard. Owners and viticulturists Buffy and Michael Eaton are inimitable hosts: Michael is a renowned artist and Buffy's multiple skills include gourmet cooking and interior design. The residence and winery have been cleverly converted out of former railway buildings and transformed into a gracious, Mediterranean-style complex, with a large, white-pebbled central courtyard overlooking the rows of grapes. The heart of the building is the dining room, with its handcrafted, wrought-iron fixtures, slate floors, high ceiling, and native timber furnishings. From here you can access the comfortable guest lounge or head up the twisting, kauri wood stairs to the rooms above. The rooms have balconies and are spacious, with lime-wash kauri furniture and exposed beams that go well with the sage-and-white color scheme. Rates include breakfast and dinner, as well as predinner and dinner drinks. ✉ *Omihi Rd., State Hwy. 1, Waipara,* ☎ *03/314–6819,* 𝔽𝔸𝕏 *03/314–6820. 2 rooms. AE, DC, MC, V. MAP.*

Hanmer Springs

⑯ *120 km (75 mi) northwest of Christchurch.*

Long before Europeans arrived in New Zealand, Maori travelers knew the Hanmer Springs area as Waitapu (sacred water). Early settlers didn't take long to discover these thermal springs, which bubble out into a serene alpine environment, just a two-hour drive from Christchurch. More than 100 years ago European visitors would "take the water" for medicinal purposes, but nowadays you will find it far more pleasant to lie back and relax in the water than to drink the stuff. From Christchurch follow Highway 1 north to Highway 7 at Waipara, 57 km (35 mi) from the city. The drive then continues through the small town of Culverden, where Highway 7A turns toward Hanmer Springs, which is well signposted.

The **Hanmer Springs Thermal Reserve** remains the number one reason to visit the area and now consists of 10 thermal pools, one freshwater pool, an activity pool, and a hydroslide. The reserve also has massage, a sauna and steam room, a fitness center, and a restaurant. ✉ *Amuri Ave., Hanmer Springs,* ☎ *03/315–7511.* 🎫 *$8, private pool $15 per person per ½-hr (minimum 2 people), sauna $15 per ½-hr, hydroslide $5.* 🕙 *Daily 10–9.*

The forest around Hanmer Springs, planted by convict labor in the early 1900s, has a distinctly European look. You'll find European larch, Austrian pine, European alder, and other varieties. The **Hurunui Visitor Information Centre** (⊠ Amuri Ave., ☎ 03/315–7128) has maps and fact sheets detailing several walks.

THE SOUTHERN ALPS

The Canterbury Plains, which ring Christchurch and act as a brief transition between the South Pacific and the soaring New Zealand Alps, are the country's finest sheep pastures, as well as its largest area of flat land. But although this may be sheep- and horse-trekking heaven, the drive south along the plain is mundane by New Zealand standards until you leave Highway 1 and head toward the Southern Alps. By contrast, the drive to Arthur's Pass quickly takes you up into the hills, and Route 73 is a good way to get to Westland and the glaciers at Fox and Franz Josef, but it would be the long way to Queenstown.

Arthur's Pass

⑰ *153 km (96 mi) northwest of Christchurch.*

Arthur's Pass National Park is another of New Zealand's spectacular alpine regions, and hiking opportunities abound. On the way to the pass, the **Castle Hill Conservation Area** is littered with interesting rock formations. You'll find the parking lot for Castle Hill on the left several miles past Lake Lyndon. Along with nearby Craigieburn Forest Park, Castle Hill gets less rainfall than Arthur's Pass National Park. Craigieburn itself has wonderful beech and fern forests.

Arthur's Pass National Park has plenty of half- and full-day hikes and 11 backcountry tracks with overnight huts for backpacking amid local natural wonders: waterfalls, gorges, alpine wildflowers, grasslands, and stunning snowcapped peaks.

The pass is the major mid-island transit to the West Coast. The west side of the pass is unbelievably steep—be warned that this may be the most hair-raising paved road you'll ever drive. The village of Arthur's Pass itself isn't much to speak of, and in foul weather it looks rather forlorn. There are a restaurant and a store for basic food supplies.

Lodging

$$$$ 🏨 **Wilderness Lodge Arthur's Pass.** That pot of gold at the end of the rainbow is in fact a Southern Alps lodge surrounded by spectacular peaks, beech forests, tawny tussock grassland, rare plants, unique bird life, serene lakes, and wild rivers. Ecologist Dr. Gerry McSweeney's second back-to-nature hotel-lodge (the other is Wilderness Lodge Lake Moeraki, ☞ Chapter 3) is a 6,000-acre sheep farm in a valley called Te Ko Awa a Aniwaniwa (Valley of the Mother of Rainbows) by its first Maori visitors. From a hillside perch it overlooks the huge meandering Waimakariri River, which has carved a gaping swath through the pass. By taking trips to nearby lakes, limestone caves, and desert landscapes—and from evening talks and slide shows—staying here constitutes a superb short course in rare, high-country ecology and sheep farming. Rates include breakfast, dinner, shorter guided activities, and use of nearly 30 km (19 mi) of walking tracks. Longer guided trips, lunch, and drinks are an additional charge. ⊠ *130 km (81 mi) west of Christchurch on State Hwy. 73 (Box 33, Arthur's Pass 8190), Canterbury,* ☎ *03/318–9246,* 🖷 *03/318–9245. 20 rooms. Lounge, boating, fishing, library, laundry service. AE, DC, MC, V. MAP.* 🐾

Aoraki (Mt. Cook)

330 km (205 mi) southwest of Christchurch.

⑱ You will know you have reached the **Mackenzie Country** after you cross Burkes Pass, and the woodland is suddenly replaced by high-country tussock grassland, which is dotted with lupines in the summer months. The area is named for James ("Jock") Mckenzie (the man is Mckenzie, but the region that took his name is *Mackenzie*), one of the most intriguing and enigmatic figures in New Zealand history. Mckenzie was a Scot who may or may not have stolen the thousand sheep that were found with him in these secluded upland pastures in 1855. Arrested, tried, and convicted, he made several escapes from jail before he was granted a free pardon nine months after his trial—and disappeared from the pages of history. Regardless of his innocence or guilt, there can be no doubt that Mckenzie was a master bushman and herdsman.

⑲ Approaching the snowy peaks of the Southern Alps, the long, narrow expanse of **Lake Tekapo** is one of the most photographed sights in New Zealand. Its extraordinary milky-turquoise color comes from rock flour—rock ground by glacial action and held in a soupy suspension.

⑳ On the east side of the lakeside power station is the tiny **Church of the Good Shepherd,** which strikes a dignified note of piety in these majestic surroundings. A nearby memorial commemorates the sheepdogs of the area, who made farming this vast countryside possible in the early pioneering days and still do so today. As you drive into the small town, you'll notice a knot of restaurants with tour buses parked outside. It's rather an off-putting image if you've come for peace and quiet, but it's relatively easy to keep the township at your back and your eyes turned on the lake and mountains—and get a tasty meal when you'd like one.

At the **Tekapo Information Centre** (✉ Main Highway, ☎ 03/680–6686) you can pick up a walking track map and hike the **Domain to Mt. John Lookout** track. In a couple of hours you can be well above the township, enjoying views of the Mackenzie Basin, Southern Alps, and Lake Tekapo.

㉑ **Mount Cook Village** (pop. 300) consists of a visitor center, a grocery store, and a couple of hotels. The national park surrounds the village. Aoraki National Park includes 22 peaks that top the 10,000-ft mark,
㉒ the tallest of which is **Aoraki (Mt. Cook).** At approximately 12,283 ft, it is the highest peak between Papua New Guinea and the Andes. The mountain's Maori name is Aoraki, after one of three brothers who were the sons of Rakinui, the sky father. Legend has it that their canoe was caught on a reef and frozen, forming South Island. In these parts, South Island's oldest Maori name is Te Waka O Aoraki (Aoraki's canoe) and the highest peak is Aoraki, himself frozen by the south wind, then turned to stone. The officially recognized name of this mountain and many other South Island places have been changed to their original Maori names as part of a 1998 settlement between the government and the major South Island Maori tribe, Ngai Tahu.

Aoraki was dramatically first scaled in 1894 by three New Zealanders—Fyfe, Graham, and Clarke—just after it was announced that an English climber and an Italian mountain guide were about to attempt the summit. In a frantic surge of national pride, the New Zealand trio resolved to beat them to it, which they did on Christmas day. The mountain is still considered a difficult ascent. In the summer of 1991 a chunk of it broke away, but fortunately there were no climbers in the path of the massive avalanches. High Peak, the summit of the mountain, is now about 66 ft. lower, but its altered form makes for a much more difficult ascent.

If the sun is shining, the views are spectacular, and even unambitious walks are inspiring. If the cloud ceiling is low, however, you may wonder why you came. Because the mountain weather is notoriously changeable, and because a lengthy detour is required to reach Mount Cook Village, it is advisable to contact the **Mt. Cook Visitor Information Centre** (☎ 03/435–1818) to check weather conditions. The center is open daily 8–5.

Radiating from the Mt. Cook Visitor Information Centre is a network of **hiking trails** offering walks of varying difficulty, from the 10-minute Bowen Track to the 5½-hour climb to the 4,818-ft summit of Mt. Sebastapol. Particularly recommended is the walk along the **Hooker Valley,** a two- to four-hour round-trip. There are frequent ranger-guided walks from the visitor center, with informative talks on flora, fauna, and geology.

A unique hands-on educational experience is to take a half-hour hike to the fast-growing 2-square-km (¾-square-mi) **Terminus Lake of the Tasman Glacier.** Fed by the glacier and the Murchison River, the lake was only formed in the last 17 years, due to the retreat of the glacier. It is milky-white in color as a result of the powdery white residue it contains, rock flour. From Terminus Lake, which is officially growing by a foot a week, you can examine up close the terminal face of the glacier, which is 3 km (1 mi) wide. Experienced guides Kylie Wakelin and Brent Shears of Glacier Encounters (☞ Guided Tours *in* Southern Alps A to Z, *below*) have sound knowledge of the glacier and can take you by boat to explore some of the large floating icebergs that have calved (fallen away) from the Tasman Glacier. It's an eerie experience skimming across the milky-white water and closing in on icebergs— even riding *through* where they have melted—to touch rocks caught in the ice that have never before been felt by human hands.

The other main activity at Mt. Cook is "flightseeing." From the airfield at Mount Cook Village, helicopters and fixed-wing aircraft make spectacular scenic flights across the Southern Alps. One of the most exciting is the one-hour trip aboard the ski planes that touch down on the **Tasman Glacier** after a gorgeous scenic flight. The 10-minute stop on the glacier doesn't allow time for much more than a snapshot, but the sensation is tremendous. The moving tongue of ice beneath your feet—one of the largest glaciers outside the Himalayas—is 29 km (18 mi) long and up to 2,000 ft thick in places. The intensity of light on the glacier can be dazzling, and sunglasses are a must. Generally, the best time for flights is early morning. During winter the planes drop skiers on the glacier at 10,000 ft, and they ski down through 13 km (8 mi) of powder snow and fantastic ice formations. With guides, this run is suitable even for intermediate skiers. Ski-plane flights cost about $240; helicopter flights range from $140 to $315. Ski planes are flown by **Mount Cook Ski Planes** (☎ 03/435–1026, ✈). The **Helicopter Line** (☎ 03/435–1801) offers helicopter trips. Or take a breathtaking 50-minute scenic flight traversing Mt. Cook National Park and the Fox and Franz Josef glaciers with **Air Safaris** (☎ 03/680–6880). **Alpine Guides Ltd.** (☎ 03/435–1834) can assist with guides for all treks and ski trips in the national park.

Dining

$$$ ✕ **Panorama Room.** You couldn't ask for a better view—floor-to-ceiling windows that put you right at nature's feet. The menu leans toward Pacific Rim cuisine, and service can be quite formal. Try the whitebait

fritters if they're in season, or crayfish, which you can order as sashimi or broiled with herb and garlic butter. The less expensive ($$) Alpine restaurant also belongs to the Hermitage (☞ Lodging, *below*). It operates a buffet service in summer, and an à la carte menu in winter, when the Panorama Room is closed. ☒ *Mount Cook Village,* ☎ *03/435–1809. Reservations essential. AE, DC, MC, V. Closed Apr.–Sept. No lunch.*

$$ ✗ **Reflections Café.** This rustically decorated restaurant has great views of the lake from almost every table. Red meat is treated well—Reflections has been awarded the Hallmark of Excellence for beef, lamb, and venison for four years in a row—but there are plenty of other choices. Salmon from a nearby hatchery is fresh and delicious, and other seafood also stars regularly. ☒ *Lake Tekapo Scenic Resort, State Hwy. 8,* ☎ *03/680–6808. AE, DC, MC, V.*

$–$$ ✗ **The Garden Courtyard.** An impressive buffet is the major feature of this pleasantly laid-out dining room. It's set up three times a day, and at lunch and dinner times always includes two soups, six main course dishes, the same number of vegetable dishes, a selection of salads, and several desserts. Salmon and other local produce is used as much as possible (if you've caught one, the restaurant kitchen will cook it for you). The cost is $30. At other times of the day, a snack menu offers burgers, burritos, and the like, all for well under $10. ☒ *The Godley, State Hwy. 8, Lake Tekapo,* ☎ *03/680–6848. AE, DC, MC, V.*

$–$$ ✗ **Kohan Japanese Restaurant.** Masato Itoh has the only Japanese restaurant in town, which gives him guaranteed access to tour loads of tourists from his home country. Despite his monopoly, he runs a class act—and his prices are very reasonable. All the usual sushi, sashimi, and tempura options are available, but he is also happy to prepare your own, fresh-caught salmon or trout. One popular snack is salmon *don*, which dresses the fish in a tasty sauce and sits it on a bowl of steamed rice. ☒ *State Hwy. 8, Lake Tekapo,* ☎ *03/680–6688. AE, DC, MC, V. No dinner Sun.*

$ ✗ **Breadcrumb Bakery.** Mark Gillespie doesn't get a lot of sleep. He's at his busy bakery-café before dawn most mornings, and is often still there well into the evening. Almost everything sold here is baked on the premises—seven or eight different styles of bread, croissants, muffins, scones, cake, and 12 different kinds of pies. Sandwiches have yummy fillings like seafood, chicken and mayonnaise, or bacon and eggs, and the scones are legendary (try the cheese and pineapple). Just in case that's not enough, Mark will rustle up a full breakfast (bacon, two eggs, tomato), and charge around $8 for it. ☒ *State Hwy. 8, Lake Tekapo,* ☎ *03/680–6655. No credit cards. No dinner.*

Lodging

Lodging at Mount Cook Village is controlled by a single company, and it tends to be overpriced. Unless you really want to be very close to the mountain, Lake Tekapo is a better bet. It has a variety of well-priced accommodations, from luxury lodges and modern B&Bs to high-country farm stays and motels. Other nearby township like Fairlie or Twizel also have good accommodation options.

$$$$ ▦ **The Hermitage.** Famed for its stupendous mountain views, this rambling hotel is the luxury option at Mount Cook Village. Generally speaking, the layout and ambience of the hotel do not match its surroundings, and you might find it disappointing. Still, you're not going to wake up every day staring at such a stunning view or to the sound of keas (those large, cheeky mountain parrots) fighting it out in the parking lot. Rooms 601–613 and 701–713 have the best mountain views. ☒ *Mount Cook Village,* ☎ *03/435–1809,* 𝐅𝐀𝐗 *03/435–1879. 104 rooms. 2 restaurants, bar, café, sauna, shops. AE, DC, MC, V.*

$$$$ ⊞ **Lake Tekapo Lodge.** When you have the magnificent natural beauty of Lake Tekapo, the Southern Alps, and the sprawling MacKenzie country at your doorstep it might be a daunting challenge to build a lodge to match. John and Lynda van Beek met that challenge and, with the help of top New Zealand craftsman, have created a luxurious, earth-brick complex with fabulous views and a sumptuous decor reminiscent of medieval England. The first arresting feature, and there are many, is the entranceway's arched antique church doors, complete with studs and heavy, metal latch and hinges. Once inside, heavy trusses and lintels oversee your welcome, along with a unique mix of fine art and farming paraphernalia. Lighting is provided by a cleverly transformed wheelbarrow-wheel "chandelier," suspended by heavy chains. The lodge uses wrought-iron embellishments and natural wood throughout, with most furnishings made of oak or elm. The front rooms are spacious and open out to a covered veranda, the garden, and the best views. ⊠ *24 Aorangi Crescent, Lake Tekapo,* ☎ *03/680–6566,* FAX *03/ 680–6599. 4 rooms. AE, DC, MC, V.* ⊛

$$ ⊞ **The Chalet.** The Chalet's six fully self-contained apartments are lo-
★ cated beside the turquoise waters of Lake Tekapo. The best are those with spacious living rooms and lake views. Owners Walter and Zita Speck have ensured that each unit has individuality. The clown room, for example, has rag rugs spread over timber floors and a collection of clowns. Most rooms feature adobe plaster walls, native timbers, and refreshing color schemes. Although two of the rooms have no appreciable views, they open onto a small patio area and lovely alpine gardens. Walter is an experienced hunting, fishing, and nature guide with an extensive knowledge of the area; you can arrange any number of exciting, customized expeditions with him. Zita also arranges for accommodations in private vacation homes. Tekapo township is a scenic five-minute walk away. ⊠ *Pioneer Dr., Box 2 Lake Tekapo,* ☎ *03/ 680–6774,* FAX *03/680–6713. 6 units. Hiking, fishing, laundry service. MC, V. BP.* ⊛

$$ ⊞ **Holbrook Station.** A 35,000-acre, high-altitude sheep station that has 9,500 Merino sheep, Holbrook lets you feel like you can play at farming while on vacation. The farm cottage is fully self-contained, and comfortably furnished in modern country style. A large window in the front lounge room has a great view of Mt. Edward, which you can enjoy next to a roaring log fire. You are welcome to look around the farm, and hosts Lesley and Alister France might be able to arrange involvement in station activities. Anglers will enjoy the farm's 3-acre lake that is well stocked with rainbow trout. You can stay on a bed-and-breakfast basis—the meal is served at the main house—or you can prepare your own meals. Lesley will also cook a three-course dinner with wine for $35 per person by arrangement. The cottage has three rooms and can accommodate up to eight people, but bookings are limited to one group at a time regardless of size. ⊠ *State Hwy. 8, 12 km (7½ mi) east of Lake Tekapo, Box 4, Fairlie,* ☎ *03/685–8535 or 025/387–974,* FAX *03/685–8534. 3-bedroom cottage. MC, V.* ⊛

Outdoor Activities and Sports

BICYCLING

Exploring the area on a bicycle is the only way to see it all up close—the range of scenery is impressive. *See* Chapter 5 for operators and trip information.

CLIMBING

The Mt. Cook National Park area is ideal for rock climbing. Experienced climbers and beginners alike can sign up for the appropriate level of **Alpine Guides'** (⊠ Box 20, Mt. Cook, ☎ 03/345–1834) 7- to 10-day mountaineering courses, which begin around $1,600.

FARM STAYS AND RURAL NEW ZEALAND

I T'S A TIRED CLICHÉ, but it's true: you can't truly experience New Zealand if you stay only in the cities and towns. As you leave metro Auckland, heading north or south, you'll quickly realize that this is still a country that relies heavily on agriculture. New Zealand was built on sheep farming, with dairy, beef, and more recently, deer farming also playing their parts. Today there are 47 million sheep and less than 4 million humans in this green, clean country! Sheep are, quite simply, everywhere.

In past years, the farming sector had what some people regarded as a charmed (though not necessarily easy) life, with favorable trading terms with Britain and financial subsidies from the government. But over the past 20 or 30 years, the agricultural sector has had its fair share of knocks. Export markets are tougher and government assistance has dried up. Farmers have looked for ways to supplement their incomes, and one of these has been to open up their homes and properties to overseas guests. Because of New Zealand's burgeoning popularity as a travel destination, it's a match made in heaven. Farmers get an economic boost—and a chance to meet the world—and visitors get a chance to get up close to the heart of this predominately agricultural country.

The country has about 3,000 farm stays and rural homes open to visitors. Their aim, first and foremost, is to provide country hospitality and the opportunity to meet and talk to New Zealanders who make a living from the land. On arrival to a farm stay you'll usually be met by your hosts, given a welcoming cup of coffee or tea, and then a tour by foot or four-wheel-drive of the property's main attributes. Be prepared to talk farming, Kiwi-style. These people love what they do and take pride in it. For many it's been a way of life for generations.

Many farm stays emphasize a hands-on experience. Don't be surprised if you're given the chance to partake in a sheep muster or to help with milking the cows at 5 AM. And don't worry, the "farmwork" is voluntary!

An added bonus of heading to a farm is that you'll probably be completely surrounded by spectacular countryside—the kind of scenery that draws visitors to New Zealand in the first place. An extended stay out in the country gives you the pleasure of really getting to know the local landscape. With most farm stays you'll have the chance to walk or tramp in the nearby wilderness, go horseback riding, rafting, kayaking, and fishing. You'll go off on your adventures fortified by a full, cooked breakfast. And, in many of the best farm stays and country lodges, a three-course dinner with wine will await you at the end of your active day. Best of all, the cost of a farm stay tends to be far lower than the rates for comparable accommodations in crowded resort areas.

HORSE TREKKING

Pukaki Horsetreks (✉ Pukaki Canal Rd., Twizel, ☎ 025/280–7353, 0800/245–549 in N.Z.) has half-hour to half-day guided trips ($65 per half day) in winter and half-hour to two-day treks in summer up Mt. Ruataniwha, which overlooks Lake Ohau in the MacKenzie Basin.

STARGAZING

Star Gazing (✉ Box 8, Lake Tekapo, ☎ 03/680–6565, ✍) beside Lake Tekapo or at Mt. Cook National Park is a most pleasurable and educational way to better understand the Southern Hemisphere skies. Japanese astronomer Hideyuki Ozawa expertly interprets the night sky while you await a shooting star to make a wish upon.

Shopping

Go to the main street of Lake Tekapo for all your necessities. Though Tekapo has its share of typical souvenir shops, there are a few exceptions. **Tekapo High Country Crafts** (✉ Main Rd., ☎ 03/680–6895) features the unique work of local artists such as Olive Small, who creates framed pictures of the MacKenzie country using natural wool as her medium. **Studio 25** (✉ 25 Murray Pl., Tekapo, ☎ 03/680–6514) displays and retails the enchanting watercolors of talented artist Shirley O'Connor, whose work reflects the radiant colors of her environment.

Southern Alps A to Z

Arriving and Departing

BY BUS AND TRAIN

InterCity (☎ 03/377–0951) operates a daily bus service between Christchurch and Queenstown via Mount Cook Village, with a one-hour stop at the **Hermitage Hotel** (☞ Lodging, *above*) for lunch. InterCity also operates the daily **TranzAlpine Express** train from Christchurch to Arthur's Pass Village departing at 9 AM. A coach will meet this train and take you on to Greymouth and elsewhere in the West Coast. The **Coast to Coast Shuttle** bus (☎ 0800/800–847) goes to Arthur's Pass Village from Christchurch.

BY CAR

Arthur's Pass is a 2½- to 3-hour drive southwest out of Christchurch on Highway 73.

The 330-km (205-mi) drive from Christchurch straight through to **Mount Cook Village** takes five hours. Take Highway 1 south out of Christchurch. At the tiny town of Rangitata turn right onto Highway 79 to Lake Tekapo. Pass through Lake Tekapo and look on the right for Highway 80 to Mount Cook Village.

BY PLANE

Air New Zealand Link (☎ 0800/737–000 in N.Z.) flies from Christchurch to Mt. Cook.

Contacts and Resources

GUIDED TOURS

Air Safaris' specially designed "flightseeing" aircraft and experienced pilots will take you from Lake Tekapo on a breathtaking alpine flight, the Grand Traverse. This outstanding flight features Aoraki (Mt. Cook), Westland National Park, Fox and Franz Josef glaciers, the Tasman and Murchison glaciers, and the main divide of New Zealand—all in 50 minutes. That's 200 km (125 mi) of mountains, ice, ski slopes, and turquoise-blue, glacier-fed lakes. The fare is $210 per adult. If you miss the flight at Lake Tekapo, consider catching it at Franz Josef. ✉ *Main Rd., Box 71, Tekapo,* ☎ *03/680–6880.* ✍

Glacier Encounters leave from the Hermitage Hotel or Mount Cook
YHA (✉ Bowen at Kitchener Dr.) for tours of Tasman glacier and guided
boat trips on its lake. ✉ *Box 18, Mount Cook Village,* ☎ *03/435–1809
or 03/435–1077.* 🖾 *$60.* ☉ *Oct.–May.* ✎

Lake Tekapo Adventures & Cruises offers fishing and boat cruises and
a range of adventurous trips, including kayaking, mountain-biking, horse-
trekking, tramping, and four-wheel-drive vehicle excursions. ✉ *Tekapo
Information Centre, Main St., Lake Tekapo,* ☎ *03/680–6721 or 03/
680–6629.* ✎

Mid Southern Tracks organizes and provides experienced guides for fishing trips, hunting safaris, and nature tours both locally and to destinations all over New Zealand. ✉ *Pioneer Dr., Box 2, Lake Tekapo,*
☎ *03/680–6774.*

VISITOR INFORMATION

Lake Tekapo Information. ✉ *Main Rd., Lake Tekapo,* ☎ FAX *03/680–
6686.* ☉ *May–Aug., daily 9–9; Sept.–Apr., daily 10–6.*
Mt. Cook–Mackenzie Visitor Information Centre. ✉ *Wairepo Rd.,
Twizel,* ☎ *03/435–0801; 0800/435–0801 in N.Z.* ☉ *Nov.–Apr., daily
8:30–6:30; May–Oct., weekdays 9–5.* ✎

SOUTHLAND

Most of Southland, the western lobe of lower South Island, is taken
up by two giant national parks, Fiordland and Mt. Aspiring. Fiordland, the name generally given to the southwest coast, is a majestic wilderness of rocks, ice, and beech forest, where glaciers have carved mile-deep
notches into the coast. The scenic climax of this area—and perhaps of
the whole country—is Milford Sound. A cruise on the sound is a must.
But if you really want to take in the raw grandeur of Fiordland, hike
one of the many trails in the area, among them the famous four-day
Milford Track, what some call the finest walk in the world. The accommodations base and adventure center for the region is Queenstown.

Wanaka

㉔ *70 km (44 mi) northeast of Queenstown, 87 km (54 mi) south of Haast
Pass.*

Set on the southern shore of Lake Wanaka, with some of New Zealand's
most impressive mountains stretched out behind it, Wanaka is the
welcome mat for Mt. Aspiring National Park. It is a favorite of Kiwis
on vacation, an alternative of sorts to Queenstown. The region has numerous trekking opportunities, a choice of ski areas, and a diverse selection of other outdoor activities. The town has a couple of unusual
cultural attractions as well, if you arrive on a rainy day.

Because of Queenstown's well-established publicity machine, Wanaka
has tended to be overlooked by many people in the past. For that reason it manages to retain an almost sleepy-village atmosphere for most
of the year. This changes during the December to January summer vacations. Some of the popular bars and restaurants get lively in the middle of the ski season as well. At those times it pays to book
accommodations ahead of time.

Spectacularly sited on the shores of Lake Wanaka, **Rippon Vineyard** is
one of the most photographed in the country. Lois and Rolfe Mills
planted a "fruit-salad" vineyard in the mid-1970s and spent the next
few years sorting out which varieties best suited the region. Now their
portfolio includes sparkling wine, riesling, gewürztraminer, chardon-

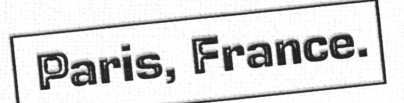

Paris, France.

Paris, Texas.

When it Comes to Getting
Local Currency at an ATM,
Same Thing.

Whether you're in Yosemite or Yemen, using your Visa® card or ATM card with the PLUS symbol is the easiest and most convenient way to get local currency. For example, let's say you're in France. When you make a withdrawal, using your secured PIN, it's dispensed in francs, but is debited from your account in U.S. dollars. This makes it easy to take advantage of favorable exchange rates. And if you need help finding one of Visa's 627,000 ATMs in 127 countries worldwide, visit **visa.com/pd/atm**. We'll make finding an ATM as easy as finding the Eiffel Tower, the Pyramids or even the Grand Canyon.

It's Everywhere You Want To Be.®

SEE THE WORLD IN FULL COLOR

Fodor's Exploring Guides bring all the great sights vividly to life with hundreds of photographs, fascinating historical background, and colorful anecdotes. Detailed maps and practical information keep you headed in the right direction.

Pair a **Fodor's** Exploring Guide with your trusted Gold Guide for a complete planning package.

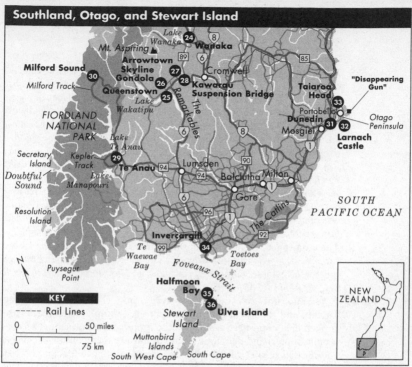

Southland, Otago, and Stewart Island

nay, sauvignon blanc, and fine (but expensive) pinot noir. Head west from Wanaka along the lake on Mt. Aspiring Road for 4 km (2½ mi). ✉ *Mt. Aspiring Rd., Box 175,* ☎ *03/443–8084,* FAX *03/441–8034.* ⊙ *Dec.–Apr., daily 11–5; July–Nov. 1–4:30.*

On your way into town on Highway 6 you'll pass the **New Zealand Fighter Pilots Museum**—a good place to take a joyride "flightseeing" the region in a Tiger Moth, Pitt Special, Harvard, or even a World War II P-51 Mustang, though the latter, at a cost of $2,000, is a little steeper than the $320 Harvard ride. Also available to fly in are the Hawker Hurricane and Supermarine Spitfire, as well as, the very rare Polikarpov 1-16 and 1-153. The museum is a tribute to New Zealand fighter pilots, of whom the country contributed more per capita than any other nation in World Wars I and II. This airport is the base for an annual international air show—Warbirds over Wanaka—usually held at Easter. It's a great opportunity to see these magnificent aircraft in the air. ✉ *Hwy. 6,* ☎ *03/443–7010,* FAX *03/443–7011.* 🎟 *$7.* ⊙ *Daily 9–4.*

Don't make **Stuart Landsborough's Puzzling World** your first stop in Wanaka—you may get hooked trying to solve one of the myriad brain-teasers and not leave until closing. The complex includes the amazing Tumbling Towers and Tilted House, which is on a 15-degree angle (is the water really running uphill?), as well as the Leaning Tower of Wanaka. The maze can be as demanding as you want to make it by setting individual challenges. Most people spend from 30 minutes to one hour in the maze and, understandably, a little less time in the Following Faces room: it's an eerie feeling to have so many famous people watch your every move. The place to take your time is the popular Puzzle Centre. Just take on the puzzle of your choice, order a cup of coffee, and proceed to get worked up. The place is 2 km (1 mi) east of town—just look for the cartoonlike houses on funny angles. ✉ *Hwy.*

89, ☎ 03/443–7489. 📷 *Puzzle Centre free; Tilted House and Holo-
gram Hall $4; Tilted House, Hologram Hall, Leaning Tower of Wanaka,
and Maze $6.* ⊙ *Daily 8:30–5:30.*

Dining and Lodging

$–$$$ ✕ **Wanakai.** Fun, funky surroundings set the scene for an eclectic
menu that includes the usual nachos, buffalo potato wedges, kebabs,
and so on. Wanakai also ups the adventure ante with dishes like gin-
gered tofu fritters and soy-ginger chicken, and even goes classical with
cervena (venison) steak, sitting on a red currant and Dijon mustard sauce.
Pasta and salads are abundant, and plenty of local wine is served by
the glass or bottle. It's open all day, every day through the winter sea-
son, but is often closed at night in summer, so it's best to phone first.
⊠ *Helwick and Ardmore Sts.,* ☎ *03/443–7795. AE, DC, MC, V.*

$$ ✕ **White House.** Mediterranean and North African influences are evident on the menu of this aptly named eatery. Honest food, served with-
out pretension, is the order of the day—recent listings have included
harissa chicken and hogget *tagine,* both loaded with Moroccan spices.
The atmosphere is casual, with outdoor seating in the summer. Come
for a meal, or you can just sit with a cuppa—coffee, that is. There are
quite a few wines available by the glass. ⊠ *Dunmore and Dungarvon
Sts.,* ☎ *03/443–9595. AE, DC, MC, V.*

$–$$ ✕ **Toscana.** Italy rules in this tiny restaurant. The decor is decidedly
Tuscan, and the menu follows suit. Properly thin-crusted pizzas are
cooked in a wood-fired oven, and the toppings are authentic (what—
no pineapple?) and delicious. Some pastas are made on the premises,
and the sauces they're tossed in or topped with have loads of honest
flavor. Main course meats include venison, ostrich, and wild boar. The
wine list mixes Otago bottles with Italian imports. ⊠ *76 Golf Course
Rd.,* ☎ *03/443–1255. AE, MC, V. Closed Oct.–Apr. No lunch.*

$$$ 🏠 **Willow Cottage.** Built from stone and cob (a commonly used mix-
★   ture of mud, straw, and horse manure) in the 1870s, this charming white
cottage is set on a farm five minutes' drive from Wanaka amid moun-
tains and farmlands. The cottage has been lovingly restored by hosts Kate
and Roy Summers, who have filled it with period furnishings. One treat
is sitting out on the veranda with a glass of wine or coffee; another is
having breakfast with the Summers in their farmhouse. Kate also runs
an antiques shop in a converted historic stable on the property, where
she has gathered an eclectic mix of New Zealand and English antiques.
The cottage is suitable for a couple or party of four. ⊠ *Maxwell Rd.,
Mt. Barker,* ☎ 📠 *03/443–8856. 1 cottage. AE, DC, MC, V. BP.*

$$ 🏠 **Wanaka Motor Inn.** Close to the lake and 2 km (1 mi) from town,
this family-run motor inn has a friendly and casual atmosphere. The
rooms' natural color schemes—with timber walls and green carpets—
work well with the views. Upstairs rooms have private terraces from
which you can enjoy the scenery. Its restaurant and bar are quite cozy.
⊠ *Mt. Aspiring Rd., Wanaka,* ☎ *03/443–8216,* 📠 *03/443–9108. 36
rooms. Restaurant, bar. AE, DC, MC, V.*

Outdoor Activities and Sports

FISHING

Locals will tell you that fishing on Lake Wanaka and nearby Lake Hawea
is better than the more famed Taupo area. You won't want to enter
that argument, but chances are good you'll catch fish if you have the
right guide. **Harry Urquhart** (☎ 03/443–1535) has trolling excursions
for rainbow trout, brown trout, and quinnat salmon on Lake Hawea,
and he has fly-fishing trips as well. **Gerald Telford** (☎ 03/443–9257)
will take you fly-fishing, including night fishing. For more information on trout fishing around Wanaka, *see* Chapter 5.

RAFTING AND KAYAKING

At **Pioneer Rafting** you can finally do some white-water rafting at a calm pace. Lewis Verduyn is New Zealand's leading eco-rafting specialist, with many years' experience as a white-water rafter. Lewis had his share of adrenaline pumping high-grade trips, and then got tired of missing out on what he sees as the real adventure, the environment he was tearing past. That's why he's put together a highly informative eco-rafting adventure, suitable for most ages. The trip retraces an historic pioneer log-raft route and includes interpretation of the human and natural history of the riverscape. Your guide talks about ecology, geology, flora and fauna, gold-panning, and how to safely maneuver a raft over white-water falls. The full-day trip includes lunch and departs at 10, returning at 4:30. The half-day departs at 1 and returns at 5:30. ⊠ *Box 124, Wanaka,* ☎ *03/443–1246 or 025/295–0418.* 🖃 *Full day $145, half day $95.* ☉ *Sept.–Apr.*

Exploring this beautiful region's rivers with **Alpine River Guides** Alan and Kirsty Hoffman is a must while in Wanaka. Unlike many of the large-scale operations of neighboring Queenstown, the couple caters to smaller groups, which means a lot of attention for beginners. You'll learn how to glide for a rest into a calm eddy, to wave surf, and to safely charge down the center of the white water. You *will* spill and for this reason all your gear, right down to the polypropylene underwear, is provided. Alan has an in-depth knowledge of the area and a great sense of humor. The full-day trip is $120 per person and includes lunch and afternoon tea. ⊠ *11 Mt. Iron Dr., Wanaka,* ☎ *03/443–9023 or 025/ 382–475.* 🐟

SKYDIVING

New Zealand is definitely the place to experiment with wild adventures, and with **Tandem Skydive Lake Wanaka** (⊠ Wanaka Airport, Hwy. 6, Wanaka, ☎ 03/443–7207 or 025/796–877) you're in capable hands. The 9,000-ft jump over gorgeous scenery is $225 and you can have a video of your exploits for $45 and photos on the ground and as you exit the plane for $20.

WALKING AND TREKKING

You could stay for a week in Wanaka, take a different walk into the bush and mountains each day, and still come nowhere near exhausting all options. If you have time for only one walk, **Mt. Iron** is relatively short and rewarding. A rocky hump carved by glaciers, its summit provides panoramic views of lakes Wanaka and Hawea, plus the peaks of the Harris Mountains and Mt. Aspiring National Park. The access track begins 2 km (1 mi) from Wanaka, and the walk to the top takes 45 minutes. To avoid going over old ground, descend on the alternative route down the steep eastern face.

Mt. Roy is a daylong commitment. A track starts at the base of the mountain, 6 km (4 mi) from Wanaka on the road to Glendhu Bay. The round-trip journey takes about six hours. The track is closed from early October to mid-November.

For maps and information on these and other local walks, contact the **Department of Conservation** (⊠ Ardmore St., ☎ 03/477–0677).

Queenstown

㉕ *70 km (44 mi) southeast of Wanaka, 530 km (330 mi) southwest of Christchurch.*

Set on the edge of a glacial lake beneath the sawtooth peaks of the Remarkables, Queenstown is the most popular tourist stop on South Island. Once prized by the Maori as a source of greenstone, the town boomed when gold was discovered in the Shotover, which quickly became famous as "the richest river in the world." Queenstown could easily have become a ghost town when gold gave out—except for its location. With ready access to mountains, lakes, rivers, ski slopes, and the glacier-carved coastline of Fiordland National Park, the town has become the adventure capital of New Zealand. Its shop windows are crammed with skis, Polartec, Asolo walking boots, and Marin mountain bikes. Along Shotover Street, travel agents tout white-water rafting, jet boating, caving, trekking, heli-skiing, parachuting, and parapenting (rappeling). New Zealanders' penchant for bizarre adventure sports reaches a climax in Queenstown, and it was here that the sport of leaping off a bridge with a giant rubber band wrapped around the ankles—bungy jumping—took root as a commercial enterprise. Taking its marvelous location for granted, Queenstown is mostly a comfortable, cosmopolitan base for the outdoor activities around it.

Some of the best views of the town and the mountains all around are from the **Queenstown Gardens,** on the peninsula that encloses Queenstown Bay. The **Skyline Gondola** whisks you to the heights of Bob's Peak, 1,425 ft above the lake, for a panoramic view of the town and the Remarkables. You can also walk to the top on the **One Mile Creek Trail.** The summit terminal has a cafeteria, a buffet restaurant, and *Kiwi Magic,* a rather silly 25-minute aerial film that uses stunning effects to provide a tour of the country. The latest addition to the complex is a luge ride—start with the scenic track, then work your way up to the advanced track. If even that isn't exciting enough, you can bungy jump from the summit terminal (☞ AJ Hackett Bungy *in* Outdoor Activities and Sports, *below*). ⊠ *Brecon St., Queenstown,* ☎ *03/442–7860,* FAX *03/442–6391.* 🎟 *Gondola $12, Kiwi Magic $7, luge ride $4.50.* ☾ *Daily 10–10; Kiwi Magic screens every hr on the hr, 11–9.*

Gibbston Valley Wines is the best-known winery in central Otago—the world's southernmost wine-producing region. In 1995 a wine cave was blasted out from the side of the hill behind the winery. Wine-tasting tours are held in the cave regularly and are now one of the most interesting aspects of a visit to Gibbston. The showcase wine here is pinot noir, which suits the hot days, cold nights, and the lack of coastal influence. Other varieties available include riesling, chardonnay, pinot gris, and that classic New Zealand white, sauvignon blanc. The attached restaurant offers good preparations of mostly local produce and lots of wine by the glass. ⊠ *State Hwy. 6, Gibbston,* ☎ *03/442–6910,* FAX *03/442–6909.* 🎟 *Wine cave tour and tasting $8.50, less for larger groups.* ☾ *Tasting room daily 9:30–5:30, restaurant daily 12–3.*

Dramatically situated **Chard Farm** perches on a rare flat spot on the edge of the Kawarau Gorge, not far from Gibbston Valley. The portfolio includes a couple of excellent chardonnays, sauvignon blanc, gewürztraminer, pinot gris, and three variations of pinot noir. Production is large by central Otago standards but still tiny in the national scheme of things. ⊠ *Chard Rd., R.D. 1, Gibbston,* ☎ *03/442–6110,* FAX *03/441–8400.* ☾ *Daily 10–5.*

Dining and Lodging

$$–$$$ ✗ **The Bathhouse.** It's exactly that—an English-style Victorian bathhouse, built in 1911. Now, it acts as a casual café in the mornings and afternoons, and a full-fledged restaurant for lunch and dinner. The surroundings remain Victorian but the kitchen is pretty up-to-date, offering starters like citrus-dusted crab cakes with crispy wontons, and a selection of generous mains—cervena (venison) served with red cabbage

and a German-style smoked sausage on the side is typical. ✉ *Marine Parade,* ☎ *03/442–5625. AE, DC, MC, V. Closed Mon.*

$$–$$$ ✕ **Gourmet Express.** This sunny spot at the front of a shopping center is popular for breakfast, when pancakes with maple syrup, eggs any way you want, and heart-starting coffee are all on call. Later in the day, come here for gourmet sandwiches, hamburgers, and a huge selection of salads, grills, casseroles, and omelets—a good number featuring chilli in some shape or form. The wine list has an emphasis on local bottles. ✉ *Bay Centre, Shotover St.,* ☎ *03/442–9619. AE, DC, MC, V.*

$$–$$$ ✕ **H.M.S. Britannia.** The timber floors and fishing nets on the walls of this nautically themed restaurant are designed to give guests the impression of dining in an English galleon, and the food is suitably seaward-leaning. Choose from prawns, crayfish, calamari, or mussels, all prepared in predictable but flavorsome ways, or go for one of the many meat dishes. This is one of the few eateries in town that can take a booking for up to 20 people and seat them at one large table. Lunch is available by arrangement only. ✉ *The Mall,* ☎ *03/442–9600. AE, DC, MC, V.*

$$–$$$ ✕ **The 19th.** No restaurant has a better situation—this bright and breezy eatery is perched right on the end of the wharf that juts out into Lake Wakatipu. The menu changes regularly, but it always includes flavorsome dishes like panfried calamari with roasted plum tomatoes, garlic, and calamata olives, or linguine pasta tossed with sun-dried tomato pesto. The wine list is extensive. ✉ *Steamer Wharf,* ☎ *03/442–4006. AE, DC, MC, V.*

$$ ✕ **Avanti.** In the heart of Queenstown, Avanti serves better-than-average Italian dishes at a far lower price than most in this resort area. Pasta and pizza are prominent, but so are more substantial meals such as braised lamb shanks and several steak options with Italian-style sauces. Servings are designed for appetites honed on the mountain slopes. ✉ *The Mall,* ☎ *03/442–8503. AE, MC, V. Licensed and BYOB.*

$$ ✕ **The Boardwalk.** You might want to eat here just for the view. On
★ the second floor of the steamer wharf building, the restaurant looks over Lake Wakatipu toward the Remarkables. Nothing can quite beat that, but the menu makes a good attempt, and this restaurant has become a favorite with both locals and visitors—even Bill Clinton tried the goods during a presidential visit. Seafood is the specialty, including dishes such as the Provençal classic bouillabaisse, and crispy fried squid rings and prawns. If you want to try what Bill had, ask for the kingfish, layered between grilled Mediterranean vegetables. Meat eaters can enjoy dishes like lamb loin in puff pastry. Reservations are recommended. ✉ *Steamer Wharf,* ☎ *03/442–5630. AE, DC, MC, V.*

$$ ✕ **The Bunker.** Log fires, leather armchairs, and a clubby atmosphere make the Bunker the coziest place in town. Guests can enjoy a good range of predinner drinks in the bar before heading downstairs for a meal that might include a salad of smoked cervena (venison) served with a chilli pear and plum chutney, or something more traditional like duck confit. ✉ *Cow La.,* ☎ *03/441–8030. Reservations essential. AE, DC, MC, V.*

$$ ✕ **The Cow.** The pizza and pasta at this tiny restaurant are some of the best-value meals in town, but the place is immensely popular, so be prepared to wait for a table. A roaring fire and stone walls provide a cozy atmosphere on chilly evenings, but patrons aren't encouraged to linger over dinner, and you may be asked to share your table. ✉ *Cow La.,* ☎ *03/442–8588. AE, DC, MC, V. Licensed and BYOB.*

$ ✕ **Naff Caff.** This is the first café open in town most mornings, and it serves food until the early evening. Emma, the owner, searches around for great breads like *ciabatta* and *fougasse* and fills them with magical combos like pesto, chicken, and tomato. Salads are imaginative, muffins are baked every day, and there's a big range of cookies, plus a cake of the day. Coffee and tea are available hot or iced. Emma doesn't do cooked breakfasts, but her egg-and-bacon sandwiches are decent and solid. ⊠ *1/62 Shotover St.,* ☎ *03/442–8211. No credit cards.*

$$$$ 🏨 **Blanket Bay.** Philip Jenkins, former manager of Nugget Point,
★ Wharekauhau, and Solitaire lodges, has done it again. This immense schist (stone) alpine lodge rises out of the land to meet Lake Wakatipu. At the heart of the lodge is the Great Room with its grand fireplace, high ceilings, vaulted wharf-timber beams, and antique wooden floors. Floor-to-ceiling windows open out to views of the lake and Humboldt Mountains, and a large terrace, which wraps around the front of the lodge. All four lakeside rooms have a balcony or terrace. The three suites have sitting areas, stone fireplaces, and large bathrooms with a steam shower and a separate tub. The decor is solid and sumptuous; hues of maroon and gold complement native timbers and stone. The two chalets echo the structure, size, and decor of the lodge, but have the added advantage of complete peaceful privacy. Rates include breakfast, pre- and after-dinner house drinks, dinner, and accommodation. There are a number of dining options, including an intimate dinner for two in the wine cave. Blanket Bay is situated at the northern end of Lake Wakatipu, 3 km (1½ mi) south of Glenorchy and a 35-minute drive over scenic roads from Queenstown. ⊠ *Blanket Bay, Glenorchy, Queenstown,* ☎ *03/442–9442,* FAX *03/442–9441. 4 rooms, 3 suites, 4 chalet suites. Bar, hot tub, steam room, exercise room, boating, fishing. AE, DC, MC, V. MAP.* ✆

$$$$ 🏨 **Heritage Queenstown.** Located on Fernhill, just a few minutes from
★ the town center, the Heritage Queenstown is more peaceful than other hotels in town and has great views of the Remarkables and Lake Wakatipu. The hotel was built almost entirely out of South Island materials, including central Otago schist (stone) and wooden beams from old local railway bridges. Rooms are among the most spacious in town, fitted with writing tables and comfortable sitting areas. ⊠ *91 Fernhill Rd., Queenstown,* ☎ *03/442–4988,* FAX *03/442–4989. 178 rooms. Restaurant, bar, pool, hot tub, sauna, exercise room. AE, DC, MC, V.* ✆

$$$$ 🏨 **Millbrook Resort.** A 20-minute drive from Queenstown, this glam-
★ orous alpine resort offers luxurious self-contained accommodations including two-bedroom hotel villas, villa suites, and single rooms in the resort's main hotel. Separate cottages with two, three, or four bedrooms are also available. The resort has excellent fitness facilities and a special appeal for golfers: it is surrounded by an 18-hole championship golf course that was designed by New Zealand professional Bob Charles. The hotel villas are decorated in country style: pine tables, textured walls, shuttered windows, and a cream-and-cornflower-blue color scheme. Each has a kitchen, laundry facilities, and a large lounge–dining room. The hotel rooms are spacious, and each comes with a large bathroom, private balcony, and fireplace. There are three world-class restaurants on the premises. ⊠ *Malaghans Rd., Arrowtown,* ☎ *03/441–7000,* FAX *03/442– 1145. 13 villas, 70 villa suites, 51 rooms, 24 cottage apartments. 3 restaurants, bar, café, indoor pool, outdoor hot tubs, massage, saunas, spa, 18-hole golf course, tennis court, boccie, health club, hiking, mountain bikes, baby-sitting. AE, DC, MC, V.* ✆

$$$$ 🏨 **Millennium Queenstown.** Providing luxurious accommodations close to town, the Millennium is built on the site where American scientists sighted Venus in 1870. One of the conditions of building the hotel was leaving intact the rock from which the planet was sighted. Of more tangible importance are the comfortable, well-equipped rooms, and the Observatory Restaurant, which adds an international touch to New Zealand fare. ⊠ *Franklin Rd. and Stanley St., Queen-*

stown, ☎ 03/441–8888, ℻ 03/441–8889. *220 rooms. Restaurant, bar, sauna, exercise room, baby-sitting. AE, DC, MC, V.* ⌨

$$$$ ⊞ **Nugget Point.** Poised high above the Shotover River, this stylish re-
★ treat offers some of the finest accommodations in the Queenstown area. Owner-manager Colin Smith has created an intimate and welcoming atmosphere with all the amenities of a large hotel. Rooms are luxuri-ously large, and each has a balcony, a kitchenette, and a bedroom sep-arate from the living area. Check out the open-air whirlpool perched on the edge of Shotover Valley—great with a glass of champagne and a loved one. The hotel's Birches Restaurant serves a blend of European and Pacific cuisine complemented by fine New Zealand and interna-tional wines. The lodge is a 10-minute drive from Queenstown on the road to Coronet Peak, one of the top ski areas in the country. ⊠ *Arthur's Point Rd., Queenstown,* ☎ 03/442–7273, ℻ 03/442–7308. *35 rooms. Restaurant, bar, pool, sauna, spa, tennis court, squash. AE, DC, MC, V.*

$$$ ⊞ **Stone House.** On the hillside overlooking Queenstown and the lake, this handsome, historic 1874 cottage has been brought back to life by its enthusiastic owners and is decorated in a charming country style. Breakfasts are large and rates also include evening drinks. The guest lounge has a large, welcoming open fire and there is an outdoor hot tub where you can appreciate the alpine night sky. Smoking is not per-mitted inside the house, and children are not accommodated. Three of the four rooms have a shower only. ⊠ *47 Hallenstein St., Queen-stown,* ☎ ℻ 03/442–9812. *4 rooms. MC, V. BP.*

Nightlife

Queenstown's exciting daytime activities are not matched by its nightlife. The clubs and bars are mostly in the center of town, within easy walk-ing distance of one another. Bars start to close around 11 PM, but the nightclubs stay open late into the night.

Bardeux (⊠ The Mall, ☎ 03/442–8284) is a stylish wine bar, good for an intimate, subdued evening. If you want to dance until the wee hours, check out **Chicos** (⊠ The Mall, ☎ 03/442–8439). **The Edge** night-club (⊠ Camp St., ☎ 03/442–6253) also offers late-night dancing. And for a hip, funky nightspot with a Pacific feel, try **Surreal** (⊠ Rees St., ☎ 03/441–8492).

Outdoor Activities and Sports

BUNGY JUMPING

AJ Hackett Bungy, the pioneer in the sport, offers a variety of jumps in the area. Kawarau Bridge is the original jump site, 23 km (14 mi) from Queenstown on State Highway 6. Daredevils who graduate from the 143-ft plunge might like to test themselves on the 230-ft Skippers Canyon Bridge. The highest and most recent addition is the Nevis High-wire Bungy, suspended 440-ft above the Nevis River, from which you jump in a specially designed bungy chair. Prices start at $125 for the Kawarau jump (including T-shirt), and an extra $30 for photos, $39 for a video, or $55 for both photos and video. If you want to jump in the dark, Hackett now operates from the gondola terminal in town until 8 PM—the best place to bungy if you're short on time. ⊠ *The Station, Camp and Shotover Sts., Queenstown,* ☎ 03/442–1177 or 03/442–7100. ☉ *Apr.–Sept., daily 8–7 (later in Jan. depending on demand); Oct.–Mar., daily 9–8.*

FISHING

For information on trout fishing guides around Queenstown, *see* Chapter 5.

For information on hiking the Milford and Kepler tracks, *see* Te Anau and Milford Sound, *below,* and Chapter 5.

HORSE TREKKING

Moonlight Stables has a choice of full- or half-day rides with spectacular views of the mountains and rivers around the Wakatipu-Arrow Basin. Ride across some of the 800 acres of rolling land that make up Doonholme deer farm. Both novice and experienced riders are welcome. Transportation from Queenstown is provided. The company operates a clay-bird shooting range, and you can shoot in combination with the ride. ⊠ *Box 784, Queenstown,* ☎ *03/442–1229.* ☜ *½-day trip $55 per person, from $115 including shooting and 20 clay-targets.*

JET-BOAT RIDES

The **Dart River Jet Boat Safari** is a 2½-hour journey 35 km (21 mi) upstream into the ranges of the Mt. Aspiring National Park. This rugged area is one of the most spectacular parts of South Island, and the trip is highly recommended. Buses depart daily from Queenstown, with a complimentary pick-up at your accommodation, daily at 8, 10, and noon in summer and 8 and 11:30 in winter for the 45-minute ride to the boats. ⊠ *Box 76, Queenstown,* ☎ *03/442–9992.* ☜ *$129.* ☉ *Year-round.*

The **Shotover Jet** is the most famous jet-boat ride in the country (and one of the most exciting): a high-speed, heart-stopping adventure on which the boat pirouettes within inches of canyon walls. If you want to stay relatively dry, sit beside the driver. The boats are based at the Shotover Bridge, a 10-minute drive from Queenstown. If you don't have transport, a shuttle coach departs from the Station building parking lot in central Queenstown every 15 minutes. Boats depart frequently between 7 AM and 9 PM from December through April, 9:30–4:30 the rest of the year. Reservations are essential. ⊠ *Shotover River Canyon, Queenstown,* ☎ *03/442–8570.* ☜ *$75.* ☉ *Year-round.* ☜

RAFTING

Kawarau Raft Expeditions runs various half-, full-, and two-day whitewater rafting trips in the Queenstown area. The most popular is the Grade 3½ to Grade 5 ride along the Shotover River, an unforgettable journey that ends with the rafts shooting through the 560-ft Oxenbridge Tunnel. ⊠ *35 Shotover St., Queenstown,* ☎ *03/442–9792.* ☜ *$99– $229 per person.* ☉ *Year-round.* ☜

For something even more physical on the river, **Serious Fun River Surfing** lets you jump on a body board and speed down the rapids that way. It was all started by Jon Imhoof, a backpacker from Hawaii, who now has a team of experienced guides who know their business and make sure surfers are well looked after. You'll enjoy the experience best if you have a reasonable level of fitness. Transport to and from Queenstown hotels is provided. ⊠ *33 Watts Rd., Sunshine Bay, Queenstown,* ☎ *03/442–5262,* 𝖥𝖠𝖷 *03/442–5265.* ☜ *$109.* ☉ *Departure year-round at 10 and 2.*

Arrowtown

㉗ *22 km (14 mi) northeast of Queenstown, 105 km (66 mi) south of Wanaka.*

Another gold-mining town, Arrowtown lies northeast of Queenstown. It had long been suspected that there was gold along the Arrow River, and when Edward Fox, an American, was seen selling large quantities of the precious metal in nearby Clyde, the hunt was on. Others attempted to follow the wily Fox back to his diggings, but he kept giving his pursuers the slip, on one occasion even abandoning his tent and provisions in the middle of the night. Eventually a large party of prospectors stumbled on Fox and his team of 40 miners. The secret was out, miners rushed to stake their claims, and Arrowtown was born.

After the gold rush ended, the place was just another sleepy rural town until tourism created a new boom. Lodged at the foot of the steep Crown Range, this atmospheric village of weathered timber shop fronts and white, stone churches shaded by ancient sycamores was simply too gorgeous to escape the attention of the tour buses. These days it has become a tourist trap, but a highly photogenic one, especially when autumn gilds the hillsides.

In a less-visited part of the town is the former **Chinese settlement.** Chinese miners were common on the goldfields in the late 1860s, but local prejudice forced them to live in their own separate enclave. A number of their huts and Ah Lum's Store, one of the few Chinese goldfield buildings to survive intact, have been preserved. ⊠ *Bush Creek (west end of town).* ☒ *Free.* ◷ *Daily 9–5.*

28 **Kawarau Suspension Bridge** is where bungy jumpers make their leaps—a spectacle well worth the short detour. As a promotional stunt, the AJ Hackett company once offered a free jump to anyone who would jump nude, but there were so many takers the scheme had to be abandoned. The bridge is on Highway 6, not far from Arrowtown.

Te Anau

29 *175 km (109 mi) southwest of Queenstown, 119 km (75 mi) east of Milford.*

By Philip Barnes

Lake Te Anau (tay-*ah*-no), which is 53 km (33 mi) long and up to 10 km (6 mi) wide, is the second-largest lake in New Zealand after Lake Taupo. Set on the southern shores of the lake, the town of Te Anau serves as a base for a wide range of local activities in Fiordland National Park. Fiordland, the largest national park in New Zealand, takes its name from the deep sea inlets, or sounds, on its western flank. This is the most rugged part of the country. Parts of the park are so remote that they have never been explored, and visitor activities are mostly confined to a few of the sounds and the walking trails.

The township of **Te Anau** has a few attractions and activities worth checking out if you have some lingering time on your way into or out of the park.

At **Te Ana-au Caves,** boats and walkways take you through a maze of caves containing underground whirlpools, waterfalls, and gushing streams. On the cave walls, myriad glowworms shine like constellations in a clear, night sky. The caves can only be reached by water and the entire trip takes 2½ hours. ⊠ *Fiordland Travel, Lake Front Dr.,* ☎ *03/249–7416.* ☒ *$36.* ◷ *Daily 2 and 8:15 PM.*

On the shores of Lake Te Anau, 1 km (½ mi) west of town, the **Te Anau Wildlife Centre** gives you the chance to preview some of the wildlife you're likely to encounter when tramping in Fiordland. The center houses one of New Zealand's rare flightless birds, the *takahe,* which was at one time thought to be extinct. The lakeside walk to the center makes for a pleasant afternoon or evening stroll. ⊠ *Manapouri Rd.,* ☎ *03/249–7921,* ☒ *Free, donations welcome.* ◷ *24 hours.*

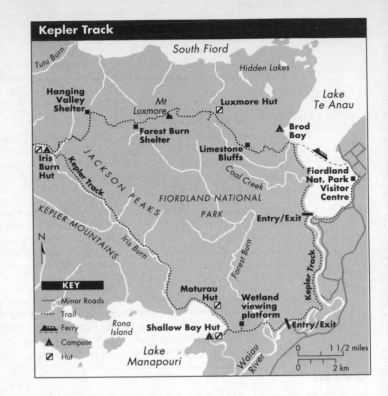

Kepler Track

From Te Anau, visitors can set out on sightseeing trips by bus, boat, or plane to Milford and Doubtful sounds, or take off on one of the park's world-class hiking tracks. Of these tracks, the most accessible to town is the the Kepler Track.

★ The 67-km (42-mi) **Kepler Track** forms a loop beginning and ending at the south end of Lake Te Anau. It skirts the lakeshore, climbs up to the bush line, passes limestone bluffs and the Luxmore Caves, goes through extensive beech forest, and has incredible views of the mountains and of South Fiord. The track features an alpine crossing, with a high point near the peak of **Mt. Luxmore**. It's a moderate walking track that takes three to four days to complete. And for those on a tight schedule it's possible to take day hikes to the Luxmore and Moturau huts.

The track was opened in 1988 to take pressure off the increasing numbers of people walking the Routeburn and Milford tracks. It features some very good quality trails and huts and is relatively easy, with only one steep climb to the alpine section by Mt. Luxmore. Trampers should beware, however, of high wind gusts while crossing the exposed saddle above the bush line. During winter and spring the alpine section may be impassable because of snow.

The track starts on the southern shores of Lake Te Anau just 4 km (2 ½ mi) from town. Although it can be walked in either direction, most people walk it counterclockwise, following the shores of the lake for 90 minutes and then climbing steeply to the Luxmore Hut. This high-standard 40-bunk hut is a 50-minute walk from where the track climbs above the tree line. The next day most people tackle the six- to seven-hour mountain-ridge walk to Iris Burn Hut. This exposed stretch of the walk offers spectacular mountain and lake views, but should not be attempted in extreme weather conditions. Keep your eyes open here for the kea, New Zealand's large and sociable mountain parrot. The following day involves a 17-km (10¾-mi) walk through beech forest and riverside clearings before you meet up with the shores of Lake Manapouri. The track follow the shoreline for two more hours, and then reaches the lodgings for the third night, the Moturau Hut. The final day is mostly easy walking on flat terrain. The 17-km (10½-mi) walk takes four to five hours, passes by rivers and forests, and crosses a wetland by boardwalk.

During the summer months, the huts are serviced and cost $15 per night for adults. During winter, when huts are unserviceable, this charge drops to $5. Inquiries and reservations can be made through **Fiordland Travel** ⊠ *Lake Front Dr., Te Anau,* ☎ *03/249–7416,* 𝖥𝖠𝖷 *03/249–7022.* ✆

Dining and Lodging

$$–$$$ ✕ **Keplers.** Described by many locals as the only serious restaurant in town, Keplers has quite a reputation to maintain. The ambience is relaxing, the view magnificent, and the food classical. Chicken croquettes are the most popular starter, and beef Wellington (how long since you've seen that on a menu?) is a big seller. Seafood is also prepared in mostly traditional ways. Crayfish arrives live in the kitchen every day, and is offered simply grilled (highly recommended), or with Mornay sauce. As nighttime falls, candles add a romantic air. ⊠ *Town Centre,* ☎ *03/249–7909. AE, DC, MC, V.*

$$ ✕ **Settlers Steakhouse.** The curtains are red, the carpet is red—and most of the meals feature red meat. Choose your own steak, perhaps rump steak or a T-bone, and the chef will cook it just the way you want it. It's not all beef—Settlers also sells chicken, lamb, ham, venison, local salmon, cod, and even crayfish, all of it cooked on a grill. The starters are dated, it's true, but they work here—this is a steak house! ⊠ *Town Centre,* ☎ *03/249–8954. AE, DC, MC, V. Closed June–July.*

$–$$ ✕ **Hollyford Boulevard.** With seating for more than 100 indoors and out, this is Te Anau's biggest nonhotel eatery. Bright colors, metal and wicker chairs, and lots of light wood give it a modern café atmosphere, and the menu strives to match the mood with a selection of big-city favorites. Pastas and salads come in all the usual variations, and main courses cover the gamut from a classical chicken Kiev to steaks with various sauces, and even a couple of curries. There's some table service, but many of the dishes are laid out, buffet style, for guests to help themselves. ⊠ *Town Centre,* ☎ *03/249–7334. DC, V. Closed winter months.*

$–$$ ✕ **La Toscana.** The wine-color walls in this cheap-and-cheerful café put you in the mood for the well-priced selection of Tuscan soups, pastas, and pizzas. You won't find geographically confused toppings like tandoori chicken or ham and pineapple—the kitchen keeps things pretty authentic. Sensibly, both pastas and pizzas are available in medium or large sizes, but remember to keep dessert in mind—the *torta di cioccolata* (chocolate cake) is a local legend. ⊠ *108 Town Centre,* ☎ *03/ 249–7756. AE, MC, V. Closed winter months. No lunch.*

$–$$ ✕ **The Olive Tree.** Sunny colors and a garden courtyard give this place a Mediterranean feel, which is entirely appropriate, because that's the style of food the kitchen says it aims for. Fair enough—but quite a few Thai flavors have sneaked into the mix. Focaccia bread, made on the premises, is filled with interesting goodies like Thai chicken salad (see!), or tomato, basil, and *bocconcini* (mozzarella nuggets). Pizzas rule at night, with equally eclectic toppings. ⊠ *52 Town Centre,* ☎ *03/249–8496. DC, MC, V.*

$–$$ ✕ **Redcliffe Café.** Exposed beams, lots of timber, and a log fire give this pleasant spot a cozy feel. The food suits the surroundings—smoked salmon on potato pancakes topped with Mornay sauce is a popular starter, and in winter the kitchen can hardly keep up with orders for braised lamb shanks, served as they would be in many local farmers' cottages, with a pile of mashed potatoes and minted peas. The adjacent bar stays open late, and has seen many riotous nights over the years. ⌧ *12 Mokonui St.,* ☎ *03/249–7431. DC, MC, V. Closed June–Aug. No lunch.*

$$$$ ⊞ **Castlerock Cookhouse.** This beautifully restored, self-contained cot-
★   tage is situated on a 4,000-acre farm one hour's drive south of Queenstown and a 50-minute drive east of Te Anau. Originally built as a station cookhouse for shearers in the 1870s, it combines traditional charm with all the modern comforts. It has a fireplace and a private garden, and is situated next to a small private lake that is equipped with a rowboat for guests and has been stocked with wild brown trout. Hosts Juliet and David Thomas, who spent two years restoring the cookhouse, are descendants of a family who moved onto the property six generations ago. David will take guests on a complimentary farm tour to view cattle, sheep, and deer. A country-style dinner can be arranged for $35 per person. ⌧ *Castlerock Rd., R.D. 2, Lumsden, Southland,* ☎ *03/248–7435 or 025/328–990,* FAX *03/248–7535. 1 cottage. MC, V.* ✑

$$$ ⊞ **The Village Inn.** Close to the lake and the town's central shopping area, this inn has a facade of a carefully reconstructed pioneer village. Behind these shop and business fronts are quality hotel rooms and suites, with modern gray and burgundy furnishings. ⌧ *Mokoroa St.,* ☎ *03/249–7911,* FAX *03/249–7003. 51 rooms. Restaurant, bar, coin laundry. AE, DC, MC, V.* ✑

$$ ⊞ **The Cats Whiskers.** Hosts Irene and Terry Maher have been running this modern and comfortable B&B for six years and succeed in creating a home-away-from-home atmosphere for their guests, complete with a resident cat. Situated on the Te Anau lakefront, Cats Whiskers is a 10-minute walk from the town center. A courtesy car is available to take you to any of the restaurants in town and your hosts will be happy to make reservations for you for day excursions. ⌧ *2 Lake Front Dr.,* ☎ *03/249–8112,* FAX *03/249–8112. 3 rooms. MC, V. BP.* ✑

$$ ⊞ **Centra Te Anau.** On the shores of Lake Te Anau, within two minutes of the downtown area, this luxurious hotel has spacious lounges, extensive gardens, individual villas, and the feel of a tropical resort, minus the palm trees. The hotel was built in 1965 and, despite its luxury, is a bit worn, though large sections were renovated in 1998. The hotel is popular with hikers who are soaking up a bit of pampering on their way to the Milford Track. The McKinnon's Restaurant serves delectable South Island seafood and game. ⌧ *64 Lake Front Dr.,* ☎ *03/249–7411,* FAX *03/249–7947. 80 rooms, 15 villa rooms, 15 villa suites. Restaurant, bar, pool, sauna, spa, baby-sitting, laundry service. AE, DC, MC, V.* ✑

Outdoors Activities and Sports

CRUISING

Peaceful **Doubtful Sound** is three times as long as Milford Sound and sees far fewer visitors. **Fiordland Travel** (⌧ Lake Front Dr., ☎ 03/249–7416) runs a range of combined bus and boat trips there. Tours include a 2-km (1-mi) bus trip down a spiral tunnel to the Lake Manapouri Power Station machine hall, an extraordinary engineering feat built deep beneath the mountain. Most people take a 9½-hour day trip from Lake Manapouri. Between November and March you can overnight on the sound, aboard the *Kay Dee II*. Rates for the day excursion are $171 per person, and for the overnight cruise, $271.

FLYING

Air Fiordland offers a range of scenic flights on its fixed-wind aircraft
to Milford Sound ($199) and Doubtful Sound ($155). It also has combined packages offering the option of flying to Milford Sound and then
taking a cruise boat or kayaking on the water before returning to either Te Anau or Queenstown. The company also runs flights to Mt.
Cook and Mt. Aspiring ($260). ✉ *Box 38, Te Anau,* ☎ *03/249–7505,*
FAX *03/249–7080.* ✍

Waterwings Airways offers scenic flights with a floatplane that takes
travelers to some of the region's most inaccessible areas. The company
has a Catch a Crayfish package where passengers are flown to a licensed
crayfishing vessel on Doubtful Sound. After cruising along the rugged
coastline observing seals, penguins, and (most days) dolphins, passengers
then enjoy a champagne lunch eating the crayfish they are guaranteed
to catch. They can also take crayfish home. The four-hour trip costs
$475 per person and a minimum of three passengers is required. Wa-
terwings Airways offers a range of other scenic flights, including a 10-
minute trip over Lake Te Anau, Lake Manapouri, and the Kepler
Track and longer flights over Doubtful, Dusky, and Milford sounds.
✉ *Box 222, Te Anau,* ☎ *03/249–7405,* FAX *03/249–7939.*

HIKING

Information and maps for the plethora of hikes near Te Anau can be
obtained from the **Fiordland National Park Visitor Centre.** ✉ *Lake Front
Dr., Te Anau,* ☎ *03/249–7924,* FAX *03/249–7613.*

En Route   The **Milford Road,** from Te Anau to Milford Sound, winds through deep,
stony valleys where waterfalls cascade into mossy beech forests. The
120-km (75-mi) road starts with a fast 29-km (18-mi) stretch along
the shores of Lake Te Anau to Te Anau Downs. This is where the ferry
leaves for those wishing to hike the **Milford Track.**

Past Te Anau Downs, the road cuts away from the lake and after 20
km (12½ mi) it enters **Fiordland National Park.** On its way to the Divide, some 85 km (53 mi) from Te Anau, the road passes some great
photo-ops at **Mirror Lakes, Knobs Flat,** and **Lake Gunn.** The Divide,
a watershed between rivers flowing both east and west, marks the starting point for the **Routeburn Track,** one of New Zealand's designated
Great Tramps. Four kilometers (2½ miles) past the Divide, the road
passes the turnoff for another fine trail, the **Hollyford Track.** From here
you can take the 3-km (2-mi) walk to **Lake Marion,** which is a good
alternative if you are on a tight schedule and unable to do the more
extensive tramps in the area.

The Milford road continues 4 km (2½ mi) to the **Homer Tunnel.** Work
on the tunnel started in 1935 as a Depression-era government work
project. After the lengthy tunnel, the road descends sharply for 16 km
(10 mi) before reaching the small settlement at Milford Sound. Allow
at least 2½ hours for the trip from Te Anau.

Milford Sound

③⓪   *120 km (75 mi) northwest of Te Anau, 290 km (180 mi) west of
Queenstown.*

Fiordland National Park's greatest appeal and busiest attraction is **Milford Sound,** the sort of overpowering place where poets run out of words
and photographers out of film. Hemmed in by walls of rock that rise
from the waterline sheer up to 4,000 ft, the 13-km-long (18-mi-long)
inlet was carved by a succession of glaciers as they gouged a track to
the sea. Its dominant feature is the 5,560-ft pinnacle of Mitre Peak,

which is capped with snow for all but the warmest months of the year. Opposite the peak, Bowen Falls tumbles 520 ft before exploding into the sea. On a clear day this is a spectacular place. Luxuriant rain forest clings to the sheer precipices that are washed with waterfalls. But Milford Sound is also spectacularly wet: the average annual rainfall is around 20 ft and it rains an average of 183 days a year. In addition to a raincoat you'll need insect repellent—the sound is renowned for its voracious sand flies.

Still, even in heavy rain and storms Milford Sound is magical. Rainfall is so excessive that a coat of up to 20 ft of freshwater floats on top of the surface of the saltwater sound. This creates a unique underwater environment similar to that found at a much greater depth in the open ocean. You can observe this at the **Milford Deep Underwater Observatory,** moored a 15-minute boat ride from Milford at Harrison Cove. From the underwater, windowed gallery you'll see rare red and black coral and a range of deepwater species. The observatory is open year-round. The 30-minute visit and round-trip boat trip from Milford take about one hour and cost $35.

For more information on exploring the Milford Sound on boat cruises, scenic flights, and kayak trips, *see* Outdoor Activities and Sports, *below.*

★ If you plan to walk the **Milford Track**—a wholly rewarding, four-day bushwalk through Fiordland National Park—understand that it is one of New Zealand's most popular hikes. The 53-km (31-mi) track is strictly one-way, and because park authorities control access, you can feel as though you have the wilderness more or less to yourself. Independent and guided groups stay in different overnight huts. Be prepared for rain and snow, but also for what many call the finest walk in the world. This is still wild country, largely untouched by humanity. Mountains rise vertically for several thousand feet out of valleys carved by glaciers. Forests tower above you, and myriad cascading waterfalls plunge into angry, fast-flowing rivers.

To hike independent of a tour group, call the **Fiordland National Park Visitor Centre** (✉ Box 29, Te Anau, ☎ 03/249–8514, 🖷 03/249–8515) and book well in advance—up to a year if you plan to go in December or January. Freedom walking, without a guide, requires that you bring your own food, utensils, and bedding. You stay in clean, basic Department of Conservation huts and you can fish along the way for trout if you have a license. The cost is $210 for three nights in the huts and the fare for the ferry rides to and from the trailheads.

Going with a guide requires deep pockets (the service costs $1,590, $1,490 in low season) and provides comfortable beds and someone who does the cooking. Food and wine are flown in by plane or helicopter to the remote lodgings, which are equipped with generators to provide electric power. Trampers enjoy quality meals, hot showers, and evening entertainment including books and games in spacious lounge rooms. As meals and bed linen are provided, guided walkers need not carry a lot of gear. The guided tramp package ends with a night's accommodation at **Mitre Peak Lodge** in Milford Sound and a cruise on Milford Sound the next day. Also included in the fee is transport to and from Queenstown. Book your guided walk with **Milford Track Guided Walk New Zealand** ✉ *Box 259, Queenstown,* ☎ *03/441–1138,* 🖷 *03/441–1124.* ✍

The trailheads for the track are remote. Both guided and unguided walks begin with a two-hour ferry ride from Glade Wharf on Lake Te Anau and end with a ferry taking you from Sandfly Point over to the Milford Sound dock. Because of the good condition of the track, the walk

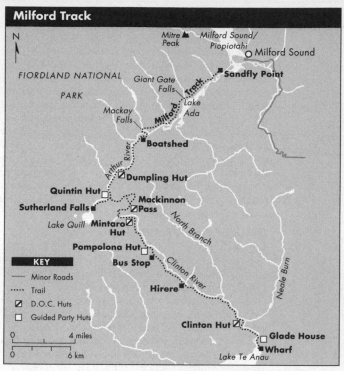

Milford Track

is rarely demanding. Much of the first days's shortish hike to the Clinton Hut entails walking along river valleys through lovely beech forests. The second day's four- to five-hour hike to the Minataro hut is also mostly easy, but the crossing of the Mackinnon Pass on the third day can be a challenge. It involves a steady climb and then a rapid descent, some of it on a lengthy, wooden staircase, past roaring rivers and waterfalls. The view from the Mackinnon Pass, however, is stunning. Also on day three, be sure to take the detour at Quintin Hut to view the world's fifth-highest waterfall, Sutherland Falls, which plunges 1,900 ft in three leaps. It's possible to walk behind the curtain of water as the waterfall reaches the valley floor, a truly unforgettable experience. Your last day entails the lengthy 21-km (13-mi) hike from Quintin Lodge to the track end at Sandfly Point. It requires an early start, but this last leg provides a glorious finale, since—especially after a rain—Arthur River and the many waterfalls flow abundantly.

Because the track is often blocked by snow in winter, there is a restricted hiking season from November until mid-April.

Lodging

Accommodations are scant at Milford Sound, and it's best to stay in Queenstown or Te Anau and make your visit a very long day trip. A pleasant alternative is to reserve on one of the overnight cruises (☞ Outdoor Activities and Sports, *below*).

$$$$ 🏨 **Mitre Peak Lodge.** This hotel's primary function is to serve walkers on Milford Track Guided Walk New Zealand (☞ Guided Tours *in* Southland A to Z, *below*), who sleep here on the final night of their hike. If the guided walk has a full quota of trampers, the hotel is full. Staff only knows if rooms will be available three days in advance, so this is only a spontaneous option. You can't count on staying here. Still, with its views of Milford Sound and surrounding mountains, the lodge

offers one of the finest views from a hotel lounge in all of New Zealand. Rates include a four-course dinner with a bottle of wine and continental breakfast. ⊠ *Milford Sound,* ☎ *03/249–7907,* ℻ *03/249–9240. 30 rooms. Restaurant, bar, coin laundry. AE, DC, MC, V. MAP.*

$ 🏠 **Milford Sound Lodge.** Just 1 km (½ mi) out of the Milford settlement, off the main Milford–Te Anau road, this backpacker hostel offers very basic accommodations, though new owners David Kluken, Amanda Simper, and Mike and Jackie McConachie are busy upgrading the lodge. The range of accommodations includes twin and double units with linen for $45 a person, four-person bunk rooms at $20 per bed, and dormitories for 6 to 12 people at $18 a bed. All bathrooms are shared though there are plans to add private bathrooms to the twin and double units. The lodge serves inexpensive breakfast and dinner or people can cook for themselves in the on-site kitchen. ⊠ *Milford Sound,* ☎ *03/249–8071,* ℻ *03/249–8075. 23 rooms without bath. Restaurant, coin laundry. MC, V. MAP.*

Outdoor Activities and Sports

CRUISING

The view from the water is mind-bendingly beautiful, which accounts for the popularity of **cruising** here. It's essential to book ahead between mid-December and March. Day cruises generally last 1½–3 hours, cost around $45, and usually go out to the Tasman Sea, stopping at waterfalls along the way. Some include a visit to the **Underwater Observatory** (☞ *above*). All boats leave from the Millford wharf area. If you can, avoid the midday sailings as they link with tour buses and are most crowded. The two main companies, **Red Boat Cruises** and **Fiordland Travel** (☞ Guided Tours *in* Southland A to Z, *below*), run over a dozen cruises a day, between them, in the summertime.

Fiordland Travel's (☞ Guided Tours *in* Southland A to Z, *below*) overnight cruises on the *Milford Wanderer,* an attractive replica of an old trading scow, take up to 70 passengers. The more intimate MV *Friendship* takes 14 passengers. On top of the usual sightseeing on the sound, the boats offer kayaking, shore visits, and swimming. Staff on board try hard to create an atmosphere of down-to-earth Kiwi hospitality with barbecues, onboard games, and anecdotes about the history of the sound and its wildlife. Rates for berths start at $120. The boats leave Milford wharf at 5 PM and return by 9 AM.

Red Boat Cruises (☞ Guided Tours *in* Southland A to Z, *below*) offers a more luxurious overnight cruise on the *Red Boat Lady of the South Pacific,* a large double-decker catamaran. The comfortable berths cost from $129 to $199.

KAYAKING

Milford Sound Kayaks offers guided kayaking on the sound that includes a hike along part of the Milford track. Prices range from $49 to $79 per person. No experience is required. ⊠ *Box 19, Milford Sound,* ☎ *0800/476–726 in N.Z. only,* ℻ *03/249–7695.* ✆

SCENIC FLIGHTS

You can avoid the four-hour bus journey from Queenstown to Milford by taking a "flightseeing" option. This combines a round-trip flight from Queenstown to Milford with a scenic cruise. Flights are weather-dependent and should be booked through **Fiordland Travel** (☞ Guided Tours *in* Southland A to Z, *below*).

Southland A to Z

Arriving and Departing

From Queenstown, **Newmans** (☎ 03/442–8238) runs into Milford Sound. **InterCity** (☎ 03/442–8238) buses also go to Nelson via the West Coast glaciers and run daily to Christchurch, Mt. Cook, and Dunedin.

Hazlett Tours (☎ 03/442–0099) runs service from Queenstown to Invercargill.

Highway 6 enters Queenstown from the West Coast; driving time for the 350-km (220-mi) journey from Franz Josef is eight hours. From Queenstown, Highway 6 continues south to Invercargill—a 190-km (120-mi) distance that takes about three hours to drive. The fastest route from Queenstown to Dunedin is via Highway 6 to Cromwell, south on Highway 8 to Milton, then north along Highway 1, a distance of 280 km (175 mi), which can be covered in five hours.

Queenstown is linked with Auckland, Christchurch, Rotorua, and Wellington by both **Ansett New Zealand** (☎ 03/442–6161) and **Air New Zealand Link** (☎ 03/442–7650), which also flies several times daily to Mt. Cook. Queenstown Airport is 9 km (5½ mi) east of town. The **Johnston's Shuttle Express** (☎ 03/442–3639) meets all incoming flights and charges $6 per person to hotels in town. The taxi fare is about $15.

Contacts and Resources

Dial 111 for **fire, police, and ambulance** services.

The **Double Decker** (☎ 03/442–6067) is an original London bus that makes a 2½-hour circuit from Queenstown to Arrowtown and the bungy-jumping platform on the Karawau River. Tours ($27) depart Queenstown daily at 10 and 2 from the Mall.

Fiordland Travel has a wide choice of fly-drive-cruise tour options to Milford and Doubtful sounds from Queenstown, Te Anau, and Milford. ⊠ *Lake Front Dr., Te Anau,* ☎ *03/249–7416,* 𝔽𝔸𝕏 *03/249–7022* or ⊠ *Steamer Wharf, Queenstown,* ☎ *03/442–7500.* ✆

Outback New Zealand has fascinating safaris into Skippers Canyon (28 km/18 mi north of Queenstown) and farther afield. Owner-operator David Gatward-Ferguson is knowledgeable about the area and is not afraid to debunk some of the local gold rush days' legends. The Skippers trip ends at the Skippers settlement, schoolhouse, and cemetery and includes a morning or afternoon tea at this historic setting. The straightforward tour costs $55, but you can add on helicopter rides, bungy jumping, rafting, and jet-boat rides at an extra cost. ⊠ *Box 341, Queenstown,* ☎ *03/442–7386,* 𝔽𝔸𝕏 *03/442–7346.*

Milford Track Guided Walk New Zealand provides guided walks on the Milford Track. The walk costs $1,590 and $1,490 in the low season. ⊠ *Box 259, Queenstown,* ☎ *03/441–1138,* 𝔽𝔸𝕏 *03/441–1124.* ✆

Red Boat Cruises offers day and overnight cruises on Milford Sound. The comfortable berths cost from $129 to $199. ⊠ *Milford Sound,* ☎ *03/441–1137,* 𝔽𝔸𝕏 *03/441–1197.* ✆

The **TSS *Earnslaw*** is a vintage lake steamer that has been restored to brassy, wood-paneled splendor and put to work cruising Lake Wakatipu from Queenstown. A lunch cruise, an afternoon cruise across the lake to a sheep station, and a dinner cruise are available from July through May. ✉ *Steamer Wharf, Queenstown,* ☎ *03/442–7500.*

Fiordland National Park Visitor Centre. ✉ *Box 29, Te Anau,* ☎ *03/ 249–7921.* ◷ *Dec. 26–Jan., daily 8–8; Feb.–Mar. and Oct.–Dec. 24, daily 8–6; Apr.–Sept., daily 9–4:30.*
Queenstown Visitor Information Centre. ✉ *Clocktower Centre, Shotover and Camp Sts.,* ☎ *03/442–4100.* ◷ *Daily 7–7.*

DUNEDIN AND OTAGO

The province of Otago stretches southeast of Queenstown to the Pacific. Flatter than Southland—as most of the world is—it looks more like parts of North Island. Its capital, Dunedin (dun-*ee*-din), is one of the unexpected treasures of New Zealand: a harbor city of steep streets and prim Victorian architecture, with a royal albatross colony on its doorstep. Invercargill is the southern anchor of the province, essentially a farm service community and for visitors a gateway to Fiordland or a stopover on the way to Stewart Island (☞ *below*).

Dunedin

③ *280 km (175 mi) east of Queenstown, 362 km (226 mi) south of Christchurch.*

Clinging to the walls of the natural amphitheater at the west end of Otago Harbour, South Island's second-largest city is blessed with inspiring nearby seascapes and wildlife. Its considerable number of university students give the city a vitality far greater than its population of 120,000 might suggest. And its size makes it easy to explore on foot.

Dunedin is the Gaelic name for Edinburgh, and the city's Scottish roots are evident. It was founded in 1848 by settlers of the Free Church of Scotland, a breakaway group from the Presbyterian Church. Today it has the only kilt shop in the country and the only whiskey distillery— and a statue of Scottish poet Robert Burns. The city prospered mightily during the gold rush of the 1860s. For a while it was the largest city in the country, and the riches of the Otago goldfields are reflected in the bricks and mortar of Dunedin's handsome Victorian townscape, most notably in the Italianate **Municipal Chambers** building.

The **Octagon,** at the center of town, is the city's hub. The **statue of Robert Burns** sits in front of the cathedral. On Stuart Street at the corner of Dunbar, take notice of the late-Victorian **Law Courts.** Above the Stuart Street entrance stands the figure of Justice, scales in hand but without her customary blindfold (though the low helmet she wears probably has the same effect).

One wonders how the city survived without the **Dunedin Public Art Gallery** until 1996, when it opened. Natural light streams into the glass ceiling foyer, which forms the heart of the multilevel complex. Native-wood parquet flooring and handcrafted wrought iron give a modern and spacious feel to the galleries. The collection includes old masters such as Turner and Gainsborough and a work by impressionist Claude Monet. New Zealand and Otago artists are well represented and the gallery has a reputation for innovative contemporary shows. ✉ *30 The Octagon,* ☎ *03/474–3450.* ✍ *Free.* ◷ *Weekdays 10–5, weekends 11–5.*

The **Dunedin Railway Station,** a cathedral to the power of steam, is a massive bluestone structure in Flemish Renaissance style, lavishly decorated with heraldic beasts, coats of arms, nymphs, scrolls, a mosaic floor, and even stained-glass windows portraying steaming locomotives. This extravagant building earned its architect, George Troup, the nickname Gingerbread George from the people of Dunedin and a knighthood from the king. The station has far outlived the steam engine and for all its magnificence receives few trains these days. ⊠ *Anzac Ave. at Stuart St.* ⊘ *Daily 7–6.*

The **First Presbyterian Church** on the south side of Moray Place is perhaps the finest example of a Norman Gothic building in the country. The **Otago Early Settlers Museum** preserves an impressive collection of artifacts, from the years when this was a whaling station, to the days of the early Scottish settlers, to the prosperous gold-rush era of the late-19th century. ⊠ *220 Cumberland St.,* ☎ *03/477–5052.* ⊡ *$4.* ⊘ *Weekdays 10–5, weekends 1–5.*

The **Otago Museum** is housed in an 1877 Victorian building. Because natural light was the only way to enhance such displays in the 19th century, most museums of this era had huge skylight windows. This museum also has a restored, magnificent kauri-timbered gallery. The museum's first curator, Captain F. W. Hutton, was a zoologist and many of the original animals collected from 1868 are still on display. You'll find a substantial collection of articulated moa skeletons, the eye of a humpback whale, and a large number of Maori artifacts. The Maritime Hall has an extensive collection of ship models and nautical objects on display. ⊠ *419 Great King St.,* ☎ *03/477–2372,* ⨍⨍ *03/477–5993.* ⊡ *$4.* ⊘ *Weekdays 10–5, weekends 12–5.*

The 35-room Jacobean-style **Olveston** mansion was built between 1904 and 1906 for David Theomin, a wealthy businessman and patron of the arts who amassed a handsome collection of antiques and contemporary furnishings. The house and its furnishings are undoubtedly a treasure from an elegant age, but, apart from some paintings collected by Theomin's daughter, there is very little in it to suggest that it's in New Zealand. Even the oak staircase and balustrade were prefabricated in England. The one-hour guided tour is recommended. ⊠ *42 Royal Terr.,* ☎ *03/477–3320.* ⊡ *$10.* ⊘ *Daily 9–5; tour daily at 9:30, 10:45, noon, 1:30, 2:45, and 4.*

Dining and Lodging

$$$ ✕ **Bellpepper Blues.** One of the country's most respected chefs, Michael Coughlin uses flair and time-honed skills to craft dishes that regularly win him major awards. Cervena (venison) is seared and served warm over a salad of *masala* (Indian spice)-dusted new potatoes, butternut squash is partnered with roasted bell peppers in a soup that is served with an herb-filled empanada, and farmed salmon is oven-roasted and drizzled with a salsa of lemon, tomato, and Italian parsley. The setting, inside a converted pub, is casual and attractive. ⊠ *474 Princes St., Dunedin,* ☎ *03/474–0973. AE, DC, MC, V. Closed Sun. No lunch.*

$$$ ✕ **Ombrello's.** Clever design means diners can eat in a sheltered courtyard between two cottages at this popular eatery. The menu is of the usual Mediterranean-leaning modern New Zealand stripe, presenting dishes like a layered tower of eggplant and bell pepper with mozzarella and arugula, or a roasted half chicken on couscous with sweet and sour onions and raisins. Several pasta dishes are also available. ⊠ *10 Clarendon St.,* ☎ *03/477–8773. AE, DC, MC, V. Closed Mon. No dinner Sun.*

$$$ ✕ **Restaurant Ninety Five.** This restaurant has had a few owners over the years, but it's as good now as it has even been. The chef is French, and traditional dishes make regular appearances on the frequently changed menu. Mostly, though, the menu appeals to modern preferences with combinations like panfried baby snapper with scallops in

a soy dressing, or lamb rump on a mesclun salad, served with new potatoes and a red pepper coulis. ⊠ *95 Filleul St.,* ☎ *03/471–9265. AE, DC, MC, V. Closed Sun. No lunch.*

$$–$$$ ✕ **Abalone.** A superlong bar dominates this quirkily decorated restaurant, but the emphasis is as much on food as ingestion of the more liquid kind. And it's not only the decor that's quirky—recent menus have seen grilled salmon fillet served with rosemary potatoes and caramelized eggplant, cervena (venison) medallions with a beet sauce on crispy noodles, and lamb rumps with ratatouille and a blue cheese crepe. Staff members are hearteningly adept at making wine recommendations for specific dishes. ⊠ *44 Hanover St.,* ☎ *03/477–6877. AE, DC, MC, V. Closed Sun. No lunch Sat.*

$$–$$$ ✕ **Two Chefs.** With terra-cotta walls, polished wooden flooring, and a log fire, this restaurant has a cozy, intimate feel. The food, from Helen Mason and Grant Cockroft, is some of the best in Dunedin. Blue swimmer crabs are partnered with shaved coconut and chilli crisps; meaty venison ribs are accompanied by a shiitake mushroom pie, and drizzled with a Szechuan pepper glaze. ⊠ *428 George St.,* ☎ *03/477–9117. AE, DC, MC, V. Closed Sun. No lunch.*

$$ ✕ **Palms Cafe.** Vegetarians and meat-eaters are both served well at this casual café with views over Queens Gardens. The menu changes regularly and around half of the dishes contain meat. Recent listings have included an eggplant and vegetable curry, and kumara, hazelnuts, and pineapple in phyllo pastry, served on a pile of spiced vegetables. Carnivores are kept happy with dishes like beef bayou—a tenderloin served with Portuguese sausage and red onion sauce. The restaurant, which is no-smoking, is open nightly for dinner and for lunch depending on reservations. ⊠ *84 Lower High St.,* ☎ *03/477–6534. AE, DC, MC, V.*

$$$$ ✕🏠 **Southern Cross Hotel.** Originally named the Grand Hotel and built in 1883, this hotel was then considered one of the finest guest houses in the southern hemisphere. It has hosted the Queen of England, the Beatles, and a long line of English and New Zealand prime ministers. Today, although it has been completely refurbished and modernized, much of the ornate Victorian architecture and detail is still in evidence, not least in the recently created, multimillion-dollar casino. Even if you don't want to gamble, it's well worth walking up the sweeping ornate staircase to ogle the chandeliers, the opulent gold and red furnishings, and the ornate plaster ceilings. The Otago scallops are excellent at the hotel's **Carlton Restaurant,** as are the central Otago wines. The 24-hour **Deli-Cafe** makes healthy snacks, smoothies, and comfort food when you've opted to stay in. But going out is easy, since you're in the heart of the city, just minutes from galleries, theaters, and shopping. ⊠ *Princess and High Sts.,* ☎ *03/477–0752,* ℻ *03/477–5776. 144 rooms, 8 suites. 3 restaurants, 2 bars, health club, casino. AE, DC, MC, V.*

$$$ 🏠 **Lisburn House.** Listed with the Historic Trust, this Victorian-Gothic
★ inn is a romantic and stately retreat set amid lovingly tended gardens. Many of its 1865 details are intact, such as the decorative Irish brickwork and fishtail slate roof tiles. Inside, there are high, molded plaster ceilings, a marble floored foyer, an impressive turn-of-the-20th-century stained-glass entrance, and a welcoming fireplace. The three spacious bedrooms are sumptuous affairs, each with beautiful four-poster queen beds and fine linen. You'll have a delicious breakfast on fine china in the stately dining room. ⊠ *15 Lisburn St., Caversham,* ☎ *03/455–8888,* ℻ *03/455–6758. 3 rooms. Dining room, lounge, in-room VCRs. AE, DC, MC, V. BP.*

$$ 🏠 **Hulmes Court Bed & Breakfast.** Housed in an 1860 home, built for one of the founders of the Otago Medical School, this B&B is comfortable, gracious, affordable, and friendly. A hearty continental break-

fast is served in the large drawing room that also doubles as a guest lounge. It's just a short walk to the center of town. Children are welcome, and there is a resident cat named Solstice. ⊠ *52 Tennyson St.,* ☎ *03/477–5319,* FAX *03/477–5310. 6 rooms. Lounge, mountain bikes. AE, DC, MC, V. BP.* ◈

The Arts

The **Marshall Seifert Gallery** (⊠ 1 Dowling St., ☎ 03/477–520) is housed in an turn-of-the-20th-century, triangular-shape building with a dizzying spiral staircase. It's literally overflowing with rare and collectible fine art, antiques, prints, and contemporary New Zealand art. Marshall Seifert is a former sports television broadcaster, who readily admits to being more interested in collecting than running the business.

Milford Galleries (⊠ 18 Dowling St., ☎ 03/477–8275) is the largest fine art dealer gallery in New Zealand. The gallery carries the work of every major New Zealand artist including the large-scale abstract expressionist paintings of Neil Frazer and Elizabeth Rees's telling oil studies of New Zealand machismo. Also represented are Colin McCahon, Para Matchitt, and Dunedin-based Ralph Hotere. Ask about the gallery's lectures on New Zealand art history.

En Route If you're driving along the coast north of Dunedin, the **Moeraki Boulders** are good to stop and gawk at for a while. These giant spherical rocks are concretions, formed by a gradual buildup of minerals around a central core. Some boulders have sprung open, revealing—no, not alien life forms—interesting calcite crystals. The boulders populate the beach north of the town of Moeraki and south as well at Katiki Beach off Highway 1, about 60 km (37 mi) above Dunedin, or 40 km (25 mi) south of Oamaru.

Otago Peninsula

The main areas of interest on the claw-shape peninsula that extends northeast from Dunedin are the albatross colony and Larnach Castle. On the return journey to Dunedin, the Highcliff Road, which turns inland at the village of Portobello, is a scenic alternative to the coastal Portobello Road. Allow an hour to drive from the city.

㉜ Set high on a hilltop with commanding views from its battlements, **Larnach Castle** is the grand baronial fantasy of William Larnach, an Australian-born businessman and politician. The castle was a vast extravagance even in the free-spending atmosphere of the gold rush. Larnach imported an English craftsman to carve the ceilings, which took 12 years to complete. The solid marble bath, marble fireplaces, tiles, glass, and even much of the wood came from Europe. The mosaic in the foyer depicts Larnach's family crest and the modest name he gave to his stately home: the Camp. Larnach rose to a prominent position in the New Zealand government of the late 1800s, but in 1898, beset by a series of financial disasters and possible marital problems, he committed suicide in Parliament House. (According to one romantic version, Larnach's third wife, whom he married at an advanced age, ran off with his eldest son; devastated, Larnach shot himself.) A café in the castle ballroom serves Devonshire teas and light snacks. There are 35 acres of grounds around the castle that include a rhododendron garden; a rain forest garden with kauri, rimu, and *totara* trees; statues of *Alice in Wonderland* characters; an herbaceous walk; and a plant shop. ⊠ *Camp Rd.,* ☎ *03/476–1616.* ⊠ *$10.* ☉ *Daily 9–5.*

㉝ **Taiaroa Head,** the eastern tip of the Otago Peninsula is the site of a breeding colony of royal albatrosses. Among the largest birds in the world, with a wingspan of up to 10 ft, they can take off only from steep slopes with the help of a strong breeze. Except for here, at Taiaroa Head, and at the Chatham Islands to the east, the birds are found only on windswept islands deep in southern latitudes, remote from human habitation. Under the auspices of the **Trust Bank Royal Albatross Centre,** the colony is open for viewing from October through August, with the greatest number of birds present shortly after the young hatch around the end of January. Between March and September parents leave the fledglings in their nests while they gather food for them. In September, the young birds fly away, returning about eight years later to start their own breeding cycle. From the visitor center you go in groups up a steep trail to the Albatross Observatory, from which you can see the birds through narrow windows. They are only rarely seen in flight. Access to the colony is strictly controlled, and you must book in advance. ⊠ *Taiaroa Head, Dunedin,* ☎ *03/478–0499.* 🎟 *1½-hr tour (including fort) $27, 1-hr tour (excluding fort) $22.* ☉ *Nov.–Mar., daily 9– dusk; Apr.–Oct., daily 10–dusk; tours late Nov.–Aug., daily 10:30–4, every ½ hr in summer, hourly in winter.*

In the same area as the colony is the **"Disappearing" Gun at Fort Taiaroa,** a 6-inch artillery piece installed during the Russian Scare of 1888. When the gun was fired, the recoil would propel it back into its pit, where it could be reloaded out of the line of enemy fire. The gun has been used in anger only once, when it was fired across the bow of a fishing boat that had failed to observe correct procedures before entering the harbor during World War II. ⊠ *Taiaroa Head, Dunedin,* ☎ *03/478–0499.* 🎟 *$12.*

If you'd like to observe the world's most endangered penguin in its natural habitat, visit the **Yellow-Eyed Penguin Conservation Reserve,** where a network of tunnels have been disguised so you can get up close to this rare and protected species. Experienced guides will interpret the birds' behavior and seasonal habits as you creep through the tunnels. ⊠ *Harrington Point, Dunedin,* ☎ *03/478–0286,* 🖷 *03/478–0257.* 🎟 *$25.* ☉ *Daily 9–5.*

Lodging

$–$$$$ 🏨 **Larnach Lodge.** It's hard to beat this setting—panoramic sea views,
★   35 acres of gardens and grounds to stroll in, the Larnach Castle next door to explore, and astounding luxury theme suites. The Scottish Room is fitted with deep red wallpaper that sets off classic tartan bedcovers and curtains, heavy brass bedsteads, and a Robbie Burns rug. The Enchanted Forest Room's enchanting feature is 1879 William Morris wallpaper. Breakfast is served in the former stables, and lunch or dinner can be arranged at the castle. Very affordable rooms with shared facilities are available in the converted 1870 coach house. ⊠ *Camp Rd., Otago Peninsula, Dunedin,* ☎ *03/476–1616,* 🖷 *03/476–1574. 12 rooms. AE, DC, MC, V.* 🐾

En Route   The **Southern Scenic Route** is 215 km (135 mi) of mostly paved road that stretches from Balclutha, south of Dunedin, through the Catlins— known for its stands of native forest and glorious coastline—on through Invercargill to Milford Sound in Fiordland. Pick up a Southern Scenic Route Brochure at the Dunedin visitor center if you want to explore all or part of this spectacular route.

Invercargill

🔟 *182 km (115 mi) south of Queenstown, 190 km (120 mi) southwest of Dunedin.*

Originally settled by Scottish immigrants, Invercargill has retained much of its turn-of-the-last-century character, with a broad main avenue and streetscapes with richly embellished buildings. You'll find Italian and English Renaissance styles, Gothic stone tracery, and Romanesque designs in a number of well-preserved buildings. The city also has botanic gardens. The pyramid-shape **Southland Museum and Art Gallery** (⊠ 108 Gala St., ☎ 03/218–9753) houses the largest public display of live tuatara—New Zealand's extremely rare, ancient lizard. It has also established the world's most successful captive breeding program.

Dining and Lodging

$$$ ✕ **Donovan's.** If you've ever dreamed of going back in time, here's your chance. Donovan's is built in a restored Edwardian home, and the dining areas are spread through six rooms, each with its original ambience. Fortunately, the kitchen is pure new-century. Fingers of chicken meat are served with a roasted plum and tomato chilli jam, and pork loin is sliced and draped over honey-mustard greens, accompanied by a kumara and green pea puree, and drizzled with mango-bourbon sauce. ⊠ *220 Bainfield Rd.,* ☎ *03/215–8156. AE, DC, MC, V. Closed Sun.–Mon. No lunch.*

$$–$$$ ✕ **The Rocks.** Exposed brick walls and terra-cotta tiles increase the noise level in this compact suburban eatery, but they add a pleasantly rustic feel. The kitchen makes good use of local seasonal ingredients. Fettuccine is topped with smoked salmon in a creamy sauce. Cervena (venison) is infused with rosemary before being dusted with black pepper and baked, then served with kumara *rösti* (sweet-potato fritters), panfried greens, and a beet-and-red-onion confit. Some combinations crowd the plate, but the flavors are mostly honest and interesting. ⊠ *Courtville Pl. at 101 Dee St.,* ☎ *03/218–7597. AE, DC, MC, V. Closed Sun. No dinner Tues.–Wed. No lunch Sat.*

$$$ ✕🏨 **Ascot Park Hotel.** This large, rambling complex is a welcome sight if you've just battled the rugged, gravel roads of the Catlins. The hotel is the largest in town; its rooms are spacious and modern, and most have recently been refurbished. Service is attentive. The fine on-site restaurant offers traditional New Zealand fare, as well as contemporary cuisine. ⊠ *Tay St. and Racecourse Rd.,* ☎ *03/217–6195,* FAX *03/217–7002. 64 rooms, 24 motel units, 2 suites, 4 studio rooms. Restaurant, bar, pool, hot tub, sauna, exercise room. AE, DC, MC, V.*

$$$ 🏨 **Homestead Villa Motel.** The Homestead's fully self-contained units are spacious and have contemporary furnishings and decor. All have whirlpools. The U-shape motor lodge is a 10-minute walk from the city center and five minutes to Queens Gardens and the Southland Museum and Art Gallery. ⊠ *Avenal and Dee Sts.,* ☎ *03/214–0408 or 0800/ 488–588,* FAX *03/214–0478. 25 units. Kitchenettes, laundry. AE, DC, MC, V.*

Dunedin and Otago A to Z

Arriving and Departing

BY BUS

Dunedin is served by **InterCity** buses (⊠ 205 St. Andrew's St., ☎ 0800/ 664–545 or 03/477–8860).

BY CAR

Driving time along the 280 km (175 mi) between Queenstown and Dunedin (via Highway 6 and Highway 1) is four hours. The main route between Dunedin and Invercargill is Highway 1—a 3½-hour drive. A slower, scenic alternative is along the coast, which adds another 90 minutes to the journey.

BY PLANE

Dunedin is linked with all other New Zealand cities by **Ansett New Zealand** (☎ 0800/800–146 or 03/477–4146) and **Air New Zealand** (☎ 03/477–5769). **Dunedin Airport** lies 20 km (13 mi) south of the city. **Johnston's Shuttle Express** (☎ 03/476–2519), a shuttle service between the airport and the city, meets all incoming flights and charges $10 per person. Taxi fare to the city is about $30.

Contacts and Resources

EMERGENCIES

Dial 111 for **fire, police, and ambulance** services.

GUIDED TOURS

Another way to get to know about the prolific wildlife of this area is to take a boat trip with **Monarch Wildlife Cruises.** Experienced guides help you identify species and interpret their behavior. The hour-long cruise includes visits to the breeding sites of the northern royal albatross, New Zealand fur seals, and three species of shags (cormorants). Depending on the season, you are likely to see sooty shearwaters (mutton birds), blue penguins, variable oyster catchers, and two varieties of gulls. If you are lucky, an albatross will fly over your boat—a spectacular sight with that huge wingspan. ⊠ *Wharf and Fryatt Sts., Dunedin,* ☎ *03/477–4267.* ⊡ *$23 for a 1-hr cruise leaving from Wellers Rock.* ⊙ *Cruises start at 3:20 and 4:30 in summer, 2:10 and 3:20 in winter.*

Twilight Tours offers various minibus tours of Dunedin and its surroundings, including an afternoon tour that focuses on the albatrosses, penguins, and seals of the Otago Peninsula. This is a good way to see the rare yellow-eyed and little blue penguins if you don't have a car. The tour price does not include admission to the albatross colony. Tours depart from the Dunedin Visitor Information Centre (☞ *below*). ⊠ *Box 963, Dunedin,* ☎ *03/474–3300.* ⊡ *$50.* ⊙ *Tour departs Apr.–Oct., daily at 1:30; Nov.–Mar., daily at 2:30.*

VISITOR INFORMATION

Dunedin Visitor Information Centre. ⊠ *48 the Octagon,* ☎ *03/474–3300,* FAX *03/474–3311.* ⊙ *Weekdays 8:30–5, weekends 9–5; extended hrs in summer.* ☜

Invercargill Visitor Information Centre. The center is in the foyer of the Southland Museum and Art Gallery. ⊠ *Victoria Ave., Box 1012,* ☎ *03/214–6243,* FAX *03/218–9753.* ⊙ *Weekdays 9–5, weekends 1–5.*

STEWART ISLAND

The third and most southerly of New Zealand's main islands, Stewart Island is separated from South Island by the 24-km (15-mi) Foveaux Strait. Its original Maori name, Te Punga o Te Waka a Maui, means "the anchor stone of Maui's canoe." Maori mythology says the island's landmass held Maui's canoe secure while he and his crew raised the great fish—the North Island. Today it is more commonly referred to by its other Maori name, Rakiura, which means "the land of the glowing skies"—which refers both to the spectacular sunrises and sunset and to the southern sky's equivalent of the northern lights.

The island covers some 1,700 square km (650 square mi). It measures about 64 km (40 mi) from north to south and about the same distance across at its widest point. On the coastline, sharp cliffs rise from a succession of sheltered bays and beaches. In the interior, forested hills rise gradually toward the west side of the island. Seals and penguins frequent the coast, and the island's prolific bird life includes a number of species rarely seen in any other part of the country. In fact, it is one of the surest places to see the Stewart Island brown kiwi, the largest of New Zealand's kiwis. Unlike its mainland cousins, the Stewart Island brown kiwi can be seen during the day as well as at night. It's a rare and amusing experience to watch these aerodynamically challenged birds scampering about on a remote beach as they feed on sand hoppers and grubs.

Archaeologists' studies of 13th-century Maori middens (refuse heaps) indicate that the island was a rich, seasonal resource for hunting, fishing, and gathering seafood. A commonly eaten delicacy was and, interestingly, still is the *titi,* also known as the sooty shearwater or mutton bird.

In the early 19th century, explorers, sealers, missionaries, and miners settled the island. They were followed by fishermen and sawmillers who established settlements around the edges of Paterson Inlet and Halfmoon and Horseshoe bays. In the 1920s the Norwegians set up a whaling enterprise, and many descendants of these seafaring people remain. Fishing, aquaculture, and tourism are now the mainstays of the island's economy.

Even by New Zealand standards, Stewart Island is remote, raw, and untouched. Roads total about 20 km (13 mi), and apart from the tiny
③⑤ township of Oban at **Halfmoon Bay** on Paterson Inlet, the place is practically uninhabited. The appeal is its seclusion, its relaxed way of life, and—despite the once-busy whaling and lumber-milling industry—its untouched quality.

The smallest playhouse in New Zealand is in Oban. Nikki Davis—self-proclaimed Southland-born lunatic-whose-ego-craves-the-limelight—puts on her one-woman show at the **Gumboot Theatre.** The raving and raved-about *Day in the Life of Stewart Island* parodies four common local activities: fishing, *paua* (abalone) diving, hunting, and the activities of the Stewart Island housewife. A new play called *The Wedding* follows the antics of a Swedish girl who marries a Stewart Islander. In a town that some might mistake for a cultural backwater, this 20-seat theater is small proof that it's alive and fishing. ⊠ *Main Rd.,* ☎ *03/210–1116.* ⊠ *$5.* ☼ *½-hr shows begin running daily at 11 AM.*

③⑥ One of the best spots for bird-watching is **Ulva Island,** a one-hour launch trip around the coast from Halfmoon Bay (☞ Guided Tours *in* Stewart Island A to Z, *below*).

Dining and Lodging

$$ ✕ **Church Hill Cafe Bar.** At this recent addition to Stewart Island, hosts Deanne McPherson and Allan Booth specialize in preparing tantalizing cuisine from the sea's rich bounty. Outdoor dining is recommended, as are reservations. ⊠ *36 Kamihi Rd., Oban,* ☎ *03/219–1323. AE, DC, MC, V.*

$ ✕ **Justcafé.** American Britt Moore has set up her cyber café in paradise. Stop in for great coffee, muffins, quiche, and cold smoked-salmon sandwiches—and surf the net while you nibble and sip. ⊠ *Main Rd., Oban,* ☎ *03/219–1422. No credit cards.*

$$ ✕☷ **South Sea Hotel.** Right in the heart of Oban with views onto Halfmoon Bay, this waterfront hotel has the air of having heard many a fish story, and its bar is a gathering spot for many island residents. Naturally, seafood is the specialty in the restaurant—try fresh blue cod. Or taste the local delicacy, mutton bird. It's not the Ritz, but the staff is welcoming and friendly and modern units have recently been added. ⊠ *Box 25, Oban,* ☎ *03/219–1059,* ᶠᴬˣ *03/219–1120. 17 rooms. AE, MC, V.*

\$\$\$ ⊡ **Port of Call.** Phillippa Fraser-Wilson and Ian Wilson are sixth-generation Stewart Islanders who have opened the doors of their stunningly appointed home to visitors. Overlooking Halfmoon Bay and the Foveaux Strait and just a few minutes' drive from Oban, this modern B&B is surrounded by abundant bird life and beautiful forest. There is an historic 1840 stone house on the property, the second oldest of its kind in New Zealand. Ian provides a water-taxi service and customized trips around the island. ⊠ *Leask Bay Rd., Halfmoon Bay, Oban,* ☏ *03/219–1394,* 𝕱𝕬𝕏 *03/219–1394. 1 room. Lounge. AE, DC, MC, V.*☜

\$\$ ⊡ **Miro Cottage.** Set atop a hill surrounded by bush, this modern, self-contained cottage has room for a family or a group (six maximum) but could equally serve as an intimate hideaway for a couple. Not that you'll be the only inhabitants in this piece of paradise in summertime—native birds such as *tui, kaka* (a native parrot), and the protected *kereru* (wood pigeon) call the surrounding wilderness home, too. Your host, Jan Lequesne, will help you settle in and provide information about activities on the island. The cottage is only a three-minute walk from Oban. ⊠ *Lonnekers Point,* ☏ 𝕱𝕬𝕏 *03/219–1180. 1 cottage. MC, V.*

\$\$ ⊡ **The Nest.** Amid the rambling native bush of Halfmoon Bay appears a B&B right out of the English countryside. Built in 1938, it has typical low ceilings, with exposed beams, mullioned windows, and Canadian wood paneling. Lindsay and Lorraine Squires, born and bred Stewart Islanders, have a commercial fishing background, and they'll gladly help out with information on the island. Bedrooms are furnished in period style, and through the diamond-paned leaded windows are views of Halfmoon Bay. There are also a comfortable guest lounge, a patio, and a beautiful garden. ⊠ *Lonnekers Point, Halfmoon Bay,* ☏ 𝕱𝕬𝕏 *03/219–1310. 2 rooms. MC, V.*

Outdoor Activities

FISHING

For information on deep-sea fishing out of Halfmoon Bay, *see* Chapter 5.

HIKING

A network of walking trails has been established on the northern half of the island, leaving the south as a wilderness area. A popular trek is the **Northern Circuit,** a 10-day walk from Halfmoon Bay that circles the North Coast and then cuts through the interior to return to its starting point. The island's climate is notoriously changeable, and walkers should be prepared for rain and mud. For information on walks, contact the **Department of Conservation** (⊠ Main Rd., Halfmoon Bay, ☏ 03/219–1218).

For a \$995 all-inclusive four-day/five-night guided Kiwi Wilderness Walk of Stewart Island, contact the **Riverton Rock** (⊠ 136 Palmerston St., Riverton, ☏ 03/234–8886, 𝕱𝕬𝕏 03/234–8816).

SEA-KAYAKING

Stewart Island Sea Kayak Adventures. Some of the best and most remote sea-kayaking abounds around Stewart Island. Paterson Inlet is 100 square km (38 square mi) of bush-clad, sheltered waterways, mostly uninhabited. It has 20 islands, four Department of Conservation huts, and two navigable rivers. ⊠ *Innes Dunstan, Innes Backpackers, Argyle St., Oban,* ☏ 𝕱𝕬𝕏 *03/219–1080.*

Stewart Island A to Z

Arriving and Departing

BY BOAT

Stewart Island Marine (☎ 03/212–7660, FAX 03/212–8377) runs the *Foveaux Express* between the island and Bluff, the port for Invercargill. The one-way fare is $42.50. Ferries depart Bluff weekdays at 9:30 and 4 between May and August (winter) and from Monday to Saturday at 9:30 and 5 the rest of the year. On Sunday there is a 5 PM departure only (4 PM in winter). The crossing takes one hour.

BY PLANE

Southern Air (☎ 03/218–9129) has several flights daily between Invercargill and Halfmoon Bay. The scenic 20-minute flight costs $120 round-trip. For the best views ask to sit up front with the pilot. There is also direct service from Dunedin to Stewart Island ($180 round-trip). The free baggage allowance is 15 kilograms (33 pounds) per passenger.

Contacts and Resources

EMERGENCIES

Dial 111 for **fire, police, and ambulance** services.

GUIDED TOURS

For guided, twilight kiwi spotting, a short hike through native bush, and a boat cruise, contact Phillip and Dianne Smith of **Bravo Adventure Cruises** (☎ FAX 03/219–1144). The excursion costs $69 and happens on alternate nights. You'll need sturdy footwear and warm clothing. Bring a flashlight. A reasonable level of fitness is required.

For information and bookings on fishing trips, kiwi spotting, bird-watching trips to Ulva Island, taxis, water taxis, and boat trips around Paterson Inlet, contact **Oban Taxis & Tours.** The company also rents out motor scooters and dive gear and tanks. ⊠ *Box 180, Stewart Island,* ☎ FAX *03/219–1456.*

Want to learn more about aquaculture, visit salmon and mussel farms, or just get a better idea of the fascinating marine life in Stewart Island's waters? **The Seabuzzz Experience** offers one- and two-hour trips in a glass bottom boat. Rates start at $20 per person. ⊠ *Box 91, Stewart Island,* ☎ *03/2191–282,* FAX *03/219–1382.*

Thorfinn Charters' (☎ 03/219–1210) owner Bruce Story has an excellent knowledge of the area's natural and human history. Scenic and historic trips start at $50 per person and guided nature trips from $50 for a half day.

VISITOR INFORMATION

Stewart Island Visitor Information Centre. ⊠ *Main Rd., Halfmoon Bay,* ☎ *03/219–1218.* ⊙ *Weekdays 8–4:30.*

5 ADVENTURE VACATIONS

Bicycling

Canoeing and Sea-Kayaking

Cross-Country Skiing

Diving

Fishing

Hiking and Tramping

Horse Trekking

Rafting

Sailing

By David
McGonigal,
Doug
Johansen, and
Jan Poole

Y OU WILL MISS the most vital part of New Zealand if you don't explore the magnificent outdoors. The mountains and forests in this clean, green land are made for hiking and climbing, the rivers for rafting, and the low-traffic roads for bicycling. The rugged coastline looks wonderful from the deck of a small vessel or, even closer to the water, a sea kayak. And this is the country that invented jet boating.

These activities are commonly split into soft and hard adventures. Hard adventure requires some physical stamina, although you usually don't have to be perfectly fit; in a few cases, prior experience is a prerequisite. In soft adventures the destination is often the adventurous element—you can sit back and enjoy the ride.

With most companies, the adventure guides' knowledge of flora and fauna—and love of the bush—is matched by a level of competence that ensures your safety even in dangerous situations. The safety record of adventure operators is very good. Be aware, however, that most adventure-tour operators require you to sign waivers absolving the company of responsibility in the event of an accident or a problem. Courts normally uphold such waivers except in cases of significant negligence.

You can always choose to travel without a guide, and the material in this chapter complements information in the rest of the book on what to do in different parts of the country. Still, in unfamiliar territory you'll learn more about what's around you by having a knowledgeable local by your side than you could traveling on your own.

Bicycling

Cycling is an excellent way to explore a small region, allowing you to cover more ground than on foot and to observe far more than you would from the window of a car or bus. Cycling rates as hard adventure because of the amount of exercise you get.

New Zealand's combination of spectacular scenery and quiet roads is ideal for cycling. Traditionally, South Island, with its central alpine spine, has been more popular, but Auckland is where most people arrive, and North Island has enough back roads and curiosities—the Waitomo Caves and the coast beyond, the stunning Coromandel Peninsula, and the hot mud pools of sulfurous Rotorua—to fill days. The average daily riding distance is about 60 km (37 mi), and support vehicles are large enough to accommodate all riders and bikes if circumstances so demand. Rides in South Island extend from the ferry port of Picton to picturesque Queenstown, the center of a thriving adventure day-trip industry. New Zealand Pedaltours operates on both islands, with tours of 9–19 days. New Zealand Backroad Cycle Tours has South Island tours of 4–10 days.

Season: October–March.
Locations: Countrywide.
Cost: From $1,150 including lodging, meals, and support vehicle.
Tour Operators: Adventure Center (✉ 1311 63rd St., #200, Emeryville, CA 94608, ☎ 510/654–1879, FAX 510/654–4200); **New Zealand Backroad Cycle Tours** (✉ Box 33–153, Christchurch, ☎ 03/332–1222, FAX 03/332–4030); **New Zealand Pedaltours** (✉ Box 37–575, Parnell, Auckland, ☎ 09/302–0968, FAX 09/302–0967, Info@Pedaltours.co.nz).

Canoeing and Sea-Kayaking

Unlike rafting, where much of the thrill comes from negotiating white water, commercial canoeing involves paddling down gentle stretches of river. Canoeing is soft adventure, as is sea-kayaking, which is excellent in Northland, the Coromandel Peninsula, the Whanganui River area, the top of South Island, Kaikoura, and as far south as Stewart Island.

The tour with Ocean River Adventure Company in the sheltered waters of Abel Tasman National Park provides a waterline view of a beautiful coastline. It allows you to explore otherwise inaccessible golden-sand beaches and remote islands and to meet fur seals on their home surf. When wind conditions permit, paddles give way to small sails, and the kayaks are propelled home by an onshore breeze.

Season: December–May.
Locations: Northland, the Coromandel Peninsula, Whanganui River, Marlborough Sounds, Kaikoura, Abel Tasman National Park, the Southland.
Cost: Around $95 for a one-day tour, $350–$475 for three-day tours.
North Island Tour Operators: Bay of Islands Kayak Co. (✉ Box 217, Russell, ☎ FAX 09/403–7672); **Canoe Safaris** (✉ Box 180, Ohakune, ☎ 06/385–9237); **Mercury Bay Sea Kayaks** (✉ 17 Arthur St., Whitianga, Coromandel Peninsula, ☎ FAX 07/866–2358).

South Island Tour Operators: Fiordland Wilderness Experience (✉ 66 Quinton Dr., Te Anau, ☎ 03/249–7700, FAX 03/249–7768, 🖎); **Marlborough Sounds Adventure Company** (✉ The Waterfront, Box 195, Picton, ☎ 03/573–6078, FAX 03/573–8827, 🖎); **Ocean River Adventure Company** (✉ Main Rd., Marahau Beach, R.D. 2, Motueka, ☎ 0800/732–529 or 03/527–8266, FAX 03/527–8006, 🖎); **Stewart Island Sea Kayak Adventures** (✉ Box 32, Stewart Island, ☎ FAX 03/219–1080).

Cross-Country Skiing

Cross-country skiing is arguably the best way to appreciate the winter landscape, and New Zealand's is spectacular. Going cross-country, you'll get away from the downhill hordes and feel like you have the mountains to yourself. Cross-country skiing is hard adventure—the joy of leaving the first tracks across new snow and the pleasure afforded by the unique scenery of the snowfields is tempered by the fatigue that your arms and legs feel at the end of the day. Multiday tours are arranged so that you stay in lodges every night.

Aoraki (Mt. Cook) and its attendant Murchison and Tasman glaciers offer wonderful ski touring, with terrains to suit all skiers. Tours typically commence with a flight to the alpine hut that becomes your base; from there the group sets out each day for skiing and instruction.

Season: July–September.
Locations: Aoraki, South Island.
Cost: Around $380 for two days, $895 for five days.
Tour Operator: Alpine Recreation Canterbury (✉ Box 75, Lake Tekapo 8770, ☎ 03/680–6736, FAX 03/680–6765, 🖎).

Diving

The Bay of Islands is perhaps New Zealand's best diving location. In the waters around Cape Brett, you can encounter moray eels, stingrays, grouper, and other marine life. Surface water temperatures rarely dip below 60°F. One of the highlights of Bay of Islands diving is the wreck of the Greenpeace vessel *Rainbow Warrior,* which French agents sunk in 1985. It is about two hours from Paihia by dive boat. From September through November, underwater visibility can be affected by a plankton bloom.

The clear waters around New Zealand make for good diving in other areas as well, such as the Coromandel Peninsula, where the Mercury and Aldermen islands have interesting marine life. With Hahei Explorer, dive in the newly created marine reserve or right off the coast. Whangamata, with three islands just off the coast, also has very good diving.

Season: Year-round.
Locations: Bay of Islands and the Coromandel Peninsula.
Cost: Around $135 per day.
Tour Operators: Hahei Explorer (⊠ Hahei Beach Rd., Hahei, Coromandel Peninsula, ☎ 07/866–3532 or 025/424–306); **Knight Diver Tours** (⊠ 30 Whangarei Heads Rd., Whangarei, ☎ 09/436–2584 or 0800/766–756, ℻ 09/436–2758, ✎); **Paihia Dive Hire and Charter** (⊠ Box 210, Paihia, Bay of Islands, ☎ 09/402–7551, ℻ 09/402–7110, ✎).

Fishing

Fishing means different things to different people. For some it is the simple joy of being away from it all in some remote spot, at a stunning beach, or on a beautifully clear river. For others it's the adrenaline rush when a big one strikes, and the reel starts screaming. Still others say it's just sitting on a wharf or a rock in the sun with a line in hand. Fishing in New Zealand is as good as it gets, so don't pass up an opportunity to drop a line in the water.

Most harbor towns have reasonably priced fishing charters available. They are generally very good at finding fish, and most carry fishing gear you can use if you do not have your own. Inland areas usually have streams, rivers, or lakes with great trout fishing, where guides provide their knowledge of local conditions and techniques. With the aid of a helicopter, you can get into places few people have ever seen.

Freshwater Fishing: Trout and salmon, natives in the northern hemisphere, were introduced into New Zealand in the 1860s and 1880s. Rainbow and brown trout in particular have thrived in the rivers and lakes, providing arguably the best trout fishing in the world. Salmon do not grow to the size that they do in their native habitat, but they still make for good fishing. There is free access to all water. You may have to cross private land to fish certain areas, but a courteous approach for permission is normally well received.

The three methods of catching trout allowed in New Zealand are flyfishing, spinning or threadlining, and trolling. In certain parts of South Island using small fish, insects, and worms as bait is also allowed. Deep trolling using leader lines and large capacity reels on short spinning rods is widely done on Lakes Rotoma, Okataina, and Tarawera around Rotorua and on Lake Taupo, with the most popular lures being tobies, flatfish, and cobras. Streamer flies used for trolling are normally the smelt patterns: Taupo tiger, green smelt, ginger mick, Jack Sprat, Parsons glory, and others. Flies, spoons, or wobblers used in conjunction with monofilament and light fly lines on either glass fly rods or spinning rods are popular on all the other lakes.

The lakes in the Rotorua district—Rotorua, Rotoiti, and Tarawera are the largest—produce some of the biggest rainbow trout in the world, which get to trophy size because of an excellent food supply, the absence of competition, and a careful and selective breeding program. In Lake Tarawera, fish from 6 to 10 pounds can be taken, especially in the autumn and winter, when bigger trout move into stream mouths before spawning.

The season around Rotorua runs from October 1 to June 30. In the period between April and June, just before the season closes, flies work very well on beautiful Lake Rotoiti. From December to March fly-fishing is good around the stream mouths on Lake Rotorua. The two best areas are the Ngongotaha Stream and the Kaituna River, using nymph, dry fly, and wet fly. Lake Rotorua remains open for fishing when the streams and rivers surrounding the lake are closed.

Lake Taupo and the surrounding rivers and streams are world renowned for rainbow trout—the lake has the largest yields of trout in New Zealand, an estimated 500 tons. Trolling on Taupo and fishing the rivers flowing into it with a guide are almost surefire ways of catching fish. Wind and weather on the lake, which can change quickly, will determine where you can fish, and going with local knowledge of the conditions on Taupo is essential. The streams and rivers flowing into the lake are open for fly-fishing from October 1 to May 31. The lower reaches of the Tongariro, Tauranga-Taupo, and Waitahanui rivers, and the lake itself, remain open year-round. Lake Waikaremoana in Urewera National Park southeast of Rotorua is arguably North Island's most scenic lake, and its fly-fishing and trolling are excellent.

South Island has excellent rivers with very clear water. Some of them hardly ever see anglers, and that untouched quality is particularly satisfying. South Island's best areas for trout are Marlborough, Westland, Fiordland, Southland, and Otago.

The Canterbury district has some productive waters for trout and salmon—along with the West Coast it is the only part of New Zealand where you can fish for salmon, the quinnat or Pacific chinook salmon introduced from North America. Anglers use large metal spoons and wobblers on long, strong rods with spinning outfits to fish the Waimakariri, Waitaki, Rakaia, Ashburton, and Rangitata rivers around Christchurch, often catching salmon of 20 to 30 pounds.

Trout fishing is normally tougher than in North Island, with trout being a little smaller on average. But occasionally huge browns are caught. You can catch brown and rainbow trout in South Island lakes using flies, or by wading and spinning around lake edges or at stream mouths.

Saltwater Fishing: No country in the world is better suited than New Zealand for ocean fishing. Its coastline—approximately as long as that of the mainland United States—has an incredible variety of locations, whether you like fishing off rocks, on reefs, surf beaches, islands, or harbors. Big-game fishing is very popular, and anglers have taken many world records over the years. All the big names are here—black, blue, and striped marlin, both yellowfin and bluefin tuna, and sharks like mako, thresher, hammerhead, and bronze whaler.

The most sought-after fish around North Island are snapper (sea bream), kingfish, *hapuka* (grouper), *tarakihi*, John Dory, *trevally*, *maomao*, and *kahawai*, to name a few. Many of these also occur around the top of South Island. Otherwise, South Island's main catches are blue cod, butterfish, hake, *hoki*, ling, *moki*, parrot fish, pigfish, and trumpeter, which are all excellent eating fish.

Perhaps the most famous angler to fish New Zealand's waters was adventure novelist Zane Grey, who had his base on Urupukapuka Island in the Bay of Islands. On North Island, the top areas are the Bay of Islands, the nearby Poor Knights Islands, Whangaroa in Northland, the Coromandel Peninsula and its islands, and the Bay of Plenty and White Island off its coast.

Licenses: Different districts in New Zealand for require different licenses. For example, Rotorua is not in the same area as nearby Lake Taupo. So it pays to check at the local fish and tackle store to make sure you are fishing legally. Fees are approximately $50 per year, but at most tackle stores you can purchase daily or weekly licenses. They can also advise you about local conditions, lures, and methods.

Publications: *How to Catch Fish and Where*, by Bill Hohepa, and *New Zealand Fishing News Map Guide*, edited by Sam Mossman, both have good information on salt- and freshwater fishing countrywide.

Season: Generally from October through June in streams and rivers; year-round in lakes and at sea.

Locations: Countrywide.

Cost: Big-game fishing: $800 to $1,200 per day. Saltwater sportfishing: $40 to $60 per half day, depending on how many are on the boat. Heli-fishing: from $495 per person, per day. Trolling and fly-fishing for lake trout: from $75 per hour (one–four people), on rivers and streams from $55 per hour.

North Island Freshwater Operators: Mark Aspinall (✉ Lake Taupo, ☎ 07/378–4453); **Bryan Colman** (✉ Rotorua, ☎ 07/348–7766); **Mark Draper Fishing Outdoors** (✉ Box 445, Opotiki, Bay of Plenty–East Cape, ☎ FAX 07/315–8069, Mark.Draper@xtra.co.nz); **Clark Gregor** (✉ 33 Haumoana St., Rotorua, ☎ 07/347–1730 or 07/347–1123, FAX 07/347–1313 fish@troutnz.co.nz); **Helicopter Line** (Lance Donnelly and Joanne Spencer, ✉ Box 3271, Auckland, ☎ 09/377–4406, FAX 09/377–4597); **Belinda Hewiatt** (✉ Lake Taupo, ☎ 07/378–1471, FAX 07/377–2926); **Chris Jolly Outdoors** (✉ Box 1020, Taupo, ☎ 07/378–0623, FAX 07/378–9458 chrisj@chrisjolly.co.nz); **Taupo Commercial Launchman's Association** (✉ Box 1386, Taupo, ☎ 07/378–3444, FAX 07/377–2926); **Trout Safaris (N.Z.) Ltd.** (✉ 6 Manuariki Ave., Rotorua, ☎ 07/357–4974, FAX 07/357–4974, ✎).

North Island Saltwater Operators: Bream Bay Charters (Steve and Brenda Martinovich, ✉ 59 Bream Bay Dr., Ruakaka, Northland, ☎ 09/432–7484); **Kerikeri Fish Charters** (Steve Butler, ✉ 23 Mission Rd., Kerikeri, Bay of Islands, ☎ 09/407–7165, FAX 09/407–5465); **Land Based Fishing** (✉ Box 579, Kaitaia, Northland, ☎ 09/409–4592); **Ma Cherie** (John Baker, ✉ Bay of Plenty, ☎ 07/307–0015 or 025/940–324); **Mako Charters** (Graeme McIntosh, ✉ Russell Harbour, ☎ FAX 09/403–7770); **MV Taranui** (✉ 17 Pacific Dr., Tairua, Coromandel Peninsula, ☎ 07/864–8511); **Outrigger Charters** (✉ 45 Williams Rd., Paihia, Bay of Islands, ☎ 09/402–6619 or 0800/485–584, FAX 09/402–7273); **Predator** (Bruce and Ann Martin, ✉ Box 120, Paihia, ☎ FAX 09/405–9883); **Sea Spray Charters (N.Z.) Ltd.** (Daryl Edwards, ✉ Box 13060, Tauranga, Bay of Plenty, ☎ 07/572–4241 or 025/477–187); **Seeker** (Ross Mossman, ✉ Hawke's Bay, ☎ 06/835–1397 or 025/442–082); **Te Ra-The Sun** (✉ Whangamata Harbor, Whangamata, Coromandel Peninsula, ☎ 07/865–8681); **Waipounamu Sport Fishing** (John Leins, ✉ Ferry Landing, Whitianga, Coromandel Peninsula, ☎ 07/866–2053, FAX 07/866–5275); **Whangarei Deep Sea Anglers Club** (✉ Box 401, Whangarei, Northland, ☎ 09/434–3818, FAX 09/434–3755).

South Island Freshwater Operators: Alpine Trophies (Dave Hetherington, ✉ Box 34, Fox Glacier, West Coast, ☎ 03/751–0856, FAX 03/751–0857); **Fishing & Hunting Services** (Gerald Telford, ✉ 210 Brownston St., Wanaka, Central Otago, ☎ FAX 03/443–9257); **4 In Fiordland** (Mike Molineux, ✉ 14 Cathedral Dr., Lake Manapouri, Fiordland, ☎ 03/249–8070, FAX 03/249–8470 infiord@ihug.co.nz); **Chris Jackson** (✉ Nelson Lakes district, ☎ 03/545–6416); **Kamahi Tours** (Bill Hayward, ✉ Box 59, Franz Josef, West Coast, ☎ 03/752–0793, FAX 03/752–0699);

Southern Lakes Guide Service (Murray and Margaret Knowles, ✉ Box 84, Te Anau Fiordland, ☎ 03/249–7565, FAX 03/249–8004); **Western Safaris** (Vern Thompson and Maggie Carlton, ✉ 34 McKerrow St., Te Anau, Fiordland, ☎ 03/249–7226); **Wilderness Fly Fishing N. Z.** (Stephen Couper, ✉ Box 149, Wakatipu, Queenstown, Central Otago, ☎ FAX 03/442–3589).

South Island Saltwater Operators: FV *Bounty* (✉ 8 Kotuku Rd., Kaikoura, ☎ 03/319–6682, FAX 03/319–5542, ✍); **Haast Fish and Dive** (✉ Box 58, Haast, West Coast, ☎ 03/750–0004, FAX 03/750–0869); **Kenepuru Tours** (Gary and Ellen Orchard, ✉ Kenepuru Sounds, R.D. 2, Picton, Marlborough Sounds, ☎ FAX 03/573–4203); **Miss Portage Charters** (✉ 144 Wailkawa Rd., Picton, Marlborough, ☎ 03/573–7883); **MV *Spirit of Golden Bay 2*** (✉ Golden Bay Charters, Box 206, Takaka, Golden Bay, ☎ FAX 03/525–9135); **Thorfinn Charters** (Bruce Story, ✉ Box 43, Halfmoon Bay, Stewart Island, ☎ FAX 03/219–1210, ✍).

Hiking and Tramping

There isn't a better place on earth for hiking—called tramping here— than New Zealand. If you're looking for short tramps, you may want to head off on your own. For long treks, however, it can be a big help to go with a guide. The New Zealand wilderness is full of a profusion of interesting flora and fauna that you won't even notice if you're in the country for the first time—unless you have someone along who knows the native bush. Many guides have a humorous streak that can be entertaining as well. Book trips at least three weeks in advance.

Particularly in the peak months of January and February, trails can be crowded enough to detract from the natural experience. One advantage of a guided walk is that companies have their own tent camps or huts, with such luxuries as hot showers—and cooks. For the phobic, it's worth mentioning one very positive feature: New Zealand has no snakes or predatory animals, no poison ivy, poison oak, leeches, or ticks. In South Island, especially on the West Coast, in central Otago, and in Fiordland, be prepared for voracious sand flies—some call it the state "bird." Pick up insect repellent in New Zealand—their repellent repels their insects.

One of the top areas in North Island for hiking and walking is the rugged Coromandel Peninsula, with 3,000-ft volcanic peaks clothed with semitropical rain forest and some of the best stands of the giant kauri tree, some of which are 45 ft around, and giant tree ferns. There is also gold-mining history on the peninsula, and today the flicker of miners' lamps has given way to the steady green-blue light of millions of glowworms in the mines and the forest. Kiwi Dundee Adventures, Ltd., has a variety of hiking trips that cover all aspects of the peninsula, as well as New Zealand–wide eco-walks away from the usual tourist spots.

Tongariro National Park in central North Island has hiking with a difference—on and around active volcanoes rising to heights of 10,000 ft, the highest elevation on the island. It is a beautiful region of contrasts: deserts, forests, lakes, mountains, and snow. Sir Edmund Hillary Outdoor Pursuits Centre of New Zealand guides hikes and more strenuous tramping around Ruapehu, as well as other activities at Turangi at the south end of Lake Taupo.

The three- to six-day walks on the beaches and in the forests of the Marlborough Sounds' Queen Charlotte Walkway and in Abel Tasman National Park (in northern South Island) are very popular, relatively easy, and well suited to family groups: your pack is carried for you, and you stay in lodges. Another option is the Alpine Recreation Canterbury 15-day minibus tour of South Island, with two- to six-hour walks daily along the way. It provides an extensive and scenic cross section, with visits to three World Heritage areas and six national parks and discussions of natural history. Of course, it misses the magic of completing a long single walk.

If you want to get away from the more standard hiking routes, check out the very northwest corner of the South Island, Cape Farewell and the Farewell Spit, the longest naturally occurring sand spit in the world. The area has magnificent coastline and the lush rain forest of the Kahurangi National Park. The Original Farewell Spit Safari leads tours on the 20 km (35 mi) spit.

The most famous New Zealand walk, the Milford Track—a three- to four-day trek through Fiordland National Park—covers a wide variety of terrains, from forests to high passes, lakes, a glowworm grotto, and the spectacle of Milford Sound itself. As the track is strictly one-way (south to north), you rarely encounter other groups and so have the impression that your group is alone in the wild. Independent and escorted walkers stay in different huts about a half day's walk apart. Escorted walkers' huts are serviced and very comfortable; independent walkers' huts are basic, with few facilities. There are other walks in the same area: the Hollyford Track (five days), the Kepler Track (three days), the Greenstone Valley (three days), and the Routeburn Track (three days). Greenstone and Routeburn together form the Grand Traverse.

If you want to get up close and personal with a mountain, Alpine Guides has a renowned seven-day course on the basics of mountaineering around Aoraki, the highest point in the New Zealand Alps. There is also a 10-day technical course for experienced climbers. New Zealand is the home of Sir Edmund Hillary, who, with Tenzing Norgay, made the first ascent of Mt. Everest, in 1953. The country has a fine mountaineering tradition, and Alpine Guides is its foremost training school.

Season: October–March for high-altitude walks, year-round for others.
Locations: Coromandel Peninsula and Tongariro National Park in North Island, Aoraki, Westland, Abel Tasman and Fiordlands National Parks in South Island.
Cost: One- to three-day hikes range from $130 to $950; from $1,490 for the six-day guided Milford Track walk; from $2,600 for 13 days. The climbing school costs $1,650 for seven days, including aircraft access, meals, accommodations, and transportation.
Tour Operators: Abel Tasman Enterprises (✉ 265 High St., Box 351, Motueka, South Island, ☎ 03/528–7801 or 0800/223–582, ℻ 03/528–6087, ✍); **Alpine Guides Ltd.** (✉ Box 20, Mount Cook, South Island, ☎ 03/435–1834, ℻ 03/435–1898); **Alpine Recreation Canterbury** (✉ Box 75, Lake Tekapo, South Island, ☎ 03/680–6736, ℻ 03/680–6765 alprec@voyager.co.nz); **Hollyford Track** (✉ Box 360, Queenstown, Otago, South Island, ☎ 03/442–3760, ℻ 03/442–3761, ✍); **Kiwi Dundee Adventures, Ltd.** (✉ Box 198, Whangamata, Coromandel Peninsula, North Island, ☎ ℻ 07/865–8809, ✍); **Marlborough Sounds Adventure Company** (✉ The Waterfront, Box 195, Picton, South Island, ☎ 03/573–6078, ℻ 03/573–8827); **Milford Track Guided Walk** (✉ Box 259, Queenstown, South Island, ☎ 03/441–1138, ℻ 03/441–1124, ✍); **The Original Farewell Spit Safari** (✉ Box 15, Collingwood, Golden Bay, South Island, ☎ 03/524–8257, ℻ 03/524–8939, ✍); **Routeburn Walk Ltd.** (✉ Box 568, Queenstown, South Island, ☎ 03/442–8200, ℻ 03/442–6072, ✍); **Sir Edmund Hillary Outdoor Pursuits Centre of New Zealand** (✉ Private Bag, Turangi, North Island, ☎ 07/386–5511, ℻ 07/386–0204); **Wild West Adventure Co.** (✉ Clifton Rd., Greymouth, South Island, ☎ 0800/223–456 or 03/768–6649, ℻ 03/768–

9149, ✈); **World Expeditions** (✉ 441 Kent St., 3rd floor, Sydney, New South Wales 2000, ☎ 02/264–3366, FAX 02/261–974).

Horse Trekking

Operators all over New Zealand take people horseback riding along beaches, in native forests, on mountains, and up rivers through pine plantations to all sorts of scenic delights. In North Island, Pakiri Beach Horse Rides & Overnight Safaris north of Auckland, and Rangihau Ranch and the Ace Hi Ranch in the Coromandel Peninsula run trips from several hours to several days.

In South Island, the sweep of the Canterbury Plains around Christchurch—and the surrounding mountain ranges—creates some of New Zealand's most dramatic scenery. One of the best ways to explore the area in some detail is on horseback. Hurunui Horse Treks and Alpine Horse Safaris have a variety of rides, including 8- and 10-day horse treks into remote backcountry in groups of six or fewer, on which you'll stay in rustic huts (without electricity, showers, or flush toilets). The feeling of riding in so much open air, watching the trail stretch to the distant horizon, is unparalleled. Terrain varies from dense scrub to open meadows and alpine passes. In the Nelson area at the top of South Island contact Stonehurst Farm Treks.

Season: October–March.
Locations: Northland, Coromandel Peninsula, Nelson, and Canterbury high country.
Cost: From $135 for a day to $1,675 for eight days.
Tour Operators: Ace Hi Ranch (✉ State Hwy. 25, R.D. 1, Whitianga, Coromandel Peninsula, North Island, ☎ FAX 07/866–4897); **Alpine Horse Safaris** (✉ Waitohi Downs, Hawarden, North Canterbury, South Island, ☎ FAX 03/314–4293); **Hurunui Horse Treks** (✉ Taihoa Downs, R.D. Hawarden, South Island, ☎ 03/314–4204, FAX 03/314–4204, ✈); **Pakiri Beach Horse Rides & Overnight Safaris** (✉ Pakiri Beach, R.D. 2, Wellsford, North Island, ☎ 09/422–6275, FAX 09/522–6277, ✈); **Rangihau Ranch** (✉ Rangihau Rd., Coroglen, Coromandel Peninsula, North Island, ☎ 07/866–3875); **Stonehurst Farm Treks** (✉ R.D. 1, Richmond, South Island, ☎ 03/542–4121, FAX 03/542–3823).

Rafting

The exhilaration of sweeping down into the foam-filled jaws of a rapid is always tinged with fear—white-water rafting is, after all, rather like being tossed into a washing machine. As you drift downriver during the lulls between the white water, it's wonderful to sit back and watch the wilderness unfold, whether it's stately *rimu* or *rata* trees overhanging the stream or towering cliffs with rain forest on the surrounding slopes. Rafting means camping by the river at night, drinking tea brewed over a fire, going to sleep with the sound of the stream in the background, and at dawn listening to the country's wonderful bird music. The juxtaposition of action and serenity gives rafting an enduring appeal that leads most who try it to seek out more rivers with more challenges. Rivers here are smaller and trickier than the ones used for commercial rafting in North America, and rafts usually hold only four to six people. Rafting companies provide all equipment—you only need clothing that won't be damaged by water (cameras are carried in waterproof barrels), a sleeping bag (in some cases), and sunscreen. Rafting qualifies as hard adventure.

In North Island, near Rotorua, the Rangitaiki offers exciting Grade-4 rapids and some good scenery. Nearby, the Wairoa offers Grade 5—the highest before a river becomes unraftable—and the Kaituna River has the highest raftable waterfall in the world: a 21-ft free fall. The Tongariro River flows from between the active 10,000-ft volcanic peaks of Tongariro National Park into the south end of Lake Taupo, New Zealand's largest lake. The Tongariro, as well as the mighty Motu River out toward the East Cape, is great for rafting.

In South Island, the great majority of activity centers on Queenstown. The most popular spot here is the upper reaches of the Shotover River beyond tortuous Skippers Canyon. In winter the put-in site for the Shotover is accessible only by helicopter, and wet suits are essential year-round, as the water is very cold. Some of the rapids are Grade 5. The Rangitata River south of Christchurch is fed by an enormous catchment basin, and rafting is serious at all water levels.

The two-day white-water-and-wilderness Danes trip, down the Landsborough River, flows through Aoraki National Park past miles of virgin forest into some very exciting rapids.

Season: Mainly October–May.
Locations: Rotorua, Taupo, the Canterbury, and Queenstown.
Cost: Around $99 for a half day, $110 for one day, $600 for two days (with helicopter set-down), including all equipment (wet suits, helmets, footwear).
Tour Operators: Challenge Rafting & Queenstown Combos (✉ Box 634, Queenstown, South Island, ☎ 03/442–7318, 🖷 03/441–8563, 🖱); **Kaituna Cascades** (✉ Box 2217, Rotorua, North Island, ☎ 0800/524–8862 or 07/357–5032, 🖷 07/357–4370, 🖱); **Rangitata Rafts** (✉ Peel Forest, R.D. 20, South Canterbury, South Island, ☎ 03/696–3735, 0800/251–251, 🖷 03/696–3534, 🖱).

Sailing

Varied coastline and splendid waters have made sailing extremely popular in New Zealand. Admittedly, your role as a passenger on a commercial sailing vessel is hardly strenuous. You are likely to participate in the sailing of the vessel more than you would on a regular cruise line, but for all intents and purposes this is a soft adventure in paradise. The best sailing areas in New Zealand are undoubtedly from the Bay of Islands south to the Coromandel Peninsula and the Bay of Plenty. This coastline has many islands and a wrinkled shoreline that make for wonderful, sheltered sailing. You can take a piloted launch, or if you have the experience, captain a sailboat yourself.

At the bottom of South Island, Southern Heritage Expeditions uses a Finnish-built, 236-ft, 19-cabin, ice-strengthened vessel, the *Akademik Shokalski,* to explore the islands of the southern Pacific Ocean and beyond to Antarctica, with one short voyage each season (November to mid-March) through the deeply indented coastline of Fiordland. It's a wonderful voyage for wildlife viewing, and you may see royal albatross, Hookers sea lions, elephant seals, and several penguin species.

Season: Year-round.
Locations: Bay of Islands in North Island, lower South Island.
Cost: Bay of Islands from $600 to $725 per night depending on the craft; Doubtful Sound from $1,500 for five days; Fiordland National Park area from $3,050 for eight days; sub-Antarctic islands of Australia and New Zealand from $8,900 for 13 days.

Tour Operators: Moorings Yacht Charters (⊠ 23B Westhaven Dr., West-haven, Auckland; mooring address, ⊠ The Jetty, Opua, Bay of Plenty, North Island, ☎ 09/402–7821, 813/530–5424 reservations in the U.S., FAX 813/530–9747); **Southern Heritage Expeditions** (⊠ Box 6282, Christchurch, South Island, ☎ 03/338–9944, FAX 03/338–3311, ✍); **Straycat Day Sailing Charters** (⊠ Doves Bay Rd., Kerikeri, Bay of Islands, North Island, ☎ 09/407–7342 or 025/96–9944).

6 BACKGROUND AND ESSENTIALS

Maps of New Zealand

Portraits of New Zealand

Books and Videos

Chronology

Smart Travel Tips A to Z

Kiwi and Maori Vocabularies

North Island

Cape Reinga
Kerr Point
Te Kao

NORTH ISLAND

Ninety Mile Beach

Kaitaia
Bay of Islands
Russell

NORTHLAND
Whangarei

Dargaville
Matakohe

Great Barrier Island

Port Jackson
Coromandel

Hauraki Gulf

Coromandel Peninsula
Whitianga
Coroglen
Auckland
Tapu
Tairua
Waiuku
Firth of Thames
Thames
Whangamata
Port Waikato
Cape Runaway
Paeroa
Tauranga
Te Araroa

Te Puke
Bay of Plenty
Hamilton
Cambridge
Whakatane
Opotiki
Raglan
EAST CAPE
Waitomo Caves
Rotorua
Tokomaru Bay
Marakopa
Gisborne
Awakino
UREWERA N.P.
Lake Taupo
Taupo
North Taranaki Bight
TONGARIRO

Tasman Sea

HAWKE'S BAY
New Plymouth
Hawke Bay
Inglewood
TONGARIRO N.P.
Cape Egmont *Egmont*
Mt. Egmont
Stratford
Mt. Ruapehu
Taihape
Napier
Hastings
WANGANUI
Wanganui
Bulls
54
2
Palmerston North
MANAWATU

ABEL TASMAN NATIONAL PARK
WAIRARAPA

Cape Farewell
Farewell Spit
TARARUA FOREST PARK
Waikane
Masterton
Golden Bay
Upper Hutt
Martinborough
KAHURANGI NATIONAL PARK
Tasman Bay
Cook Strait
Lower Hutt
Motueka
★ Wellington
NELSON BAYS
Nelson
Blenheim
Seddon
6
MARLBOROUGH

Cape Foulwind
Murchison
NELSON LAKES FOREST PARK
Kekerengu

Punakaiki
Grey R.
Kaikoura

Greymouth
Hanmer Springs
LAKE SUMMER FOREST PARK

ARTHUR'S PASS N.P.

MT. COOK N.P.
Christchurch
SOUTH PACIFIC OCEAN
Dunedin

KEY
— Rail Lines
N
0   100 miles
0   150 km

THE EDEN DOWN UNDER

I first laid eyes on New Zealand in 1967, near the end of an ocean voyage from Los Angeles to Australia. For a long morning, we skirted the New Zealand coastline north of Auckland, slipping past a land of impossibly green hills that seemed to be populated entirely by sheep. When the ship berthed in Auckland, I saw parked along the quay a museum-quality collection of vintage British automobiles, the newest of which was probably 15 years old. The explanation was simple enough: the alternative would be new imports, and imports were taxed at an enormous rate. But to a teenager fresh from the United States, it seemed as though we had entered a time warp. When we took a day tour into the hills, the bus driver kept stopping for chats with other drivers; in those days it seemed possible to know everyone in New Zealand.

Since then, Auckland has caught up with the rest of the world. Its cellular-phone-toting execs, its waterfront restaurants with sushi and French mineral water, its newly revitalized nightclub scene all exist, unmistakably, in the new millennium. Yet the countryside still belongs to a greener, cleaner, friendlier time. Nostalgia is a strong suit in New Zealand's deck—second, of course, to its incomparable scenery. You'll still find people clinging sentimentally to their Morris Minors, Wolseley 1300s, VW Beetles, or Austin Cambridges—even though inexpensive used Japanese imports have flooded the market in recent years. Some of New Zealand's most notable cultural achievements have been made in conjunction with nature—in the spectacular displays of its gardens, the growing reputation of its wineries, the fascinating lives and artifacts of the Maori (pronounced *moh*-ree), even the respect for nature

shown in its current eco-tourism boom. Auckland, Christchurch, and Wellington may never rival New York, Paris, or Rome, but that's probably not why you're considering a trip to New Zealand. And when you are in the cities, you're likely to find just as much warmth, calm, and graciousness as you will in rural areas.

Humanity was a late arrival to New Zealand. Its first settlers were Polynesians who reached its shores about AD 850, followed by a second wave of Polynesian migrants in the 14th century. These were not carefree, grass-skirted islanders living in a palmy utopia, but a fierce, martial people who made their homes in hilltop fortresses, where they existed in an almost continual state of warfare with neighboring tribes. That fierceness turned out to ensure them more respect from the *Pakeha*—the Maori word for Europeans—than that received by many other native groups around the world in their encounters with colonial powers. The first Europeans to come across New Zealand were on board the Dutch ships of explorer Abel Tasman, which anchored in Golden Bay atop South Island on December 16, 1642. Miscommunication with a local Maori group the next day resulted in the death of four Europeans. The famous Captain James Cook was the next to explore New Zealand, in the 18th century, but it wasn't until the 1840s that European settlers, primarily from England, arrived in numbers.

Compared with other modern immigrant societies such as the United States and Australia, New Zealand is overwhelmingly British—in its love of gardens, its architecture, its political system, and its food. Even so, changes are afoot. Momentum is gathering toward New Zealand becoming a republic, though it would undoubtedly remain within the British Commonwealth. In 1993, the country held a referendum that threw out the "first past the post" electoral system inherited from Westminster, adopting instead a mixed-member proportional (MMP) election, the first of which was held in 1996. This means that each voter now casts two votes, one for a local representative and the other for the party of his or her choice. To govern, a party (or combination of parties) must have at least 50% of the actual vote—not just 50% of parliamentary seats. So rather than being dominated by just two strong parties, with various minor political entities filling out the numbers, New Zealand is now governed by party coalitions. Currently it has a Labour/Alliance party coalition and its prime minister is Helen Clark, the country's second woman PM.

The Maori remain an assertive minority of around 14%, a dignified, robust people whose oral tradition and art bears witness to a rich culture of legends and dreams. That culture comes dramatically to life in performances of songs and dances, including the *haka*, or war dance, which was calculated to intimidate and demoralize the enemy. It's little wonder that the national rugby team performs a haka as a prelude to its games. It would be a mistake, however, to feel that the Maori people's place in New Zealand is confined to history and cultural performances for tourists. They are having considerable impact in a modern political sense, reclaiming lost rights to land, fisheries, and other resources. Former deputy Prime Minister and Treasurer Winston Pe-

ters is a Maori, as are several current government ministers. You'll see Maori who are prominent television newscasters, literary figures, and major athletes, at the same time keeping their cultural traditions alive.

The New Zealand landmass consists of two principal islands, with other outlying islands as well. Most of the country's 3.42 million people live on North Island, and South Island has the lion's share of the national parks (more than one-tenth of the total area has been set aside as parkland). In a country about the size of Colorado—or just slightly larger than Great Britain—nature has assembled active volcanoes, subtropical rain forests, geysers, streams now filled with trout, fjords, beaches, glaciers, and some two dozen peaks that soar to more than 10,000 ft. The country has spectacular scenery from top to bottom, but while North Island often resembles a pristine, if radically hilly, golf course, South Island is wild, majestic, and exhilarating.

Experiencing these wonders is painless. New Zealand has a well-developed infrastructure of hotels, motels, and tour operators—but the best the country has to offer can't be seen through the windows of a tour bus. A trip here is a hands-on experience: hike, boat, fish, hunt, cycle, raft, and breathe some of the freshest air on earth. If these adventures sound a little too daunting, the sheer beauty of the landscape and the clarity of the air will give you muscles you never knew you had.

–Michael Gebicki

FLORA AND FAUNA

New Zealand is a fascinating evolutionary case. Its islands are a chip off the onetime Gonwanaland supercontinent—a vast landmass that consisted of current-day South America, Africa, and Australia that started breaking up some 100 million years ago, well before the evolution of mammals. Since then, floating on its own some 1,200 mi southeast of Australia, this cluster of islands might seem to have developed quietly on its own, away from the hungry predatory jaws of the rest of the world.

But powerful forces of change have been constantly working on New Zealand. Plate tectonics created the rugged, 12,000-plus-ft mountains of South Island. And the Pacific Rim's wild geothermal eruptions left their mark on North Island. For eons volcanic activity has built mountainous cones and laid carpets of ash, making tremendously rich soil for the plant kingdom. The great, rumbling Mt. Ruapehu near Lake Taupo is a living reminder of this subterranean fury.

Global climatic variations haven't spared the islands, either, and on numerous occasions the Antarctic ice cap has edged north from the pole. In these times, glaciers covered South Island and much of North Island, significantly affecting the character of plant life. Some plants adapted, and some couldn't survive. Except for the northern portions of North Island that weren't iced over—interestingly enough the rough extent of New Zealand's glorious kauri trees—after each glacial retreat the country's flora has recolonized the areas previously covered by ice in different ways.

Animals on the islands were, at least until the arrival of humans, almost like living fossils. The only mammal was a tiny bat, and there were no predators until the Maori first came, around AD 700. Bird life included the 12-ft flightless moa, which the Maori hunted to extinction. This happened relatively quickly, because the birds had never needed to develop evasive behavior to stay alive. The Maori brought dogs and rats, and Europeans brought deer, possums, goats, trout, and other fauna, some of which were used for their pelts, others for sport. In almost all cases, the exotic fauna have done tremendous damage to the landscape. And, of course, the human presence itself has dramatically altered the land. Early Maori farming practices involved burning, which reduced a portion of the forests. When Europeans settled the country, they brought sheep, cattle, and the grasses that their livestock needed to eat. And they cut down the forests for, among other uses, ship masts. The kauri served this purpose better than any other wood in the world and paid in numbers for that virtue.

None of this makes the forests that cover New Zealand any less exotic, or any less fascinating. Some plants have adapted growth cycles in which the plant completely changes appearance—lancewood is an example—some of them two or three times until they reach maturity. As a result, botanists at one time believed there to be two or three species where in fact there was only one. If you have never been in a rain forest, the sheer density of vegetation in various subtropical areas will be dazzling. There are species here that exist nowhere else on earth. And keep in mind that one-fifth of the country is set aside as parkland. In those wild woods, you will still find no predators, and native species are alive and well, in many cases making comebacks very dramatic indeed.

Here is a short list of plants and animals that you might encounter in New Zealand.

The New Zealand forest has a different sound than any other, and it's the welcoming, chiming song of the **bellbird,** together with that of the *tui,* that make it unique.

It's a lot easier to get into the grips of a **bush lawyer** plant than out of them. It is a thorny, viny thing that grows in dense forest, climbing in and out of whatever it chooses.

The odd plant clumps fastened to the sides of trees throughout forests are **epiphytes,** not parasites. They grow on the trees but make their own living off water and other airborne particles. Some are orchids, a marvelous sight if you catch them in bloom.

The abundance of **ferns** may be what you most readily associate with the New Zealand bush. Two of the most magnificent are the *mamaku* and the *punga.* The former also goes by the English name black tree fern, and it is the one that grows up to 60 ft tall and is found countrywide, with the exception of the east coast of South Island. The Maori used to cook and eat parts of the plant that are said to taste a bit like applesauce. The punga is shorter than the mamaku, reaching a height of 30 ft. Its English name, silver tree fern, comes from the color of the undersides of the fronds. Their silvery whiteness illuminates darker parts of the bush. The punga is the ferny emblem of New Zealand's international sports teams and Air New Zealand.

The **Hector's dolphin** is rare and confined to New Zealand waters. You might have the luck of seeing one near Kaikoura or off the Banks Peninsula. They have a distinctive rounded fin.

The *horoeka* (also called lancewood) tree is one of the freakish New Zealand natives par excellence. In its youth, its long, serrated, almost woody leaves hardly look alive, hanging down from their scrawny trunk. *Horoekas* inch their way skyward like this for as many as 20 years before maturing, flowering profusely, and bearing black berries.

The towering **kahikatea** (ka-*hee*-ka-tee-ah) is the tallest tree in the country, reaching as high as 200 ft with its slender and elegant profile. A mature tree bears a tremendous amount of berries, which Maori climbers used to harvest by ascending 80 branchless ft and more to pluck. These days wood pigeons are the prime consumers of the fruit.

There are still **kauri** trees in Northland and the Coromandel Peninsula that are as many as 1,500 years old, with a girth of at least 30 ft and height upward of 150 ft. The lower trunks of the trees are branchless, and branches on an old tree begin some 50 ft above the ground. Lumberjacks in the 1800s spared some of these giants, and their presence is awesome. Like so many other native trees, kauris are slow growers—a mere 80-year-old will stand just 30 ft tall. Kauris were valued for their gum as well as their wood. The gum doesn't rot, so balls of gum of any age were usable to make varnish and paint. It is now illegal to cut down a kauri, and as a result the trees are making a solid comeback. Visitors with limited time can see impressive kauri trees in the Waitakere ranges, just west of Auckland, but the oldest and largest examples are in the Waipoua Forest in Northland. The southernmost kauri trees are found just south of Katikati in the Bay of Plenty.

Much is said of the formidable South Island **kea** (kee-ah), a mountain parrot, which, because it has been accused of killing sheep, has in the last century barely escaped extinction. Its numbers are significant today, much to the dismay of campers and anyone who lives under a tin roof. Keas love to play, which means anything from ripping tents to shreds, to clattering around on metal roofs at all hours, to peeling out the rubber gaskets around car windows. They are smart birds, smart enough, perhaps, to delight in taking revenge on those who tried to wipe them out. Observe their behavior keenly; it may be the only way to maintain a sense of humor if harassed.

It takes effort and more than a fair share of luck to spot a **kiwi** in the wild.

These nocturnal, bush-loving birds are scarce and shy, and their numbers had dwindled significantly with the felling of forests over the last 150 years. Predator eradication programs have helped them make a slight resurgence over the last few years. Along with the now-extinct giant moa and other species, the kiwi is one of the remarkable New Zealand natives that live (or lived) nowhere else on earth. If you're keen on seeing one in the feather, plan a trip to Stewart Island and hire a guide to take you on a search, or stop at a wildlife park. Your best chance of sighting one on the North island is to pitch a tent in the Waipoua forest camping ground.

The **mohua** or yellowhead is a small insect-eating bird you'll only find in the forests of the South island and Stewart Island. The bird is easily identifiable from the splash of bright yellow that covers its head and breast. The rest of the body is brown with varying tinges of yellow and olive.

The **manuka** is a small tree shrub found throughout the country in tough impenetrable thickets. Early settlers made a tea from the plant until something tastier came along. The tea tree's white or rosy blossoms attract bees in profusion, and they in turn produce the popular, strong-tasting manuka honey that you can find in stores just about everywhere.

The **nikau palm** is one of the country's most exotic-looking trees, growing to a height of about 30 ft. The Maori used different parts of the leaves both for food and for thatch in shelters.

Phormium tenax, also called New Zealand flax—even though it isn't a true flax, has been used in traditional and contemporary weaving. It favors damp areas and hillsides. Its thick, spiky, dark green leaves originate from a central saddle and can grow to 6 ft. The telltale flower stalk can reach 15 ft and bears dark red flowers. A number of varieties are ornamental and are very popular in New Zealand gardens.

The **pohutukawa** (po-*hoo*-too-*ka*-wa) tree is a sight both for its gnarly roots that like watery places and its red blossoms, which burst forth toward the end of December—hence its Kiwi name: New Zealand's Christmas tree.

Currently about 80 million in number, **possums** are an introduced species that is gobbling up New Zealand forests. Try as they may to get rid of them, Kiwis are having a rough go with the tree dwellers. Their nickname, squash 'ems, comes from seeing so many splayed out on roads throughout the country.

The **pukeka** (poo-*keh*-ka) is a bird that kicks around on farms and roadsides often enough that you're likely to see plenty of them. They're blue, with a red bill, and they stand about 15 inches tall.

You'll get to know the **rangiora** (rang-ee-*ohr*-ah) plant better if you remember it as "bushman's friend"—its soft, silvery underside is the forest's best tissue for your underside.

There are a couple of species of **rata.** The northern rata is a parasite plant, climbing a host tree and eventually cutting off its light and water supplies. The rata and its host wage a long-term struggle, and the rata doesn't always win. The southern rata is a free-standing tree, yielding beautiful red lumber. Rata flowers are a pretty red themselves, resembling the pohutukawa tree's blooms but coming out about a month earlier in November.

If you're in the country in November, you'll first see evidence of the **rewarewa** (*re*-wa-*re*-wa) tree in its fallen blossoms on the ground. They are tightly woven, magenta bottle-brush-like flowers, with touches of chartreuse and black, that are some of the most enchanting in the country, in part for their uniqueness.

One of those ingenious New Zealand plants that goes through three distinct stages on its way to maturity, the **rimu** red pine is a valuable source of timber. It spends its first stage in life as a delicate treelet, with pale green, weeping branches that look something like an upright moss. It then turns itself into a conical shape before finishing its growth as a soaring, 100-plus-ft wonder with a branchless trunk and a rounded head. Charcoal from rimu was used in traditional Maori tattooing.

Supplejack vines just hang about in the forest, so dense in places that they make passage next to impossible. You'll often find that their soft, edible tips have been nipped off by the teeth of wild goats that *Pakeha* (Europeans) introduced. Believe it or not, this is a member of the lily family.

New Zealand's living dinosaur, the *tuatara,* is an ancient reptile found on protected offshore islands such as Stephens Island in Marlborough Sounds. It feeds on insects, small mammals, and birds' eggs and has a vestigial third eye. The combination of its nocturnal habits and its rarity means that the likelihood of seeing one in the wild is virtually nil. Your best bet is to see one in captivity at a zoo. Auckland Zoo has a particularly good tuatara display in its Kiwi House.

Along with the bellbird, the **tui** is the chanteuse extraordinaire that fills Aotearoa's woods with its magically clear melodies. You may have never thought of birds as actually singing, but you certainly will when you hear a tui.

Wekas (weh-kah) are funny birds. They can appear to be oblivious to what's going on around them as they walk about pecking at this or that, looking bemused. They are flightless rails, and they'll steal your food if you're camping, so hide it away. Generally speaking, they're pleasant to have around, particularly if you're looking for some entertainment.

Wetas are large insects, some species of which are only topped in size by the African goliath beetle. If you chance upon one, it is likely to throw its spiny back legs up in the air as a defense, giving it a particularly ferocious look. However, wetas are not as fearsome as they look and in the unlikely event that you do get nipped, it will only result in a slight stinging sensation. The largest species is found on Little Barrier Island near Auckland. You may well see specimens in the wild in forests such as the Waitakere Ranges near Auckland, but if you like your fierce-looking insects safely behind glass they can be viewed at the Arataki Visitors Centre, west of Auckland.

You'll have no trouble figuring out that the **wood pigeon** is indeed a pigeon, but your jaw will drop at the size—they look like they've been inflated like balloons. They're beautiful birds.

—Stephen Wolf, Barbara Blechman, and Stu Freeman

WHAT TO READ AND WATCH BEFORE YOU GO

Books

Because of the limited availability of many first-rate books on New Zealand outside the country, there is only so much that you'll be able to read before you go. So leave room in your suitcase for pickup reading once you arrive, and bring something home to make your trip linger longer. One caveat: because of economies of scale in the New Zealand publishing industry, books tend to be expensive. That's one reason to do some secondhand shopping; another is the stores' usually knowledgeable staff, which can make recommendations.

History

The *Oxford Illustrated History of New Zealand,* edited by Keith Sinclair, provides a comprehensive and highly readable account of the country's social, political, cultural, and economic evolution from the earliest Maori settlements up to 1989. James Belich's *Making Peoples* looks at New Zealand history from a 1990s perspective, with more emphasis on the Maori view than some earlier publications. The *Colonial New Zealand Wars,* by Tim Ryan and Bill Parham, is a vivid history of the Maori-British battles. Lavishly illustrated with photographs of colonial infantry and drawings of Maori hill forts, flags, and weapons, the book makes far more compelling reading than the dry military history suggested by the title. Another highly readable military-historical book is James Belich's the *New Zealand Wars.* J. C. Beaglehole's the *Discovery of New Zealand* is an authoritative and scholarly analysis of the voyages of discovery, from the first Polynesians to the Europeans of the late 18th century.

Fiction

New Zealand's best-known short-story writer is **Katherine Mansfield** (1888–1923), whose early stories were set in and around the city of Wellington, her birthplace. The *Best of Katherine Mansfield* is a fine compilation of stories from five collections. Reading her journals will give you a sense of her passionate romantic side, and as much as she disliked the small-minded provincial qualities of New Zealand, she loved the country deeply.

New Zealand's most distinguished living writer is **Janet Frame.** Her works are numerous, from novels such as her successful *The Carpathians,* to a three-part autobiography, which is a lyrical evocation of growing up in small-town New Zealand in the 1920s and 1930s and of the gradual awakening of a writer of great courage. Kiwi filmmaker Jane Campion adapted the middle of it for the screen into *An Angel at My Table.* **Maurice Gee** is another distinguished novelist. His *Plumb* won the James Tait prize for the best novel in Britain when it was published. *Plumb* reaches back to the early 20th century for its story of a renegade parson and his battle with old-world moral pieties. One particularly compelling scene is set in a mining town, where Plumb happens to be the man to hear the last testament of a notorious murderer. Gee is also known for his young adult fiction, in which he often plays out a fantasy–science fiction story in a New Zealand setting. Best examples include *Half Men of O* and *Under the Mountain.*

Two of the finest and most exciting writers at work in the country today are **Patricia Grace** and **Witi Ihimaera,** both Maori whose story collections and novels are on a par with the best fiction in the United Kingdom and the States. Grace's stories are beautifully and fluidly related, very much from inside her characters. Look for *The Dream Sleepers and Other Sto-*

ries and her novel *Mutuwhenua*. Ihimaera (ee-hee-may-ra) also uses very clear prose and Maori experience. His early novel *Tangi* opens with the death of a father and moves through the 22-year-old son's experience of loss and innocence to his acceptance of his role as a man. Maori elements of the story are fascinating both culturally and emotionally. Also look for his *Bulibasha* and *Nights in the Garden of Spain*.

The most internationally celebrated work of fiction to come from New Zealand in recent years is **Keri Hulme**'s the *Bone People*, winner of the Booker McConnell Prize in 1985. Set on the isolated West Coast of the South Island, this challenging, vital novel weaves Polynesian myth with Christian symbolism and the powerful sense of place that characterizes modern Maori writing. More recently, **Alan Duff's** *Once Were Warriors* is a frank, uncompromising, and ultimately transcendent look at urban Maori society. Both the novel and the film were real sensations in New Zealand. The sequel, *One Night Out Stealing*, as well as *What Becomes of the Broken Hearted*, and Duff's most recently published *Both Sides of the Moon*, have also been hugely successful.

Poetry

100 New Zealand Poems by 100 New Zealand Poets, edited by New Zealand's current Poet Laureate, Bill Manhire, ranges from the country's earliest poems to the new poets of the 1990s. The final poem in the book is by six year-old Laura Ranger, who went on to publish, at age 10, the outstanding best-seller *Laura's Poems*, which has now sold more than any previous book of New Zealand poetry. Greg O'Brien and Jenny Bornholdt's *My Heart Goes Swimming* is a charming selection of New Zealand love poems. A more wide-ranging and weighty collection is *An Anthology of New Zealand Poetry in English*, edited by Mark Williams, Greg O'Brien, and Jenny Bornholdt.

Garden Guides

If you are serious about visiting gardens while in New Zealand, any of the books listed below would be helpful. These are not typically stocked in U.S. bookstores or even on-line, so make a well-supplied store one of your first stops when you arrive. Hundreds of gardens are listed in Alison McRae's *Garden's to Visit in New Zealand* and Beverly Bridge's *Register of New Zealand Private Gardens Open to the Public, Volume 2*. They both give descriptions of gardens and list addresses, telephone numbers, and visiting times. *The Native Garden*, by Isobel Gabites and Rob Lucas, offers a superb vision of what constitutes a truly New Zealand garden, which of course is dominated by unique indigenous flora. Two other books are more limited in providing information but offer glossy photographs and make good souvenirs: Julian Matthews and Gil Hanly's *New Zealand Town and Country Gardens* and Premier Books's *Glorious New Zealand Gardens*. A superb monthly magazine, *New Zealand Gardener*, highlights several of the country's gardens in each issue. It is available at newspaper shops and bookstores countrywide.

Specialized Guidebooks

Strictly for wine lovers, *The Wines and Vineyards of New Zealand*, by Michael Cooper, is an exhaustive evaluation in words and pictures of every vineyard in the country. For travelers who plan to make hiking a major component of their vacations, *Tramping in New Zealand*, published by Lonely Planet, is an invaluable guide. *A Field Guide to Auckland* is a wonderful introduction to the natural and historic attractions of the Auckland region. It includes an overview of natural and human history and details of over 140 interesting places to visits within easy distance of the city.

Art Books

Three companion volumes—on painting, sculpture, printmaking, photography, ceramics, glass, and jewelry—provide a superb introduction to New Zealand art: *100 New Zealand Paintings, Another 100 New Zealand Artists,* and *100 New Zealand Craft Artists*. Greg O'Brien's

Hotere: Out the Black Window covers the work of one of the country's most respected artists.

Illustrated Books

Salute to New Zealand, edited by Sandra Coney, is a coffee-table book that intersperses lavish photographs with chapters by some of the country's finest contemporary writers. *Wild New Zealand,* published by Reader's Digest, is a pictorial account of the country's landscape, flora, and fauna, supplemented by an informative text with such a wealth of detail that it turns the sensory experience of the landscape into a cerebral one.

Videos

New Zealand's film industry has had a relatively small output, but the quality of its films has been quite high. Jane Campion's *The Piano* (1993) is a prime example, as are her earlier *An Angel at My Table* (1990) and *Sweetie* (1988), which was made in Australia. Roger Donaldson's 1977 thriller *Sleeping Dogs* was the first New Zealand film released in the United States, followed by the equally worthy *Smash Palace* (1982). The tough, urban portrayal of *Once Were Warriors* (1995) is one of the most recent to make it across the Pacific. Its portrait of urban Maori life, unfortunately, makes New Zealand look a little too much like Los Angeles. *Scarfies,* a black comedy about Otago University students, received positive feedback at the 2000 Sundance Film Festival, following success in local cinemas. Filming started on Peter Jackson's *The Lord of the Rings* in 1999 and continued at press time. The cast is international and it's being shot at various locations around New Zealand.

Hardly high culture, but still a major success for New Zealand's film and television industry, was the *Hercules* television series starring Kevin Sorbo. The show was axed in the United States in 1999 but its spin-off series *Xena: Warrior Princess* survived to kick butt in the new millennium. Both series were filmed in West Auckland, doing its best to look like ancient Greece.

NEW ZEALAND AT A GLANCE

ca. AD 750 The first Polynesians arrive, settling mainly in South Island, where they find the moa, a flightless bird and an important food source, in abundance.

950 Kupe, the Polynesian voyager, names the country Aotearoa, "land of the long white cloud." He returns to his native Hawaiki, believed to be present-day French Polynesia.

1300s A population explosion in Hawaiki triggers a wave of immigrants.

1642 Abel Tasman of the Dutch East India Company becomes the first European to sight the land—he names his discovery Nieuw Zeeland. But after several of his crew are killed by Maori, he sails away without landing.

1769 Captain James Cook becomes the first European to set foot on New Zealand. He claims it in the name of the British crown.

1790 Sealers, whalers, and timber cutters arrive, plundering the natural wealth and introducing the Maori to the musket, liquor, and influenza.

1814 The Reverend Samuel Marsden establishes the first mission station, but 11 years pass before the first convert is made.

1832 James Busby is appointed British Resident, charged with protecting the Maori people and fostering British trade.

1840 Captain William Hobson, representing the crown, and Maori chiefs sign the Treaty of Waitangi. In return for the peaceful possession of their land and the rights and privileges of British citizens, the chiefs recognize British sovereignty.

1840–41 The New Zealand Company, an association of British entrepreneurs, establishes settlements at Wanganui, New Plymouth, Nelson, and Wellington.

1852 The British Parliament passes the New Zealand Constitution Act, establishing limited self-government. The country's first gold strike occurs in Coromandel town in the Coromandel Peninsula.

1861 Gold is discovered in the river valleys of central Otago, west of Dunedin.

1860–72 Maori grievances over loss of land trigger the Land Wars in North Island. The Maori win some notable victories, but lack of unity ensures their ultimate defeat. Vast tracts of ancestral land are confiscated from rebel tribes.

1882 The first refrigerated cargo is dispatched to England, giving the country a new source of prosperity—sheep. A century later, there will be 20 sheep for every New Zealander.

1893 Under the Liberal government, New Zealand becomes the first country to give women the vote.

1914 New Zealand enters World War I.

1931 The Hawke's Bay earthquake kills 258 and levels the city of Napier.

1939 New Zealand enters World War II.

1950 New Zealand troops sail for Korea.

1965 Despite public disquiet, troops are sent to Vietnam.

1973 Britain joins the European Economic Community, and New Zealand's loss of this traditional export market is reflected in a crippling balance-of-payments deficit two years later.

1981 Violent antigovernment demonstrations erupt during a tour by a South African rugby team.

1984 David Lange's Labour Government wins a landslide majority in the general election, at least partly due to its pledge to ban nuclear armed vessels from New Zealand waters.

1985 The Greenpeace ship *Rainbow Warrior* is sunk by a mine in Auckland Harbour, and a crewman is killed. Two of the French secret service agents responsible are arrested, jailed, transferred to French custody—then soon released.

Sir Paul Reeves is sworn in as the first Maori governor-general.

Relations with the United States sour when the government bans visits by ships carrying nuclear weapons. The U.S. government responds by ejecting New Zealand from the ANZUS alliance.

1986 Goods and Services Tax (GST) is introduced at 10% (later to be raised to 12.5%). Tourists are not exempt from the tax, although many exports and foreign exchange earners are.

1989 David Lange resigns as prime minister.

1990 The National Party replaces the Labour Party in government.

1993 The country votes for a major constitutional change, replacing the "first past the post" electoral system inherited from Britain with a "mixed-member proportional" (MMP) system. The election sees the National Party clinging to power within a coalition.

1995 New Zealand's *Black Magic* wins the America's Cup yachting regatta. The country goes into party mode over the win, which signals both a sporting triumph and a coming of age technologically.

Mt. Ruapehu in North Island's Tongariro National Park bubbles and sputters, attracting interested onlookers from around the world.

New Zealanders' abhorrence of all things nuclear comes to the fore again with major floating protests against France's resumed nuclear testing in the South Pacific.

1996 Noisy Ruapehu spews debris into the air, covering nearby towns with a few inches of ash.

New Zealand elects its first MMP government, having voted for constitutional change three years earlier. New Zealand First holds the balance of power and goes into government with the National Party.

1997 New Zealand starts to feel the effect of weakening Asian currencies, particularly as the number of Korean and Japanese tourists falls.

Jenny Shipley becomes the country's first woman PM.

1998 The Government introduces a controversial "work for the dole" scheme, in which people on unemployment benefit are required to work or train 20 hours a week or risk having their income slashed.

As the Asian economic crisis continues to bite, industrial strikes on Australia's waterfront also impact New Zealand's economy. The country's economic fundamentals remain strong, but these outside influences cause the N.Z. dollar to lose value against U.S. currency.

1999 The New Zealand cricketers record their first test-win over England at Lords, regarded as the spiritual home of the game. New Zealand goes on to win the series.

New Zealand contributes personnel and machinery to a United Nations peace-keeping force in Indonesia.

A Labour-Alliance coalition wins the general election but a close vote means it still needs the support of the Green Party in matters of national importance. Helen Clark becomes New Zealand's second successive female prime minister.

Chronology

ESSENTIAL INFORMATION

AIR TRAVEL

BOOKING

When you book **look for nonstop flights** and **remember that "direct" flights stop at least once.** Try to avoid connecting flights, which require a change of plane.

CARRIERS

Air New Zealand and Qantas fly from Los Angeles to New Zealand, nonstop and direct. **United** and **Air Canada** connect from points in North America with flights of their own out of Los Angeles. Air New Zealand is the only carrier with direct flights from North America to Christchurch as well as Auckland.

British Airways, Cathay Pacific, Japan Airlines, Qantas, and Singapore Airlines operate between London and Auckland, with a stopover in Asia. **Air New Zealand** and **United** operate between London and Auckland by way of the United States.

Within New Zealand, **Air New Zealand** and **Ansett New Zealand** compete on intercity trunk routes.

➤ MAJOR AIRLINES: **Air New Zealand** (☎ 310/615–1111, 800/262–1234 in the U.S., 800/663–5494 in Canada). **Qantas** (☎ 800/227–4500 in the U.S. and Canada). **United** (☎ 800/241–6522). **Air Canada** (☎ 800/776–3000).

➤ FROM THE U.K.: **Air New Zealand** (☎ 020/8741–2299). **British Airways** (☎ 0345/222–111). **Cathay Pacific** (☎ 020/7747–8888). **Japan Airlines** (☎ 0345/747–700). **Qantas** (☎ 0345/747–767). **Singapore Airlines** (☎ 020/7439–8111). **United** (☎ 020/8990–9900).

➤ DOMESTIC AIRLINES: **Air New Zealand** (☎ 09/357–3000). **Ansett New Zealand** (☎ 0800/267–388 in N.Z.).

CHECK-IN & BOARDING

Assuming that not everyone with a ticket will show up, airlines routinely overbook planes. When everyone does, airlines ask for volunteers to give up their seats. In return, these volunteers usually get a certificate for a free flight and are rebooked on the next flight out. If there are not enough volunteers, the airline must choose who will be denied boarding. The first to get bumped are passengers who checked in late and those flying on discounted tickets, so **get to the gate and check in as early as possible,** especially during peak periods. For domestic flights within New Zealand, check in no later than 20 minutes before departure.

Always **bring a government-issued photo ID to the airport.** You may be asked to show it before you are allowed to check in.

CUTTING COSTS

The least expensive airfares to New Zealand usually must be purchased in advance and are nonrefundable. It's smart to **call a number of airlines, and when you are quoted a good price, book it on the spot**—the same fare may not be available the next day. Always **check different routings** and look into using different airports. Travel agents, especially low-fare specialists (☞ Discounts & Deals, *below*), are helpful.

Consolidators are another good source. They buy tickets for scheduled international flights at reduced rates from the airlines, then sell them at prices that beat the best fare available directly from the airlines, usually without restrictions. Sometimes you can even get your money back if you need to return the ticket. Carefully read the fine print detailing penalties for changes and cancellations, and **confirm your consolidator reservation with the airline.**

When you **fly as a courier,** you trade your checked-luggage space for a ticket deeply subsidized by a courier service. There are restrictions on when you can book and how long you can stay.

Budget air travel within New Zealand is still expensive compared with the cost of bus or train travel, but you can **save a substantial amount of money if you buy multitrip tickets. Ansett New Zealand** (☞ Carriers, *above*) has a **New Zealand Airpass** entitling you to fly between three and eight sectors (i.e., point-to-point flights) starting from $450 for a three-sector pass and costing $150 for each additional sector. The pass is valid for the duration of your stay in New Zealand and should be purchased prior to arrival to avoid New Zealand sales tax. Also inquire about Ansett's 4-in-1 InterCity New Zealand Travelpass. **Air New Zealand** offers similar discount tickets, available through travel agents.

➤ CONSOLIDATORS: **Cheap Tickets** (☎ 800/377–1000). **Discount Airline Ticket Service** (☎ 800/576–1600). **Unitravel** (☎ 800/325–2222). **Up & Away Travel** (☎ 212/889–2345). **World Travel Network** (☎ 800/409–6753).

ENJOYING THE FLIGHT

For more legroom, **request an emergency-aisle seat.** Don't sit in the row in front of the emergency aisle or in front of a bulkhead, where seats may not recline. If you have dietary concerns, **ask for special meals when booking.** These can be vegetarian, low-cholesterol, or kosher, for example. On long flights, try to maintain a normal routine, to help fight jet lag. At night, **get some sleep.** By day, **eat light meals, drink water** (not alcohol), and **move around the cabin** to stretch your legs.

All New Zealand domestic flights and flights between New Zealand and Australia are nonsmoking. **Air New Zealand** has banned smoking on all of its flights worldwide.

FLYING TIMES

From New York to Auckland (via Los Angeles) it takes about 19 hours; from Chicago, about 17 hours; from

Los Angeles to Auckland (nonstop), about 12 hours. From the United States and Canada, you will have to connect to a New Zealand–bound flight in L.A.

Flights from London to Auckland take about 24 hours, either via the United States or via Southeast Asia. These are all actual air hours and do not include ground time.

HOW TO COMPLAIN

If your baggage goes astray or your flight goes awry, complain right away. Most carriers require that you **file a claim immediately.**

➤ AIRLINE COMPLAINTS: U.S. Department of Transportation **Aviation Consumer Protection Division** (✉ C-75, Room 4107, Washington, DC 20590, ☎ 202/366–2220, www.dot.gov/airconsumer). **Federal Aviation Administration Consumer Hotline** (☎ 800/322–7873).

RECONFIRMING

It is not required that you reconfirm outbound flights from or within New Zealand.

AIRPORTS

The major airport is **Auckland International Airport** (☎ 09/275–0789).

➤ AIRPORT INFORMATION: **Christchurch International Airport** (☎ 03/374–7100). **Wellington International Airport** (☎ 04/385–5123).

DUTY-FREE SHOPPING

Auckland International Airport has some of the best duty-free deals (on liquor, cigarettes, and cosmetics) in the South Pacific and even compares favorably with many Asian countries.

BIKE TRAVEL

New Zealand is a sensational place to take cycling tours. For information on multiday trips throughout the country, *see* Chapter 5.

➤ BIKE MAPS: *The New Zealand Cyclers' Guide to Cycle Touring* by J. B. Ringer has North Island and South Island editions and is available in some bike shops and major book stores around the country.

➤ BIKE RENTALS: **NZ Pedaltours** (✉ 4/156 Parnell Rd., Parnell, Auckland,

☎ 09/302–0968) rents bikes in Auckland and Christchurch and can also provide contacts for companies that arrange bike rental in other cities and towns. NZ Pedaltours conducts guided cycle tours and can customize itineraries for special interest groups.

BIKES IN FLIGHT

Most airlines accommodate bikes as luggage, provided they are dismantled and boxed. For bike boxes, often free at bike shops, you'll pay about $5 from airlines (at least $100 for bike bags). International travelers can sometimes substitute a bike for a piece of checked luggage at no charge; otherwise, the cost is about $100. Domestic and Canadian airlines charge $25–$50.

BOAT & FERRY TRAVEL

To travel between North Island and South Island take **Tranz Scenic's** the **Interislander** ferry or the faster, slightly more expensive **Lynx**ferry between Wellington and Picton. Both ferries carry cars. They also connect with Tranz Scenic's trains and a free shuttle is available between the railway station and ferry terminal in both Wellington and Picton. The Interislander travels five times a day, the Lynx, two to three times. The one-way fare for the Interislander ranges from $23 to $46 depending on the time of year. The fare for a medium-size sedan ranges from $83 to $165. Be sure to ask about specials, including ferry/train deals, when you book.

FARES & SCHEDULES

Schedules are available at train stations and visitor information centers around the country. Most will arrange Interislander ferry bookings. Be sure to reserve in advance, especially during holiday periods.

➤ BOAT & FERRY INFORMATION: **Tranz Scenic** (☎ 0800/802–802).

BUS TRAVEL

New Zealand is served by an extensive bus network; for many travelers, buses offer the optimal combination of cost and convenience. **InterCity** and **Newmans** are the main bus lines.

CUTTING COSTS

➤ DISCOUNT PASSES: The InterCity Travelpass allows unlimited travel on all InterCity buses and trains and on the Interislander ferries that link the North and South Islands (☞ Train Travel, *below*). Both **Newmans** and **Intercity** offer a 20% discount to students and Youth Hostel members. Identification cards are required. A 30% discount is available for passengers over the age of 60.

➤ BUS INFORMATION: **InterCity** (☎ 09/639–0500). **Mount Cook Landline** (☎ 310/640–2823, 800/468–2665 in the U.S., 800/999–9306 in Canada, 020/8741–5652 in the U.K., 0800/800–287 in N.Z.). **Newmans** (☎ 09/309–9738).

PAYING

Credit cards and traveler's checks are accepted by the major bus companies.

RESERVATIONS

Reservations are recommended.

BUSINESS HOURS

BANKS & OFFICES

Banks are open weekdays 9–4:30, but trading in foreign currencies ceases at 3.

GAS STATIONS

Gas stations are usually open, at the least, from 7 AM to 7 PM. Large stations on main highways are commonly open 24 hours.

MUSEUMS & SIGHTS

Museums around the country do not have standard hours but many are open from 10 AM to 5 PM. Hours for individual museums are denoted in this book by the ☉ icon.

PHARMACIES

Pharmacies are open from 9 AM to 5 PM. In larger cities, you will find basic nonprescription drugstore items in supermarkets, many of which are open until 8 PM. During off-hours there will usually be emergency-hour pharmacies in the major cities. Phone the local hospital for details.

SHOPS

Shops are generally open Monday–Thursday 9–5:30, Friday 9–9, and

Saturday 9–noon. Sunday trading is becoming more common but still varies greatly from place to place. Most Auckland shopping centers are open at least Sunday mornings.

CAMERAS & PHOTOGRAPHY

New Zealanders are usually happy to have their photograph taken, but if you're getting up close, it pays to ask permission first.

If you are taking photos of mountains and lakes, avoid the glare of the afternoon—dusk and dawn are the best times. In the North Island, the West Coast has some spectacular sunsets. In the South Island, particularly in Fiordland, thick fog wraps itself around moss-laden trees on winter mornings, providing for eerie-looking photographs. For a spectacular wide-angled photograph, be sure to **travel to the top of Bob's Peak** by the Skyline Gondola and takes a shot of Queenstown and the Remarkables mountain range. For a close-up, attend a Maori dance performance in Rotorua and take a photo of a tatooed warrior as he thrusts his tongue out during the *haka*.

➤ PHOTO HELP: **Kodak Information Center** (☎ 800/242–2424). *Kodak Guide to Shooting Great Travel Pictures,* available in bookstores or from Fodor's Travel Publications (☎ 800/533–6478; $16.50 plus $5.50 shipping).

EQUIPMENT PRECAUTIONS

Always **keep your film and tape out of the sun.** Carry an extra supply of batteries, and **be prepared to turn on your camera or camcorder** to prove to security personnel that the device is real. Always **ask for hand inspection of film,** which becomes clouded after repeated exposure to airport X-ray machines, and **keep videotapes away from metal detectors.**

FILM & DEVELOPING

Film is readily available in airport duty-free shops, pharmacies, department stores, tourist shops, and gas stations. **Kodak** and **Fuji** are widely available. A roll of 36-exposure film costs about $13. Twenty-four-hour film developing is available even in smaller towns and some pharmacies and photo shops wili develop in an hour or two.

VIDEOS

The local standard for videotape is PAL and a three-hour tape will cost around $8.

CAR RENTAL

Japanese brands dominate rental agencies in New Zealand. Cars in the "economy" ranges are likely to include Honda Logos, Honda Civics, Toyota Corollas, or similar types. They are suitable for two or three people. At the luxury end of the scale you will find Honda Legends. **For some local flavor, rent a Holden Commodore,** a popular car in New Zealand. Most major agencies will have this as a luxury option.

Rates in New Zealand begin at $60 a day and $350 a week for an economy car with unlimited mileage. This does not include tax on car rentals, which is 12.5%.

➤ MAJOR AGENCIES: **Alamo** (☎ 800/522–9696, 020/8759–6200 in the U.K.). **Avis** (☎ 800/331–1084, 800/879–2847 in Canada, 02/9353–9000 in Australia, 09/525–1982 in New Zealand). **Budget** (☎ 800/527–0700, 0144/227–6266 in the U.K.). **Dollar** (☎ 800/800–6000; 020/8897–0811 in the U.K., where it is known as Eurodollar; 02/9223–1444 in Australia). **Hertz** (☎ 800/654–3001, 800/263–0600 in Canada, 020/8897–2072 in the U.K., 02/9669–2444 in Australia, 03/358–6777 in New Zealand). **National InterRent** (☎ 800/227–3876; 0345/222–525 in the U.K., where it is known as Europcar InterRent).

➤ LOCAL AGENCIES: **Mauitours** (☎ 800/351–2323 in the U.S., 800/663–2002 in Canada, 01737/843242 in the U.K., 09/275–3013 in New Zealand) rents cars as well as the popular campervans.

CROSS-ISLAND RENTALS

Most major international companies have a convenient service if you are taking the ferry between North and South islands and want to continue your rental contract. You simply drop off the car in Wellington and on the same contract pick up a new car in

Picton, or vice-versa. It saves you from paying the considerable fare for taking a car across on the ferry (and it's easier for the company to keep track of its rental fleet). Your rental contract is terminated only at the far end of your trip, wherever you end up. In this system, there is no drop-off charge for one-way rentals, making an Auckland–Queenstown rental as easy as it could be.

CUTTING COSTS

To get the best deal, **book through a travel agent who will shop around.** Do **look into wholesalers,** companies that do not own fleets but rent in bulk from those that do and often offer better rates than traditional car-rental operations. Payment must be made before you leave home.

➤ WHOLESALERS: **Auto Europe** (☎ 207/842–2000 or 800/223–5555, FAX 800–235–6321, www.autoeurope. com). **Kemwel Holiday Autos** (☎ 800/678–0678, FAX 914/825–3160, www.kemwel.com).

INSURANCE

When driving a rented car you are generally responsible for any damage to or loss of the vehicle as well as for any property damage or personal injury that you may cause. Before you rent see what coverage your personal auto-insurance policy and credit cards already provide.

In New Zealand, it is usual to have the insurance included in the rental price, but you will almost certainly be expected to pay what Kiwis call an "excess" if you badly damage the car. This will be about $1,200. Since deductibles are very high with the most basic coverage, you may want to opt for total coverage. Be sure to get all of the details from the rental agent before you decide.

REQUIREMENTS & RESTRICTIONS

In New Zealand your own driver's license is acceptable. An International Driver's Permit is a good idea; it's available from the American or Canadian automobile association, and, in the United Kingdom, from the Automobile Association or Royal Automobile Club. These international permits are universally recognized,

and having one in your wallet may save you a problem with the local authorities.

The minimum age for renting a car in New Zealand is 25. This requirement is waived if the driver has held a driver's license for one year or more. Even then, the young driver is liable for an extra "underage drivers fee" of $25 plus the 12.5% general sales tax (GST) in addition to the quoted rates. Rental car companies may ask drivers not to take their cars onto certain roads, but this is rare and tends to only apply in the rough and rugged hill country around the Southern Alps.

SURCHARGES

Before you pick up a car in one city and leave it in another, **ask about drop-off charges or one-way service fees,** which can be substantial. Note, too, that some rental agencies charge extra if you return the car before the time specified in your contract. To avoid a hefty refueling fee, **fill the tank just before you turn in the car,** but be aware that gas stations near the rental outlet may overcharge.

CAR TRAVEL

Nothing beats the freedom and mobility of a car for exploring. Even for those nervous about driving on the "wrong" side of the road, motoring here is relatively easy.

Remember this simple axiom: drive left, look right. That means keep to the left lane, and when turning right or left from a stop sign, the closest lane of traffic will be coming from the right, so look in that direction first. By the same token, pedestrians should look right before crossing the street. Americans and Canadians can blindly step into the path of an oncoming car by looking left as they do when crossing streets at home. So repeat this several times: drive left, look right. You'll find yourself in a constant comedy of errors when you go to use directional signals and windshield wipers—in Kiwi cars it's the reverse of what you're used to. You won't be able to count how many times those wipers start flapping back and forth when you go to signal a turn (it'll happen in reverse when you get back home). You can be sure it's time to call it a day when you reach over your left shoulder for the seat belt and grab a handful of air.

AUTO CLUBS

➤ IN AUSTRALIA: **Australian Automobile Association** (☎ 02/6247–7311).

➤ IN CANADA: **Canadian Automobile Association** (CAA, ☎ 613/247–0117).

➤ IN NEW ZEALAND: **New Zealand Automobile Association** (☎ 09/377–4660).

➤ IN THE U.K.: **Automobile Association** (AA, ☎ 0990/500–600). **Royal Automobile Club** (RAC, ☎ 0990/722–722 for membership, 0345/121–345 for insurance).

➤ IN THE U.S.: **American Automobile Association** (☎ 800/564–6222).

EMERGENCY SERVICES

In the case of serious accident, immediately pull over to the side of the road and phone 111. You will find New Zealanders quick to help if they are able to, particularly if you need to use a phone. Minor accidents are normally sorted out in a calm and collected manner at the side of the road. However, "road rage" is not unknown. If the driver of the other vehicle looks particularly angry or aggressive, you are within your rights to take note of the registration number and then report the accident at the local or nearest police station.

➤ CONTACTS: **The New Zealand Automobile Association** offers emergency road service and is associated with the Automobile Association of America (AAA). If you are an AAA member, you will be covered by the service as long as you register with a NZAA office in New Zealand and present your membership card. The central Auckland office (☎ 09/302–1825) is at 99 Albert Street.

GASOLINE

On main routes you'll find stations at regular intervals. However, if you're traveling on back roads where the population is sparse it's best not to let your tank get too low—it can be a long walk to the nearest helpful farmer if you run out of gas.

The price of gas (Kiwis say "petrol") in New Zealand is more volatile than the fuel itself. At press time prices had recently rocketed from 82 cents per liter to about $1 a liter. Credit cards are widely accepted, though not necessarily at small country gas stations, so ask before you fill up.

Unleaded gas is widely available and is often referred to as 91. Leaded gas is 96. Unleaded is usually a couple of cents cheaper than leaded and most rental cars run on unleaded gas. Virtually all gas stations will have staff on hand to pump gas or assist motorists in other ways, however they tend to have self-service facilities for anyone in a hurry. These are simply operated by pushing numbers on a console to coincide with the dollar value of the gas required. When you pump the gas, the pump will automatically switch off when you have reached the stated amount. Pay at the counter inside the station. For gas station opening hours, *see* Business Hours, *above*.

ROAD CONDITIONS

Roads are well maintained and generally uncrowded, though signposting, even on major highways, is often poor. Because traffic in New Zealand is relatively light, there has been little need to create major highways, and there are few places where you get straight stretches for very long. So don't plan on averaging 100 km (62 mi) per hour in too many areas. Most of the roads pass through beautiful scenery—so much in fact that you may be constantly agog at what you're seeing. The temptation is strong to look at everything, but keep your eyes on the road. Rest areas, many in positions with great views, are plentiful. Some roads are incredibly windy; others, like the road from Wanaka to Arrowtown outside of Queenstown, are off-limits for rental cars. Ask your rental company in advance where you can and cannot drive if you plan to go off the beaten path.

The only city with a serious congestion problem during rush hour is Auckland, particularly on inner-city motorway on and off ramps. Avoid driving between 7:30 AM and 9 AM, and 5 PM and 6:30 PM. Traffic around other cities, such as Wellington and Christchurch, builds up at these times too and it is worth taking this into account if you have important appointments or a plane to catch. Give yourself a spare 15 or 20 minutes to be on the safe side.

New Zealanders are seldom as good at driving as they think they are, so the best policy is just to keep at a safe distance. Dangerous overtaking, speeders, lack of indication, and slow drivers in passing lanes are all afflictions you will have to suffer on New Zealand highways. In saying that, driving has improved over recent years due to increased education about speeding and drunk driving and bad driving in general.

ROAD MAPS

Road maps are widely available in gas stations, at airports, and in bookshops around the country. Rental car companies will hand you a road map on request, and local city guidebooks available at airports and information centers usually have passable maps on the back pages. In the unlikely event you can't find what you want, phone the **New Zealand Automobile Association** (☎ 09/302–1825).

RULES OF THE ROAD

The speed limit is 100 km per hour (62 mi per hour) on the open road and 50 kph (31 mph) in towns and cities. A circular sign with the letters LSZ (Limited Speed Zone) means speed should be governed by prevailing road conditions, but still not exceed 100 kph. Watch out for speed cameras, particularly in city suburbs and on approaches to and exits from small towns. These are a relatively new phenomena in New Zealand and the police force (not to mention the money counters) have taken to them with relish. Fines start at about $60 for speeds 10 km over the speed limit.

Right turns are not permitted on red lights. The law states that **you must always wear a seat belt** in New Zealand, whether you are driving or a passenger in a car. If you are caught without a seat belt and you are clearly not a New Zealander, the result is likely to be a friendly but firm warning.

Drunk drivers are not tolerated in New Zealand. The blood alcohol limit is 0.05 and it's safest to avoid driving altogether if you've had a drink. If you are caught driving over the limit you will be taken to the nearest police station to dry out, and required to pay a high fine. Repeat offences or instances of causing injury or death while under the influence of alcohol are likely to result in jail terms. Don't try it unless you really want to ruin your vacation.

When driving in rural New Zealand, cross one-lane bridges with caution—there are plenty of them. A yellow sign on the left will usually warn that you are approaching a one-lane bridge, and another sign will tell you whether you have the right-of-way. A rectangular blue sign means you have the right-of-way, and a circular sign with a red border means you must pull over to the left and wait to cross until oncoming traffic has passed. Even when you have the right-of-way, slow down and take care. Some one-lane bridges in South Island are used by trains as well as cars. Trains always have the right-of-way.

The usual fine for parking over the time limit on meters is $10 to $15. Make sure to observe all "no parking" signs. If you don't, your car will almost certainly be towed away. It will cost about $100 to have the car released, and most tow companies won't accept anything but cash.

CHILDREN IN NEW ZEALAND

New Zealand may not have the high-tech theme parks of many other destinations, but children will love it here all the same. The big appeal is the same as it is for adults: wide, open spaces. The forests are safe to explore (there are no poisonous snakes, spiders, or even poison ivy); remote beaches have secret coves to discover; and there are lakes to kayak on and cool clear rivers to swim in. Many city attractions are child-friendly as well, with museums adding "discovery" centers where young people can have hands-on learning experiences. These and other sights and attractions of special interest to children are highlighted in this book by a ☺ icon. New Zealand is a safe place for children, but don't get careless. Especially around water, make sure you accompany children at all times. And like adults, children who wander off marked paths and tracks in forested or mountainous areas can get lost for a long time.

If you are renting a car, don't forget to **arrange for a car seat** when you reserve.

➤ BABY-SITTING: Most hotels and resorts have baby-sitters available at a charge of around $10 to $15 per hour. Baby-sitting services are also listed in the yellow pages of city telephone directories.

FLYING

If your children are two or older, **ask about children's airfares.** As a general rule, infants under two not occupying a seat fly at greatly reduced fares or even for free. When booking, **confirm carry-on allowances** if you're traveling with infants. In general, for babies charged 10% of the adult fare you are allowed one carry-on bag and a collapsible stroller; if the flight is full, the stroller may have to be checked or you may be limited to less.

Experts agree that it's a good idea to use safety seats aloft for children weighing less than 40 pounds. Airlines set their own policies: U.S. carriers usually require that the child be ticketed, even if he or she is young enough to ride free, since the seats must be strapped into regular seats. Do **check your airline's policy about using safety seats during takeoff and landing.** And since safety seats are not allowed just everywhere in the plane, get your seat assignments early.

When reserving, **request children's meals or a freestanding bassinet** if you need them. But note that bulkhead seats, where you must sit to use the bassinet, may lack an overhead bin or storage space on the floor.

FOOD

New Zealand children are included in most of their parents' social activities. Children are welcome in all restaurants throughout the country. However, they are rarely seen in those restaurants that appear in Fodor's very expensive (**$$$$**) and expensive (**$$$**) price categories. These restaurants may not have high chairs or be prepared to make special children's meals.

LODGING

Most hotels in New Zealand allow children under a certain age to stay in their parents' room at no extra charge, but others charge for them as extra adults; be sure to **find out the cutoff age for children's discounts.**

In hotels, roll-away beds are usually free, and children under 12 sharing a hotel room with adults either stay free or receive a discount rate. Few hotels have separate facilities for children.

Home hosting provides an ideal opportunity for visitors to stay with a local family, either in town or on a working farm. For information on home and farm stays, home exchange, and apartment rentals, *see* Lodging, *below*.

SIGHTS & ATTRACTIONS

Places that are especially appealing to children are indicated by a rubber duckie icon (🦆) in the margin.

SUPPLIES & EQUIPMENT

Baby products such as disposable diapers (ask for napkins or nappies), formula, and baby food can be found in chemists' shops (pharmacies). They are less expensive in supermarkets.

➤ STROLLER AND BASSINET RENTAL: **Royal New Zealand Plunket Society** (✉ 5 Alexis Ave., Mt. Albert, Auckland, ☎ 09/849–5652).

COMPUTERS ON THE ROAD

Traveling with a laptop does not present any problems in New Zealand, where the electricity supply is reliable. However, you will need a converter and adapter as with other electronic equipment (☞ Electricity, *below*). It pays to **carry a spare battery and adapter,** since they're expensive and can be hard to replace.

City hotels and even provincial hotels and motels are well equipped to handle computers and modems. You may get a little stuck in family-run bed-and-breakfasts and farm stays in remote areas, but even these places will probably be able to sort something out for you.

CONSUMER PROTECTION

Whenever shopping or buying travel services in New Zealand, **pay with a major credit card** so you can cancel payment or get reimbursed if there's a problem. If you're doing business with a particular company for the first time, **contact your local Better Business Bureau and the attorney general's offices** in your own state and the company's home state, as well. Have any complaints been filed? If you're buying a package or tour, always **consider travel insurance** that includes default coverage (☞ Insurance, *below*).

➤ BBBs: **Council of Better Business Bureaus** (✉ 4200 Wilson Blvd., Suite 800, Arlington, VA 22203, ☎ 703/ 276–0100, FAX 703/525–8277, www. bbb.org).

CRUISE TRAVEL

For years, New Zealand was almost the forgotten destination of cruise lines, tucked away at the bottom of the South Pacific. This has changed since the 1990s with more and more companies taking advantage of not only Auckland's superb harbor but also the scenic opportunities in places such as Bay of Islands and Marlborough Sounds. New Zealand is now included on world cruise itineraries by vessels such as *QEII* but some of the best cruising programs are those that concentrate entirely on the South Pacific and combine New Zealand with destinations such as Fiji, New Caledonia, Tonga, and Samoa. **P & O Holidays** operates the *Fair Princess,* which runs about 12 cruises out of Auckland from November to March. It offers a few cruises that take in six New Zealand destinations before traveling on to Sydney. More frequently, the cruises start and finish in Auckland and visit South Pacific Islands in between. **Pacific Sky** is a less frequent, and more upmarket, visitor to New Zealand that runs a Kiwi Adventure cruise that visits Bay of Islands, Auckland, Napier, Wellington, Christchurch, Dunedin, and Milford Sound.

➤ CRUISE LINES: **Pacific Sky** (✉ Level 8, 6B Cawley St., Ellerslie, Auckland, ☎ 09/526–3855. **P & O Holidays** (✉ Level 10, Quay Towers, Auckland, ☎ 0800/441–766).

CUSTOMS & DUTIES

When shopping, **keep receipts** for all purchases. Upon reentering the country, **be ready to show customs officials what you've bought.** If you feel a duty is incorrect or object to the way your clearance was handled, note the inspector's badge number and ask to see a supervisor. If the problem isn't resolved, write to the appropriate authorities, beginning with the port director at your point of entry.

IN AUSTRALIA

Australian residents who are 18 or older may bring home $A400 worth of souvenirs and gifts (including jewelry), 250 cigarettes or 250 grams of tobacco, and 1,125 milliliters of alcohol (including wine, beer, and spirits). Residents under 18 may bring back $A200 worth of goods. Prohibited items include meat products. Seeds, plants, and fruits need to be declared upon arrival.

➤ INFORMATION: **Australian Customs Service** (Regional Director, ✉ Box 8, Sydney, NSW 2001, ☎ 02/9213– 2000, FAX 02/9213–4000).

IN CANADA

Canadian residents who have been out of Canada for at least 7 days may bring home C$500 worth of goods duty-free. If you've been away less than 7 days but more than 48 hours, the duty-free allowance drops to C$200; if your trip lasts 24–48 hours, the allowance is C$50. You may not pool allowances with family members. Goods claimed under the C$500 exemption may follow you by mail; those claimed under the lesser exemptions must accompany you. Alcohol and tobacco products may be included in the 7-day and 48-hour exemptions but not in the 24-hour exemption. If you meet the age requirements of the province or territory through which you reenter Canada, you may bring in, duty-free, 1.14 liters (40 imperial ounces) of wine or liquor *or* 24 12-ounce cans or bottles of beer or ale. If you are 16 or older you may bring in, duty-free, 200 cigarettes and 50 cigars. Check ahead of time with Revenue Canada or the Department of Agriculture for policies regarding meat products, seeds, plants, and fruits.

You may send an unlimited number of gifts worth up to C$60 each duty-free to Canada. Label the package UNSOLICITED GIFT—VALUE UNDER $60. Alcohol and tobacco are excluded.

➤ INFORMATION: **Revenue Canada** (✉ 2265 St. Laurent Blvd. S, Ottawa, Ontario K1G 4K3, ☎ 613/993–0534, 800/461–9999 in Canada, FAX 613/ 957–8911, www.ccra-adrc.gc.ca).

IN NEW ZEALAND

New Zealand has stringent regulations governing the import of weapons, foodstuffs, and certain plant and animal material. Anti-drug laws are strict and penalties severe. In addition to personal effects, nonresidents over 17 years of age may bring in, duty-free, 200 cigarettes or 250 grams of tobacco or 50 cigars, 4.5 liters of wine, one bottle containing not more than 1,125 milliliters of spirits or liqueur, and personal purchases and gifts up to the value of US$440 (NZ$700).

Don't stash any fruit in your carry-on to take into the country. The agricultural quarantine is serious business. So if you've been hiking recently and are bringing your boots with you, clean them before you pack. The authorities for very good reason don't want any nonnative seeds haplessly transported into the country. It's a small and fragile ecosystem, and Kiwis rightfully want to protect it.

IN THE U.K.

From countries outside the EU, including New Zealand, you may bring home, duty-free, 200 cigarettes or 50 cigars; 1 liter of spirits or 2 liters of fortified or sparkling wine or liqueurs; 2 liters of still table wine; 60 milliliters of perfume; 250 milliliters of toilet water; plus £136 worth of other goods, including gifts and souvenirs. If returning from outside the EU, prohibited items include meat products, seeds, plants, and fruits.

➤ INFORMATION: **HM Customs and Excise** (✉ Dorset House, Stamford St., Bromley, Kent BR1 1XX, ☎ 020/ 7202–4227).

IN THE U.S.

U.S. residents who have been out of the country for at least 48 hours (and who have not used the $400 allowance or any part of it in the past 30 days) may bring home $400 worth of foreign goods duty-free. U.S. residents 21 and older may bring back 1 liter of alcohol duty-free. In addition, regardless of your age, you are allowed 200 cigarettes and 100 non-Cuban cigars. Antiques, which the U.S. Customs Service defines as objects more than 100 years old, enter duty-free, as do original works of art done entirely by hand, including paintings, drawings, and sculptures.

You may also send packages home duty-free: up to $200 worth of goods for personal use, with a limit of one parcel per addressee per day (except alcohol or tobacco products or perfume worth more than $5); label the package PERSONAL USE and attach a list of its contents and their retail value. Do not label the package UNSOLICITED GIFT or your duty-free exemption will drop to $100. Mailed items do not affect your duty-free allowance on your return.

➤ INFORMATION: **U.S. Customs Service** (✉ 1300 Pennsylvania Ave. NW, Washington, DC 20229, www.customs.gov; inquiries ☎ 202/354–1000; complaints c/o ✉ Office of Regulations and Rulings; registration of equipment c/o Resource Management, ☎ 202/927–0540).

DINING

Some restaurants offer a fixed-price dinner, but the majority are à la carte. It's wise to make a reservation and inquire if the restaurant has a liquor license or is "BYOB" or "BYO" (Bring Your Own Bottle)—many places have both.

Properties indicated by a ✕☑ are lodging establishments whose restaurant warrants a special trip.

Attire countrywide is pretty casual; unless you're planning to dine at the finest of places, men won't need to bring a jacket and tie. At the same time, the most common dinner attire is usually one level above jeans and sports shirts.

The restaurants we list are the cream of the crop in each price category. Price categories are as follows:

CATEGORY	COST*
$$$$	over $45
$$$	$35–$45
$$	$25–$35
$	under $25

*per person, excluding drinks, and service

MEALS & SPECIALTIES

When in New Zealand, try lamb. Restaurants offer it roasted, grilled, barbecued, or almost any other way you could think of. *Cervena,* or farm-raised venison, is local delicacy available all over New Zealand. Of course, seafood is a speciality in this island country, and one of the tastiest fish around is snapper. Orange roughy is another favorite. As for shellfish: don't miss the wonderful Bluff oysters (in season March–August), Greenshell mussels (also known as green-lipped or New Zealand green mussels), scallops, crayfish (spiny lobster), and two local clamlike shellfish, *pipi* and *tuatua.* Whitebait (known to Maori as *inanga*), which are the juvenile of several fish species, are featured in many restaurants in the springtime. They are eaten whole, usually in an omelet-like fritter. Be sure to try *kumara,* a local sweet potato that's sacred to the Maori. If you see *pavlova* on the dessert menu, give it a go. It's a large slice of meringue, usually stuffed with cream and garnished with fruit.

MEALTIMES

Restaurants serve breakfast roughly between 7 and 9:30. Lunch usually starts up at about noon and is over by 2. Dinners are usually served from 5 PM onward but the most popular dining time is around 7. Restaurants in cities and resort areas will serve dinner well into the night, but some places in small towns or rural areas still shut their doors at around 9.

Unless otherwise noted, the restaurants listed in this guide are open daily for lunch and dinner.

PAYING

Credit cards are widely accepted in restaurants and even small cafés. You may find exceptions to this rule, so check first.

RESERVATIONS & DRESS

Reservations are always a good idea: we mention them only when they're essential or not accepted. Book as far ahead as you can, and reconfirm as soon as you arrive. We mention dress only when men are required to wear a jacket or a jacket and tie.

WINE, BEER & SPIRITS

New Zealand's wine industry has leaped forward over the last decade. Best known for its white wines, particularly sauvignon blanc, riesling, and chardonnay, the country is now gaining a reputation for red wines such as cabernet and merlot. The main wine producing areas are West Auckland, Hawke's Bay, Martinborough, Marlborough, and Nelson. Emerging regions include Canterbury and central Otago. Restaurants almost without exception feature New Zealand products on their wine list.

Only 10 or 15 years ago people ordering a beer in New Zealand had a choice of two—Lion Red or DB Draught. Now those two breweries have substantially improved their range, and small microbreweries have added to the mix. Monteith Breweries and Macs are South Island–based breweries that distribute around the country and have a strong local following. Steinlager, probably the most famous of New Zealand beers, is brewed by Lion Breweries and is widely available. Most restaurants and liquor stores sell beers from Australia, the United States, Europe, and other parts of the world.

The only spirit New Zealand can really call its own is Wilson's Whisky, distilled in Dunedin—a city with a strong Scottish heritage.

Since 1999 it is possible to purchase beer and wine in supermarkets as well as specialized shops and to do so seven days a week. People under 18 are not permitted by law to purchase alcohol, and shops, bars, and restaurants strictly enforce this. If you look younger than you are, carry photo identification to prove your age.

DISABILITIES & ACCESSIBILITY

The **New Zealand Tourism Board** publishes ***Access: A Guide for the Less Mobile Traveller,*** listing accommodations, attractions, restaurants, and thermal pools with special facilities.

➤ LOCAL RESOURCES: **New Zealand Tourism Board** (☎ 04/472–8860).

AIR TRAVEL

In addition to making arrangements for wheelchair-using passengers, both **Qantas** and **Ansett Airlines** accommodate trained dogs accompanying passengers with sight- and hearing-impairments. On **Air New Zealand,** wheelchairs for in-flight mobility are standard equipment; seat-belt extensions, quadriplegic harnesses, and padded leg rests are also available. Ask for the company's brochure "Air Travel for People with Disabilities" (☞ Air Travel, *above*) .

CAR RENTAL

Only **Budget** offers cars fitted with hand controls, but these are limited. **Hertz** will fit hand-held controls onto standard cars in some cities. *See* Car Rental, *above*.

LODGING

In New Zealand, all accommodations are required by law to provide at least one room with facilities for guests with disabilities. Even independent lodgings with more than eight rooms should provide at least one room with such facilities. The major hotel chains (such as **Parkroyal**) provide three or four rooms with facilities for guests with disabilities in most of their properties. In Auckland, the **Centra** and the **Carlton** are recommended, and in Rotorua, the **Royal Lakeside Novotel** is a good option.

RESERVATIONS

When discussing accessibility with an operator or reservations agent, **ask hard questions.** Are there any stairs, inside *or* out? Are there grab bars next to the toilet *and* in the shower/tub? How wide is the doorway to the room? To the bathroom? For the most extensive facilities meeting the latest legal specifications, **opt for newer accommodations.**

TAXIS

Companies have recently introduced vans equipped with hoists and floor clamps, but these should be booked several hours in advance if possible; contact the **Plunket Society** (☞ Children in New Zealand, *above*) for more information.

TRAIN TRAVEL

Passengers on mainline passenger trains in New Zealand can request collapsible wheelchairs to negotiate narrow interior corridors. However, compact toilet areas and platform access problems make long-distance train travel difficult.

TRANSPORTATION

➤ COMPLAINTS: **Disability Rights Section** (✉ U.S. Department of Justice, Civil Rights Division, Box 66738, Washington, DC 20035-6738, ☎ 202/514–0301 or 800/514–0301; TTY 202/514–0301 or 800/514–0301, FAX 202/307–1198) for general complaints. **Aviation Consumer Protection Division** (☞ Air Travel, *above*) for airline-related problems. **Civil Rights Office** (✉ U.S. Department of Transportation, Departmental Office of Civil Rights, S-30, 400 7th St. SW, Room 10215, Washington, DC 20590, ☎ 202/366–4648, FAX 202/366–9371) for problems with surface transportation.

TRAVEL AGENCIES

In the United States, the Americans with Disabilities Act requires that travel firms serve the needs of all travelers. Some agencies specialize in working with people with disabilities.

➤ TRAVELERS WITH MOBILITY PROBLEMS: **Access Adventures** (✉ 206 Chestnut Ridge Rd., Rochester, NY 14624, ☎ 716/889–9096), run by a former physical-rehabilitation counselor. **CareVacations** (✉ 5-5110 50th Ave., Leduc, Alberta T9E 6V4, ☎ 780/986–6404 or 877/478–7827, FAX 780/986–8332, www.carevacations.com), for group tours and cruise vacations. **Flying Wheels Travel** (✉ 143 W. Bridge St., Box 382, Owatonna, MN 55060, ☎ 507/451–5005 or 800/535–6790, FAX 507/451–1685, www.flyingwheels.com).

DISCOUNTS & DEALS

Be a smart shopper and **compare all your options** before making decisions. A plane ticket bought with a promotional coupon from travel clubs, coupon books, and direct-mail offers may not be cheaper than the least expensive fare from a discount ticket agency. Keep in mind that what you get is just as important as what you save.

DISCOUNT RESERVATIONS

To save money, **look into discount reservations services** with toll-free numbers, which use their buying power to get a better price on hotels, airline tickets, even car rentals. When booking a room, always **call the hotel's local toll-free number** (if one is available) rather than the central reservations number—you'll often get a better price. Always ask about special packages or corporate rates.

When shopping for the best deal on hotels and car rentals, **look for guaranteed exchange rates,** which protect you against a falling dollar. With your rate locked in, you won't pay more, even if the price goes up in the local currency.

➤ AIRLINE TICKETS: ☎ **800/FLY–4–LESS.**

➤ HOTEL ROOMS: **Travel Interlink** (☎ 800/888–5898, www.travelinterlink. com).

PACKAGE DEALS

Don't confuse packages and guided tours. When you buy a package, you travel on your own, just as though you had planned the trip yourself. Fly/drive packages, which combine airfare and car rental, are often a good deal.

ECOTOURISM

For anyone passionate about the natural world, a journey to New Zealand offers the chance to step back in time to a primeval era. Isolated from other landmasses for at least 80 million years, New Zealand has enormous biological diversity.

Learn about flora and fauna with eco-sensitive tour operators from the 100% Pure Nature network, a group that works with Tourism New

Zealand to promote nature tourism. These are knowledgable tour operators who are actively involved in conservation.

➤ 100% NATURE ECO-TOURISM OPERATORS: **Akaroa Harbour Cruises** (✉ Akaroa, ☎ 03/304–7641). **Bush & Beach** (✉ Auckland, ☎ 09/478–2882). **Dolphin Discoveries** (✉ Bay of Islands, ☎ 09/402–8234). **Guided Nature Walks** (✉ Queenstown, ☎ 03/442–7126). **Heritage Expeditions Ltd.** (✉ Christchurch, ☎ 03/338–9944). **Kiwi Dundee Adventures** (✉ Coromandel, ☎ 07/865–8809, www. kiwidundee.co.nz). **Monarch Wildlife Cruises** (✉ Dunedin, ☎ 03/477–4276). **Mt. Bruce National Wildlife Center** (✉ Masterton, ☎ 06/375–8004). **Nature Connection** (✉ Rotorua, ☎ 07/347–1705). **NZ Marine Studies Centre** (✉ Dunedin, ☎ 03/479–5826). **100% Pure Nature Network** (www.purenz.com). **Otago Peninsula trust** (✉ Dunedin, ☎ 03/478–0497). **Stewart Island Lodge** (✉ Stewart Island, ☎ 03/478–0286). **Waimangu Valley** (✉ Rotorua, ☎ 07/366–6137). **Whalewatch Kaikoura** (✉ Kaikoura, ☎ 03/319–5045). **Wilderness Lodge Arthur's Pass** (✉ Canterbury, ☎ 03/318–9246). **Wings of Kotuku** (✉ Dunedin, ☎ 03/454–5169).

ELECTRICITY

To use your U.S.-purchased electric-powered equipment, **bring a converter and adapter.** The electrical current in New Zealand is 240 volts, 50 cycles alternating current (AC); wall outlets take slanted three-prong plugs (but not the U.K. three-prong) and plugs with two flat prongs set at a "V" angle.

If your appliances are dual-voltage, you'll need only an adapter. Don't use 110-volt outlets, marked FOR SHAVERS ONLY, for high-wattage appliances such as blow-dryers. Most laptops operate equally well on 110 and 220 volts and so require only an adapter.

EMBASSIES

➤ AUSTRALIA: (✉ 72-78 Hobson St., Thorndon, Wellington, ☎ 04/473–6411).

➤ CANADA: (✉ 61 Molesworth St., Wellington, ☎ 04/473–9577).

➤ U.K.: (✉ 44 Hill St., Wellington, ☎ 04/472–6049).

➤ U.S.: (✉ 29 Fitzherbert Terr., Thorndon, Wellington, ☎ 04/472–2068).

EMERGENCIES

➤ CONTACTS: Dial 111 for fire, police, or ambulance services.

GAY & LESBIAN TRAVEL

Discrimination on the grounds of sexual orientation is illegal in New Zealand and Kiwis in general are accepting of gays and lesbians. As in North America, Britain, and Australia, gay and lesbian travelers may feel comfortable in many urban areas, but might want to be more cautious in rural areas.

➤ GAY- & LESBIAN-FRIENDLY TRAVEL AGENCIES: **Different Roads Travel** (✉ 8383 Wilshire Blvd., Suite 902, Beverly Hills, CA 90211, ☎ 323/651–5557 or 800/429–8747, FAX 323/651–3678). **Kennedy Travel** (✉ 314 Jericho Tpk., Floral Park, NY 11001, ☎ 516/352–4888 or 800/237–7433, FAX 516/354–8849, www.kennedytravel.com). **Now Voyager** (✉ 4406 18th St., San Francisco, CA 94114, ☎ 415/626–1169 or 800/255–6951, FAX 415/626–8626, www.nowvoyager.com). **Skylink Travel and Tour** (✉ 1006 Mendocino Ave., Santa Rosa, CA 95401, ☎ 707/546–9888 or 800/225–5759, FAX 707/546–9891, www.skylinktravel.com), serving lesbian travelers.

HEALTH

Nutrition and general health standards in New Zealand are high, and it would be hard to find a more pristine natural environment. There are no venomous snakes, and the only poisonous spider, the *katipo,* is a rarity.

DIVERS' ALERT

Do not fly within 24 hours of scuba diving.

FOOD & DRINK

There is one surprising health hazard in New Zealand: don't drink the water in New Zealand's outdoors. While the country's alpine lakes might look like backdrops for mineral-water ads, some in South Island harbor a tiny organism that can cause "duck itch," a temporary but intense skin irritation. The organism is found only on the shallow lake margins, so the chances of infection are greatly reduced if you stick to deeper water. Streams can be infected by giardia, a water-borne protozoal parasite that can cause gastrointestinal disorders, including acute diarrhea. Giardia is most likely contracted when drinking from streams that pass through an area inhabited by mammals (such as cattle or possums). There is no risk of infection if you drink from streams above the tree line.

PESTS & OTHER HAZARDS

The major health hazard in New Zealand is sunburn or sunstroke. Even people who are not normally bothered by strong sun should cover up with a long-sleeve shirt, a hat, and pants or a beach wrap. At higher altitudes you will burn more easily, so apply sunscreen liberally before you go out—even for a half-hour—and wear a visor or sunglasses.

Dehydration is another serious danger that can be easily avoided, so be sure to carry water and drink often. Limit the amount of time you spend in the sun for the first few days until you are acclimatized, and avoid sunbathing in the middle of the day.

One New Zealander you will come to loathe is the tiny black sand fly, common to the western half of South Island, which inflicts a painful bite that can itch for several days (some call it the state bird). In other parts of the country, especially around rivers and lakes, you may be pestered by mosquitoes. Be sure to use insect repellent.

HOLIDAYS

On Christmas Day, everything closes down in New Zealand except for a few gas stations, some shops selling essential food items, and emergency facilities. On other public holidays (often referred to as bank holidays) many museums and attractions will stay open, as will transportation systems, though on a reduced schedule. Around Christmas and New Year's Kiwis pack up and go to the beach, so seaside resorts will be difficult to visit unless you have booked well in advance. You'll get plenty of sunshine and far fewer crowds if you visit from late January through to the colder period of late March. Cities such as Auckland and Wellington are quite pleasant over Christmas and New Year's. Fewer cars are on the road and you'll get good prices from hotels trying to make up for the lack of corporate guests.

INSURANCE

The most useful travel insurance plan is a comprehensive policy that includes coverage for trip cancellation and interruption, default, trip delay, and medical expenses (with a waiver for preexisting conditions).

Without insurance you will lose all or most of your money if you cancel your trip, regardless of the reason. Default insurance covers you if your tour operator, airline, or cruise line goes out of business. Trip-delay covers expenses that arise because of bad weather or mechanical delays. Study the fine print when comparing policies.

If you're traveling internationally, a key component of travel insurance is coverage for medical bills incurred if you get sick on the road. Such expenses are not generally covered by Medicare or private policies. U.K. residents can buy a travel insurance policy valid for most vacations taken during the year in which it's purchased (but check preexisting-condition coverage). British and Australian citizens need extra medical coverage when traveling overseas. Always **buy travel policies directly from the insurance company**; if you buy them from a cruise line, airline, or tour operator that goes out of business you probably will not be covered for the agency or operator's default, a major risk. Before making any purchase, **review your existing health and homeowner's policies** to find what they cover away from home.

➤ TRAVEL INSURERS: In the U.S.: **Access America** (✉ 6600 W. Broad St., Richmond, VA 23230, ☎ 804/285–3300 or 800/284–8300, FAX 804/673–1583, www.previewtravel.com),

Travel Guard International (✉ 1145 Clark St., Stevens Point, WI 54481, ☎ 715/345–0505 or 800/826–1300, FAX 800/955–8785, www.noelgroup.com). In Canada: **Voyager Insurance** (✉ 44 Peel Center Dr., Brampton, Ontario L6T 4M8, ☎ 905/791–8700, 800/668–4342 in Canada).

➤ INSURANCE INFORMATION: In the U.K.: **Association of British Insurers** (✉ 51–55 Gresham St., London EC2V 7HQ, ☎ 020/7600–3333, FAX 020/7696–8999). In Australia: **Insurance Council of Australia** (☎ 03/9614–1077, FAX 03/9614–7924).

LANGUAGE

To an outsider's ear, Kiwi English can be mystifying. Even more so, the Maori (pronounced *moh*-ree) language has added to the New Zealand lexicon words that can seem utterly unpronounceable. It is still spoken by many New Zealanders of Polynesian descent, but English is the everyday language for all people. A number of Maori words have found their way into common usage, most noticeably in place-names, which often refer to peculiar features of the local geography or food supply. The Maori word for New Zealand, Aotearoa, means "land of the long white cloud." The South Island town of Kaikoura is famous for its crayfish—the word means "to eat crayfish." Whangapiro (fang-ah-pee-ro), the Maori name for the Government Gardens in Rotorua, means "an evil-smelling place," and if you visit the town you'll find out why. A Polynesian word you'll sometimes come across in Maori churches is *tapu* "sacred," which has entered the English language as the word taboo. Another Maori word you will frequently encounter is *Pakeha*, which means you, the non-Maori. The Maori greeting is *kia ora*, which can also mean "good-bye," "good health," or "good luck." *See* the Kiwi and Maori glossaries in Chapter 6.

LODGING

The **New Zealand Tourism Board** (☞ Visitor Information, *below*) publishes an annual Where to Stay directory listing more than 1,000 properties.

The lodgings we list are the cream of the crop in each price category. We always list the facilities that are available—but we don't specify whether they cost extra: when pricing accommodations, always ask what's included and what costs extra. The price categories are as follows:

CATEGORY	COST*
$$$$	over $200
$$$	$125–$200
$$	$80–$125
$	under $80

All prices are for a standard double room.

Assume that hotels operate on the **European Plan** (EP, with no meals) unless we specify that they use the **Continental Plan** (CP, with a Continental breakfast), **Breakfast Plan** (BP, with a full breakfast), **Modified American Plan** (MAP, with breakfast and dinner), or the **Full American Plan** (FAP, with all meals).

Properties marked ✕🖬 are lodging establishments whose restaurants warrant a special trip.

B&BS

Hospitality Plus is a one-number booking system for bed-and-breakfasts, as well as homestays and farm stays, around New Zealand. The company has about 300 places on its books. Once in New Zealand you will find the *New Zealand Bed and Breakfast Book* in most major bookstores. It lists about 1,000 bed-and-breakfasts, but be aware that the editorial copy in the book has been provided by the property owners themselves, rather than providing independent assessments as this Fodor's guide does.

➤ RESERVATION SERVICES: **Hospitality Plus** (✉ Box 56-175, Auckland 3, ☎ 09/810–9175, ℻ 09/810–9445).

CAMPING

There are almost 900 backcountry huts in New Zealand. They provide basic shelter but few frills. Huts are usually placed about four hours apart, although in isolated areas it can take a full day to get from one hut to the next. They are graded 1 to 4, and cost varies from nothing to $14 per person per night. Category 1

huts (the $14 ones) have cooking equipment and fuel, bunks or sleeping platforms with mattresses, toilets, washing facilities, and a supply of water. At the other end of the scale, Category 4 huts (the free ones) are simple shelters without bunks or other facilities. Pay for huts with coupons, available in books from Department of Conservation offices. If you plan to make extensive use of huts, an annual pass giving access to all Category 2 and 3 huts for one year is available for $65.

➤ EXCHANGE CLUBS: **HomeLink International** (✉ Box 650, Key West, FL 33041, ☎ 305/294–7766 or 800/638–3841, ℻ 305/294–1448, www.homelink.org; $98 per year). **Intervac U.S.** (✉ Box 590504, San Francisco, CA 94159, ☎ 800/756–4663, ℻ 415/435–7440, www.intervac.com; $89 per year includes 2 catalogs).

HOME AND FARM STAYS

Home and farm stays, which are very popular with visitors to New Zealand, offer not only comfortable accommodations but a chance to **get to know the countryside and its people**—a great thing to do because Kiwis are so naturally friendly. Most operate on a bed-and-breakfast basis, though some also offer an evening meal. Farm accommodations vary from modest shearers' cabins to elegant homesteads. Guests can join in farm activities or explore the countryside. Some hosts offer day trips, as well as horseback riding, hiking, and fishing. For two people, the average cost is $90–$150 per night, including all meals. Homestays, the urban equivalent of farm stays, are less expensive. Most New Zealanders seem to have vacation homes, called *baches* on North Island, *cribs* on South Island, and these are frequently available for rent.

➤ RESERVATIONS & INFORMATION: **New Zealand Farm Holidays Ltd.** (✉ Box 256, Silverdale, Auckland, ☎ 09/307–2024) or **Homestay Ltd. Farmstay Ltd.** (✉ Box 25–115, Auckland, ☎ 09/575–9977). *Baches and Holiday Homes to Rent*, by Mark and Elizabeth Greening ($14.95; ✉ Box 3017, Richmond, Nelson, ☎ ℻ 03/

544–5799), lists 430 self-contained holiday homes.

HOSTELS

No matter what your age, you can **save on lodging costs by staying at hostels.** In some 5,000 locations in more than 70 countries around the world, Hostelling International (HI), the umbrella group for a number of national youth-hostel associations, offers single-sex, dorm-style beds and, at many hostels, rooms for couples and family accommodations. Membership in any HI national hostel association, open to travelers of all ages, allows you to stay in HI-affiliated hostels at member rates; one-year membership is about $25 for adults (C$26.75 in Canada, £9.30 in the United Kingdom, $30 in Australia, and $30 in New Zealand); hostels run about $10–$25 per night. Members have priority if the hostel is full; they're also eligible for discounts around the world, even on rail and bus travel in some countries.

In addition to the International Youth Hostels, a network of low-cost, independent backpacker hostels operates in New Zealand. They can be found in nearly every city and tourist spot, and they offer clean, twin- and small-dormitory–style accommodations and self-catering kitchens, similar to those of the Youth Hostel Association (or YHA, the Australian version of IYH), with no membership required.

➤ ORGANIZATIONS: **Hostelling International—American Youth Hostels** (✉ 733 15th St. NW, Suite 840, Washington, DC 20005, ☎ 202/783–6161, FAX 202/783–6171, www.hiayh.org). **Hostelling International—Canada** (✉ 400–205 Catherine St., Ottawa, Ontario K2P 1C3, ☎ 613/237–7884, FAX 613/237–7868, www.hostellingintl.ca). **Youth Hostel Association of England and Wales** (✉ Trevelyan House, 8 St. Stephen's Hill, St. Albans, Hertfordshire AL1 2DY, ☎ 01727/855215 or 01727/845047, FAX 01727/844126, www.yha. uk). **Australian Youth Hostel Association** (✉ 10 Mallett St., Camperdown, NSW 2050, ☎ 02/9565–1699, FAX 02/9565–1325, www.yha.com.au). **Youth Hostels Association of New Zealand** (✉ Box 436, Christchurch, New Zealand, ☎ 03/379–9970, FAX 03/365–4476, www.yha.org.nz).

In New Zealand, hostelling information and registration are available at **YHA Travel Centres** (✉ 36 Customs St. East or Box 1687, Auckland, ☎ 09/379–4224; ✉ corner of Gloucester and Manchester Sts., Christchurch, ☎ 03/379–8046). To find out about backpacker hostels, contact **Budget Backpackers Hostels NZ, Ltd.** (✉ Rainbow Lodge, 99 Titiraupenga St., Taupo, ☎ 07/378–5754; or ✉ Foley Towers, 208 Kilgore St., Christchurch, ☎ 03/366–9720).

HOTELS

All hotels listed have private bath unless otherwise noted.

➤ TOLL-FREE NUMBERS: **Best Western** (☎ 800/528–1234, www.bestwestern.com). **Choice** (☎ 800/221–2222, www.hotelchoice.com). **Clarion** (☎ 800/252–7466, www.choicehotels.com). **Comfort** (☎ 800/228–5150, www.comfortinn.com). **Holiday Inn** (☎ 800/465–4329, www.holiday-inn.com). **Quality Inn** (☎ 800/228–5151, www.qualityinn.com).

MOTELS

Motels are the most common accommodations, and most offer comfortable rooms for $60–$90 per night. Some motels have two-bedroom suites for families. All motel rooms come equipped with tea- and coffee-making equipment, many have toasters or electric frying pans, and full kitchen facilities.

MOTOR CAMPS

The least expensive accommodations in the country are the tourist cabins and flats in most of the country's 400 motor camps. Tourist cabins offer basic accommodation and shared cooking, laundry, and bathroom facilities. Bedding and towels are not provided. A notch higher up the comfort scale, tourist flats usually provide bedding, fully equipped kitchens, and private bathrooms. Overnight rates run about $6–$20 for cabins and $25–$70 for flats.

SPORTING LODGES

At the high end of the price scale, a growing number of luxury sporting lodges offer the best of country life,

fine dining, and superb accommodations. Fishing is a specialty at many of
them, but there is usually a range of
outdoor activities for nonanglers.
Tariffs run about $350–$800 per day
for two people; meals are generally
included.

MAIL & SHIPPING

Airmail should take around 6 or 7
days to reach the United Kingdom or
the United States, and 2 or 3 days to
reach Australia.

OVERNIGHT SERVICES

Overnight services are available
between New Zealand and Australia,
but to destinations further afield
"overnight" will in reality be closer to
48 hours. Even to Australia, truly
overnight services is only offered
between major cities and can be
subject to conditions, such as the time
you call in. A number of major operators are represented in New Zealand
and the services are reliable, particularly from cities.

➤ MAJOR SERVICES: **DHL World
Express** (✉ 29 Mahunga Dr., Man-
gere, ☎ 09/633–0077 or 0800/557–
777). **Federal Express (Fedex)** (✉
Airport Freight Centre, Auckland
Airport, ☎ 0800/733–339). **TNT
International Express** (✉ 6 Doncaster
St., Mangere, ☎ 09/255–0500).

POSTAL RATES

Post offices are open weekdays 9–5.
The cost of mailing a letter within New
Zealand is 40¢ standard post, 80¢ fast
post. Sending a standard size letter by
air mail costs $1.50 to North America,
$1.80 to Europe, and $1 to Australia.
Aerogrammes and postcards are $1 to
any overseas destination.

RECEIVING MAIL

If you wish to receive correspondence,
have mail sent to New Zealand held
for you for up to one month at the
central post office in any town or city
if it is addressed to you "c/o Poste
Restante, CPO," followed by the
name of the town. This service is free.

SHIPPING PARCELS

You can use the major international
overnight companies listed above or
purchase packaging and pre-paid mail
services from the post office. Major
duty-free stores and stores that deal

frequently with travelers will be able
to help with international shipping,
but if you purchase from small shops,
particularly in country areas, **arrange
shipping with a company in the nearest city.**

MEDIA

New Zealand has its share of scandal
sheets and gossip magazines, but in
general the standard of journalism is
high. Because it is a small and isolated
country, you'll find the interest in
international news greater than you
may expect. Any major stories coming out of the United States and the
United Kingdom—or major sports
events around the world—are likely
to receive full coverage.

NEWSPAPERS & MAGAZINES

There are daily metropolitan newspapers in all cities (two in Wellington),
smaller local dailies in provincial
towns, and many, many community
and local papers. The *New Zealand
Herald* is the daily with the country's
largest circulation. Although it has a
distinctly Auckland slant to it, the
Herald does a good job on national
and international news. The *Dominion* is Wellington's morning paper
and is the best source for the nation's
political events. In Christchurch, the
Press is highly regarded.

The country has a massive array of
locally published magazines—there
are more local magazine titles per
capita than in any other country in
the world. *Women's Weekly,
Women's Day,* and *New Idea* will
keep you current with royal scandals
from Britain and who's doing what to
whom among the local celebrities. For
more serious reading, pick up a copy
of *North & South* (monthly) or the
Listener (weekly). Both have in-depth
articles on issues facing New Zealand.
Metro magazine is slightly more
lighthearted and concentrates on
Auckland issues.

RADIO & TELEVISION

For news, views, and talk back (talk
radio) try Newstalk ZB at AM1080,
and for sports coverage (including
American sports events in the middle of
the night NZ time) tune to AM1332.
There's a good array of music stations.
For the latest hits, go to the ZM network (FM91 in Auckland).

New Zealand has four main television channels: TV 1, 2, 3, and 4, plus other free channels (Prime and Triangle) that you'll find in main centers. Channels 1 and 3 have news at 6 PM. Channels 2 and 4 are targeted at the youth market and this is where you'll find popular U.S. programs.

Most hotels have Sky TV, including the news channel that takes a feed from CNN.

MONEY MATTERS

For most travelers, New Zealand is not an expensive destination. The cost of meals, accommodation, and travel is slightly higher than in the United States but considerably less than in Western Europe. At about $1 per liter—equal to about U.S.$2.10 per gallon—premium-grade gasoline is expensive by North American standards, but not by European ones.

Inflation, which reached a peak of almost 20% in the late 1980s, has now been reduced to less than 5%.

The following are sample costs in New Zealand at press time:

Cup of coffee $2.50; glass of beer in a bar $2.50–$4; take-out ham sandwich or meat pie $2.50; hamburger in a café $5–$8; room-service sandwich in a hotel $12; a 2-km (1¼-mi) taxi ride $5. Prices throughout this guide are given for adults. Substantially reduced fees are almost always available for children, students, and senior citizens. For information on taxes, *see* Taxes, *below.*

ATMS

ATMs are widely found in city and town banks and in some shopping malls. The number of ATMs is growing all the time. All the major banks in New Zealand (Bank of New Zealand, Westpac, and Auckland Savings Bank) accept cards in the Cirrus and Plus networks. The norm for PIN numbers in New Zealand is four digits. If the PIN for your account has a different number of digits, you must **change your number before you leave for New Zealand.**

CREDIT CARDS

Throughout this guide, the following abbreviations are used: **AE**, American Express; **DC**, Diners Club; **MC**, MasterCard; and **V**, Visa.

➤ REPORTING LOST CARDS: American Express (☎ 09/367–4247); Diners Club (☎ 09/359–7796); MasterCard (☎ 0800/449–140); Visa (☎ 0800/445–594).

CURRENCY

All prices quoted in this guide are in New Zealand dollars.

New Zealand's unit of currency is the dollar, divided into 100 cents. Bills are in $100, $50, $10, and $5 denominations. Coins are $2, $1, 50¢, 20¢, 10¢, and 5¢. At press time the rate of exchange was NZ$2.17 to the U.S. dollar, NZ$1.46 to the Canadian dollar, NZ$3.26 to the pound sterling, and NZ$1.27 to the Australian dollar. Exchange rates change on a daily basis.

CURRENCY EXCHANGE

U.S. dollars are widely accepted in New Zealand, but for the most favorable rates, **change money through banks.** Although ATM transaction fees may be higher abroad than at home, ATM rates are excellent because they are based on wholesale rates offered only by major banks. You won't do as well at exchange booths in airports or rail and bus stations, in hotels, in restaurants, or in stores. To avoid lines at airport exchange booths, **get a bit of local currency before you leave home.**

➤ EXCHANGE SERVICES: International Currency Express (☎ 888/278–6628 for orders, www.foreignmoney.com). Thomas Cook Currency Services (☎ 800/287–7362 for telephone orders and retail locations, www.us. thomascook.com).

TRAVELER'S CHECKS

Do you need traveler's checks? It depends on where you're headed. If you're going to rural areas and small towns, go with cash; traveler's checks are best used in cities. Lost or stolen checks can usually be replaced within 24 hours. To ensure a speedy refund, buy your own traveler's checks. The person who bought the checks should make the call to request a refund.

OUTDOORS & SPORTS

For information on guided bicycling, canoeing and sea-kayaking, cross-country skiing, diving, fishing, hiking, horseback riding, rafting, and sailing tours and tour operators, *see* Chapter 5.

FISHING

Wherever you fish, and whatever you fish for, you will profit immensely from the services of a local guide. On Lake Taupo or Rotorua, a boat with a guide plus all equipment will cost around $130 for two hours. In South Island, a top fishing guide who can supply all equipment and a four-wheel-drive vehicle will charge about $400 per day for two people. In the Bay of Islands region, an evening fishing trip aboard a small boat can cost as little as $35. For a big-game fishing boat, expect to pay between $600 and $1,000 per day. There are also several specialist lodges that provide guides and transport to wilderness streams sometimes accessible only by helicopter.

For more information on fishing, *see* Chapter 5.

GOLF

Generally speaking, clubs can be rented, but you'll need your own shoes. Greens fees range from $5 at country courses to $60 at exclusive city courses. The better urban courses also offer resident professionals and golf carts for rent.

For more information, contact the Executive Director, **NZ Golf Association** (✉ Box 11–842, Wellington).

HIKING

The traditional way to hike in New Zealand is freedom walking. Freedom walkers carry their own provisions, sleeping bags, food, and cooking gear, and sleep in basic huts. A more refined alternative—usually available only on more popular trails—is the guided walk, on which you trek with just a light day pack, guides do the cooking, and you sleep in heated lodges. If you prefer your wilderness served with hot showers and an eiderdown on your bed, the guided walk is for you.

If you plan to walk the spectacular Milford or Routeburn tracks in December or January, book at least six months in advance. At other times, three months is usually sufficient. (If you arrive without a booking, there may be last-minute cancellations, and parties of one or two can often be accommodated.) The Milford Track is closed due to snowfall from the end of April to early September.

Plan your clothing and footwear carefully. Even at the height of summer weather can change quickly, and hikers must be prepared—especially for the rainstorms that regularly drench the Southern Alps. (The Milford Sound region, with its average annual rainfall of 160 inches, is one of the wettest places on earth.) The most cost-effective rain gear you can buy is the U.S. Army poncho.

Wear a hat and sunglasses and put on sun block to protect your skin against the sun. Keep in mind that at higher altitudes, where the air is thinner, you will burn more easily. Sun reflected off of snow, sand, or water can be especially strong. Apply sunscreen liberally before you go out—even if only for a half-hour.

Also, be careful about heatstroke. Symptoms include headache, dizziness, and fatigue, which can turn into convulsions, unconsciousness, and can lead to death. If someone in your party develops signs of heat stroke, have one person seek emergency help while others move the victim into the shade, and wrap him or her in wet clothing (is a stream or lake nearby?) to cool him or her down.

Temperatures can vary widely from day to night. Be sure to bring enough warm clothing for hiking and camping, along with wet weather gear. Exposure to the degree that body temperature dips below 95°F (35°C) produces the following symptoms: chills, tiredness, then uncontrollable shivering and irrational behavior, with the victim not always recognizing that he or she is cold. If someone in your party is suffering from any of this, wrap him or her in blankets and/or a warm sleeping bag immediately and try to keep him or her awake. The fastest way to raise body temperature is through skin-to-skin contact in a sleeping bag. Drinking warm liquids also helps.

Avoid drinking from streams or lakes, no matter how clear they may be. Giardia organisms can turn your stomach inside out. And in South Island a tiny organism found on the shallow margins of lakes can cause "duck itch," a temporary but intense skin irritation. The easiest way to purify water is to dissolve a water purification tablet in it. Camping equipment stores also carry purification pumps. Boiling water for 15 minutes is always a reliable method, if time- and fuel-consuming.

For information on camping, *see* Lodging, *above*.

PACKING

In New Zealand, be prepared for temperatures varying from day to night and weather that can turn suddenly, particularly at the change of seasons. The wisest approach to dressing is to wear layered outfits. You'll appreciate being able to remove or put on a jacket. Take along a light raincoat and umbrella, but remember that plastic raincoats and nonbreathing polyester are uncomfortable in the tropics. Don't wear lotions or perfume in the tropics either, since they attract mosquitoes and other bugs; carry insect repellent. Bring a hat with a brim to provide protection from the strong sunlight (☞ Health, *above*). You'll need warm clothing for South Island.

Dress is casual in most cities, though top resorts and restaurants may require a jacket and tie. In autumn, a light wool sweater and/or a jacket will suffice for evenings in coastal cities, but winter demands a heavier coat—a raincoat with a zip-out wool lining is ideal. Comfortable walking shoes are a must. You should have a pair of running shoes or the equivalent if you're planning to trek, and rubber-sole sandals or canvas shoes are needed for walking on reef coral.

In your carry-on luggage, **pack an extra pair of eyeglasses or contact lenses** and **enough of any medication you take** to last the entire trip. You

may also ask your doctor to write a spare prescription using the drug's generic name, since brand names may vary from country to country. In luggage to be checked, **never pack prescription drugs or valuables.** To avoid customs delays, carry medications in their original packaging. And don't forget to carry with you the addresses of offices that handle refunds of lost traveler's checks.

CHECKING LUGGAGE

How many carry-on bags you can bring with you is up to the airline. Most allow two, but not always, so make sure that everything you carry aboard will fit under your seat or in the overhead bin, and get to the gate early. Note that if you have a seat at the back of the plane, you'll probably board first, while the overhead bins are still empty.

If you are flying internationally, note that baggage allowances may be determined not by piece but by weight—generally 88 pounds (40 kilograms) in first class, 66 pounds (30 kilograms) in business class, and 44 pounds (20 kilograms) in economy.

Airline liability for baggage is limited to $1,250 per person on flights within the United States. On international flights it amounts to $9.07 per pound or $20 per kilogram for checked baggage (roughly $640 per 70-pound bag) and $400 per passenger for unchecked baggage. You can buy additional coverage at check-in for about $10 per $1,000 of coverage, but it excludes a rather extensive list of items, shown on your airline ticket.

Before departure, **itemize your bags' contents** and their worth, and label the bags with your name, address, and phone number. (If you use your home address, cover it so potential thieves can't see it readily.) Inside each bag, **pack a copy of your itinerary.** At check-in, **make sure that each bag is correctly tagged** with the destination airport's three-letter code. If your bags arrive damaged or fail to arrive at all, file a written report with the airline before leaving the airport.

PASSPORTS & VISAS

When traveling internationally, **carry your passport even if you don't need** one (it's always the best form of I.D.) and **make two photocopies of the data page** (one for someone at home and another for you, carried separately from your passport). If you lose your passport, promptly call the nearest embassy or consulate and the local police.

ENTERING NEW ZEALAND

U.S., Canadian, and U.K. citizens need only a valid passport to enter New Zealand for stays of up to 90 days.

PASSPORT OFFICES

The best time to apply for a passport or to renew is in fall and winter. Before any trip, check your passport's expiration date, and, if necessary, renew it as soon as possible.

➤ AUSTRALIAN CITIZENS: **Australian Passport Office** (☎ 131–232 (from anywhere in Australia), www.dfat. gov.au/passports).

➤ CANADIAN CITIZENS: **Passport Office** (☎ 819/994–3500 or 800/567–6868, www.dfait-maeci.gc.ca/passport).

➤ U.K. CITIZENS: **London Passport Office** (☎ 0990/210–410) for fees and documentation requirements and to request an emergency passport.

➤ U.S. CITIZENS: **National Passport Information Center** (☎ 900/225–5674; calls are 35¢ per minute for automated service, $1.05 per minute for operator service).

REST ROOMS

Shopping malls in cities, major bus and train stations, gas stations, and many rest areas on main highways have public toilets. Look for a blue sign with white figures (ladies and gents) for directions to a public toilet. New Zealanders often use the word "loo."

Most New Zealand public rest-room facilities are clean and tidy, and often have a separate room for mothers with young children.

Some gas stations, shops, and hotels have signs stating that only customers can use the rest room. Kiwis are generally fair-minded folk, so if you're genuinely caught short and explain the situation you will probably not be turned away.

Most gas stations in New Zealand have toilet facilities, but their standard is variable. As a rule of thumb, the newer and more impressive the gas station, the cleaner and better the toilet facilities.

SAFETY

New Zealand is safe for travelers, but international visitors have been known to get into trouble when they take their safety for granted and let their guard down. Use common sense, particularly if walking around cities at night. Stick around other people and avoid deserted alleys. Although New Zealand is an affluent society by world standards, it has its share of poor and homeless (often referred to as "street kids" if they are young). Avoid bus and train stations or city squares late at night. The crowds in some pubs can get a bit rough late at night, so if you sense aggravation, leave.

Hotels offer safes for guests' valuables, and it pays to use them. Don't flash your wealth, and remember to lock doors of hotel rooms and cars. Unfortunately, opportunist criminals stake out parking lots at some popular tourist attractions. Put valuables out of sight under seats before you arrive at the destination.

If traveling in the countryside, you're safer as a couple. Remember, most visitors have no trouble and find the New Zealand people among the friendliest in the world. Nine times out of ten, offers of help or other friendly gestures will be genuine.

WOMEN IN NEW ZEALAND

Women will not attract more unwanted attention than in most other Western societies, nor will they be immune from the usual hassles. In cities at night, stick to well-lit areas and avoid being totally alone. Hotel staff will be happy to give tips on any areas to avoid, and the times to avoid them. New Zealand is relatively safe for women, but don't be complacent.

SENIOR-CITIZEN TRAVEL

To qualify for age-related discounts, **mention your senior-citizen status up front** when booking hotel reservations (not when checking out) and before you're seated in restaurants (not when paying the bill). When renting a car, ask about promotional car-rental discounts, which can be cheaper than senior-citizen rates.

➤ EDUCATIONAL PROGRAMS: **Elderhostel** (✉ 75 Federal St., 3rd floor, Boston, MA 02110, ☎ 877/426–8056, 🆁🅰🆇 877/426–2166, www.elderhostel.org). **Interhostel** (✉ University of New Hampshire, 6 Garrison Ave., Durham, NH 03824, ☎ 603/862–1147 or 800/733–9753, 🅵🅰🆇 603/862–1113, www.learn.unh.edu).

SHOPPING

New Zealand is not widely regarded as a shopping destination for tourists. However, the state of the Kiwi dollar at press time means that visitors from the United States and Europe will find plenty of bargains. Duty-free shopping is particularly good, and at Auckland International Airport you'll find prices to rival anywhere else in the world. Most cities and towns have outdoor markets at least once a week. You'll often find local arts and crafts at these, as well as second-hand clothing and assorted knickknacks. Ask at local visitor information centers for dates, times, and locations of markets.

If you have a car and want to meet Kiwis in a slightly unusual way, pick up a Friday-morning newspaper and look in the classified ads for Saturday- and Sunday-morning garage sales. Sometimes you'll find five or six garage sales in the space of a few suburban miles—especially in places like west and south Auckland. Some of your fellow buyers will be "professionals" who pick up bargains and resell them in second-hand stores, others are just people out looking for a good deal.

New Zealand shops have set prices, but you'll be able to bargain a bit in antiques and second-hand stores, or markets. Don't expect to be able to knock more than a few dollars off the stated price though.

KEY DESTINATIONS

Aucklanders shop in their suburbs, and a number of these have developed excellent shopping centers. Among the best are St. Lukes, Lynmall (New Lynn), and Manukau City. The most accessible shopping district in Auckland is Queen Street. Wellington's Lambton Quay has a comprehensive selection of shops. Christchurch has shops stretching off in all directions from Cathedral Square, and Dunedin's best shops are around the Octagon.

SMART SOUVENIRS

A rugby jersey, especially for the All Black team, can look more fashionable than it sounds. Expect to pay about $100.

A bottle of sauvignon blanc from the Marlborough District, particularly the attractively labeled Cloudy Bay, is a tasty souvenir and will cost between $20 and $30. It's fun to buy from the vineyard, but you can also buy New Zealand wine at general stores and in city wine shops.

Greenstone (jade) is available in tourist and souvenir shops. It's beautiful stone and is best when carved and polished. Prices vary greatly depending on the size and quality of the item.

WATCH OUT

Buy a sheepskin rug if you must, but don't do it from an inner-city souvenir shop unless you want to pay more than its worth. Look at a few shops before making a decision. New Zealand tourist shops have taken to selling toy koalas. They're adorable, so buy one if it makes you happy, but they have absolutely nothing to do with New Zealand. You won't even find koalas in the zoos here because the leaves they eat grow widely only in Australia.

SIGHTSEEING GUIDES

At some tourist attractions around Rotorua local boys will offer their services as guides. Negotiate the price at a few dollars and they will probably add a bit of color to your experience. Still, you'll find out much more about the place if you hire an official guide through a visitor information center.

STUDENTS IN NEW ZEALAND

➤ IDS & SERVICES: **Council Travel** (CIEE; ✉ 205 E. 42nd St., 14th floor, New York, NY 10017, ☎ 212/822–2700 or 888/268–6245, 🅵🅰🆇 212/822–2699, www.councilexchanges.org) for mail orders only, in the United States. **Travel Cuts** (✉ 187 College St., Toronto, Ontario M5T 1P7, ☎ 416/979–2406 or 800/667–2887, www.travelcuts.com) in Canada.

TAXES

AIRPORT

Visitors exiting New Zealand must pay a departure tax of $20.

VALUE-ADDED TAX

A goods and services tax (GST) of 12.5% is levied throughout New Zealand. It's usually incorporated into the cost of an item, but in some hotels and some restaurants it is added to the bill.

TELEPHONES

AREA & COUNTRY CODES

The country code for New Zealand is 64. When dialing from abroad, drop the initial 0 from the local area code. Dialing from New Zealand to back home, the country code is 1 for the United States and Canada, 61 for Australia, and 44 for the United Kingdom.

DIRECTORY & OPERATOR ASSISTANCE

Dial 018 for New Zealand directory assistance. For international numbers, dial 0172. To call the operator, dial 010; for international operator assistance, dial 0170.

INTERNATIONAL CALLS

To make international calls directly, dial 00, then the international access code, area code, and number required.

LONG-DISTANCE SERVICES

AT&T, MCI, and Sprint access codes make calling long distance relatively convenient, but you may find the local access number blocked in many hotel rooms. First ask the hotel operator to connect you. If the hotel operator balks, ask for an international operator, or dial the international operator yourself. One way to improve your odds of getting connected to your long-distance carrier is to travel with more than one company's calling card (a hotel may block Sprint, for example, but not MCI). If all else fails, call from a pay phone.

➤ ACCESS CODES: **AT&T Direct** (☎ 000–911). **MCI WorldPhone** (☎ 000–912). **Sprint International Access** (☎ 000–913).

PUBLIC PHONES

Most pay phones now accept Phone Cards or major credit cards rather than coins. PhoneCards, available in denominations of $5, $10, $20, or $50, are sold at shops displaying the green PhoneCard symbol. To use a Phone Card, lift the receiver, put the card in the slot in the front of the phone, and dial. The cost of the call is automatically deducted from your card; the display on the telephone tells you how much credit you have left at the end of the call. A local call from a public phone costs 20¢ per minute. Don't forget to take your PhoneCard with you when you finish your call. You may end up making some very expensive calls by leaving it behind.

TIME

Trying to figure out just what time it is in New Zealand can get dizzying, especially because of cross-hemisphere daylight savings times and multi-time-zone countries. Without daylight savings times, Auckland is 17 hours ahead of New York; 18 hours ahead of Chicago and Dallas; 20 hours ahead (or count back four hours and add a day) of Los Angeles; and 12 hours ahead of London.

From Canada and the States, **call New Zealand after 5 PM.** From the United Kingdom or Europe, it isn't quite as complicated: call early in the morning or very late at night. **When faxing,** it's usually not a problem to ring discreet fax numbers at any time of day.

TIPPING

Tipping is not widely practiced in New Zealand. Only in the better city restaurants and international hotels will you be expected to show your appreciation for good service with a 10% tip.

Taxi drivers will appreciate rounding up the fare to the nearest $5 amount, but don't feel you have to do this. Porters will be happy with a $1 or $2 coin. Most other people, like theater attendants, gas station attendants, or barbers, will probably wonder what you are doing if you try to give them a tip.

TOURS & PACKAGES

Because everything is prearranged on a prepackaged tour or independent vacation, you'll spend less time planning—and often get it all at a good price.

BOOKING WITH AN AGENT

Travel agents are excellent resources. But it's a good idea to collect brochures from several agencies as some agents' suggestions may be influenced by relationships with tour and package firms that reward them for volume sales. If you have a special interest, **find an agent with expertise in that area**; ASTA (☞ Travel Agencies, *below*) has a database of specialists worldwide.

Make sure your travel agent knows the accommodations and other services of the place they're recommending. Ask about the hotel's location, room size, beds, and whether it has a pool, room service, or programs for children, if you care about these. Has your agent been there in person or sent others whom you can contact?

Do some homework on your own, too: local tourism boards can provide information about lesser-known and small-niche operators, some of which may sell only direct.

BUYER BEWARE

Each year consumers are stranded or lose their money when tour operators—even large ones with excellent reputations—go out of business. So **check out the operator.** Ask several travel agents about its reputation, and try to **book with a company that has a consumer-protection program.** (Look for information in the company's brochure.) In the United States, members of the National Tour Association and the United States Tour Operators Association are required to set aside funds to cover your payments and travel arrangements in the event that the company defaults. It's also a good idea to choose a company that participates in the American Society of Travel Agents' Tour Operator Program (TOP); ASTA will act as mediator in any disputes between you and your tour operator.

Remember that the more your package or tour includes the better you can predict the ultimate cost of your vacation. Make sure you know exactly what is covered, and **beware of hidden costs.** Are taxes, tips, and transfers included? Entertainment and excursions? These can add up.

➤ TOUR-OPERATOR RECOMMENDATIONS: **American Society of Travel Agents** (☞ Travel Agencies, *below*). **National Tour Association** (NTA; ✉ 546 E. Main St., Lexington, KY 40508, ☎ 606/226–4444 or 800/682–8886, www.ntaonline.com). **United States Tour Operators Association** (USTOA; ✉ 342 Madison Ave., Suite 1522, New York, NY 10173, ☎ 212/599–6599 or 800/468–7862, FAX 212/599–6744, www.ustoa.com).

TRAIN TRAVEL

New Zealand's Tranz Scenic trains travel, as a rule, north and south along the main trunk of New Zealand. If you want to crisscross the country, then you'll have to abanden the country's rail network. There are some exceptions, most notably the famous Tranz-Alpine Express, a spectacular scenic ride across Arthur's Pass and the mountainous spine of South Island between Greymouth and Christchurch.

For day excursions from Auckland, consider the Kamai Express to Tauranga or the Geyserland to Rotorua.

Even the most popular services tend to run only once daily. They do leave and arrive on time as a rule. Trains have one class, and they have standard, comfortable seats, and a basic food service offering light meals, snacks, beer, wine, and spirits. Special meals (diabetic/wheat free/vegetarian) can be arranged but you have to order at least 48 hours before you board the train. Most carriages have large windows from which to view the spectacular passing scenery, and some routes have a commentary on points of interest. Most trains also have a special viewing carriage at the rear.

CUTTING COSTS

To save money, **look into rail passes.** But be aware that if you don't plan to cover many miles you may come out ahead by buying individual tickets.

Travelers can purchase an New Zealand Travelpass for unlimited travel by train, bus, and Interislander ferry for a variety of periods. The 4-in-1 New Zealand Travelpass, available for purchase outside New Zealand only, includes one flight sector on Ansett New Zealand between assigned city pairs. The flight may be at any time after the date of issue of the Travelpass and up to seven days after expiration of the Travelpass. Two additional flight sectors may be purchased at $255 per sector. For Youth Hostel Association members, the InterCity Youth Hostel Travel Card ($75 for 14 days, $99 for 28 days) gives a 30% discount on most train service, all InterCity coach service, and on Interislander ferries. Students with an International Student Identity Card (ISIC) get a 20% discount. Senior citizens (over 60) get a 30% discount with proof of age.

➤ BUYING PASSES: **InterCity Travel Centres** (☎ 09/639–0500 in Auckland, 03/379–9020 in Christchurch, 04/472–5111 in Wellington). In the United States, **ATS Tours** (☎ 818/841–1030) or **Austravel Inc.** (☎ 800/633–3404).

FARES & SCHEDULES

You can obtain both schedules and tickets at visitor information centers and at train stations.

➤ TRAIN INFORMATION: **Tranz Scenic** (☎ 0800/802–802).

PAYING

Major credit cards are accepted, as are cash and traveler's checks.

RESERVATIONS

Reservations are advised, particularly in the summer months. **Book at least 48 hours in advance.**

TRANSPORTATION AROUND NEW ZEALAND

Trains provide a relaxing mode of travel in New Zealand, but stick very much to the beaten track and have limited schedules. Buses cover the country far more extensively and depart more frequently (especially from main centers). If you really want

to see New Zealand properly you'll have to grit your teeth and be prepared to drive on the left side of the road. Even so, it is a good idea to combine driving with some scenic public transport and tour opportunities—such as a ferry trip on the Auckland Harbour, or the journey across the Southern Alps by train.

TRAVEL AGENCIES

A good travel agent puts your needs first. Look for an agency that has been in business at least five years, emphasizes customer service, and has someone on staff who specializes in your destination. In addition, **make sure the agency belongs to a professional trade organization.** The American Society of Travel Agents (ASTA), with 27,000 agents in some 170 countries, is the largest and most influential in the field. Operating under the motto "Integrity in Travel," it maintains and enforces a strict code of ethics and will step in to help mediate any agent-client disputes if necessary. ASTA also maintains a Web site that includes a directory of agents. (If a travel agency is also acting as your tour operator, *see* Buyer Beware *in* Tours & Packages, *above*.)

➤ LOCAL AGENT REFERRALS: **American Society of Travel Agents** (ASTA; ☎ 800/965–2782 24-hr hot line, FAX 703/684–8319, www.asta.net). **Association of British Travel Agents** (✉ 68–71 Newman St., London W1P 4AH, ☎ 0171/637–2444, FAX 0171/637–0713, www.abtanet.com). **Association of Canadian Travel Agents** (✉ 1729 Bank St., Suite 201, Ottawa, Ontario K1V 7Z5, ☎ 613/521–0474, FAX 613/521–0805). **Australian Federation of Travel Agents** (✉ Level 3, 309 Pitt St., Sydney 2000, ☎ 02/9264–3299, FAX 02/9264–1085, www.afta.com.au). **Travel Agents' Association of New Zealand** (✉ Box 1888, Wellington 10033, ☎ 04/499–0104, FAX 04/499–0827).

TRIP PLANNING

The difficulty with planning a trip to New Zealand is exquisite agony—nearly every square mile of the country is spectacular. And nearly everyone who comes back from the country wishes he or she had planned to spend more time there. Yet if you try to see too much, you may end up feeling like you haven't seen anything at all. So give yourself time to really savor two or three areas and get to know them and meet a few locals. Four days to a week per locale will leave you feeling that you have actually been somewhere.

VISITOR INFORMATION

➤ NEW ZEALAND TOURISM BOARD: **In the U.S.** (✉ 501 Santa Monica Blvd., Los Angeles, CA 90401, ☎ 310/395–7480 or 800/388–5494, FAX 310/395–5454). **In Canada** (✉ 888 Dunsmuir St., Suite 1200, Vancouver, BC V6C 3K4, ☎ 800/888–5494, FAX 604/684–1265). **In the U.K.** (✉ New Zealand House, Haymarket, London SW1Y 4TQ, ☎ 020/7930–1662, FAX 020/7839–8929).

➤ U.S. GOVERNMENT ADVISORIES: **U.S. Department of State** (✉ Overseas Citizens Services Office, Room 4811 N.S., 2201 C St. NW, Washington, DC 20520, ☎ 202/647–5225 for interactive hot line, 301/946–4400 for computer bulletin board, FAX 202/647–3000 for interactive hot line); enclose a self-addressed, stamped, business-size envelope.

WEB SITES

Do check out the World Wide Web when you're planning. You'll find everything from current weather forecasts to virtual tours of famous cities. Fodor's Web site, www.fodors.com, is a great place to start your on-line travels. When you

see a 🐚 in this book, go to www.fodors.com/urls for an up-to-date link to that destination's site.

WHEN TO GO

New Zealand is in the Southern Hemisphere, which means that seasons are reversed—it's winter down under during the American and European summer. The ideal months for comfortable all-round travel are October–April, especially if you want to participate in adventure activities. Avoid school holidays, when highways may be congested and accommodation is likely to be scarce and more expensive. Summer school holidays (the busiest) fall between mid-December and the end of January; other holiday periods are mid-May to the end of May, early July to mid-July, and late August to mid-September.

CLIMATE

Climate in New Zealand varies from subtropical in the north to temperate in the south. Summer (December–March) is generally warm, with an average of seven to eight hours of sunshine per day throughout the country. Winter (June–September) is mild at lower altitudes in South Island, but heavy snowfalls are common in South Island, particularly on the peaks of the Southern Alps. Rain can pour at any time of the year. (Some areas on the west coast of South Island receive an annual rainfall of more than 100 inches.)

The following are average daily maximum and minimum temperatures for some major cities in New Zealand.

AUCKLAND

Jan.	74F	23C	May	63F	17C	Sept.	61F	16C
	61	16		52	11		49	9
Feb.	74F	23C	June	58F	14C	Oct.	63F	17C
	61	16		49	9		52	11
Mar.	72F	22C	July	56F	13C	Nov.	67F	19C
	59	15		47	8		54	12
Apr.	67F	19C	Aug.	58F	14C	Dec.	70F	21C
	56	13		47	8		58	14

CHRISTCHURCH

Jan.	70F	21C	May	56F	13C	Sept.	58F	14C
	54	12		40	4		40	4
Feb.	70F	21C	June	52F	11C	Oct.	63F	17C

	54	12		36	2		45	7
Mar.	67F	19C	July	50F	10C	Nov.	67F	19C
	50	10		36	2		47	8
Apr.	63F	17C	Aug.	52F	11C	Dec.	70F	21C
	45	7		36	2		52	11

QUEENSTOWN

Jan.	72F	22C	May	52F	11C	Sept.	56F	13C
	49	9		36	2		38	3
Feb.	70F	21C	June	47F	8C	Oct.	61F	16C
	50	10		34	1		41	5
Mar.	67F	19C	July	46F	8C	Nov.	65F	18C
	47	8		34	− 1		45	7
Apr.	61F	16C	Aug.	50F	10C	Dec.	70F	21C
	43	6		34	1		49	9

➤ FORECASTS: **Weather Channel Connection** (☎ 900/932–8437), 95¢ per minute from a Touch-Tone phone.

FESTIVALS AND SEASONAL EVENTS

Sport features heavily in New Zealand's festival calendar. Horse and boat races, triathlons, and fishing competitions are far more prominent than celebrations of the arts. Just about every town holds a yearly agricultural and pastoral (A and P) show, and these proud displays of local crafts, produce, livestock, and wood-chopping and sheep-shearing prowess provide a memorable look at rural New Zealand. An annual calendar, *New Zealand Special Events*, is available from government tourist offices.

➤ DEC. 25–26: On **Christmas Day** and **Boxing Day** the country virtually closes down.

➤ JAN. 1: **New Year's Day** is a nation-wide holiday.

➤ LAST MON. IN JAN.: For the **Auckland Anniversary Day Regatta,** Auckland's birthday party, the City of Sails takes to the water. ☎ 09/579–0923.

➤ FEB. 3–14: The **Festival of Romance** is held in Christchurch—the city where lovers can stroll through an old English garden and enjoy a punt ride on the Avon River. ☎ 03/379–9629.

➤ FEB. 5–6: **Speights Coast to Coast** is the ultimate iron-man challenge—a two-day, 238-km (148-mi) marathon of cycling, running, and kayaking that crosses South Island from west to east. *Information: Robin Judkins,* ☎ 03/326–5493.

➤ FEB. 6: **Waitangi Day,** New Zealand's national day, commemorates the signing of the Treaty of Waitangi between Europeans and Maori in 1840. The focus of the celebration is, naturally enough, the town of Waitangi in the Bay of Islands.

➤ FEB. 14–22: Christchurch's **Garden City Festival of Flowers,** the country's largest flower show, finds the city bursting with blossoms and activity, with plenty of related events, displays, and exhibitions. ☎ 03/379–5977

➤ LATE FEB.: **The Devonport Food and Wine Festival** showcases some of the country's best restaurants and is easily reached by a ferry trip from Auckland city. ☎ 09/445–3011.

➤ FEB. 26: The **Pacifika Festival** highlights the many Pacific Island cultures found in Auckland with plenty of color, music, and dance. The main activity is at Western Springs lakeside, near the Auckland Zoo. ☎ 09/379–2620.

➤ 1ST THURS.–SAT. OF MAR.: **Golden Shears International Shearing Championship** is a three-day event that pits men armed with shears against the fleecy sheep in Masterton, just north of Wellington. *Information:* ✉ *Masterton Visitor Information Centre, 5 Dixon St.,* ☎ 06/378–7373.

➤ MAR. 21: Auckland's **Round the Bays Run** is one of the world's largest 10-km (6-mi) fun runs. A few people take it seriously, but thousands of others run, walk, or ride about the course in their own time. The run starts in the city, follows Tamaki Drive around the waterfront, and finishes in the plush suburb of St. Heliers. ☎ 09/525–2166.

➤ MAR. OR APR.: The **Easter** holiday weekend lasts from Good Friday through Easter Monday. Dates change each year and generally fall in March or April. The Royal Easter Show is held in Auckland over the holiday. ☎ 09/638–9969.

➤ APR. 25: **Anzac Day** honors the soldiers, sailors, and airmen and women who fought and died for the country.

➤ EARLY MAY: The **Fletcher Marathon** around Lake Rotorua is New Zealand's premier long-distance event. ☎ 07/347–1419.

➤ 1ST MON. IN JUNE: The **Queen's Birthday** is celebrated nationwide.

➤ EARLY TO MID-JULY: At the **Queenstown Winter Festival,** the winter-sports capital hits the slopes for a week of competition by day and entertainment by night. ☎ 03/442–5746.

➤ LATE JULY: **Mad, Mad Mid-Winter Festival** is a mixture of sporting events held in Rotorua, from outrigger canoeing to nighttime mountain biking to a mountain-rafting championship contest. ☎ 07/347–1419.

➤ OCT. 15–22: **Dunedin Rhododendron Festival** opens the city's gardens for tours and offers lectures and plant sales. ☎ 03/474–3300.

➤ OCT. 23: **Labour Day** is observed throughout the country.

➤ NOV. 1–10: **Taranaki Rhododendron Festival** in and around New Plymouth is a major event. One hundred–plus private gardens are open to the public, there are lectures, and the vast Pukeiti Rhododendron Trust holds a series of cultural events and festivities. ☎ 06/752–4141.

➤ MID- TO LATE NOV.: **Ellerslie Flower Show** in Auckland is one of the headline events on New Zealand's gardening calendar. It is modeled on London's Chelsea Flower Show. In a confusing twist, the show recently moved from the suburb of Ellerslie to the Botanic Gardens at Manurewa, farther south, while retaining its old name. ☎ 09/309–7875.

➤ 2ND WEEK IN NOV.: **Canterbury Agricultural and Pastoral Show** spotlights the farmers and graziers of the rich countryside surrounding Christchurch. *Information:* ✉ *Christchurch–Canterbury Visitor Information Centre, Worcester St. and Oxford Terr., Christchurch,* ☎ *03/379–9629.*

➤ 2ND WEEKEND IN NOV.: The city of Blenheim's **Garden Marlborough** has local garden tours and a fête with products for sale. The festival follows Auckland's Ellerslie Flower Show, which gives the international experts who attended the Auckland event time to get to South Island and give excellent lectures and workshops. ☎ 03/572–8707.

WORDS AND PHRASES

A Kiwi Glossary

Talking Kiwi is hardly a daunting prospect for anyone traveling abroad with the English language under their belts. You'll seldom be at a complete loss, and if a phrase does confuse you, the locals will delight in explaining its meaning. The word "kiwi" itself can be a source of confusion—it can mean the brown flightless bird that lives in New Zealand forests, the people of New Zealand, a furry fruit that is one of the country's best-known exports, a quick lottery ticket, or even a rugby league team. You'll have to figure it out in context. Despite being half a world away, New Zealanders are in many ways still fairly protective of the Queen's English and have resisted the Americanization of the language to a greater extent than their cousins in Australia. In newspapers and magazines you will read "colour" instead of "color," and "programme" not "program." New Zealanders are prone to shorten names, and also to give nicknames, but this is not as prevalent as in Australia. And Kiwis have developed a few quirky terms of their own. Here are a few translations that will help:

Across the Ditch: Over the Tasman Sea in Australia
Aubergine: Eggplant
Aussi: An Australian
Bach: Vacation house (North Island) (pronounced *batch*)
Battle on: Try hard with limited success
Bludger: Someone who lives off other people's effort
Bush: The outdoors, wilderness
Capsicum: Bell pepper
Carpark: Parking lot
Chilly bin: A cooler
Choka (or choka block): Full
Courgette: Zucchini
Cuppa: Cup of tea or coffee
Crib: Vacation house (South Island)
Crook: Sick
Dag: Amusing person or happening
Dairy: Convenience or corner store
Devonshire tea: Cream tea with scones (served morning and afternoon)
En suite: Bathroom attached to your hotel room
Fair dinkum: It's really true
Fair go: Fair chance
Fair suck of the sav: Fair deal
Fanny: Woman's privates (obscene)
Footie: Rugby football
Footpath: Sidewalk
Give a wide berth: Leave alone
Greenie: Conservationist
Home and hosed: Successful
Jandal: Open topped footwear
Loo: Toilet (bathroom is only for bathing)
Mainlander: Resident of the South Island

Metal road: Gravel road
Motorway: Freeway or highway
Mozzie: Mosquito
Mug: Goodhearted to the point of being foolish
Nappie: Diaper
Ocker: An Australian
Pavlova: A meringue cake
Pom or pommie: Native of England
Rubber: Eraser (also condom)
Sealed road: Paved road
Serviette: Napkin
Shout: Buy a round of drinks
Sink a few: Drink some beer
Smoko: Tea or coffee break
Take aways: Food to go, takeout
Tall poppy: One who excels
Tea: Dinner (also the beverage)
Togs: Swimsuit
Track: Hiking trail
Tramping: Hiking
Up with the play: Knows what is going on
Ute: Pickup truck
Whinger: Whiner or moaner

A Maori Glossary

The use of the *Te Reo Maori* (the Maori language) is experiencing a resurgence in contemporary New Zealand, with nearly 90% of Maori children enrolled in some form of Maori language early childhood education. This is a heartening outcome for a language that has stood for decades tenuously at the brink of extinction.

Though the language was never officially legislated against, the great-grandparents of today's generation were beaten at school for speaking Maori. Not until the 1980s was government funding made available for Maori language education.

The realms of Maori language use are slowly moving out of the *marae* and into schools, parliament, and broadcasting. While you're in New Zealand, make a point to watch Sunday-morning television. It's the only time you'll see Maori language programs. Except for when you're involved in a specifically Maori activity or event you won't be hearing it much in everyday use. (Though expressions like "kia ora" have made their way into general Kiwi speech.)

Still, knowing how to pronounce Maori words can be important when trying to say place-names in New Zealand. Even if you have a natural facility for picking up languages, you'll find many Maori words to be quite baffling. The West Coast town of Punakaiki (pronounced poon-ah-*kye*-kee) is relatively straightforward, but when you get to places like Whangamata, the going gets tricky—the opening *wh* is pronounced like an *f*, and the accent is placed on the last syllable: "fahng-ah-ma-*ta.*" Sometimes it is the mere length of words that makes them difficult, as in the case of Waitakaruru (why-ta-ka-ru-ru) or Whakarewarewa (fa-ka-*re*-wa-*re*-wa). You'll notice that the ends of both of these have repeats—of "ru" and "rewa," which is something to look out for to make longer words more manageable. Town names like Waikanea (*why*-can-eye) you'll just have to repeat to yourself a few times before saying them without pause.

The Maori *r* is rolled so that it sounds a little like a *d*. Thus the Northland town of Whangarei is pronounced "fang-ah-day," and the word *Maori* is pronounced "mo-dee," with the *o* sounding like it does in the word mould, and a rolled *r*. All of this is a little too complicated for some *Pakeha* (pahk-eh-ha) who choose not to bother with Maori pronunciations. So in some places, if you say you've just driven over from "fahng-ah-ma-*ta*," the reply might be: "You mean 'wang-ah-*ma*-tuh.'" You can pronounce these words either way, but more and more non-Maori New Zealanders are saying Maori words as the Maori do.

Ae: Yes
Ahau: I, me
Aotearoa: Land of the long white cloud (New Zealand)
Atua: Spirit, god
Awa: River
Awhi: Help
Haere atu: Go away, farewell, depart
Haere mai: Welcome, come here
Haere ra: Farewell, good-bye
Haka: Fierce rythmical dance made internationally famous by the country's rugby team, the All Blacks, and performed before each game.
Hakari: Feast, gift
Hangi: Earth oven, food from an earth oven
Hapu: Sub-tribe
Harakeke: Flax leaf (also used to refer to woven flax items)
Heitiki: Greenstone pendant
Hongi: Press noses in greeting
Hui: Gathering
Ika: Fish
Iwi: People, tribe
Kahore: No
Kai: Food, eat, dine
Kai moana: Seafood
Ka pai: Good
Karakia: Ritual chant, prayer, religious service
Kaumatua: Elder
Kete: Flax bag
Kino: Bad
Koha: Customary gift, donation
Kohanga reo: Language nest, Maori pre-school
Kumara: Sweet potato
Kura kaupapa: Total immersion Maori language school
Mana: Influence, prestige, power
Manu: Bird
Manuhiri: Guest, visitor
Maoritanga: Maori culture, perspective
Marae: Traditional gathering place
Maunga: Mountain
Mauri: Life principle, source of vitality and mana
Mihi: To greet, congratulate
Moana: Sea, lake
Moko: Tattoo
Motu: Island
Pa: Fortress

Pakeha: Non-Maori, European, Caucasian
Poi: Light ball attached to string
Rangatira: Chief, person of rank
Roto: Lake
Taiaha: Long, two-handed weapon, blade at one end and point at the other
Tangata whenua: People of the land
Taniwha: Spirits-monsters living in the sea, and inland waters
Taonga: Treasure
Tapu: Sacred, under religious restriction
Tauiwi: Foreigner
Tino rangatiratanga: chief's authority, self-determination
Toa: Warrior
Tohunga: Priest, expert
Tupuna: Ancestor
Wai: Water, liquid
Waiata: Sing, song
Wairua: Soul, spirit
Waka ama: Outrigger canoe
Whaikorero: Speech
Whakapapa: Genealogy, cultural identity
Whanau: Family
Whare: House
Whenua: Land

Greetings and Expressions

Tena koe (korua) (koutou): Hello to one person (to two people) (to three or more people)
Kia ora: Hello
Haere mai: Welcome
Haere ra: Goodbye (from the person staying to the one leaving)
E noho ra: Goodbye (from the person leaving to the person staying)
Ka pai: Good, excellent
Kei te pehea koe: How are you? (to one person)

Maori Place-Names

Kirikiriroa: Hamilton
Otautahi: Christchurch
Otepoti: Dunedin
Rakiura: Stewart Island
Tamaki-makau-rau: Auckland
Te Ika-A-Maui: North Island
Te Waipounamu–Te-Waka-A-Aoraki: South Island
Whanganui-a-tara: Wellington

INDEX

NOTES

NOTES

FODOR'S NEW ZEALAND

EDITOR: Beatrice Aranow

Contributors: Jules Brown, Michael Gebicki, Stu Freeman, Doug Johanson, Jan Poole, Mere Wetere, Vic Williams

Editorial Production: Stacey Kulig

Maps: David Lindroth, *cartographer;* Rebecca Baer and Robert Blake, *map editors*

Design: Fabrizio La Rocca, *creative director;* Guido Caroti, *art director;* Jolie Novak, *photo editor;* Melanie Marin, photo researcher

Cover Design: Pentagram

Production/Manufacturing: Robert B. Shields

COPYRIGHT

Sixth Edition

ISBN 0–679–00666–4

ISSN 1531–0450

SPECIAL SALES

Fodor's Travel Publications are available at special discounts for bulk purchases for sales promotions or premiums. Special editions, including personalized covers, excerpts of existing guides, and corporate imprints, can be created in large quantities for special needs. For more information, contact your local bookseller or write to Special Markets, Fodor's Travel Publications, 280 Park Avenue, New York, NY 10017. Inquiries from Canada should be directed to your local Canadian bookseller or sent to Random House of Canada, Ltd., Marketing Department, 2775 Matheson Boulevard East, Mississauga, Ontario L4W 4P7. Inquiries from the United Kingdom should be sent to Fodor's Travel Publications, 20 Vauxhall Bridge Road, London SW1V 2SA, England.

PRINTED IN THE UNITED STATES OF AMERICA
10 9 8 7 6 5 4 3 2 1

IMPORTANT TIP

Although all prices, opening times, and other details are based on information supplied to us at press time, changes occur all the time in the travel world, and Fodor's cannot accept responsibility for facts that become outdated or for inadvertent errors or omissions. So **always confirm information when it matters,** especially if you're making a detour to visit a specific place.

PHOTOGRAPHY

Stone: *Larry Ulrich cover (Seaward Kaikoura Range, South Island)*

Abel Tasman National Park Enterprises, *2 bottom left, 10C, 15C*

Andris Apse, *7F.*

Art Resource, New York: *Werner Forman Archive, 16.*

Auckland Art Gallery, *John McIver, 6C.*

Clean Green Images: *Gilbert van Reenen, 2 top right.*

Corbis: 3 bottom left. *Hans Georg Roth, 7E. Vince Streano, 1.*

Dennis Cox, *13E.*

Cox Graphic Design, *14A.*

Ric Ergenbright Photography: *Byron Crader, 12B. Floyd Norgaard, 8C.*

Blaine Harrington III, *9E, 12C.*

Houserstock: *Dave G. Houser, 3 top left.*

Hunter's Wines, *11E.*

Bob Krist, *13D.*

Legend Photography: *Andy Belcher, 9D, 10B, 11D, 11F, 13F.*

Liaison International: *Steven Burr Williams, 6B, 7D.*

Museum of New Zealand Te Papa Tongarewa: *Michael Hall, 8B.*

Laurence Parent, *10A, 12A.*

Photosport: *Andrew Cornaga, 6A.*

Polynesian Spa, *3 bottom right.*

Stone: *Ken Graham, 8A. Philip & Karen Smith, 4–5.*

Stoneleigh Vineyards, *2 bottom right.*

Tourism Auckland, *2 bottom center, 3 top right.*

Whale Watch®, *2 top left, 14B.*

ABOUT OUR WRITERS

Our success in helping to make your trip the best of all possible vacations is a credit to the hard work of our extraordinary writers and editors.

Jules Brown is an experienced travel writer with countless newspaper features and a dozen guidebooks to his credit. During a year in New Zealand, he never learned to love rugby, but he soon warmed to the joys of Kiwi pinot noirs, kayaking, tramping, and the cafés of Wellington. No one will ever convince him, however, that beets are a fitting addition to a burger.

Stu Freeman, like most Kiwis, loves to get out into the bush on a regular basis, watch rugby, toss back a pint every now and then. He escaped the life of a daily newspaper journalist in the early 1980s, threw a pack on his back, and tramped through Asia and Europe. Since then he's been freelance writing about New Zealand and the South Pacific and publishing an incentive travel magazine.

Doug Johansen and Jan Poole, who contributed to our Adventure Vacations chapter, are owner-operators of Kiwi Dundee Adventures Ltd., which offers a variety of off-the-beaten-path hiking trips on the Coromandel Peninsula and around New Zealand. They are two nature-loving Kiwis who have a deep respect for the mountains, forests, and coastlines of New Zealand. Doug is known as one of New Zealand's pioneers of nature tourism, and in 1992 won the inaugural New Zealand Eco-Tourism Award.

Mere Wetere brings to her writing the perspective of her Maori heritage, and we are very pleased to make that a part of our *New Zealand*. Formerly a journalist, Mere is the owner-manager of an employment consultant business for women and also provides media services and training on the Treaty of Waitangi for educational and community groups. Her partner, **Philip Barnes,** journalist and avid tramper, contributed to the section on the Milford Sound walk in Fiordland.

Vic Williams is all over the New Zealand food and wine map. He is a columnist and restaurant critic for *Cuisine* and *Fashion Quarterly* magazines, Cellar Director for the New Zealand Wine Society, and New Zealand wine consultant for Cathay Pacific Airways. Author of the popular annual *Penguin Good New Zealand Wine Guide,* he has appeared as a wine and food presenter on several television and talk-radio programs, including *Weekend, Summer Cooking with Vic Williams, Breakfast,* and *5:30 Live.* His pen and his superb taste are behind all of our restaurant and winery selections.

Don't Forget to Write

We love feedback—positive and negative—and follow up on all suggestions. So contact the New Zealand editor at editors@fodors.com or c/o Fodor's, 280 Park Avenue, New York, NY 10017. Have a wonderful trip!

Karen Cure

Karen Cure
Editorial Director